AF754899

Language Engineering

Language Engineering

Hristo Georgiev

continuum

Continuum
The Tower Building
11 York Road
London
SE1 7NX

80 Maiden Lane
Suite 704
New York
NY 10038

© Hristo Georgiev 2007

All rights reserved. No part of this publication may be reproduced or transmitted in any form or by any means, electronic or mechanical, including photocopying, recording, or any information storage or retrieval system, without prior permission in writing from the publishers.

British Library Cataloguing-in-Publication Data
A catalogue record for this book is available from the British Library.

ISBN: HB: 0-8264-8294-5

Typeset by Free Range Book Design & Production Limited
Printed and bound in Great Britain by Biddles Ltd., King's Lynn, Norfolk

Contents

Preface

This book is the result of merging two disciplines: study of language (linguistics) and computer programming. The new discipline is called 'linguistic programming' known also as 'computational linguistics' (a term used to include statistical methods as well), which some prefer to call either 'natural language processing' or 'language engineering' or 'linguistic engineering', because of the ever increasing role of computers in language study, teaching, technology and computerisation of all aspects of language. In many languages exists a parallel term calling this branch of linguistics 'computer linguistics'. We will concentrate upon those linguistic aspects of language that need to be programmed for one or another purpose. In view of this, we hope that our readers will know either linguistics or programming or both.

This book will describe written language only and will not concern spoken language at all. However, since spoken language and written language have many things in common, we hope that the subject matter of this book will find successful application to spoken language as well.

This book will not discuss all languages in the world. This is impossible to do in a single book. However, we will do our best to show techniques that will be applicable to most languages. We will show which techniques are common to most languages and which are language specific. So far as the language-specific techniques are concerned, we will apply them to English, French and German languages only, but we will give examples, wherever necessary, in Italian, Turkish, Bulgarian and Russian.

For example, universal grammatical features are number and gender. Some of the language-specific grammatical features are the Case and the expression of Verbal Tenses. Russian, for example, has only three Verbal Tenses, English has over 30 (in all different Moods). Russian and German have Cases, Bulgarian and English, not. Vietnamese varies the meaning of a word by changing the tone with which it is pronounced, etc. Our aim is not to make a comparative study, it is to show natural language processing techniques, applicable to most languages.

The programming language to express the natural language processing techniques will be C. It is not possible to do that in all programming languages, but we hope, that the reader and the programmer familiar with other programming languages will find the necessary parallels and will draw the appropriate conclusions. C remains one of the most widely used among the programming languages. Ideas that have found practical implementation in one programming language and on one platform (Operating System), as is the case here, can be successfully applied to other programming languages and other platforms.

The examples in C will be explained so that those readers not familiar with it, or not knowing any programming language, will still be able to understand the grammatical, etc. rules expressed in C. On the other hand, those programmers who are not familiar with linguistics do not have to learn it before they read this book. Here, they will learn what they need to know about linguistics with programming examples. So far as the linguists are concerned, they will learn from this book what they need to know about programming linguistic and language-related tasks. This will help them present linguistic knowledge in a way more understandable for the programmers and for the computer and will show them in what areas of linguistics their research is most needed.

The book will offer practical programming solutions for software development in the sphere of language engineering. These solutions are already tested and work efficiently in a number of software programs developed by the author. The book is intended for programmers, software developers, linguists involved in Natural Language Processing (NLP) and as a textbook for all NLP courses.

Language Engineering is a vast subject. We will ignore the theories and concentrate upon the practice of Dictionary making for computational purposes, including tagging (the fundament in all applications), Parsing (the grammatical and syntactical analysis of the sentence used by all other applications), Orthographical and Grammatical Spell-checking, Lexical Semantics for computational purposes as found in the Thesauri and other dictionaries, Machine Translation and natural language understanding, namely Question Answering and Text Attribution. It is the practice, the achievement, the comparison with other results and achievements that matters in the end. Theories only help to achieve a better result. Intelligent searching for information on the Internet, robotics and language-related Artificial Intelligence (thinking, understanding, reasoning, decision taking etc.), and future applications can also profit from this book.

All this considered, the reader will find Language Engineering an appropriate title for this book.

Part one

PREPARATORY WORK

1 Dictionary of Wordforms

Any text-processing system needs a word-list, called a Dictionary or Lexicon, or lately called 'lingware'. The dictionary is part of a database; in certain cases, it is all the database one has or needs. Some text-processing systems use a Dictionary which comprises all wordforms of each individual word. For example, the English word *book*, the German word *Buchständer*, the French word *abolition* will be presented in the respective language Dictionary with its basic form and with its wordforms:

English	**German**	**French**
book	Buchständer	abolition
books	Buchständern	abolitions
booked	Buchständers	
booker		
bookers		
booking		

The wordform is sometimes called, in the respective literature, running word or word from space to space, in order to avoid any misunderstanding. All the wordforms of a word, within the same part of speech and meaning, make its paradigm. The paradigm of the Adjective *rich* (English), *richtig* (German) and *vert* (French) will be presented in the respective Dictionaries as follows:

English	**German**	**French**
rich	richtig	vert
richer	richtige	verte
richest	richtigem	vertes
	richtigen	
	richtiger	
	richtiges	

The English Adverb *richly* and the Nouns *richness* and *riches* will be also registered in the Dictionary separately. In yet another example, the English Verb *come* the German *kommen* and the French *valoir* will be presented with all its Present, Past and Participle forms:

English	**German**	**French**
come	komme	valoir
comes	kommst	valu
came	kommt	valus
coming	kommen	etc.
	gekommen	
	etc.	

Each such registered wordform is called word entry. All wordforms of a given word, as we have said above, constitute its paradigm. So, in the above examples, we have listed the paradigms of the following words: *book, rich, come, Buchständer, richtig, kommen, abolition, vert, valoir*.

One can well imagine, that such a Dictionary will be huge. We can roughly say, that such an English Dictionary will contain at least 130,000 entries. Inflective languages such as German or French will need a Dictionary of more than one million word entries. Therefore, in the past, for lack of sufficient memory, Dictionaries were usually made by listing only one form of the word, which the lexicographers call 'basic form' or 'representative form'. In our examples above, the words *book, rich, come, Buchständer, valoir*, etc. will be basic forms. What must be added at the end of the basic form to make wordforms is called 'word ending', or rather 'grammatical ending'. This is a common feature, met in many languages, which must be taken into consideration when constructing the dictionary. The Dictionary presents its word entries in an alphabetical order. This is because it is easier and quicker to find the word we want.

At present, memory is no longer a problem, so we can list all the words with their paradigms. At least, by doing so, we will eliminate many ambiguities on the word level. For example, the English wordforms *affirmative, affordable, agile*, etc. will be Adjectives only. In this case, the basic form and the wordform coincide. An English wordform such as *addicts* or *addle* will remain ambiguous: they will be either Noun or Verb (*addicts*) or Adjective or Verb (*addle*). The German wordforms *billiges, billigem, billiger* will be Adjectives only, but the wordforms *billige* and *billigen* will remain ambiguous: they will be either an Adjective or a Verb. The French wordforms *vectoriel, vendable, verbal* will be Adjectives only, but the wordforms *vermille* and *vermilles* will remain ambiguous: they will be either Noun or Verb. So, in each language which wordforms are ambiguous must be established individually (Note: In this book we will call the basic form of the word simply word, in order to distinguish it from wordform.)

Ambiguous wordforms are listed in the so called 'Electronic Dictionaries', used by the computers for text processing purposes. In our opinion, it will be better to adopt a 'mixed' approach to construct the Dictionary. This means making a list of all basic forms and adding only the ambiguous and the irregular wordforms. In this case, the English basic form will be *addict* and the wordforms *addicts* (Noun or Verb), *addicted* (Adjective or Past Form of the Verb or Participle Form of the Verb), *addicting* (Adjective or Present Participle or Noun) will be added, because they are ambiguous. The wordforms *addiction* and *addictness* do not have to be registered in the Dictionary, because the programmer can write an instruction to tell the computer that *-ion, -ness* can be added to the basic form of a word to make a Noun. However, since this instruction will apply to all words it will lead to errors, since we cannot add *-ion, -ness* to all words indiscriminately. Therefore, the programmer cannot always write such generalizing instructions. For example, as a rule, we can add the ending *-ly* to an Adjective to form an Adverb, but we cannot make this rule general because there are many exceptions. Whether we can write generalizing rules or not depends on our aims. If our aim is simply to recognize the word *addiction* on the basis of the word *addict* without registering *addiction* in the Dictionary, we can write a generalizing rule to tell the computer that *-ion* is an ending of a Noun. Similarly, we can write such a generalizing rule to form unregistered Adverbs from Adjectives already registered in the dictionary by adding *-ly* to the registered Adjectives. Consider, for example, *indestructible* and *high* (Adjectives, basic forms, registered in the Dictionary) and *indestructibly* and *highly* (Adverbs, unregistered in the Dictionary, but still recognized as such by the program). If our aim is higher, in other words if we want to be more specific and accurate, we must teach the computer that *-ion* cannot be added to *address* (Verb or Noun) to form *addression*, and *-ly* cannot be added to *adventuresome* to form *adventuresomely*. As far as machine translation, question answering, information retrieval and text attribution are concerned, generalizing rules have place, because it is important to recognize the wordform even when it is misspelt.

Some rules can be universal. For example, if we have registered in the Dictionary of Wordforms (DW) *generalize* we don't have to register *generalise* as well, because we can make a generalizing rule to tell the computer that all Verbs that end in *-ize* can have *-ise* forms as well. Generalizing rules have no place in a spell-checking software program.

In order to make a parallel with the German language, the basic form will be *billig* and the wordforms *billige*, *billigen* will be added, because they are ambiguous. The wordforms *billiges, billigem, billiger* will not be registered in the Dictionary, because the programmer will write an instruction to tell the computer that *-es, -em, -er* can be added to the basic form of an Adjective. This instruction will apply to all Adjectives.

The same applies to the French language, but the rules for each word are specific and language dependent. The French basic forms will be *vermille* (Noun or Verb) and *vermiller* (Verb only) and the wordforms *vermilles* (Noun or Verb), *vermillé* (Participle or Adjective), etc. will be added, because they are ambiguous. The wordforms *vermillez, vermillions* will not be registered in the Dictionary, because the programmer will write an instruction to tell the computer that *-ez, -ions,* etc. can be added to the basic form of the Verb. This instruction will apply to all Verbs.

We will return frequently to the Dictionary of Wordforms in the course of this book to discuss each point as it arises in the respective chapter.

1 Construction of the Dictionary of Wordforms

The construction of the Dictionary of Wordforms is inseparably connected with writing the source code of the program, because it is the computer program that uses this dictionary. There are many possibilities to make a Dictionary of Wordforms, but we will choose just one, the one that is easiest to understand.

In the Dictionary of Wordforms we will list the word entries in alphabetical order. Each word entry will have a description. The description is the information we want to have registered about this particular word entry. This is mainly grammatical information (for example: Part of Speech, number, gender, etc.), in some cases semantical information (for example: human being, geographical name, word denoting time, etc.), or even syntactical information about the word entry (for example, its combinatorics with the next word(s)). The word entry and its description we will separate with the sign =. By doing so, we tell the computer program that what follows after = is the information about this particular word entry. Each item of information will have a code. We are free to choose the codes and we must always use the same code for the same thing.

For example, the word entries *adventurer*, *Buchständer* and *abolition* for the respective languages will be entered as follows:

English	**German**	**French**
adventurer=N	buchständer=N	abolition=N

The code **N** means that the word entry here is a Noun. Note that we have written *Buchständer* with a small letter, contrary to German spelling norms for nouns. In German the nouns are written with a capital letter. This is not important here for the dictionary. Later, we will write a general rule and the computer program will 'know', that *Buchständer* is written with a capital letter, because it is a noun.

The word entries *abandon, abändern, abaisser* for the respective languages will be entered as follows:

English	**German**	**French**
abandon=V	abändern =V	abaisser =V

The code **V** means that the word entry is a Verb.

The word entries *abroad, abends, abondamment* for the respective languages will be entered as follows:

English	**German**	**French**
abroad=D	abends=D	abondamment=D

The code **D** means that the word entry here is an Adverb. This coding is valid for all languages when the word belongs to only one part of speech.

However, in those cases when the word entry can belong to more than one part of speech, we are faced with a problem. For example, the English word *abstract* and the German word *plumpen* can be a Verb, a Noun or an Adjective, and the French word *annexe* can be a Verb or a Noun. We can register the word entry separately, with each one of its grammatical meanings:

English	**German**	**French**
abstract=N	plumpen=N	annexe=N
abstract=V	plumpen=V	annexe=V
abstract=A	plumpen=A	

where the code **A** means Adjective.

However, this type of coding for ambiguous words will increase the volume of the Dictionary enormously, will make the programming task more difficult and will not help us differentiate in which context *abstract* or *plumpen* is used as a Verb, and in which context it is used as a Noun or Adjective. The same applies to the French word *annexe*. Therefore, it will be better, from our point of view, to register these words as a single entry in the following way:

English	**German**	**French**
abstract=Z/N/A	plumpen=Z/N/A	annexe=Z/N

where **Z** denotes the ambiguity Verb or another Part of Speech, **N** denotes a Noun, **A** denotes an Adjective, the sign **/** separates each item of information about the word. The codes used are language independent and the programmer is free to decide what codes to use, but the coding of each particular word is language specific. The coding of the information about the word is called tagging.

Often we need to know more about the Noun, the Verb, the Adjective, etc. We can add the additional grammatical, semantical, syntactical and even pragmatical information, contained in this word or in a group of words, in the following way:

English	**German**	**French**
adventurer=N[H]	buchständer=N[M]	abolition=N[F]
adventuress=N[HF]	plumpen=Z/N[F]/A	aboutement=N[M]
borneo=N[N]	examen=N[U]	aboulique=N[0]/A
come=u[i]	abscheu=N[0]	annexe=Z/N[F]
him=R[3SM]		
jelly-fish=N[C]		

where **H** means human being, **C** means singular or plural, **i** means irregular, **S** means singular, **3** means third person, **0** means no Gender or ambiguous Gender (0 can also mean 'no information about this word'), **M** means Masculine, **F** means Feminine, **U** means Neuter, **N** means 'name'. The square brackets are used to enclose additional information about the part of speech of this particular word. The coded information before the square bracket as Part of Speech (N, A, V, etc.), and that enclosed within square brackets, indicates membership to a list of words: all words marked with **N** before the square brackets belong to the list of nouns, all words marked with **H** in the square brackets belong to the list of words denoting a 'human being', all words marked with **N** in square brackets belong to the list of names, etc. There is no ambiguity between the code **N** before the square brackets and the code **N** within the square brackets, because the difference is defined with a source code in the software program.

One word entry can belong, simultaneously, to many such word-lists; for example, *him* belongs to the list of Personal Pronouns, to the list of Personal Pronouns 3rd person, to the list of Personal Pronouns in singular, to the list of Personal Pronouns, masculine gender. In other words, the list is a file and the code is the name of this file. The file is part of the Dictionary (the database). The only difference is that here we cannot use long file names. Only one letter is used for a file name.

Note that the coding of gender is very important for German, Russian, Bulgarian and French. In Turkish there is no gender. In English only a small number of words have gender. If there is no word agreement in gender, there is no reason to code it unless we need it. In other words, the coding of the grammatical features is language specific.

Note that the German word *Buchständer* above is written with Umlaut (ä). Often, specially on the Internet, the Umlaut ä, ö, ü is written *ae, oe, ue* and the double consonant ß in Swiss German is 'ss'. In this case, we have three possibilities to register the Umlaut, depending on whether our program will run on DOS, Windows or other platforms:

buchstander=N[M]
buchständer=N[M]
buchstaender=N[M]

which we can reduce to two:

buchständer=N[M]	or	buchstander=N[M]
buchstaender=N[M]		buchstaender=N[M]

Finally, we can reduce these possibilities to a single one, by coding the word written with Umlaut and writing a rule in the program to instruct it to recognize the Umlaut (DOS):

buchstander=^N[M]

where ^ indicates the presence of an Umlaut in this word. The rule in the program will say 'when you meet a word with this coding, take into consideration that the vowels can be equal to vowels with Umlaut'. However, from orthographical point of view, it will not be correct to register *buchstander*, if we want to make a spell-checking program.

There is yet another possibility (DOS), to write

buchstaender=N[M]

and tell the computer software program that ae = ä, oe = ö, ue = ü. There will be a number of German words (consider, for example, the words starting with *ae*, where *ae* is not equal to *ä*, like *aerob, Aerodynamik, aerodynamisch, Aerogramm*, etc.) that should not come under this rule. We can exclude these words from the rule if we are to make an orthographical spell-checker for German.

The last choice is when the program will run on Windows or another platform:

buchständer=N[M]

What we have said above for German, applies also to Turkish

gölcük=N (*pond*)

to the French accent

colorimètre=N[M]
colorimétrie=N[F]
garçon=N[M]

and to all other languages that use accentuated letters.

An important piece of grammatical information about the Noun is its singular or plural. In the Dictionary of Wordforms, as a rule, Nouns are registered in their singular form. The plural form is recognized automatically, by a rule written in the software program. This rule can only recognize automatically regular Nouns (those Nouns that form their plural according to a well-defined rule, applicable to most Nouns). For example:

English	**German**	**French**
algorithm=N	frau=N[F]	caféier=N[M]
alternative=N	frauen=n[F]	caféiers=n[M]
alternatives=n	or	caféière=N[F]
boss=N	frauen=N[FP]	caféières=N[FP]
bosses=N[P]		

where **n** means Noun plural and **[P]** means plural. The rule will be:

for English, make the Plural Form of the Noun, by adding
-s or *-es* (*-es* when the Noun ends in *-ch*, *-ss*);

for German, make the Plural Form of a Feminine Noun, by adding
-en or *-n* (*-n* when the Noun ends in *-e*);

for French, make the Plural Form of the Noun, by adding
-es or *-s* (*-s* when the Noun ends in *-e*).

So, the rule governing how to make a plural from a regular singular form is language specific, it applies only to a particular language and to a particular set of words within this language.

For example, the plural form of regular German Nouns depends on the gender. Masculine or Neuter Nouns, unlike feminine nouns, form their plural by adding the ending *-e*. For example:

spiel=N[U]
spiele=n[U]
spinat=N[M]
spinate=n[M]
etc.

Some Nouns form their plural form in an irregular way, for example:

English	**German**	**French**
alveolus=N	examen=N[U]	acini=n[M]
alveoli=n	examina=n[U]	acinus=N[M]
bacillus=N	absorptionsspektren=n	adamien=N
bacilli=n	absorptionsspektrum=N	adamienne=n
bacterium=N	abstandsgeld=N[U]	alleu=N[M]
bacteria=n	abstandsgelder=n[U]	alleux=N[MP]
man=N	abstichloch=N[U]	
men=n	abstichloecher=n[U]	

etc.

As evident from the examples shown above, there is no general rule for the formation of irregular Nouns and this poses a problem in text processing. Therefore, the best way will be to register the plural form of the irregular Nouns in the DW, as we have done above, rather than write complicated rules in the program.

For certain specific tasks, we have to 'tell' the computer software program which Noun is irregular and how it forms its irregular forms. This information we can add in the following way:

for English
alveolus=N[i](alveolus->alveoli)
alveoli=n
bacillus=N[i](bacillus->bacilli)
bacilli=n
bacterium=N[i](bacterium->bacteria)
bacteria=n
man=N[i](man->men)
men=n

for German
examen=N[USi](examen; examina)
spektrum=N[USi](spektrum; spektra; spektren)

for French
acinus=N[MSi](acinus->acini)
adamien=N[Si](adamien->adanienne)
alleu=N[MSi](alleu->alleux)

etc., where [i] means irregular, S means singular only, the semicolon and the sign -> are codes chosen by the programmer to separate the words in the list.

Some Nouns can be both singular and plural. There is no morphological feature within the word itself to tell us whether the Noun is singular or plural. For example:

English	**German**	**French**
sheep=N[C]	brausen=Z[s]/N[C]	bras=N[MC]

where [C] marks the ambiguity singular or plural, Z marks the ambiguity Noun or Verb, s codes additional information about the verb.

A number of Nouns have no plural. They are used only in singular. For example:

English	**German**	**French**
borneo=N[SN]	kopfes=N[MS]	quart-de-pouce=N[S]
buddhism=N[S]	berlin=N[SN]	quart-de-rond=N[S]

where [S] marks the Noun as singular only, [N] denotes a proper or geographical name. Note, that the ending *-es* of the German word *Kopf* is a case ending. For those languages (German, Russian, etc.) that have cases, we have to register either the case endings separately, or the wordform with its case ending(s), as in the example below.

German	**Russian**
komfort=N[M]	**высший**=A
komforts=N[M]	**высшего**=A
kommandant=N[M]	**высшему**=A
kommandanten=N[MC]	etc.
kommndo=N[U]	
kommndos=N[UC]	

Note that in German the case ending often coincides with the plural of the Noun and we can differentiate these two only in context (*Kommandanten, Kommandos*). Similar ambiguities in the word endings can be found in many languages.

We code likewise the other Parts of Speech, depending on what morphological, grammatical, syntactical, semantical, etc. information we consider relevant for the text analysis. For example, we can tell the software program what are the irregular forms of an English or German irregular Verb:

speak=V[i](speak; spoke; spoken)
aussprechen=V[i](aussprechen; ausgesprochen)

which German Participles are used only with *haben* [h] and which only with *sein* [s] or which words are used only with a certain preposition [X]:

gebeten=E[h]
gefallen=E[s]
bezeichnend=A[X]

what is the new German spelling:

auswaertslaufen=V[lq]<auswaerts; laufen>

what is the irregular form of a French adjective:

accélérateur=N[M]/A[i](accélérateur->accélératice)

etc.,
where < > and ( ) are codes used by the programmer to enclose the list of words, [i] means 'irregular form', **E** means Past Participle, [h] means 'used with *haben*', [s] means 'used with *sein*', [lq] means 'this word has a new spelling', **A** means Adjective, [X] means 'used with the Preposition *für*'. Note that we can use also a combination of codes [lq] to mark a single item of information. The codes [h], [s] and [X] mark the syntactical information of the word and its syntactically allowed combinatorics with other words.

Note that certain codes, especially those within the square brackets, are language specific; for example, in another language, we can mark with [X], [h], [s] something else.

Knowing that the Verb is irregular (does not form Past Tense and Past Participle in the normal way, by adding *-ed*), it is easy to make a rule to treat *speaked* as an error and to output its correct forms (speak; spoke; spoken). In this case, we have to enter the wrong spelling *speaked* in the dictionary, in the following way:

speaked=V[e](speak; spoke; spoken)

where [e], for example, will mean 'wrongly spelt word' and the program will output its correct spelling when it meets it in the text. The same applies to all irregular words in all languages.

As we mentioned earlier, often a word can belong to more than one Part of Speech.

English	**German**	**French**
then=D/J	das=T/S	le=T/M
		accélérateur=N[M]/A

For example, the German word *das* can be an Article (T) and a Pronoun (S), the English *then* can be an Adverb or a Conjunction, the French *le* can be an Article or a Pronoun. Therefore, we have to code all possibilities, separating them, for example, with a forward slash (/). The code we register first (T) will be the code valid for all contexts, unless specified otherwise (S). The specification, stating in what context(s) *das* can be S (Pronoun) can be made only within the software program. Then, with a simple rule (statement) we tell the software program in what specific context(s) *das* is a Pronoun. This applies to all other alternatives in the examples above and to all words in all languages that belong to more than one part of speech.

The syntactical information of a word can also be defined in the following ways:

a) By registering, in the DW, the whole phrase in which the word is met. This applies to words that follow immediately one after the other, as a phrase, with a fixed meaning. For example:

keep aloof=WVw
keep away=WVw
line by line=WNPN
ab und zu=WDww
abendkleid in schwarz=WNPN
abseits pfeifen=WNV
eine andere richtung einschlagen=WTANV
eine anleihe machen=WVww
a pleine capacité=WTAN
abattage des poussieres=WNww
abattement special=WNw
acceptation conditionnel=WNA
aller chercher=WVw
etc.,

where **W** means 'a phrase', **w** denotes a word entry within the phrase, NPN denotes the sequence Noun, Preposition, Noun, TANV denotes the sequence Article, Adjective, Noun, Verb, etc.

b) By writing a syntactic structure in the DW. This applies to words that are written separately and do not follow one after the other, but have one meaning. For instance

keep <NP>'away' =@Vfernhalten\@ \
achten <NP>'hoch'=@Vappreciate\$@\

where <NP> denotes a Noun Phrase separating the Verbs *keep away* (English) and *achten hoch* (German). These syntactic structures can be used in English – German and German – English Machine Translation to tell the computer software program, that *away* is an integral part of *keep* and that its translation in German is *fernhalten*, and, that *hoch* is an integral part of *achten* and its translation in English is *appreciate*. All other codes in the above examples are needed for the recognition of the separable verbs. In other words, when the program looks in the DW and identifies these codes, then the program 'knows' that it has to deal with a separable verb. For example, consider the sentence:

We have to keep the dogs away.

where the Noun Phrase *the dogs* separates the Verb *keep away*.

These syntactic structures are very important in Machine Translation, because some frequently used English Verbs (*put, let, keep, come*, etc.) can have completely different meanings when used with a detached Adverb (*up, down, out, away, off*, etc.). The same applies to any other language that has separately written words, when these words are separated from one another by a phrase. For example, consider the huge number of German separable verbs:

bringen <NP>'ab'=@Vdissuade\@\
bringen <NP>'an'=@Vput;fix;fit\@ \
bringen <NP>'auf'=@Vraise;find;muster;rouse\@ \
bringen <NP>'aus' =@Vannounce\@ \
bringen <NP>'bei' =@Vteach\@ \
bringen <NP>'dar' =@Voffer\@ \
bringen <NP>'durch' =@Vget through\@ \
bringen <NP>'um' =@Vkill\@ \

```
bringen <NP>'unter' =@Vstore\@ \
bringen <NP>'weg' =@Vremove\@ \
bringen <NP>'weiter' =@Vfurther\@ \
bringen <NP>'wieder' =@Vbring back\@ \
bringen <NP>'zu' =@Vspend\@ \
```

where the same verb '*bringen*' (bring) can have so many different meanings, depending on the part that follows it. It is preferable to represent the structures in the Dictionary of Wordforms, rather than to write a source code for each such structure in the program.

Yet another Dictionary problem, are the compound words. The compound words are words that consist of two or three words written as one word: *greenhouse* (English), *Lernprozess* (German) or words separated with a dash (in almost every language) or with an inverted comma ' (*l'*, *d'*, *n'*, *s'*, *'une*, etc.), appended to the word in French (*'s*, *'l*, *'t*, etc.), English and other languages. For example, *line-up, long-range, long-standing, l'accord, jusqu'a, qu'une, there's, I'll, can't*, etc. The first words *green, line, long, Lern* act as a word-formation prefix, to which one can add other words to form compound words:

English	**German**	**French**
greenhouse	Lernmittel	décomposer
line-up	Lernmittelfreiheit	régénération
long-range	Lernprozess	
long-standing	Sprachkurs	

etc.

In Turkish, an agglutinative language, this phenomenon is much more pronounced. Compare, for example, *kardeşim* (my friend), in which the possessive pronoun (*im*) is part of the word and positioned at the end, *gölcükda* (in the pond) and *kardeşimda* (in my friend) which is an entire adverbial prepositional clause in which *da* here means *in (the)*. The only difference with the other three languages under discussion is that instead of a prefix, in Turkish the attached word is a postfix (suffix), which will be dealt with further in this book when we return to the word endings.

One therefore feels tempted to isolate *long, Lern, dé*, etc., and to put them in a separate Dictionary and make the computer software program link freely other words to them. However, this will lead to the formation of words that are not accepted in the language. Consider for example: *long-inserted* (English), *Lernfrau, Lernhaus* (German), etc. This approach is unacceptable, if we are planning to make a spell-checking or Machine Translation software program, which is why it is better to list all compound words as they are presented in the dictionaries (see, for example, Jones (1967) or Duden (1996), Larousse (1995)).

We will have to consider specially the word-formation ability of the Prefixes. For example: *auto, trans-, super-, hyper-, in-, multi-, un-* (English), *dé-, ré-*, (French), *an-, auf-, herum-* (German), etc. Here, we again have two possibilities:

a) To list the prefixes in a table, enabling the software program to recognize the words that start with them even when these words are not listed in the Dictionary of Wordforms.
b) To list all the words that have prefixes, thus specifying which prefix can be used with which word. This way, we will make sure that *excusable* can have the prefix *in-* to make the word *inexcusable*, and that the word *unexcusable* does not exist.

We will also have to consider the word formation ability of the epenthetic German particle *zu* and of the morpheme *ge*, acting either as prefix or infix. The particle *zu* can be either prefixed to (*zubringen*) or inserted in almost any Verb to form an Infinitival Form of the Verb. For example: *abbauen - abzubauen, abdecken abzudecken*, etc. The morpheme *ge* can be either prefixed to (*gebraucht*), or inserted in almost any Verb to form the Past Participle Form of the Verb. For example: ***altern - gealtert, abbauen - abgebaut, abdecken - abgedeckt***, etc. In addition, we can provide a *ge-, -ge-, zu-, -zu-* word formation rule in our software program, just in case we have omitted to record certain wordforms in the dictionary. Our advice is to list all possible prefixed words in the Dictionary of Wordforms if we want to make a good parsing program, a good spell-checking program or a good machine-translation program.

To sum up, we have described the composition of the word, valid for many languages (prefix, infix, word ending or suffix), what information a word can contain (part of speech, number, gender, case, semantical information, syntactical information) and how to express (code) this information: the word or wordform comes first, then comes the sign = used as a separator, then comes the code for part of speech, then the additional information about this word in square brackets and, finally, what information can be printed about this word, contained in ( ) or in < >. When we come to describe a particular language, we see that German, for example, has fewer cases than Russian, Turkish has no gender, in English only a limited number of words have gender, the Neuter in English and French is not needed in the same way as German, some languages have an additional plural attached at the end of the word to express 'both' or 'the two' (for example, a south Bulgarian dialect) and negation can be expressed with a prefix (*un-, im- не-*), a suffix (***yapılmamıştı***, Turkish, ***has not done***), or a particle (***not, nicht, ne pas***, etc.) depending on the language. So, the method of description is universal and language independent. What language features will be described depends on whether the language has these features or whether we need these features for what we want to achieve. Later in the book, when we come to discuss programming procedures, it will become clear why we need to know all this.

1.1 Protection of the Dictionary

The Dictionary of Wordforms is a text file, which the software program opens to read. This means that anybody can open it with a Text Editor and read it, even edit and copy it, and an experienced programmer from a competitor firm will see what information you have coded. So, you have betrayed to the competition part of your trade secret. It costs much time, effort and money to develop such a Dictionary for our program, therefore we must protect it. In order to do that, we need to make a Dictionary-making software program. This Dictionary-making software program can perform various tasks:

– Extract wordforms from plain text and list them in alphabetical order, deleting the extra identical wordforms. The most common example of such a Dictionary-making software program is the 'Sort Text' sub-menu item of Microsoft Word (although, it does not delete the repeated wordforms). There are other such commercial programs with the source code available on the market.
– Insert new entries (new words and wordforms) into our existing Dictionary of Wordforms, preserving the wordforms already listed.
– Print our copyright text at the beginning of the Dictionary.
– Encrypt the entire Dictionary. This will make the Dictionary illegible. No one can read it and steal it.

The simplest way to protect our Dictionary is to copyright it: print our copyright text at the beginning of the Dictionary. Then, when we write the source code for our software program, we can write a piece of source code to read our copyright when opening the Dictionary. If our copyright does not exist or is not the same (as it should be), the program will not work. This procedure serves also to authenticate the dictionary, to confirm that the dictionary is the same as we have made it. This is important, because no one should edit the dictionary except those who have made it. The coding of the new dictionary entries is, as a rule, a trade secret and so complex and intricately connected with the source code of the program, that the average user cannot be trusted to do it. The same applies to the encrypted Dictionary: the software program must have a piece of source code to decipher the encryption and read the copyright.

2. C (C++) source code associated with the morphological, grammatical, syntactical and semantical information.

The programming work needed to develop a software program that compiles and executes without error is enormous. This work does not include the making of the Dictionary used by the program. For example, one qualified person needs at least four years to make a good bilingual Machine Translation Dictionary. This person must be either the programmer of the source code himself (herself), or if not, the programmer of the source code must understand (at least, grammatically) the foreign language and work very closely with the person who creates the Dictionary.

Of course, not all source code of such a program needs to be programmed by the programmer. Most compilers, especially the expensive ones of the last decade or so, have examples, in which the programmer can find (or generate automatically) the source code of ready-made interfaces and adapt them to the program's needs. Also, during the last decade one can buy ready-made, electronic single-language or bilingual dictionaries, but one cannot use them without significant re-editing and adapting to the needs of the software program.

Note: The source code, presented further in this book, is for specialised programmers only. We have done our best to explain the programming code to those who do not know programming at all. The quoted lines of code will compile without error only when the *.c(pp) and the *.h files are complete.

Since we do not intend to teach C (C++) programming, we have not provided explanations to all source code used in the examples. The source code used in the book is of two types:

a) standard for the programming language and
b) created by the programmer. Our explanations are for non-specialists, to help them understand that part of the source code, that relates directly to the grammar of the language under discussion. This is mainly the code created by the programmer. The reader can find an useful guide to C in Paul Davies (1995).

Having constructed the Dictionary of Wordforms (our English Dictionary of Wordforms has 55,421 word entries, used in *Syntparse* (Georgiev, 1993)), we will have to teach the computer software program to recognize and interpret our codes for the morphological, grammatical, semantical and syntactical information used in the DW. Note that if we define all this information in the DW, but we do not define it with a source code in the software program, the program will function, but will not recognize the information in the DW. On the other hand, if we define all this information with a source code in the software program, but we do not code this information in the DW, the program will function, but will not find the information in the DW. So, the DW and the software program are inseparably connected – one cannot function properly without the other. In a file, named, for example, "grammar.c(c)" or "grammar.cpp", we have to define each code and the grammatical, etc. information attached to it. This file will begin as follows:

```
#include <ctype.h>
#include <stdio.h>
#include <conio.h>
#include <alloc.h>
#include <dir.h>
#include <bmenu.h>
#include <bmouse.h>
// etc. standard include files present in our compiler, as needed.
/*** Note: The sign // is used to add comments or to close source code on the same line.
```

The sign /* */ is used to to add comments or to close source code on one line or more than one lines. Using **#include <... >** we include the standard *.h files, that come with the compiler, as needed. The names of these *.h files and their contents are standard for most compilers. ***/

```
#include "dicgram.h"
```

/*** This is our file for coding of the information about the word.
Using **#include " ... "** we include the *.h file(s) developed by us for the respective *.c(pp) file(s). ***/

```
void get_gram(int lang, char *c, WORD *wrd);
int find_words(struct QUE *que[]);
DLIM *enque_dlm(struct QUE *que[], char syn, char ssyn);
WORD *enque_word(struct QUE *que[], char syn, char *word);
struct C_TAB *contr_analys(char *word, int wl, WORD *wrd);
struct M_TAB *morph_analys(char *word, int wl, WORD *wrd, char *ww);
struct PREF_TAB *pref_analys(char *word, WORD *wrd);
```

/* etc. There are two types of code words used by the program: **standard** code words for C (*void* function, integral values *int*, text characters *char*, structure variable *struct*, etc.) and code words **invented** and defined by the programmer, such as *morph_analys* (morphological analysis), *pref_analys* (analysis of the prefix), PREF_TAB (table for the prefixes), etc. */

```
#include "grammar.h"
```

// Here we define our invented codes and declare internal subroutines.

From this point on begin various morphological and grammatical functions (tasks), named struct, which the program has to perform. The function starts with an opening brace { and ends with a closing brace }. We will start with the recognition of the prefix.

2.1 Recognition of the Prefix.

In all European languages there is a large number of word-producing prefixes. This means that when we construct the Dictionary of Wordforms, we can omit the prefixed words if we list the prefixes separately.

When the program reads a text, word by word, it tries to match each wordform from the text with its corresponding wordform registered in the Dictionary of Wordforms. If the program cannot find a match, it will perform the following tasks:

– Will try to match one of the prefixes (from the List) with the prefix of the word that was not found.
– If a match is found (prefixes match), the program ignores the prefix (cuts it away) and tries to match the remaining part of the wordform with a corresponding wordform registered in the Dictionary of Wordforms.
– If a match is found, the wordform is recognized.
– If a match is not found, the wordform is not recognized. In this case the program starts another procedure – cuts off the grammatical ending of the word (if there is such) and tries to find a matching word in the DW (explained further below).

These steps of the analysis of the prefix find expression in the following source code from the file "grammar.c(pp)":

```
struct PREF_TAB *pref_analys(char *word, WORD *wrd)
{
```

/* where PREF_TAB (a template name) is our table for the prefixes of the words, 'wrd', 'word' (our parameter list). */

```
struct PREF_TAB *pref;
int l;    // the prefix has a length in letters
```

```
  for ( pref = PREFTAB; pref->prefix; pref++ )
// while pref = PREFTAB, execute pref->prefix; pref++
  {
    if ( !strncmp(word, pref->prefix, pref->len) )
// if statement
    { // marks the start of the statement block
     l = pref->len;
// length of prefix
     if (wrd->wl == l) {
// If the word is equal to the prefix (for compound words)
    strcpy(wrd->outwd, pref->rprefix);
// take the recorded prefix for the target language
    wrd->syn = 'D';
// and note that this word cannot be declined and is not inflected.
    wrd->stat = 2; // other information, as needed
    return NULL;
     }
    else
    if ( pref->prefix[0] == 'r' && pref->prefix[1] == 'e') {
// If the prefix of the source language word is 're' (English),
// the equivalent prefix of the target language word will be " "
      strcat(wrd->rprefix, " ");
// Here we have not specified it.
/* Note: the prefix of the target language word is needed only if we
   want to use this program for Machine Translation as well. */
     }
     strncat(wrd->eprefix, wrd->inword, l);
     wrd->wl -= l;
     strcpy(wrd->inword, wrd->inword + l);
     strcpy(word, word + l);
     wrd->stat = 1;
     return pref;
   } // closes if statement
  }
  return NULL;
}
```

Following the above rule, the prefixes are listed in the included file "grammar.h" as follows:

for the English language:

```
struct PREF_TAB {
char *prefix;
int len;
char *rprefix;
};
struct PREF_TAB PREFTAB[] =
{
/* List of prefixes of the source language and their equivalent in
   the target language. Since the target language can be any, we have not
   specified it. We have written again the source language prefix, as equivalent. */

{"non",   3,   "non"   },
{"sub",   3,   "sub"   },
```

```
{"pre",   3,  "pre"  },
{"de",    2,  "de"    },
{"re",    2,  "re" },
{"infra", 5,  "infra" },
{"pseudo", 6,  "pseudo" },
{"stereo", 6,  "stereo" },
{"video", 5,  "video" },
{"radio", 5,  "radio" },
{"photo", 5,  "photo"  },
{"tele",  4,  "tele"  },
{"trans", 5,  "trans" },
{"super", 5,  "super" },
{"hyper", 5,  "hyper" },
{"multi", 5,  "multi" },
{"semi",  4,  "semi"  },
// etc.
{NULL,  0,  NULL }
};
```

We can specify the prefix, if we want it, for example, for German–English Machine translation:

```
struct PREF_TAB PREFTAB[] =
{
{"abend", 5,  "evening" },
{"abwehr", 6,  "protective" },
{"alkohol", 7,  "alcohol" },
{"alpen", 5,       "alp" },
{"alters", 6,    "elderly" },
{"alt",   3,       "old" },
{"amateur", 7,  "amateur" },
{"amts", 4,  "office" },
{"anders", 6,  "different" },
{"angriffs", 8,  "offensive" },
{"antennen", 8,  "aerial" },
{"antriebs", 8,  "driving" },
// etc.
{"zukunfts", 8,  "future"  },
{NULL,  0,  NULL }
};
```

We can specify the prefix, if we want it for French–English Machine translation:

```
struct PREF_TAB PREFTAB[] =
{
{"aéro",   4,  " aero"    },
{"anti",   4,  "anti"    },
{"auto",   4,  "auto"  },
{"bio",    3,  "bio"    },
{"bi",     2,  "bi"    },
{"centi",  5,  " centi" },
{"contre",  6,  " counter" },
{"co",     2,  " co"    },
{"électro", 7,  " electro" },
{"euro",   4,  " euro"  },
```

```
{"extra",   5,   " extra" },
{"géo",    3,   " geo"   },
{"hecto",  5,   " hecto" },
{"hétéro", 6,   " hetero" },
{"idéo",   4,   " ideo"  },
// etc.
{NULL,  0,  NULL }
};
```

etc. source and target language.

The figure after the prefix shows the number of letters in the prefix. (Note: There are other ways to list the prefixes and to make the program recognize them. This is simply one possibility.)

The inclusion of some short prefixes such as ***re-***, ***un-***, ***in-***, (English), *bio-* (English, French), *alt-* (German), etc., may lead to problems if we want to construct a spell-checking software program, because such word beginnings as *re-*, *un-*, *in-*, *bio-*, *alt-*, etc. are not always prefixes. Moreover, even when they are prefixes, the spell-checking program will not be able to correct the misspelt word: for example, ***unexcusable*** (correct: *inexcusable*). Therefore, our advise is to list all prefixed words in the dictionary, if possible.

2.2 Recognition of the compound words separated with a dash.

If in an *.h file we place the following code:

```
struct T_PART {
  char *inst;
  char *outst;
  int cond;
}
  PART[] =
{
// etc.
// for the English Language
   {"H-'d'",    "Aww",   },  /* 3-d */
   {"H-'nd'",   "Aww",   },  /* 2-nd */
   {"H-'st'",   "Aww",   },  /* 1-st */
   {"H-'th'",   "Aww",   },  /* 4-th */
   {"[H?#NZ]-'based'", "A ", },
   {"[dD]-B-[ZV]",  "D-P-A", },
   {"[#?H]-[NIAZ]",  "A-A", },
   {"I-N",         "@-A", },
   {"[?#N]-A",      "A A", },
// for the German language
   {"N-",    "A", },
   {"-Z",   "@N", },
   {"Z-",    "N", },
// etc.
// for the French language
   {"V-'nous'",      "V@R",  },
   {"V-'il'",      "V@R",  },
   {"V-'elle'",      "V@R",  },
   {"V-'ils'",      "V@R",  },
   {"V-'t'-'il'",    "V@m@R",  },
```

```
   {"V-'t'-'nous'",    "V@R@m",  },
   {"V-'t'-'ils'",   "V@m@R",  },
   {"V-'t'-'elle'",    "V@m@R",  },
// etc.
{NULL,    NULL, 0}
};
```

the software program will be able to recognize the constituent words of the two-words-long and the three-words-long compound words separated with a dash. Note that we have to define every code we use in a *.h file in a *.c(pp) file first:

```
   struct T_PART *ptb;
   synset[j] = *inst;
   char synset[80];
   // etc.
```

In the examples above '-' represents the dash separating the compound word. The stand-alone codes and the codes listed in square brackets show the possible part(s) of speech that can be separated with a dash. For example, {"[H?#NZ]-'based'", "A ", } can recognize such English words as *book-based, campus-based*, etc., the second part of which is '*-based*'. The above rules can be applied to all languages that use a dash to separate the compound words. For the other abbreviations used above see the Index of Abbreviations.

2.3 *Recognition of the abbreviated compound words separated with an inverted comma (')*.

As we have said in the previous chapter, many languages use an inverted comma to separate the abridged constituent words of a compound word. To deal with this phenomenon we can use the following C source code placed in the file 'grammar.c(pp)':

```
struct C_TAB *contr_analys(char *word, int wl, WORD *wrd)
/* where C_TAB (a template name) is our table for the prefixes of the words, 'wrd', 'word' (our parameter list). */
{
struct C_TAB *mor;
int lf, i;
WORD *new;

 for ( mor = CTAB; mor->mflex; mor++ ) {
   if ((lf = isflex(word, wl, mor->mflex)) > 0 ) {
// if statement about the word ending
    wl -= lf;
    wrd->stat = 1;

    switch (mor->mgram[0]) {
// a switch statement to evaluate the expression mor->mgram[0]

   case 'X' : // for English
// when the word is marked with X, execute the if statements below
      if (!strcmp(word, "there\'s") ||
      !strcmp(word, "here\'s")  ||
      !strcmp(word, "what\'s")  ||
      !strcmp(word, "that\'s")  ||
```

```
      !strcmp(word, "who\'s"))
// if the following English words are matched
/*****
   case 'X' :  // for French
      if (!strcmp(word, "c\'est") ||
      !strcmp(word, "s\'est") ||
      !strcmp(word, "d\'une") ||
      !strcmp(word, "m\'a") ||
      !strcmp(word, "j\'ai") ||
      !strcmp(word, "m\'en") ||
      !strcmp(word, "qu\'on") ||
      !strcmp(word, "j\'y") ||
      !strcmp(word, "l\'a") ||
      !strcmp(word, "j\'en"))
// if the following French words are matched
       // etc. French *****/
      {
       word[wl] = '\0';
       break;
      }
      else { /* abridged using inverted comma */
       word[wl] = '\0';
       for (i = 0; PRTAB[i].mflex; i++)
      if (strcmp(PRTAB[i].mflex, word) == 0) break;
       if (PRTAB[i].mflex == NULL && mor->cond == 3) {
      /* inverted comma */
      word[wl] = '\'';
      wrd->stat = 0;
      return NULL;
       }
       /* abridged */
      }
   break;
   default:  /* English 'not' */
      if (!strcmp(word, "can\'t"))
         wl++;
      else if (!strncmp(word, "arn", 3)) {
// this will make the form 'arn't'
      strcpy(wrd->inword + 1, "re");
      strcpy(word + 1, "re");
// 'are not'
     wl = 3;
    }
    else if (!strncmp(word, "won", 3)) {
// this will make the form 'won't'
      strcpy(wrd->inword + 1, "ill");
      strcpy(word + 1, "ill");
// 'will not'
         wl = 4;
      }
      else if (!strncmp(word, "sha", 3)) {
// this will make the form 'shan't'
      strcpy(wrd->inword + 3, "ll");
      strcpy(word + 3, "ll");
```

```
// 'shall not'
      wl = 5;
/***** // French
      else if (!strncmp(word, "j", 1)) {
      strcpy(wrd->inword + 1, "ai");
         strcpy(word + 1, "ai");
// this will recognize 'j'ai'
      wl = 2;
      }
      else if (!strncmp(word, "c", 1)) {
         strcpy(wrd->inword + 1, "est");
         strcpy(word + 1, "est");
// this will recognize c'est
      wl = 4;
    }
     // etc. French
*****/
    }
    else if (mor->cond == 2) /* cannot */
     wl = 3;
    wrd->wl = wl;
    word[wl] = '\0';
  break;

    } /* end switch */
  }
 }
 return NULL;
```

In the respective *.h file we have to continue the above rule in the following way:

```
struct C_TAB {
char *mflex;
char *mgram;
char *iw;
char *ow;
int cond;
};

struct C_TAB CTAB[] = {
// for English
{"let\'s","M",  "us",  NULL, 4},
{"\'s",  "X",  "is",  NULL, 3},
{"n\'t", "K",  "not",  "not", 0},
{"\'ll", "X",  "will", NULL, 0},
{"\'d",  "X",  "would", NULL, 1},
{"\'m",  "T",  "am",  NULL, 0},
{"\'re", "T",  "are",  NULL, 0},
{"\'ve", "X",  "have", "have", 0},
{"cannot", "K", "not",  "not", 2},
/* where we code the word ending after the inverted comma, the part of speech of that word and
the full form of the abridged word */
// etc. English
// for French
```

```
{"\'s",  "î",  "se",  NULL, 2},
{"s\'",  "î",  "se",  NULL, 2},
{"t\'",  "T",  "te",  NULL, 2},
{"s\'",  "T",  "se",  NULL, 2},
{"j\'",  "T",  "je",  NULL, 2},
{"l\'",  "T",  "le",  NULL, 2},
{"c\'",  "T",  "ce",  NULL, 2},
{"n\'",  "K",  "ne",  NULL, 2},
{"d\'",  "T",  "de",  NULL, 2},
{"m\'",  "T",  "me",  NULL, 2},
```

/* where we code the word beginning before the inverted comma, the part of speech of that word and the full form of the abridged word */

```
{"\'ont",  "T",  "ont",  "avoir", 0},
{"\'été",  "T",  "été",  "être", 0},
{"\'étais",  "T",  "étais",  "être", 0},
{"\'était",  "T",  "était",  "être", 0},
{"\'avais",  "T",  "avais",  "avoir", 0},
{"\'ayant",  "T",  "ayant",  "avoir", 0},
{"\'aurai",  "T",  "aurai",  "avoir", 0},
```

// "avoir", "être", etc. can be replaced by
// a translation into another language

```
{"\'en",  "T",  "en",  "en", 0},
{"\'on",  "T",  "on",  "on", 0},
{"\'achète",  "T",  "achète",  NULL, 0},
```

/* Where we code the word ending after the inverted comma, the part of speech of that word and the full form of the abridged word, plus its translation into another language, as needed. */
// etc. French
/* It is impossible to list all such words, because
their number in French is huge! */

```
{NULL,  NULL,  NULL, NULL,}
};
```

In French, similar to the English examples above, two words are often written as one word, where the first word can be a Negation Particle (n'), Reflexive Pronoun (s'), Personal Pronoun Objective Case (m'), Conjunction (qu'), etc. Compare: ***n'existe pas, d'esprit, s'emparera, l'éducation, l'heure, l'émergence, l'authenticité, l'endroit***, etc.

Using the above descriptions and definitions, the program recognizes the compound apostrophized word, separates its constituent words and prints them, eventually, separately. The only problem in this case is that we do not know, at this stage, whether in French ***l'*** is ***le*** or ***la***. If needed, that can also be found out, if we make additional rules to establish the Gender of the Noun.

As an alternative to the above rules for the abridged compound words, separated with an inverted comma or dash, we can list these words directly in our DW if they are not too many (for example, in French they are too many, in German only a few):

English	**German**	**French**
arn't=X	da hapert's=WPN	l'acheter=V
can't=U	da hast du's=WPXN	j'ai=X
there's=X	war's=X	qu'ill=R
campus-based=A	dass-satz=N	abat-jour=N

However, here, we omit the part of speech of one of the constituent words (***can not, war es, je ai***, etc.), therefore, we had better list only those compound words that represent one part of speech (***l'acheter, there's, campus-based***) and those that are used in a phrase (***da hast du's***). If we want to use our program for machine translation only, we can list all such words and their translation, without exception, regardless of part of the speech.

2.4 *Recognition of the Umlaut and the accent*

As we mentioned above, the Umlaut in German plays a grammatical role and is met in two variants (*ä, ö, ü* and *ae, oe, ue*). The digraph *ss* is also met in two variants (*ss* and *ß*) differentiating the Swiss spelling from the German and Austrian spelling. Therefore, we have to consider this fact, in the software program, especially because both variants are used on the Internet.

In a file named, for example, "de_gram.cpp", we can put the following source code statement to enable recognition of the Umlaut or the French accent:

```
short CDeFinder::ConvertAccent( const char *pszWord, char *pszWordOut )
{
  short nAccent = 0;  // here we call the Umlaut "accent"
  if (!pszWord[0])
  {
    pszWordOut[0] = '\0';
     return nAccent;
  }
  for (; *pszWord; *pszWord++, *pszWordOut++)
  {
   if (pszWord[0] == (uchar)*S_DEU_AE_)  // if ä
     {
     pszWordOut[0] = 'a';  // without ¨ it is equal to a
       nAccent++;
     }
    else
   if (pszWord[0] == (uchar)*S_DEU_SS_)  // if 'ß' (ss)
     {
   pszWordOut[0] = 'ß'; // it is equal to ß
       nAccent++;
     }
  else
  if (pszWord[0] == (uchar)*S_DEU_UE_)  // if ü
     {
   pszWordOut[0] = 'u'; // without ¨ it is equal to u
      nAccent++;
     }
   else
   if (pszWord[0] == (uchar)*S_DEU_OE_)  // if ö
      {
   pszWordOut[0] = 'o';  // without ¨ it is equal to o
        nAccent++;
   }
// end for German
     else
   if (pszWord[0] == (uchar)*S_LAT_AB_)  // if à
      {
   pszWordOut[0] = 'a';  // without ' it is equal to a
        nAccent++;
   }
// etc. for French
```

```
// etc., depending on the language
   else
      *pszWordOut = *pszWord;
   }
   *pszWordOut = 0;
   return nAccent;
}
```

In a *.c(pp) file (for example: alphabet.c(pp)), we must define the codes used for the German Umlaut, in the following way:

```
#if defined __LANG_DE  // If the German alphabet is defined
const uchar S_DEU_AE_[] = {132, '\0'}; // ä
const uchar S_DEU_AE[] = {142, '\0'}; // Ä
const uchar S_DEU_OE_[] = {148, '\0'}; // ö
const uchar S_DEU_OE[] = {253, '\0'}; // Ö
const uchar S_DEU_UE_[] = {129, '\0'}; // ü
const uchar S_DEU_UE[] = {154, ''\0'}; // Ü
const uchar S_DEU_SS_[] = {225, '\0'}; // ß
// end for German
// etc., depending on the language having accentuated words
#endif
```

Then we do the same for French:

```
#if defined __INTERNAL_OEM
const uchar S_LAT_AB_[] = {133, '\0'}; // à
// etc. French
#endif
// etc. for any other language with accentuated letters
```

The numbers show the ASCII codes of the letters.

The respective alphabet.h file will contain the following codes for German:

```
extern const uchar S_DEU_AE_[];   // definition of ä
extern const uchar S_DEU_OE_[];   // definition of ö
extern const uchar S_DEU_UE_[];   // definition of ü
extern const uchar S_DEU_SS_[];   // definition of ß
extern const uchar S_DEU_AE[];    // definition of Ä
extern const uchar S_DEU_OE[];    // definition of Ö
extern const uchar S_DEU_UE[];    // definition of Ü
// etc. for German
// etc., depending on the language
```

And then again for French:

```
#if defined __INTERNAL_ANSI
const uchar S_LAT_AB_[] = {224, '\0'}; // à
// etc. for French
#endif
```

The French accent plays a grammatical and semantical role. For example, compare the difference between *eut* in *il eut* (passé simple, indicatif) and *eût* in *qu'il eût* (imparfait, subjonctif) or *mange* (présent) and *mangé* (participes); therefore, we have to make the program recognize it. Note that most European languages have accentuated letters.

The above conversion of the German Umlaut and the French accent cannot be used in a spell-checking software program, because ä = a, ö = o, ü = u, à = a, û = u, etc., which is not true. This means, that if the letter is *a* and we write *ä*, the program will understand it and will not 'think' that that is wrong. Similarly, if the letter is ä and we write *a*, the program will also understand it. This conversion can be used in Machine Translation, because there the source German or French text must be written correctly anyway. In Machine Translation this conversion is needed if we decide to register the words in the DW without using the Umlaut or the accent. That will save us some problems, but will create other problems, because the Umlaut often not only has a grammatical function but a semantical function (a word can mean different things when it is written with Umlaut or without it). We will discuss this in greater detail later in the book.

There is also another way to make the program recognize the Umlaut or any other accentuated letter in C++, without loss of information:

```
BOOL IsWordBreak(char cThisChar)
{
   BOOL bReturn = FALSE;
   if (!::isalnum(cThisChar))
   {
      bReturn = TRUE;
      if (cThisChar == 'ö')  // if the letter is ö low-case
         bReturn = FALSE;
      if (cThisChar == 'ü') // if the letter is ü low-case
         bReturn = FALSE;
      if (cThisChar == 'ä') // if the letter is ä low-case
         bReturn = FALSE;
      if (cThisChar == 'Ö') // if the letter is Ö upper-case
         bReturn = FALSE;
      if (cThisChar == 'Ü') // if the letter is Ü upper-case
         bReturn = FALSE;
      if (cThisChar == 'Ä')  // if the letter is Ä upper-case
         bReturn = FALSE;
// etc. for German
      if (cThisChar == 'è')  // if the letter is è lower-case
         bReturn = FALSE;
// etc. for French
// etc., depending on the language having accentuated words
   }
   return bReturn;
}
```

provided that we have defined
BOOL IsWordBreak(char cThisChar);
in the included *.h file.

2.5 *Recognition of the Parts of Speech by their grammatical ending*

Many languages have inflected parts of speech – usually the noun, the adjective and the verb. The pronoun in some languages is inflected, in others, not. Below we will show how the software program can recognize the part of speech exclusively on the basis of the grammatical ending of the word.

In the file "grammar.c" or "grammar.cpp" we can use the following source code statement (valid for all languages and all parts of speech):

```
struct M_TAB *morph_analys(char *word, int wl, WORD *wrd, char *ww)
{
/* The obligatory reference to the table where the grammatical endings will
be listed. */
struct M_TAB *mor, *mow;
int lf = 0, l;
   for ( mor = MTAB; mor->mflex; mor++ ) {
      if ((lf = isflex(word, wl, mor->mflex)) > 0 ) {
```

```
wl -= lf;
      if (mor->mflex[0] == 'e') {
```
/* When 'e' is a registered grammatical ending of an English word */
```
      *ww = 'e';
```
/* 'e' is the last letter of the word */
/* Earlier in the program we have defined that *ww = word[wl - 1], */
/* where 'wl' is word length */
```
   }
      wrd->syn = mor->mgram[0];
```
/* The attribution of the word to particular Part of Speech is as shown in the Table */
```
switch (mor->mgram[0]) {
```
/* Now, let's define the Parts of Speech one by one.*/
Note: this statement continues in 2.5.1 and 2.5.2.

2.5.1 Case 'N', where the code designates a Noun

a) Definition of the basic form of the Noun made in the file "grammar.c" or "grammar.cpp" (continuation after switch):

```
      case 'N' :
```
/* definition of Noun Singular, basic Form, language independent */
```
      if (mor->mflex[lf - 1] == '\'' ||mor->mflex[0] == '\'')
        word[wl] = '\0';
```
// the basic form of the word has no grammatical ending
```
      break;
```
(Remember: The signs /* */ are used to insert comments or to close source code on one or more lines to stop the compiler compiling it.)

Case 'N' states that the basic form of the Noun is presented in the Dictionary without its possible grammatical endings present in the wordforms. The possible endings are defined in the file "grammar.h", as follows:

```
struct M_TAB {
char *mflex;
char *mgram;
int cond;
};
```
(Note: the endings registered in the file "grammar.h" are language dependent.)
Presentation for the English language follows below.

```
struct M_TAB MTAB[] = {
{"s\'",   "N12",},   /* Possessive Form of the Noun */
{"\'s",   "N02",},   /* Possessive Form of the Noun */
// the backward slash marks the end of the dictionary word
// the ending of the word is what is added after the backward slash
/* the numbers 12, 02, 00, 13, etc., after 'N', etc., indicate type of Noun or
other part of speech , as applicable */
{"ment",  "N00",},   /* Noun ending in '-ment' */
{"ion",   "N00",},   /* Noun ending in '-ion' */
{"ence",  "N00",},   /* Noun ending in '-ence' */
{"s",   "Z13",},
/* Noun Plural, be aware, the same word can be also a Verb */
// etc. English word endings
{NULL,   NULL, }
};
```

Knowing this rule, the computer software program 'knows' that the above-listed English word endings can be added to the basic form to make other forms ('ment', 'ion', 'ence' forms) or the plural form 's' of the Noun. For example, if we have registered the word *ship* in the DW and have not registered *ship's*, *shipment* and its plural and verbal form *ships*, the software program will be able to recognize these wordforms when met in the text.

Nouns ending in *-age* or *-ance* and not recorded in the Dictionary of Wordforms, can be recognized if we register these endings also in the above-stated rule:

```
{"age",   "N00",},
{"ance",  "N00",},
```

Knowing this, the computer software program can recognize that *reportage* is a Noun, when met in a text, if we have registered the Verb or Noun *report* and failed to register the Noun *reportage* in the Dictionary of Wordforms. The same applies to the ending *-ance*.

Presentation of the same structure for the German language follows below.

```
struct M_TAB MTAB[] = {
{"es",  "N",},      /* Noun ending in -es */
{"s",   "N",},      /* Noun ending in -s */
{"n",   "N",},      /* Noun ending in -n */
{"e",   "Z13",},   /* Noun ending in -e */
// etc. for the German language
{NULL,   NULL, }
};
```

Knowing the above rule, the computer software program 'knows' that the above-listed German endings can be added to the basic form to make other forms (*"es"*, *"s"*, *"n"* are case forms, *"n"* is ambiguous – case or plural, therefore it will need further clarification) or to make the plural form of the Noun by adding *"e"*. Note, that *e* is not an universal plural form in German and it is ambiguous (noun plural or verb 1st person singular present tense, which is why it is coded with Z). It is a commonly used plural form for Masculine and Neuter Nouns, but not for Feminine Nouns. Therefore, to take into account all exceptions, we need to make further specifications, either in the DW or in the program itself. In our case, we have chosen to do that in the DW and leave in the program only one plural ending *e*.

Nouns ending in *-heit* or *-keit* and not recorded in the Dictionary of Wordforms, can be recognized if we register these endings in the above-stated rule:

```
{"heit",  "N",},
{"keit",  "N",},
```

Knowing this, the computer software program can recognize that *Affektiertheit* is a Noun if we have registered the Participle *affektiert* and failed to register the Noun *Affektiertheit* in the Dictionary of Wordforms. The same applies to the ending *keit*.

Presentation of the same structure for the French language follows below.

```
struct M_TAB MTAB[] = {
{"age",   "N",},
{"es\'",  "N",},
{"s\'",   "N",},
{"\'s",   "N",},
{"ies\'", "N",},
{"es",    "Z13",}, /* Noun Plural */
{"s",     "Z13",}, /* Noun Plural */
// etc. for the French language
```

```
{NULL,   NULL, }
};
```

Knowing the above rule, the computer software program 'knows' that the above-listed French endings can be added to the basic form to make other forms of the Noun. Nouns ending in *-ment* or *-isme*, etc. and not recorded in the Dictionary of Wordforms, can be recognized, if we register these endings in the above stated rule:

```
{"ment",   "N",},
{"isme",   "N",},
// etc.
```

Knowing this, the computer software program can recognize that *coulissement* is a Noun if we have registered the Noun *coulisse* and failed to register the Noun *coulissement* in the Dictionary of Wordforms. The same applies to the ending *-isme*. Note: When registering the endings of different Parts of Speech we should take care that they do not coincide, because that will confuse the program! That is why we have marked the plural Noun ending *-s* (English, French) with the sign Z13, because of the existing ambiguity with the endings of the verb. The sign Z13 marks this ambiguity. In English Z13 means plural noun or third person singular verb. In French, German, etc. language 13 marks another number or person, depending on the language.

b) Definition of the additional information (enclosed in square brackets in the DW) carried by the Noun in the file "grammar.c(pp)". The source code statement presented below defines the additional information for the Noun and until *switch* is independent of language and part of speech.

```
void get_engram(char *word, char *cw, WORD *wrd)
{
char *wdic;
char *wirr;
 if (!wrd->inbase ||wrd->inbase[0] == '\0')
   strcpy(wrd->inbase, word);              /* Source Form */
   strcpy(wrd->rprefix, cw);         /* Debug  Info */

  switch (wrd->syn)  /* switch to part of speech info */
  {

case 'N' : /* Noun Singular, registered (usually basic) Form */
   if (isdigit(*cw)) wrd->tflag = *cw++ - '0';
   if (isdigit(*cw)) wrd->gender = *cw++ - '0';
   // etc. if statements
   if (*cw == '[') {
/* If there is a square bracket opened to enclose additional information about the Noun */
    while (*cw && *cw != ']') {
// while the square bracket remains opened
/* If statements about the enclosed coded information contained in the word
follow below in the following order: = = C, S, P, H, etc, is the code placed in square brackets in
the DW , wrd->e.N.constant = 1, etc. is the code word used in the source code in a *.c(pp) file
for 'C', etc.  */
/* What follows below is language dependent, but most of this information is common for all
languages. */
      if (*cw == 'C')  wrd->e.N.constant = 1;  // can be both Singular and Plural
      if (*cw == 'S')  wrd->e.N.singular_only = 1;
          /* is registered as Singular only */
      if (*cw == 'P')  wrd->e.N.plural_only = 1;  // is registered as Plural only
```

```
      if (*cw == 'H')  wrd->e.N.human = 1; // is a human being
      if (*cw == 'N')  wrd->e.N.name = 1;       // is a name
      if (*cw == 'M')  wrd->e.N.masculin = 1; // is a masculine gender
      if (*cw == 'F')  wrd->e.N.fem = 1; // is a feminine gender
      if (*cw == 'U')  wrd->e.N.neuter = 1; // is a neuter gender
      if (*cw == 'T')  wrd->e.N.time = 1; // denotes time
      if (*cw == 'D')  wrd->e.N.grau_from = 1;
// is used with the English preposition 'from'
//    if (*cw == 'V')  wrd->kflag = 1;
/* is used with the German preposition 'am' */
// etc.
      if (*cw == 'L')  {     /* for compound words */
      wrd->e.N.compound = 1;
      wrd->gflag = 'f';
       }  /*end*/
      cw++;
   }
   cw++;
   }
/* When we exhaust all possible codes (letters of various alphabets, numbers, punctuation marks and other signs) within the square brackets and we need to enclose more additional information about the particular part of speech (in our case, here, the Noun), we can enclose more information about the noun (or any other part of speech) within arrows, as shown below: */
// if (*cw == '<') {
// if an arrow is opened
//   while (*cw && *cw != '>') {
// while the arrow stays opened and is not closed
//    if (*cw == 'C')  wrd->e.N.comp_sys = 1;
//    if (*cw == 'C')  wrd->comp_sys = 1;
/* if within the arrows we find the code C, this code will mark the meaning comp_sys (Computer Operating System: DOS, Linux, Macintosh, Windows, etc.) */
/* Note that the code C here has a different meaning compared to the meaning of C when enclosed within square brackets (see above). */
//    cw++;
//   }
//   cw++;
//    }
// and use again all possible codes
/* and when these codes are not enough, we can enclose more codes within paranthesis and assign to them different information, for example */
//    if (*cw == '{') {
// if a paranthesis is opened
//    while (*cw && *cw != '}') {
// while the paranthesis stays opened and is not closed
//    if (*cw == 'C')  wrd->e.N.comp_acc = 1;
//    if (*cw == 'C')  wrd->comp_acc = 1;
/* where comp_acc will mean Computer Accessories (modem, printer, etc.) */
/* Note again, that we have used three times the same code to mark three different meanings!
*/
//    cw++;
//   }
//   cw++;
//    }
// etc. until we exhaust all possibilities
```

```
}
   wrd->person = 3;
  break;
```

The above rule defines the following additional grammatical, semantical or syntactical information registered in the DW and enclosed in square brackets:

'C' – the same word or wordform can be used both in Singular and in Plural. For example, compare such words as: *sheep, fish* (English), *Afrikaner, Afrolooks, Agenten* (German), *anglais, beaujolais, bellis* (French), etc.
'S' – means that the word entry is used only in Singular. For example, compare such words as: *capitalism, Cardiff, cardiology*, (English), *Agnostizismus, Alkoholgehalt, Alkoholkriminalität* (German), *en-but, flagada, grand-croix* (French), etc.
'P' – means that the word entry is in Plural.
'H' – means that the word entry designates a "human being".
'N' – means that the word entry is a proper or geographical name.
'D' – means that the word entry is used with the Preposition "*from*".
'T' – means that the word entry denotes Time,

etc. We can add more such codes for every item of information we want to register and use, so long as we always use the same code for the same thing within the square brackets. (Note: The codes in the square brackets have nothing to do with the codes outside the square brackets. This means that we can use =N to mark a Noun and use the same code once again within the square brackets [N] to mark something else =N[N] – in our case above, a name.)

In order to make the computer software program 'understand' what we mean by human, compound, plural_only, etc. we have to define these code-words. We have made these definitions in a file named 'dicgram.h'. First, we start the file by declaring enumerations.

```
/* Enumeration for the Number of the Noun (N_): Singular (SG), Plural (PL) */
enum E_NUMBER_TYPE {N_SG, N_PL};
/* Enumeration of the Parts of Speech (P_): Noun (NOUN), Adjective (ADJ), etc. */
enum R_PARTS_TYPE {P_NONE, P_NOUN, P_ADJ, P_VERB, P_ADV, P_PRON, P_NUM,
P_PRE, P_PREP, P_CONJ, P_VMOD, P_PART, P_INTJ, P_ING, P_ART};
/* Enumeration of the Main Verbal Tenses (T_): present, past, future. */
enum E_TENSE_TYPE {T_PRESENT, T_PAST, T_FUTURE};
/* Enumeration of the Mood */
enum E_MOOD_TYPE {M_NULL, M_REFLEX, M_SUBJ, M_3, M_IMPER,
      M_INF = 8, M_SUBQ = 16};

/* codes for the NOUN */
typedef struct {
unsigned          name      : 1;    /*   [N]     */ /* name */
unsigned          human     : 1;    /*   [H]     */ /* human */
unsigned          compound  : 1;    /*   [L]     */ /* compound word */
unsigned          constant    : 1;  /*   [C]  */
/* both singular and plural: sheep, Abbaubagger, bras, etc. */
unsigned          time          : 1;    /*   [T]    */ /* time */
unsigned          singular_only    : 1; /*   [S]    */ /* singular */
unsigned          plural_only    : 1;   /*   [P]    */ /* plural */
// etc. codes, some language independent, some dependent on the language.
} NOUN;
```

There are often several ways to express a single grammatical feature. For example, the Plural of the Noun can be presented in the Dictionary of Wordforms as follows:

English	**German**	**French**
additions=N[P]	konzerte=N[UP]	arcs-en-ciel=N[UP]
or		
additions=n	konzerte=n[U]	arcs-en-ciel=n[U]

If we choose to express the Plural of the Noun with a small *n*, we have to define the small *n* in the program, in the file "grammar.c(pp)", like this:

```
case 'n' :  /* Noun Plural */
  l = strlen(mor->mflex);
  if (mor->mflex[l - 1] == 's')
// If the Noun ends with the letter "s" (English, French)
// if (mor->mflex[l - 1] == 'e') // If the Noun ends with the letter "e" (German)
// etc., depending on the language
    wrd->numb = 1;  // Then this Noun is in Plural
  else {
    if (word[wl - 1] == word[wl - 2]) {
     *ww = word[wl - 1];
     wl--;
    }
    word[wl] = '\0';
  }
 break;
```

or like this, depending on the language (here German):

```
case 'N': case 'n': case '#':
    if (g->W.plural) wrd->numb = 1;
// if the code word is W.plural the Noun is in plural
    if (g->W.singular_only) wrd->numb = 0;
// if the code word is W.singular_only the Noun is in singular
    else if (g->W.fgender && isflex(wrd->inword,
     wrd->wl, "en")) wrd->numb = 1;
// if the German noun is feminine and ends in 'en', it is in plural
    else if (g->W.fgender && isflex(wrd->inword,
     wrd->wl, "n")) wrd->numb = 1;
/* If the German noun is feminine and ends in 'n', it is plural. Note that here there are exceptions
– this rule does not apply to the nouns that end in 'n' and are registered in the DW as singular.
The rule applies only to the nouns not registered in the DW. Compare: Arbeiterin (registered),
Arbeiterinnen (not registered). */
else if (g->W.mgender && isflex(wrd->inword, wrd->wl, "e")) wrd->numb = 1;
// if the German noun is masculine and ends in 'e', it is in plural
else if (g->W.ngender && isflex(wrd->inword, wrd->wl, "e")) wrd->numb = 1;
// if the German noun is neuter and ends in 'e', it is in plural
/* This rule does not apply to the nouns that end in 'e' and are registered in the DW as plural.
The rule applies only to the nouns not registered in the DW. */
// etc. endings, depending on the language
    else if (syn == 'n' || g->W.plural ||
       g->W.plural_only) {
/* If the word is coded with the sign n or with the code words W.plural or W.plural_only */
       wrd->syn = 'n';
// the the sign of this word is n
       wrd->numb = 1;
// it is in plural
```

```
}
else if (g->W.singular ||
g->W.singular_only) wrd->numb = 0;
/* if the code word is W.singular or W.singular_only the Noun is in singular */
// below is some other relevant information
wrd->gender = g->W.fgender * 2 + g->W.mgender;
wrd->tcase = g->W.tcase;
wrd->person = 3;
break;
```

Since this rule is very general and there are exceptions, we have to mark all exceptions, so that we can exclude them when needed.

We can register with a small *n* any Plural Form of the Noun that forms the Plural by adding the ending "*s*" (English, French), "*e*" (German), etc. to its basic (singular) form. Some Nouns possess no formal morphological feature to express the Plural within the word itself. Their plural is expressed syntactically, by a preceding word (Numeral, Plural Form of the Article, Plural Form of the Pronoun, etc.). In the following example,

two sheep (English)
die Buerger (German)
les bras (French)

sheep, Buerger, bras will be in Plural, because of the English Numeral *two* (the singular form is *a sheep*), the French plural article *les*, the German Article *die* (the singular form in Nominative is *der Buerger*). We cannot express the Plural of the Noun *sheep, Buerger, bras* in the Dictionary of Wordforms. There, it will be registered as follows:

sheep=N[C]
Buerger=N[MC]
bras=N[MC]

where [C] means singular or plural, depending on context.

Because the plural of the noun is seen only in context (syntactically), we have to define it within the software program by writing the following piece of source code in one of the *.c (*.cpp) files:

```
case 132: /* Syntactically expressed Plural of some Nouns */
if (wrdm->numb == 1 || wrdm->e.N.plural_only == 1) break;
// exclude all plural Nouns, registered as such in the DW
wrdm->numb = 1; // the Noun is in Plural
CopySyn();
i = mpos; continue;
```

With this rule we tell the program that the 2nd word is in plural (see the continuation in the *.h file further below).

The same rule for the German language will be somewhat different:

```
case 132:
/* Syntactically expressed Plural in the German Nouns */
if (wrdm->numb == 1 || wrdm->e.N.plural_only == 1) break;
// exclude all Nouns that are already in Plural
if (wrd->e.N.fem == 1) break; // exclude all Feminine Nouns
if (isflex(wrdm->inword, wrdm->wl, "n") ||
isflex(wrdm->inword, wrdm->wl, "er")
|| isflex(wrdm->inword, wrdm->wl, "l") ||
```

```
        isflex(wrdm->inword, wrdm->wl, "en") &&
        wrdm->e.N.neuter || wrdm->e.N.masculine)
// if the 2nd word ends in -n, -en, -er or -l and is Neuter or Masculine
      wrdm->numb = 1;  // then the Noun is in Plural
      CopySyn();
      i = mpos; continue;
```

With the above rule for German, we tell the software program that if the Noun is Masculine or Neuter and if this Noun ends in "*n*", "*er*", "l" or "*en*", then this Noun is Plural. In the above rule we have included the endings "*en*" and "*n*" of the German Masculine and the Neuter Nouns, because these endings alone are not clear indication that the Noun is Plural. These endings can be Case endings and then the Masculine or the Neuter Noun is Singular. Only the German Feminine Nouns ending in "*en*" or "*n*" and not registered in the DW as singular can be, for certain Plural. Therefore, we did not include the "*n*" ending as a plural ending when we defined the German Noun earlier.

The code wrdm denotes the second word in a sequence of words (see below the instruction in the *.h file). We have to continue the above rule in the respective *.h file:

```
   {"[IH]<AdD>N", NULL, 132}, /* for any language */
      {"'these'<AD>N", NULL, 132},
/* If the Noun (2nd word) is preceded by "these" (English) */
      {"'die'<AD>N", NULL, 132},
/* If the Noun (2nd word) is preceded by "die" (German) */
         {"'les'<AD>N", NULL, 132},
/* If the Noun (2nd word) is preceded by "les" (French) */
```

(Note: the number 132 marks the case in the *.c(pp) file.)
The codes enclosed within the arrows < > list the Parts of Speech (Adjective (A) or Adverb (D)) that can be positioned between the Numeral (H), the Indicative Pronoun (I), "*these*", or the plural articles "*die*", "*les*" and the Noun (N). In other words, we tell the software program that if this Noun is preceded by a Numeral or by a plural article (note that English has no plural article) or by the English Indicative Pronoun "*these*", then this Noun is Plural. At the very beginning of case 132 we took care to exclude from the rule those Nouns that were already Plural. Note that the above rule is language dependent. The plural words that can precede the Noun, and the optional parts of speech that can be positioned before the Noun, depend on the language we describe.

We can define the Plural ending "*n*" of the German Feminine Nouns or the endings "*s*" and "*x*" of the French plural nouns in two different ways:

Either by registering the Plural Form of the Noun in the Dictionary of Wordforms:

German	**French**
Konzession=N[F]	fleurs=n[F]
Konzessionen=n[F]	jardins=n[M]

Or by writing a piece of source code to say that all German Feminine Nouns that end in "n" or all French Nouns that end in "*s*" or "*x*" are Plural (case 15).

```
         case 15: /* Plural of the German Feminine Nouns */
      if (wrd->numb == 1 || wrd->e.N.plural_only == 1) break;
// exclude all Nouns that are already in Plural
                    if (wrd->e.N.masculine == 1 || wrd->e.N.neuter == 1)
break;
// exclude the Masculine and the Neuter Nouns
         if (isflex(wrd->inword, wrd->wl, "n") ||
                    isflex(wrd->inword, wrd->wl, "en") && wrd->e.N.fem)
```

```
// if the German  word ends in -n or -en and is a Feminine Noun
                        wrd->numb = 1;  // then the Noun is in Plural
                        CopySyn();
        i = mpos; continue;
```

The above rule says that if the German Noun is Feminine and if this Noun ends in "*n*" or "*en*", it is Plural. However, a considerable number of feminine German nouns end in "*n*" but are singular, such as *Aberration, Ablaufbahn, Abnahmekommission, Abonnentin*, etc. This rule works well only because we have registered all singular and plural feminine forms in the DW. If we have problems using this rule, we have to mark in the DW all singular forms of all feminine nouns ending in *n* with [S] and add to case 15 the following exclusion:

```
      if (wrd->numb == 0 || wrd->e.N.singular_only == 1) break;
// exclude all singular Nouns
```

However, we must be very careful what we do, because [S] can mean that the Noun cannot have a plural.

```
        case 15: /* Plural of the French Nouns */
      if (wrd->numb == 1 || wrd->e.N.plural_only == 1) break;
// exit the rule if the Noun is already in Plural
      if (wrd->e.N.constant == 1 || wrd->e.N.singular_only == 1) break;
// exit the rule if the Noun is used only in Singular or both in Singular and Plural
                        if (isflex(wrd->inword, wrd->wl, "s") ||
        isflex(wrd->inword, wrd->wl, "x")
// if the Noun ends in -s or -x  (French)
                        wrd->numb = 1;  // then the Noun is in Plural
                        CopySyn();
        i = mpos; continue;  // continue with the next case
```

The above rule says, that if the French Noun ends in "*s*" or "*x*", it is Plural. The same rule can also be applied to the French Adjectives.

The code wrd means the first word of a sequence of words, or the word under consideration. In the very beginning of case 15 we took care to exclude those Nouns that were already marked as Plural, all German Masculine and Neuter Nouns and all constant or singular French nouns. Compare: *acinus* (singular), *bras* (constant), etc.

Continuation of the above rule in the *.h file:

```
{"N", NULL, 15},
```

Some English, German and French Nouns form their Plural Form in an 'irregular' way. German nouns do this most often by simply umlauting one of the vowels in the word and often adding the ending "*-e*" at the end of the basic form. For example:

English	**German**	**French**
addenda=n[P]	Apfel=N[M]	acini=n[M]
addendum=N[S]	Äpfel=n[M]	acinus=N[MS]
wife=N[S]	Kopf=N[M]	bocal=N[MS]
wives=n	Köpfe=n[M]	bocaux=n[M]
	Korb=N[M]	
	Körbe=n[M]	

etc.

Because there is no direct orthographical correspondence between the Singular Form of these Nouns and their respective Plural Forms, there is no way to make the software program recognize the Plural Form on the basis of its Singular Form, as we have done with the regular forms. Therefore we have to choose one of the following two options:

– Register the Plural Form in the Dictionary of Wordforms (DW) separately, as we have done above, and thus increase considerably our word entries.
– Write a piece of source code with which to tell the software program how to recognize the German plural when Umlaut is used to make it, without having to write the irregular Plural Forms in the DW. Here is an example of how to do it:

```
void CDeFinder::MorphCorr1( uchar dicsyn, short f_accent, T_WORD *wrd )
{
  if (f_accent)       /* If the word is written with Umlaut */
  {
  if ((dicsyn == N_SYN || dicsyn == Z_SYN))
// and if the word is marked in the DW as a Noun (N) or Noun or Verb (Z)
      {
  wrd->syn = N_SYN; // then this word is a Noun.
            if (wrd->e.N.singular_only)
// If this word is marked as Singular only [S],
              wrd->numb = 0;  // then it is in Singular
      else             // otherwise
      wrd->numb = 1;   // it is in Plural.
  }
     else
//     if (............. etc.
```

If we have registered in the DW

apfel=N[M]

and have not registered its plural form

äpfel=n[M]

the rule, shown above, will recognize *äpfel*, when met in a text, as the plural form of a*pfel*. This rule can be used in a machine translation program, but it cannot be used in a spell-checking software program, because it is very general and can lead to many errors.

There are some other irregular German plural forms, such as:

Examen=N[U]
Examens=N[US] // S denotes Singular only (Case form)
Examina=n[U]
Konten=n[U]
Konto=N[U]
Kontos=N[UC] // C denotes Singular (Case form) or Plural

and it would be better to register them as such in the DW, without writing a rule about them, because it is not easy to describe the principle used to make a plural from a singular form, especially when the number of such irregular words is insufficient for a rule.

2.5.2 *Case 'V', where the code designates a Verb.*

Note: Case 'N', Case 'V', etc. and cases for the other Parts of Speech follow one after the other after *switch* in 2.5.

Some verbal endings indicate clearly the Person and the Number (1st, 2nd, 3rd Person singular or plural). We can program this knowledge as follows:

```
case 'V' : // English verbal endings
/* Definition of the basic form of the Verb. */
  l = strlen(mor->mflex);       // length of the string of letters
  if (mor->mflex[l - 1] == 's') /* If the Verb ends in -'s' */
   wrd->person = 3;  /* then the Verb is 3rd person */
   wrd->numb = 0;    /* Singular */
  else {    // otherwise
   if (word[wl - 1] == word[wl - 2]) {
    *ww = word[wl - 1];
    wl--;
   }
   word[wl] = '\0'; // this is a basic form
  }
 break;
```

In short, **mor->mflex[l - 1] == 's'** means that if the last letter of the Verb is **s** the Verb is

> **wrd->person = 3;**
> **wrd->numb = 0;**

third person (person = 3) singular (numb = 0).

```
case 'V' :  /* German verbal endings */
  l = strlen(mor->mflex);       // length of the string of letters
  if (mor->mflex[l - 1] == 'e')  /* If the Verb ends in -'e' */
   wrd->person = 1;  /* then the Verb is 1st person */
   wrd->numb = 0;    /* Singular */
  if (mor->mflex[l - 2] == 's' && mor->mflex[l - 1] == 't')
// if the verb ends in '-st'
   wrd->person = 2; /* then the Verb is 2nd person */
   wrd->numb = 0;      /* Singular */
  if (mor->mflex[l - 2] == 'l' && mor->mflex[l - 1] == 'n')
// if the verb ends in '-ln'
   wrd->person = 1; /* then the Verb is 1st person */
   wrd->numb = 1;     /* Plural */
  if (mor->mflex[l - 2] == 'e' && mor->mflex[l - 1] == 'n')
// if the verb ends in '-en'
   wrd->person = 1; /* then the Verb is 1st person */
   wrd->numb = 1;     /* Plural */
  else {
   if (word[wl - 1] == word[wl - 2]) {
    *ww = word[wl - 1];
    wl--;
   }
   word[wl] = '\0';
  }
 break;
```

In short, **mor->mflex[l - 2] == 's' && mor->mflex[l - 1] == 't'** means that if the last but one letter of the Verb is **s** and the last letter is **t**, the Verb is

> **wrd->person = 2;**
> **wrd->numb = 0;**

second person (person = 2) singular (numb = 0).

We have not defined above the verbal ending *-et*, because of its ambiguity (3rd person singular or 2nd person plural). This verbal ending can be defined in context only, if needed. The reader will find enough examples in this book of how we define one or another grammatical feature in context, when it is ambiguous.

```
    case 'V' :  /* French verbal endings */
   l = strlen(mor->mflex);  // length of the string of letters
// define the grammatical ending and the Number or Person denoted by this ending
   if (mor->mflex[l - 2] == 's' && mor->mflex[l - 1] == 'e')
// if the verb ends in '-se'
     wrd->numb = 0;  // it is in singular
   if (mor->mflex[l - 2] == 't' && mor->mflex[l - 1] == 'e')
// if the verb ends in '-te'
     wrd->numb = 0;  // it is in singular
   if (mor->mflex[l - 2] == 'i' && mor->mflex[l - 1] == 'e')
// if the verb ends in '-ie'
     wrd->numb = 0;   // it is in singular
     wrd->tcase = 1;   // this is additional information
   if (mor->mflex[l - 3] == 'a' &&
    mor->mflex[l - 2] == 'i' && mor->mflex[l - 1] == 's')
// if the verb ends in '-ais'
     wrd->numb = 0;    // it is in singular
   if (mor->mflex[l - 3] == 'a' &&
       mor->mflex[l - 2] == 'i' && mor->mflex[l - 1] == 't')
// if the verb ends in '-ait'
     wrd->person = 3;  // it is third person
     wrd->numb = 0;  // singular
   if (mor->mflex[l - 3] == 'e' &&
    mor->mflex[l - 2] == 'n' && mor->mflex[l - 1] == 't')
// if the verb ends in '-ent'
     wrd->person = 2;  // it is 2nd person
      if (mor->mflex[l - 3] == 'i' &&
       mor->mflex[l - 2] == 'e' && mor->mflex[l - 1] == 'z')
// if the verb ends in '-iez'
     wrd->person = 2;   // it is second person
     wrd->numb = 1;   // plural
      if (mor->mflex[l - 3] == 'm' &&
       mor->mflex[l - 2] == 'e' && mor->mflex[l - 1] == 's')
// if the verb ends in '-mes'
     wrd->numb = 1;  // it is plural
     wrd->person = 1;   // 1st person
     wrd->tense = T_PAST;  // past tense
      if (mor->mflex[l - 3] == 'o' &&
       mor->mflex[l - 2] == 'n' && mor->mflex[l - 1] == 's')
// if the verb ends in '-ons'
     wrd->person = 1;   //  it is 1st person
     wrd->numb = 1;  // plural
   if (mor->mflex[l - 3] == 'o' &&
    mor->mflex[l - 2] == 'n' && mor->mflex[l - 1] == 't')
// if the verb ends in '-ont'
      wrd->person = 3;   //  it is 3rd person
      wrd->numb = 1;     // plural
      if (mor->mflex[l - 3] == 'r' &&
```

```
        mor->mflex[l - 2] == 'a' && mor->mflex[l - 1] == 'i')
// if the verb ends in '-rai'
       wrd->person = 1;  // it is 1st person
       wrd->numb = 0;    // singular
     if (mor->mflex[l - 3] == 'r' &&
        mor->mflex[l - 2] == 'a' && mor->mflex[l - 1] == 's')
// if the verb ends in '-ras'
       wrd->person = 2;  // it is 2nd person
       wrd->numb = 0;    // singular
     if (mor->mflex[l - 3] == 'r' &&
       mor->mflex[l - 2] == 'e' && mor->mflex[l - 1] == 'z')
// if the verb ends in '-rez'
       wrd->person = 2;     // it is 2nd person
       wrd->numb = 1;       // plural
     if (mor->mflex[l - 3] == 't' &&
       mor->mflex[l - 2] == 'e' && mor->mflex[l - 1] == 's')
// if the verb ends in '-tes'
       wrd->person = 2;     // it is 2nd person
       wrd->numb = 1;       // plural
       wrd->tense = T_PAST;  // past tense
     if (mor->mflex[l - 2] == 'e' && mor->mflex[l - 1] == 'z')
// if the verb ends in '-ez'
       wrd->numb = 1;   // it is in plural
     if (mor->mflex[l - 2] == 'e' && mor->mflex[l - 1] == 's')
// if the verb ends in '-es'
       wrd->numb = 1;   // it is in plural
     if (mor->mflex[l - 2] == 'a' && mor->mflex[l - 1] == 'i')
// if the verb ends in '-ai'
       wrd->numb = 0;    // it is singular
     if (mor->mflex[l - 1] == 'e')
// if the verb ends in '-e'
       wrd->numb = 0;   // it is singular
     if (mor->mflex[l - 1] == 'z')
// if the verb ends in '-z'
       wrd->numb = 1;    // it is in plural
     else {
       if (word[wl - 1] == word[wl - 2]) {
        *ww = word[wl - 1];
        wl--;
       }
       word[wl] = '\0';
     }
   break;
```

In short, **mor->mflex[l - 3] == 'r' && mor->mflex[l - 2] == 'a' && mor->mflex[l - 1] == 'i'** means that if the third letter from right to left is **r** and if the last but one letter is **a** and the last letter is **i**, the Verb is:

wrd->person = 1;
wrd->numb = 0;

first person (person = 1) singular (numb = 0).

Note that we have given precedence to the longer endings, leaving the short endings at the very end for example, the endings '-te' and '-ie' are singular, '-e' is also singular. The same interpretation applies to the other endings of the Verb, as listed above. The ambiguous endings are not listed. They can only be defined syntactically, depending on the context.

There are other ways to define the Verbal endings; this depends on what we want to know about them and what we want to do with them. For example, we can use the following source code in the file "de_gram.cpp" for the German language:

```
short CDeFinder::WordMorphFlexFound( uchar morsyn, const char *pSyn,
char *wdic, char *word )
{
  short bfmatch = -1, l;
  struct SCHRFLEX *flx = NULL;
  if (*pSyn == ,$')
    return bfmatch;
  switch (morsyn)
  {
    case 'Z' : case 'A' : case 'V' : // Definition of the Parts of Speech
      flx = DE_Vflex;         // that can have the specified endings
    break;
    case 'E' :  // Definition of the Past Form of the Verb
    if (ftype == 'E')
      {
       bfmatch = 3;
                    return bfmatch;
      }
     flx = DE_Eflex;
    break;
```

Then, the verbal endings are defined in the file 'degram.h' as follows:

```
struct SCHRFLEX DE_Vflex[] =
{
// define the form(s) of the Verb, as listed in DW
"t",                  // sagt
"et",                 // bildet
"rn",                 // abaendern
"ten",                // arbeiten
"ren",                // anfuehren
"en",                 // sagen
"n",                  // sammeln
"te",                 // brauchte
"rte",                // amusierte
NULL
};
```

The endings SCHRFLEX (shown above) are to be cut off from the word or wordform and then the endings MORPH_FLEX (shown further below) are to be added to fit the running word from the text (not found in the DW). As seen from the examples shown above, the basic form of the verb is defined alongside other forms.

Another definition of the German Verbal endings in "de_gram.cpp" will read as follows (these are the endings which we must add to the basic form when the grammatical ending is cut off from it):

```
char * CDeFinder::MorphAnalys( char *pszWord, short wl, T_WORD *wrd, char
*ww )
{
    const char *flex;
    struct MORPH_FLEX *flx;
   CStrLex strlex(" ");
   CListFile *pList;
    short l;
   T_WORD *pnew;
   pszFoundWordFlex = NULL;
   szWordFlex[0] = 0;
    if ( wrd->stat == 0 )
    {
      pList = GetStdPrefList();
      if ( pList && (pref = pList->Find(pszWord)) )
      {
// etc.
      }
   }
```

For this rule the verbal endings (MORPH_FLEX) are defined in the file "degram.h" as follows:

```
struct MORPH_FLEX de_endflex[] =
{
// define the actual endings(s) of the Verb, that may not be listed in DW
"st",                   "z",     NULL, 2,     // ambiguous ending(s)
"eten ten ete te",  "Z",     NULL, 1,     // ambiguous ending(s)
"etet tet et t",      "E",     NULL, 20,   // (prefix) ge...(e)t oder v2-3p pl.
// etc.
NULL
};
```

The same can be applied to the French verbal endings in the respective *.c(pp) and *.h files:

```
short CFrFinder::WordMorphFlexFound( uchar morsyn, const char *pSyn,
char *wdic, char *word )
{
   short bfmatch = -1, l;
   struct SCHRFLEX *flx = NULL;
   if (*pSyn == '$')
      return bfmatch;
   switch (morsyn)
   {
      case 'Z' : case 'V' : //  Definition of the Parts of Speech
         flx = FR_Vflex;          // that can have the specified endings
      break;

     case 'E' :    // Definition of the Past Form of the Verb
      if (ftype == 'E')
        {
         bfmatch = 3;
      return bfmatch;
        }
       flx = FR_Eflex;
```

```
    break;
```

Continuation in the respective *.h file:

```
struct SCHRFLEX FR_Vflex[] =
{
// define the basic form(s) of the Verb, as listed in DW
"ser",                /* propo-ser */
"ire",                /* constru-ire */
"oir",                /* recev-oir*/
"yer",                /* appu-yer*/
"re",                 /* construi-re */
"ir",                 /* fin-ir */
"ai",                 /* offrir-ai*/
"er",                 /* appeler */
NULL
};
struct SCHRFLEX FR_V3flex[] =
{
// define the basic form(s) of the Verb, as listed in DW
"enir",               /* conv-ient [S] */
"ier",                /* apprec-ient [P] */
NULL
};
```

The endings SCHRFLEX (shown above) are cut off from the word and then the endings MORPH_FLEX (shown further below) are added to fit the running word from the text (not found in the DW).

Another definition of the French Verbal endings in "grammar.cpp" will read as follows:

```
char * CFrFinder::MorphAnalys( char *pszWord, short wl, T_WORD *wrd, char
*ww )
{
   const char *flex;
   struct MORPH_FLEX *flx;
  CStrLex strlex(" ");
  CListFile *pList;
   short l;
  T_WORD *pnew;
  pszFoundWordFlex = NULL;
  szWordFlex[0] = 0;
   if ( wrd->stat == 0 )
   {
   pList = GetStdPrefList();

     if ( pList && (pref = pList->Find(pszWord)) )
     {
// etc.
     }
  }
```

For this rule the French verbal endings (MORPH_FLEX) are defined in the *.h file as follows:

```
struct MORPH_FLEX fr_endflex[] =
```

```
{
// define the actual ending(s) of the Verb, that may not be listed in DW
"ions",      "Z",    NULL, 1,  // ambiguous ending - Verb or Noun
"és",        "E",    NULL, 2,  // Past Tense
// etc.
NULL
};
```

a) Definition of the additional information carried by the Verb. The additional information about the Verb, enclosed in square brackets, is expressed in C (C++) in the following way (after *switch* in 2.5):

```
case 'V': case 'E': case 'G': case 'Z':
  case 'h': case 'v': case 'z':
/* A case for all types of verbs: verb proper, present form (V, v), past (E, h), gerund (G), ambiguous (Z, z) */
dig00:
    if (isdigit(*cw)) wrd->e.V.anim = wrd->e.V.control = *cw++ - '0';
    if (isdigit(*cw)) wrd->e.V.controli = wrd->tflag = *cw++ - '0';
    if (isdigit(*cw)) wrd->e.V.control2 = *cw++ - '0';
// if statements for verification and definition
    if (*cw == '[') {
/* If there is a square bracket opened to enclose additional information about the Verb */
    while (*cw && *cw != ']') {
// while it remains opened
      if (isdigit(*cw)) wrd->person = *cw - '0';
/* If statements about the enclosed coded information contained in the word
follow below in the following order: = = 'i', a, z, R, etc, is the code placed in square brackets in the DW , wrd->e.V.transit = 1, etc. is the code word used in the source code in a *.c(pp) file for 'a', etc. */
            if (*cw == 'i')  wrd->gflag = *cw;    // the Verb is irregular
      if (*cw == 'a')  wrd->e.V.transit = 1; /* transitive Verb */
            if (*cw == 'z')  wrd->e.V.intransit = 1;  /* intransitive V */
            if (*cw == 'R')  wrd->e.V.reflexiv  = 1;  /* Reflexive */
         if (*cw == '<')  wrd->e.V.tense = T_PAST;  /* Past Tense */
      if (*cw == 'A')  wrd->e.V.of = 1;
/* used with the English Preposition 'of' */
/* etc. prepositions, each with its own code, depending on the language */
/* below are listed the code letters and the code words typical for the German verb */
      if (*cw == 'h')  wrd->e.V.haben = 1;  /* the Verb is used with "haben" */
      if (*cw == 's')  wrd->e.V.sein = 1;  /* the Verb is used with "sein" */
      if (*cw == 'g')  wrd->e.V.genitiv = 1;   /* Genitiv */
      if (*cw == 't')  wrd->e.V.dativ = 1;   /* Dativ */
// if (*cw == 'V')  wrd->kflag = 1;
/* used with the German preposition 'am' */
// etc. prepositions and other information
      if (*cw == 'l')  {
      wrd->e.V.newspell = 1;  /* the new German spelling */
      wrd->gflag = 'q';
        }                    /*end*/
      cw++;
     }
    cw++;
    }
```

```
    if (*cw == '(') {
// if the verb has an irregular form registered in brackets
     wirr = wrd->irrform;
// this is the actual irregular form
     while (*cw && *cw != ')')
// while the bracket is not closed
       *wirr++ = *cw++;
     *wirr++ = *cw++;
     *wirr = '\0';
    }
if (wrd->syn == 'E' ||wrd->esyn == 'E' ||
     wrd->syn == 'h')  /* If the word sign is E or h */
      wrd->tense = T_PAST;  /* The word Tense is Past Tense */
if (wrd->syn == 'v')   // if the verb is marked with small 'v'
      wrd->person = 3;  // it is 3rd person singular
    if (wrd->syn == 'z'){     // if the verb is marked with small 'z'
      wrd->person = 3; // it is 3rd person singular (ambiguous)
    }
break;
```

(Note: wrd->syn = = E denotes Past or Participle, wrd->syn = = h Past only.)
The signs i, h, s, a, z, R, g, t, <, l, etc. are the signs used only in the Dictionary of Wordforms, in square brackets. The codes, wrd->tense = T_PAST, wrd->e.V.transit = 1, wrd->e.V.of = 1, wrd->e.V.haben = 1, wrd->e.V.sein = 1, etc., are used only in the source code of the software program in a *c(pp) file, when needed to make a rule about the Verbs that bear the particular sign enclosed in square brackets. We will explain later how this information is used in the program rules.

We have not coded all grammatical, syntactical etc. information related to the Verb, for example we have not provided a code for the German separable Verbs. If we want to do that, we can add the following code:

```
if (*cw == 'b')  wrd->e.V.separable = 1;
```

We have not coded the separable Verbs, because we have found another way to register them for the needs of German Foreign-Language Machine Translation. When the German verb can be used both with *haben* and with *sein*, we provide no information, because that will lead to confusion unless we define when it can be used with *haben* and *sein*, in context. When the Verb can be both transitive and intransitive, we do not mark it as such for the same reasons. (Note: When we make our rules, we make them apply to a very large group of words. There are always exceptions, which we must mark (code) and exclude, or handle separately. Too many rules, with too many exceptions often lead to a mess, and we must be very careful that the rules do not contradict one another. Also, we must not use the same code for different things.)

Now, we have to define, in the file "dicgram.h", the verb-related codes that we will be using in the program:

```
/* codes related to the VERB */
typedef struct {
unsigned       irregular  : 1;      /*  [i] irregular verb */
unsigned       reflexiv   : 1;      /*  [R] reflexive verb  */
unsigned       haben      : 1;      /*  [h] German Participle with haben */
unsigned       sein       : 1;      /*  [s] German Participle with sein */
unsigned       dativ      : 1;      /*  [t] German or other language  */
unsigned       genitiv    : 1;      /*  [g] German or other language  */
unsigned       transit    : 1;      /*  [a] transitive verb  */
```

```
unsigned      intransit  : 1;      /* [z] intransitive verb */
// etc. coded information about the verb, depending on the language
} VERB;
```

In a similar way, we have defined separately the Auxiliary Verbs with their paradigms: *have* (Y), *be* (X), *will, shall* (x), *can* (U), etc. for the English language, *haben* (Y), *sein* (X), *werden* (x), *können* (U), etc. for the German Language and *avoir* (Y), *être* (X), *pouvoir* (U), etc. for the French language and their Present, Past and Participle forms. The irregular forms of the Auxiliary Verbs we have registered in the Dictionary of Wordforms. These are:

English	**German**	**French**
am=X[S1]\be	bin=X[S1]\sein	ai=Y[S1]\avoir
are=X[P]\be	bist=X[S2]\sein	as=Y[S2]\avoir
is=X[S3]\be	ist=X[S3]\sein	a=Y[S3]\avoir
was=X[S<]\be	koennten=U[P<]	soyez=X[P2]*être*
will=x[>]/N	werden=x[>P]/N[U]	soyons=X[P1]\ *être*

The codes "\be", "\sein", "\avoir" point to the representative form of the Verb: *am* comes from *be*, *bist* comes from *sein*, *as* comes from *avoir*, etc. depending on the language. The information in square brackets shows the person and the number of the Verb, S1 means 1st person singular, P2 means second person plural, [P<] means plural, past form, etc. X represents all Auxiliary Verbs, past and present, from the paradigm *be* etc. (English), *sein* etc. (German) and *être* etc. (French), Y represents the paradigm of *avoir* (French), etc. The same applies to all other languages.

The case presented below defines the additional information about the Auxiliary Verbs, irrespective of language.

```
case 'X' : case 'x' : case 'Y' :
// case for the Auxiliary Verbs
    if (isdigit(*cw)) wrd->tense = *cw++ - '0';
    if (isdigit(*cw)) wrd->numb = *cw++ - '0';
    if (isdigit(*cw)) wrd->person = *cw++ - '0';
    if (*cw == '[') {   // info in the square brackets
     while (*cw && *cw != ']') {
      if (isdigit(*cw)) wrd->person = *cw - '0';
      if (*cw == 'P')  wrd->numb = 1;  // plural
      if (*cw == '<')  wrd->tense = T_PAST;  // past form
      if (*cw == '>')  wrd->tense = T_FUTURE;  // future form
// etc. information
      cw++;
     }
     cw++;
    }
   break;
```

b) Recognition of the epenthetic morphemes and infixes.

As an example, we will discuss the recognition of the German epenthetic morphemes "-zu-" (zu-) and "-ge-" (ge-) used with the Verbs. In those cases when we have registered the representative form of the Main Verb in the Dictionary of Wordforms (for example: *kennenlernen, bringen*), but have failed to register its infinitival form (*kennenzulernen, zubringen*), we can make the program recognize the infinitival form using the following procedure written in the appropriate *.cpp file:

```
const char *_ZU = "zu";  /* declaration of the infinitival particle "zu" */
const char *_GE = "ge";  /* declaration of the particle "ge" for past forms */
```

```
/* where _ZU, _GE are codes, zu, ge are the actual morphemes, as met in the word. */
// etc. declaration of any epenthetic morphemes or infixes in any language
char * CDeFinder::MorphAnalys( char *pszWord, short wl, T_WORD *wrd,
char *ww )
{
const char *flex;
struct MORPH_FLEX *flx;
CStrLex strlex(" ");
CListFile *pList;
short l;
T_WORD *pnew;
pszFoundWordFlex = NULL;
szWordFlex[0] = 0;
if ( wrd->stat == 0 )
{
pList = GetStdPrefList();
if ( pList && (pref = pList->Find(pszWord)) )
{
      nPrefLen = pref->m_nLen;
   if (wrd->wl > nPrefLen + 4 &&
        !strncmp(pszWord + nPrefLen, _ZU, 2))
      {
           strcpy(wrd->inword + nPrefLen, wrd->inword + nPrefLen + 2);
           strcpy(pszWord + nPrefLen, pszWord + nPrefLen + 2);
   pnew = enque_word(NULL, '?', wrd->inword);
      if (pnew == NULL)
                     {
                     wrd->stat = (uchar)-1;
                     return NULL;
      }
      pnew->stat = 1;
   pnew->mood |= M_INF;
      pnew->next = wrd->next;
      wrd->next = pnew;
                     wrd->stat = 1;
   wrd->syn = _B_SYN;
   strcpy(wrd->inword, _ZU);
                     wrd->wl = 2;
                     return NULL;
   }
}
```

The rule for "-ge-" is identical: we only have to replace _ZU (above) with _GE and the software program will recognize *kennengelernt*, *abgefertigt* (main form *abfertigen*), etc., when met in the text, without having to register them in the Dictionary of Wordforms. The same programming code can be applied to all other languages which have epenthetic morphemes. All we need to do is to replace _ZU, _GE and the actual morphemes *zu*, *ge* with other codes and morphemes, depending on the language.

2.5.3 Case 'A', where the code designates an Adjective.

The Adjective has: Degree (English), Degree, Gender and Number (French, Italian) and Degree, Gender, Number and Case (Nominative, Accusative, Genitive and Dative) in German. Other languages also have two or more of these grammatical features.

We can define some of these grammatical features using the same method as shown above for the Noun and the Verb, by making a separate case for the English Adjective (follows after *switch* in 2.5):

```
   case 'A' :    // when the word is coded with the letter A
    l = strlen(mor->mflex);
// the information below is for the English adjective
    wrd->cflag = 'a'; // can have a degree form
    if (mor->mflex[l - 2] == 'e' && mor->mflex[l - 1] == 'r')
// if the word ends in -er
      wrd->tense = 1;  // then, this is Comparative Degree of the Adjective
    else
    if (mor->mflex[l - 2] == 's' && mor->mflex[l - 1] == 't')
// if the word ends in -st
      wrd->tense = 2;    // then, this is Superlative Degree of the Adjective
    if (mor->mflex[0] == 'i' && mor->mflex[1] == 'e') {
// if the word ends in -ie
      word[wl++] = 'y';  // it comes from a word that ends in -y
      word[wl] = '\0';
// y is removed so that we can add -ie (happy -> happiest)
      }
      else {
      if (word[wl - 1] == word[wl - 2]) {
       *ww = word[wl - 1];
       wl--;
      }
      word[wl] = '\0';
      }
      break;
```

Definition of the additional information carried by the Adjective:

```
void get_engram(char *word, char *cw, WORD *wrd)
{
char *wdic;
char *wirr;
 if (!wrd->inbase || wrd->inbase[0] == '\0')
   strcpy(wrd->inbase, word);             /* Source Form */

  switch (wrd->syn)
  {
case 'A' : case 'd' :
   if (*cw == '[') {
   while (*cw && *cw != ']') {
    if (*cw == 'M')  wrd->e.A.more_most = 1;
// cannot have a degree
// etc. additional information for the English adjective
    if (*cw == 'I' || *cw == 'i') {
// if the adjective bears the code [i]
     wrd->e.A.irregular = 1;
     wrd->gflag = 'i';
// it is irregular
       }
    if (*cw == '-')  wrd->mood = 1; // cannot add -ly
```

```
      if (*cw == 'a')  wrd->e.A.all = 1;  // can have a degree
      if (*cw == 'e')  wrd->e.A.e_form = wrd->mood = 1;
// recorded in the DW with its degree form
      if (*cw == 'p')  wrd->e.A.prefer = 1;  // preferable degree form
// etc. additional information for the English adjective
      cw++;
     }
    cw++;
    if (*cw == '(') {
// if a bracket is opened
     wirr = wrd->irrform;
// the parenthesis contain the irregular form
     while (*cw && *cw != ')')
      *wirr++ = *cw++;
     *wirr++ = *cw++;
     *wirr = '\0';
    }
    }
    break;
```

Case A is language specific. We have to make similar cases for the other languages, depending on the grammatical endings of the Adjective.

(Note: We will discuss the Case endings of the German adjective and the Number endings of the German and French adjectives in greater detail later in this book when we come to the grammatical rules. The English adjective has no case and number endings. The remaining Parts of Speech are dealt with in a similar manner, in the same file (grammar.c, or grammar.cpp). We will discuss them one by one, briefly.)

2.5.4 *Definition of the Article*

Case 'T' , the Article *a, an, the*, etc. (English), *ein, eine, die, der, das*, etc. (German), *d'un, d'une, la, le, les*, etc. (French). The Article needs a definition about the following grammatical information: Definite or Indefinite, Gender, Number and Case, depending on the language under consideration.

2.5.5 *Definition of the Pronoun*

The Pronoun can be described in one case or in a number of cases, if we want to consider all types of Pronouns separately: Personal, Indicative, Possessive, Relative, Interrogative, Reflexive, etc. This depends entirely on us, on our aims and on the language we describe, because not all Pronouns have the same grammatical features. Most of the Pronouns have the following grammatical features: Person, Gender, Case and Number, depending on the language under consideration.

2.5.6 *Definition of the Adverb*

The Adverb in the languages under consideration is not inflected. We can differentiate the Adverbs according to whether they denote Place, Direction, Manner, Degree, etc., and code this differentiation, respectively if we want to use this information in our software program. If we do not want to do that, it is a simple case:

```
   case 'D' :  /* case for the Adverb, marked with the letter D */
    word[wl] = '\0';
// has no ending in English and some other languages
    wrd->cflag = 'd';
   break;
```

2.5.7 *Definition of the Auxiliary Words*

The Prepositions (P), Conjunctions (J), Interjections, etc. we have also marked and defined respectively. Here, for example is a case for the English Preposition with extensive information about it, because certain Prepositions are used only with certain words:

```
void get_engram(char *word, char *cw, WORD *wrd)
{
char *wdic;
char *wirr;
 if (!wrd->inbase ||wrd->inbase[0] == '\0')
   strcpy(wrd->inbase, word);              /* Source Form */
   strcpy(wrd->rprefix, cw);        /* Debug  Info */
  switch (wrd->syn)
  {
// start enumeration of the cases:
case 'P':  /* a case for the English Preposition */
   if (!stricmp(wrd->inword, "of"))
// of  is special, in English, because it is used in Genitive
    wrd->tflag = 1;
if (*cw == '[') {
// if there is a square bracket opened for additional informantion
    while (*cw && *cw != ']') {
/* look for the code marking the combinatorics of this Preposition */
      if (*cw == 'X')  wrd->fflag = 1;
/* wrd->fflag (etc.) names exactly which Preposition is meant when we use it in the *.c(pp) file
instruction */
      if (*cw == 'D')  wrd->xflag = 1;
// coding the English preposition 'from'
      if (*cw == 'V')  wrd->kflag = 1;
// coding the English preposition 'for'
      if (*cw == 'G')  wrd->zflag = 1;
      if (*cw == 'Q')  wrd->nflag = 1;
      if (*cw == 'Z')  wrd->qflag = 1;
      if (*cw == 'R')  wrd->bflag = 1;
      if (*cw == 'Y')  wrd->vflag = 1;
      if (*cw == 'x')  wrd->uflag = 1;
      if (*cw == 'u')  wrd->wprep = 1;
      if (*cw == 'L')  wrd->oflag = 1;
      if (*cw == 'O')  wrd->pflag = 1;
// etc. codes for the syntactical information of the English prepositions
//    if (*cw == 'V')  wrd->kflag = 1;
/* Note: the same code for 'for' above can be used to code the German preposition 'am' or any
other preposition in other languages. The choice of codes depends on the programmer and on the
language we describe. We cannot describe more than one language with the same codes. */
      cw++;
    }
```

```
    cw++;
   }
  break;
```

The same case, with slight modification can be applied to German and other languages.

2.6 *Unregistered and unrecognized words*

A number of words, met in the text, cannot be found in the Dictionary of Wordforms. A certain number of them can be recognized by their grammatical endings (as defined above) or capital letters (case 59).

```
        case 59:
/* Unrecognized word, written with capital letter, *.c(pp) file. */
        if (isupper(wrd->inword[0]))
// if the word is written with a capital letter
        {
        wrd->syn = NAME; // it is a noun, a name
        CopySyn();
        }
        i++; continue;
     {"[?#]", "N", 59},   // in the corresponding *.h file
```

or the word can be presented with its left surrounding (as defined below)

```
  {"[TIP]<ADTH>[?#]",    "@$N", },
```

in the corresponding *.h file, where [?#] is the unrecognized word, [TIP]<ADTH> are the parts of speech that can precede it, when it is used as a noun (N).

All other unrecognized words, not covered by the above rules, will remain unrecognized and will not be attributed to a particular part of speech. They will stay marked with the code ? (or # or any other convenient code). We need a code for the unrecognized words in order to be able to deal with them. For example, to collect them and register them in the DW.

2 Disambiguation Procedures

We are often faced with various sorts of ambiguity (grammatical, semantical, etc.), when we process a text, therefore we have to deal with it efficiently. The disambiguation procedures are constructed on the assumption that the computer software program uses, as a reference table, a full and comprehensive dictionary of the respective language (DW) in which every wordform is marked according to its membership to a particular Part of Speech.

Those wordforms in the Dictionary that belong to more than one Part of Speech are marked as follows: Noun or Adjective (N/A) *accusative* (English), *akut, defekt* (German), *abbatiale, absent* (French), Adjective or Verb (Z/A) *alternate, animate* (English), *billige(n)* (German), *abandonner, absente* (French), Noun or Verb (Z/N) *annex, answer, lead* (English), *gehen, geige(n), genese* (German), *embauche, emblave, enduit* (French), Adjective or Noun or Verb (Z/N/A) *abstract, account* (English), *genuge, gleiche* (German), *équivalent, abstrait, allume* (French), Verb or Adjective or Participle (e/A) *wet* (English), *delegiert, berufen* (German), *inclus* (French), Participle or Adjective or Noun or Verb (e/N/A) *cast, fell, hit* (English), *betreten* (German), *extrait* (French), Participle or Verb (e) *besonnen* (German), *exclue* (French), Adjective or Adverb (A/D) *dergleichen, dreimonatlich* (German), Verb or Noun or Participle (e/N) *bet* (English), *befahren* (German), *vis* (French). As is well seen from these examples, all three languages have ambiguous wordforms. The reader can find similar examples in all languages. We must know all ambiguous wordforms in every language in order to deal with them adequately.

The table below shows the size of the ambiguous wordforms in the DW in numbers. We present the numbers, not the percentage, because different languages have different numbers of word entries in their vocabularies. German, unlike English or French, has many unambiguous compound words, which increase considerably the size of the dictionary and decrease the percentage of ambiguous words. Therefore, the percentage is not an accurate basis for comparison.

Table 1 Number of ambiguous wordforms

Ambiguous wordforms	English	German	French
verb or other	3767	2364	3210
adjective or other	3490	9301	15387
total ambiguous	7257	11665	18597
phrases	1866	2410	2426
total entries in DW	55421	161497	80665

The information for the table above was obtained from the DW in use in Georgiev 1993, 1996, 1997. The number of phrases used in the DW is not important, as it depends on our aims and on the person who makes the DW. The above-mentioned dictionaries were used for parsing and grammar spell-checking, therefore the number of the phrases was kept to a minimum. However, a bilingual dictionary for machine translation requires as many phrases as possible, the more the phrases, the better the translation.

The number of ambiguous words does not depend on the total number of word entries in the DW. For example, German has double the number of word entries of French, but many fewer ambiguous words.

Verb or other means 'verb or noun', 'verb or noun or adjective', 'verb or adjective'. Adjective or other means mainly 'noun or adjective', which is the most common ambiguity, 'adjective or adverb' is less common and is not counted separately.

Below, we present the percentage and number (in brackets) of the ambiguous word entries 'verb or noun', 'verb or noun or adjective', 'verb or adjective' in respect of the total number of a 'verb and other' part of speech:

Table 1.1 Percentage of ambiguous wordforms

Verb or other	English	German	French
verb or noun	81.2% (3060)	86.6% (2047)	83.5% (2669)
verb or noun or adjective	14.3% (539)	6.1% (143)	10.8% (348)
verb or adjective	4.4% (166)	6.3% (150)	5.7% (182)

As seen from Table 1, the ambiguous words on the level of parts of speech are considerable in number in all three languages, and cannot be ignored in text processing. Therefore, we will pay special attention to this type of ambiguity, because we cannot resolve the semantic ambiguity later unless we resolve the part-of-speech ambiguity first.

Since the Noun in German is always written with a capital letter, the ambiguity Verb or Noun, Noun or Adjective is non-existent. However, the ambiguity Verb or Adjective, Verb or Participle remains, because the Verbs, the Participles and the Adjectives are written with a small letter.

In order to make the disambiguation procedures work, the ambiguous words in the Electronic Dictionary of Wordforms will be presented, alongside with the unambiguous, as follows:

English	**German**	**French**
speed=Z/N/A	schien=h[<S]	dame=Z/N[F]
spell=Z/N	schienbein=N[U]	dame-jeanne=N[FS]
spelling=N/G/A	schiene=Z/N[F]	damé=E/N[0]
	schienen=Z/N[FP]	damer=V[ ]
	schienenbruch=N[M]	dames=Z/N[FC]
		dames-jeannes=n[F]
		damier=N[M]
		damnable=A
		damnation=N[F]

... etc.

where G marks the Present Participle (the *-ing* form of the Verb in English, the respective Present Participle form in other languages).
(Note: the codes in brackets represent additional information about the word (gender, number, etc., as defined in the previous chapter)).

1 Disambiguation instructions programmed in C (C++)

The disambiguation described below is on the level of parts of speech, when a word or wordform belongs to more than one part of speech when in the dictionary.

1.1 General observations and rules

Since all Nouns in German and all names in English and French are written with a capital letter, the ambiguity Name (Noun, in German) or Verb is very easy to resolve. The following instruction (in a *.c or *.cpp file) makes the program check if the word is written with a capital letter:

```
          case 76: /* Noun or Verb */
                    if (isupper(wrd->inword[0]))
/* if the 1st letter [0] of the input word (wrd->inword) is written with
a capital letter (isupper) */
                                        wrd->syn = N_SYN;
// this word is a noun
                               else     // if not
                                        wrd->syn = V_SYN;
// this word is a verb
                    CopySyn();
                    i = mpos; continue;
```

where **if (isupper(wrd->inword[0]))** means if the first letter [0] of the first word (wrd) is written with a capital letter (isupper), then the first word **wrd->syn** is a Noun (**N_SYN**); else (otherwise) the first word **wrd->syn** is a Verb (**V_SYN**). The respective *.h file finalizes this instruction, showing the immediate right surrounding of the ambiguous word (used as a first word in a sequence of two words), in the following way:

```
{"Z[TOI]",   NULL, 76},   // case 76
```

where **Z** marks the ambiguity Noun or Verb (as the first word in a sequence), followed by either an Article (T) or by a Possessive Pronoun (O) or by an Indicative Pronoun (I). These alternatives are presented in square brackets [TOI] and are language dependent.

Case 76 above, with slight alteration, can be used to resolve the ambiguity between noun or adjective in German and between name and adjective in other languages. If, however, we have to resolve the ambiguity Noun or Verb, Noun or Adjective or Verb, in languages where the noun is written with a small letter, the disambiguation procedure is more complex. We have to take into account, first of all, such formal features in the context, which disambiguate with a 100 per cent accuracy this type of ambiguity. Let us take as an example the following instruction (in the respective *.h file):

```
{"[TOSI]ZN",        "@A",  },
```

where the first word in the sequence is either an Article (T) or a Possessive Pronoun (O) or a Determiner (S) or an Indicative Pronoun (I) enclosed in square brackets [TOSI], the second word is the ambiguous word (Verb or Noun or Adjective) marked with **Z**, which is immediately followed by a Noun (**N**). This rule states, that in this particular context, the second word is an Adjective (**A**). See **@A**, where **@** stands for the first word, **A** marks the second word in this sequence and replaces Z in this instruction.

We can also disambiguate individual words, if we write the ambiguous wordform in the rule, in the respective *.h file, for example:

```
   {"[Ve]'bankrupt'",    "@A",  },
   {"[VeEh]'bust'",    "@A",  },
// in English 'bankrupt', 'bust' after a Verb is an Adjective
   {"'correct'*",       "d", },
   {"'then'*",        "d", },
// in English 'correct', 'then' before a full stop is an adverb
```

```
{"'please'V",    "D", },
```
// in English 'please' before a Verb is an Adverb
```
{"X'corrupt'",    "@A", },
```
// in English '*corrupt*' after an Auxil. Verb from the '*be*' paradigm is an Adjective
```
{"'last'N",       "A", 16},
```
/* in English '*last*' before a Noun is an Adjective, 16 is the case that deals with it in the respective *.c(pp) file */
```
{"[ZV]'fort'", "@D", },
```
/* The German Adjective "*fort*" is used as an Adverb (D) after a Verb */
```
{"P'einige'[VUYXx]", "@N",  },
```
/* After Preposition and before a Verb "*einige*" in German is a Noun */
```
{"P'einigen'[VUYXx]", "@N",  }, /* same as above */
{"'warm'[Vh]",   "D",  }, // German
```
/* The German Adjective "*warm*" before a Verb is used as an Adverb (D) */
```
{"Z'lassen'", "V", },
```
/* Ambiguous word before "*lassen*" in German is a Verb (V) */
```
{"'ehe'[TNADVP]",   "J",  },
```
/* In German, the word "*ehe*" before an Article, Noun, etc. is a Conjunction (J) */
```
{"'billige'N",   "A",  },
```
/* The German word "*billige*" before a Noun is an Adjective (A) */
```
{"'billigen'N",   "A",  }, /* same as above */
{"'bleichen'N",   "A",  },
```
/* The German word "*bleichen*" before a Noun is an Adjective (A) */
```
{"'weiß'N",   "A",  },
```
/* The German word "*weiß*" before a Noun is an Adjective (A) */
```
{"'chose'Z",         "@A",  },
```
/* in French *chose* is an Adjective before N or V */
```
{"[*,]Z[VeG]",       "@N",  },
```
/* in French N or V is a N in the beginning of the Sentence or after comma, when followed by V or Participle */
```
{"[CN]'de'Z[*,]",        "@@N",  },
```
/* in French N or V (Z) at the end of the sentence [*,] is a N when preceded by a Conjunction or N [CN] followed by "*de*" */
```
{"'se'ZD",          "@V",  },
```
/* in French N or V (Z) is a V when preceded by "*se*" and followed by an Adverb */
```
{"CZ'des'",          "@V",  },
```
/* in French N or V is a V when preceded by a Conjunction and followed by "*des*" */
```
{"[RN]'a'",          "@Y",  },
```
/* in French "*a*" is an Auxiliary Verb when preceded by a Noun or by Personal Pronoun Nominal Case */
```
{"'aller'V",          "V",  },
```
/* in French "*aller*" is a Verb when followed by a Verb */
```
{"'grand'[ZN]",        "A",  },
```
/* in French "*grand*" is an Adjective, when followed by an ambiguous word or a Noun */
etc.

All rules, shown above, are language specific. Note, that the French Determiner (*le, les, se, de,* etc.) or the German preposition '*zu*' or the English preposition '*to*' can be also a Particle when used before a Verb.

The disambiguation of the ambiguous words can be done mostly on a syntactical basis. As a rule, the attribution of a word to a particular Part of Speech depends exclusively on its left surrounding. Where needed, the disambiguation can be carried out on a semantical basis, then the rules are more specific in design. In our experience, we have done disambiguation on a semantical basis only when we have needed the program for machine translation.

The disambiguation of the ambiguous words needs a description in a file called, for example, "parser.c(pp)" with a corresponding *.h file called for example "parser.h". The file "parser. c(pp)" will begin as follows:

```
#include <ctype.h>
#include <stdio.h>
#include <conio.h>
#include <alloc.h>
#include <dir.h>
// etc. standard include files
#include "dicgram.h"
#include "grammar.h"
#include "parser.h"
// etc. own include files
extern int wcount;
extern char synstr[MAXWORDS + 3];
int copysyn(struct QUE *que[], WORD *wp[]);
// etc.
WORD *wrd, *wrdm, *wrdp, *w;
// etc.
for (ptb = PART; ptb->inst; ptb++) {
   for ( i = 0; i < wcount - 1; i++ ) {
     if ( (mpos= piccmp(wp, i, ptb->inst)) ) {
       wrd  = wp[i];
       wrdm = wp[mpos];
       wrdp = wp[mpos-1];
      switch (ptb->cond) {   // start the cases

     case 1 :      /* case 1 */
// etc.
// then starts the enumeration of the disambiguation cases outlined below
```

2 Ambiguity Noun or Verb

This ambiguity cannot be resolved with one rule. One needs many rules – one for each ambiguous case, depending on context and language. Here we will consider only certain cases.

```
Case 200 : /* OZ - Noun or Verb after Possessive Pronoun */
   if (wrd->next->syn = 'O') {
// if the first word (after the full stop) is a Possessive Pronoun
     wrdm->syn = 'N';  // the second (ambiguous) word is a Noun
     }
   copysyn(que, wp);
   continue;
```

where wrd->next means the word after a full stop (*) and wrdm (the 2nd word in this sequence) is marked with Z (Noun or Verb). Continuation of the above rule in the respective *.h file:

```
{"*OZ", NULL, 200},
```

In other words, the ambiguous word, 'Noun or Verb', is always a Noun when preceded by a Possessive Pronoun at the beginning of the sentence. The following example shows how we rename the Verb when it is used as a Noun:

```
case 201:  /* rename V to N */
   if (wrdm->esyn == 'h' && strrchr(wrdm->cw, 'N')) {
/* if the word wrdm (2nd one) is marked in the DW as h (Past form of the Verb) and if the same word is marked also as N (Noun) */
      wrdm->syn = 'N'; // then, in this case, it is a Noun
      copysyn(que, wp);
   }
   i = wcount; continue;
```

Continuation of the above rule in the respective *.h file:

```
{"[TAOP][Ve]",          ".N",  201},   /* one small bit */
```

Note that in the DW the English word *bit*, the German word *abriss*, the French word *abattis*, etc., are coded with two different signs (**h** and **N**) as follows:

bit=h[i](bite; bit; bitten)/N
abriss=h/N[M]
abattis=h/N[M]

Case 201 applies to all words coded with two different signs (**h** and **N** or **E** and **N**), as well as in other languages, but the context may vary, depending on the language.

3 Ambiguity Adjective or Verb

First of all, we have to take into account such formal features in the context that disambiguate with a 100 per cent accuracy this type of ambiguity. Let us take as an example the following instruction (in the respective *.h file):

```
{"HZN",       "@A",  },
```

where the first word in the sequence is a Numeral (H), the second word is the ambiguous word (Verb or Adjective) marked with **Z**, which is immediately followed by a Noun (**N**). Depending on the language, we can vary the left surrounding by adding more alternatives [TOISAH]. This rule states that, in this particular context, the second word is an Adjective (**A**). See **@A**, where **@** stands for the first word, and **A** marks the second word in this sequence. This rule will disambiguate all Verbs or Adjectives in all languages:

English	**German**	**French**
absent=Z/A	achte=Z/A	accables=Z/A
acerbate=Z/A	bereite=Z/A	actives=Z/A
alternate=Z/A	beschaffen=Z/A	aguerri=Z/A
etc.		

4 Ambiguity Noun or Adjective

Since both the Noun and the Adjective belong to the so-called 'Nominal Group', we do not have to bother to disambiguate them, unless we want to know precisely which is the Adjective and which is the Noun. In English, the preceding Noun plays the role of an attribute (an Adjective). Therefore we can write the following generalizing rule in the *.h file:

```
{"NN",       "A",  },
```

which means, when we have two consecutive Nouns, the first one plays the role of an Adjective (attribute to the Noun). However, there are exceptions, especially in German, and we cannot use such generalizing rule for all proper and geographical names. Therefore, we can write a case to exclude the names:

```
case 202:  /* Adjective or Noun */
  if (wrd->e.N.name == 1) {
/* if the first Noun is a name, names are coded with a code in square brackets */
     wrd->syn = 'N';   // it is a Noun
  else                 // otherwise
     wrd->syn = 'A';   // it is an Adjective
     copysyn(que, wp);
  }
  i = wcount; continue;
```

Continuation of the above rule in the respective *.h file:

```
{"NN", NULL, 202},
```

Even when the name is written with a small letter in German, by mistake, the above rule will let the program know that this is a Noun. This is an example of using a semantical feature for disambiguation.

The problem is, that we cannot register all names in our dictionary. There are so many place names and names of persons in the world. Therefore we can use the following case instead:

```
case 203:  /* Adjective or Noun */
  if (isupper(wrd->inword[0])) {
// if the first word is written with a capital letter
     wrd->syn = 'N';   // it is a Noun
  else                 // otherwise
     wrd->syn = 'A';   // it is an Adjective
     copysyn(que, wp);
  }
  i = wcount; continue;
```

Continuation of the above rule in the respective *.h file:

```
{"NN", NULL, 203},
```

This rule is especially suitable for the German language, where we often have two nouns following one another without one of them being an adjective: ***Alte Welt, Beispiel Schokolade, Berg Heil***, etc. In French, the situation is slightly different, there the adjective often follows the noun and we, therefore, need to write another rule:

```
{"'le'NN",          "@@A",  },
```

where the 2nd noun is an adjective.
This rule is not very accurate, because not all nouns are also adjectives, therefore we need a more precise case for the French language:

```
case 1:  /* rename N to A */
  if (wrdm->esyn == 'N' && strrchr(wrdm->cw, 'A')) {
/* if the word wrdm (2nd one) is marked in the DW as N (Noun) and if the same word is marked
also as A (Adjective) */
```

```
        wrdm->syn = 'A'; // then, in this case, it is an Adjective
        copysyn(que, wp);
    }
    i = wcount; continue;
```

Continuation of the above rule in the respective *.h file:

```
{"NN",       "@A",  1},   /* the 2nd Noun is an Adjective in French */
```

Compare the following example:

Il vent te tailler le crayon rouge.

Where *rouge* can be a noun or adjective. When we use the above rule, *rouge* will be recognized as an adjective.

Case 1 above, after slight modification, can be applied, to any language to check whether the first noun is really an adjective, because the names, in particular, are not adjectives in this context. We can increase our requirements by checking whether the first noun is written with a capital letter, and we should not forget to include 'else' in the rule, to say what else the first word can be if not an adjective.

5 Ambiguity between Particle and Preposition or Article

In English *to*, and in German *zu*, can be either Particle or Preposition, in French '*de*', etc. can be Particle or Article. Case 64 below will deal successfully with this type of ambiguity.

```
    case 64:      /* BZ */
     if (wrdm->person ||wrdm->numb) {
/* if the 2nd word (the word after 'B') is 3rd person singular or is in plural */
        wp[i+1]->syn = 'P';
// 'B' is not a 'B', it is a 'P' (Preposition)
        copysyn(que, wp);
     }
     i = mpos; continue;
```

Continuation of the above rule in the respective *.h file:

```
{"[EV]BZ", NULL, 64},
```

For example, in the following context, '*to*' in English will be recognized as a preposition and not as a verbal particle.

'*This will lead <u>to cuts</u> in the budget.*'

The word *cuts* is registered in the DW as ambiguous (Noun plural or Verb 3rd person singular) and coded with Z or z (depending on what codes we have adopted). Case 64 can be applied, as it is, to French and German as well.

Often, the disambiguation is done without a case. The following context in the appropriate *.h file will be enough to disambiguate the French particle or article '*de*':

```
{"AZ'de'Z",   "@NPN",  },
```

The above rule says, that *'de'* after an adjective and ambiguous word and before an ambiguous word is a preposition.

6 Ambiguity of an individual word

There are many contexts where we cannot use a generalizing rule. We must be very specific. This means that we have to write a rule for a specific individual word or individual words in a specific context. Here are some examples:

For the English language

```
{"R'make'[ZVe]",     "@V",  },        /* PPNC followed by "make" etc., "make" is a V */
{"T'free'Z",    "@@N",  },            /* Z ( Noun or Verb) is a Noun */
{"[Ve]'bankrupt'",   "@A",  },        /* the word bankrupt is an attribute (A) to the Verb */
{"[VE][MR]'steady'", ".MA",  },       /* the word steady is an attribute (A) to the Verb */
{"'correct'*",       "d", },          /* correct at the end of the sentence is an Adverb */
{"'then'*",      "d", },              /* then at the end of the sentence is an Adverb */
{"'prevention'N",    "A",  },         /* prevention before a Noun is an Adjective */
{"'this'ZZ",     "@@V",  },           /* the second Z (Noun or Verb) is a Verb */
{"[RL]'like'[TNSOAMm]",    "@V",  },  /* like in this context is a Verb */
{"U<KD>'like'",  "@$V",  },
// 'like' after an auxiliary verb from the paradigm 'can'  is a verb
```

For the German language

```
{"[PTK]'guten'[PBTV]",    "@N",  },
// 'guten' after preposition, article or negation and
// before preposition, article, particle or verb is a noun
{"'einigen'I",      "A",  },
// 'einigen' before indicative pronoun or numeral is an adjective
{"[OSTK]'bleiben'",   "@N", },
// 'bleiben' after possessive or indicative pronoun, article
// or negation is a noun
{"[STK]'wollen'[VE]",   "@N", },
// 'wollen' after indicative pronoun, article or negation and before
// verb or participle is a noun
```

For the French language

```
{"'aller'V",        "V",  },
// 'aller' before a verb is a verb
{"[TAP]'car'",          "@N",  },
// 'car' after preposition, adjective or article is a noun
{"[TAP]'doit'",          "@N",  },
// 'doit' after preposition, adjective or article is a noun
{"[RNS]'fait'",          "@V",  },
// 'fait' after personal pronoun, noun or indicative pronoun
// is a verb
etc...
```

Please, see the Index of Abbreviations for the abbreviations used above.
Note that the disambiguation instructions are

a) individual, when a rule is made only for one individual word;
b) for a group of words belonging to the same part of speech and bearing the same code within square brackets [];
c) for a whole class of words (for all nouns, all Verbs, etc.), excluding the exceptions (the exceptions are coded with a code in square brackets [] when their number is large, or they are enumerated individually, as individual words).

Without proper disambiguation of the parts of speech, there cannot be efficient parsing.

3 Parsing

1 The Sentence

The sentence, in our view, is any grammatically correct and meaningful word, or word sequence, that stretches from full stop to full stop, or from full stop to a Question or Exclamation Mark.

1.1 Simple Sentence

The simple sentence is composed of:

a) The Subject (Sj) – the performer of the action.
b) The Predicate, or Verb, expressed always as a Verbal Tense – the action; compare *come, sit* (English) , *kommen, sitzen* (German), *faire, faisander* (French), etc. or state *is, was* (English), *ist, war* (German), *fut, fussent* (French), etc.
c) The Direct Object (Od) – an object towards which the action is aimed directly.
d) The Indirect Object (Oi) – an object towards which the action is aimed indirectly.

The simple sentence can consist of: a Subject only; a Verb only; a Subject and Verb only; a Subject, Verb and Object Direct only; a Subject, Verb, Object Indirect and Object Direct only. It cannot consist of: Subject, Verb and Object Indirect only; of Object only; Verb and Object only (except in Imperative sentences). Other, less important elements of the sentence are:

e) The Complement (Subject, Object) – modifying the Subject, or the Object.
f) The Infinitive, or otherwise called Infinitival Complement.
g) The Adverbs and the adverbial phrases, as modifiers of the Verb.
h) The Article, the Pronoun, the Numeral and the Adjective as modifiers of the Noun.

The Simple Sentence does not contain a Prepositional Adverbial Clause, though it contains Adverbs and Adverbial Phrases.

1.2 Clause

The Clause can be of two types. It can be equal to a Simple Sentence, or joined to another such simple sentence to form a Complex or Compound Sentence by means of a Conjunction. For example:

(i) *We waited, but she did not come.*
R V J R V k V
Sj V J Sj V

(i a) *Wir warteten, / aber / sie kam nicht an.*
R V J R V k an
Sj V J Sj V

(i b) *C'est une option / que / je fais mienne.*
I X T N J R V O
Sj V Cs Sj V Od

The Clause can be equal to a Simple sentence, having an appositional role (used as a Complement in the same way as a single word would be used as a Complement in the Simple sentence). Compare the sentence:

(ii) *We met a woman, a friend of ours.*
R V T N T N P M
Sj V Od Co

(ii a) *Wir trafen eine Frau, / einen Freund von uns.*
H V T N T N P R
Sj V Od Co

1.3 Complex Sentence

The Complex (also the Compound) Sentence consists of Clauses. There are two main types of Clauses:

a) The Principal (or Main) Clause. This is the Independent Clause. All other Clauses in the Complex (also Compound) Sentence are dependent on it and modify it in one or another way.

(iii) *They stayed a minute at the door, but they saw little choice,*
R V T N P T J R V A N
Sj V Od PAC J Sj V Od

then the workers on the nearest table asked them to come in.
J T N P T A N V M B V
Sj PAC V Od Ic

(iii a) *Sie blieben eine Minute / in der Tür stehen, / aber / die Chancen waren*
H V T N P T N V J T N X
Sj V Od PAC V J Sj
offenbar nicht gut,
D k D
V D

denn / die Arbeiter / am nächsten Tisch / schienen unsere Partei zu nehmen.
J T N P A N V O N B V

(iii b) *Cette maison-ci est plus proche / que / celle-là.*
I N X A A J I D
Sj V Cs

(iii c) *Effacez ce / qui / ne / vous paraît pas juste.*
V I J K H V K A
V Od Sj V D

The Main Clauses are underlined.

b) The Subordinate, or so-called Dependent Clause. The Subordinate Clause is linked to the Main Clause or to another Subordinate Clause by means of a Conjunction. The choice of a given Conjunction depends on the meaning we want to express with the entire Complex (or Compound) Sentence. The Dependent Clauses, depending on whether they complement (refer to) the Subject, the Predicate (the Verb) or the Object of the Main Clause, are called, respectively: Subject Clause (iv), Predicate Clause (v) and Object Clause (vi).

(iv) *She was adult, but she was afraid.*
R X A J R X D
Sj V Sj V

(iv a) *Er war einverstanden, / obwohl / er zuerst ablehnte.*
H V J H D V
Sj V Sj V

(iv b) *Sie ist das, / was / sie muß sein.*
H V I J H V
Sj V Cs

(iv c) *Tel / qui rit vendredi, / dimanche pleurera.*
I G V N N V
Sj Sj V Od Sj V
Sj Sj V D (time) D (time) V

(iv d) *Il monta un petit cheval gris, /puis / il alla tout le long / au pas.*
H V T A N A J H V D P N
Sj V Od Co J Sj V D PAC

(v) *Her mother meant what she said.*
O N V J R V
Sj V J Sj V

(v a) *Ihre Mutter meinte, / was / sie sagte.*
O N V J H V
Sj V Sj V

(v b) *Sie wußte, / was / zu sagen.*
H V J B V
Sj V Ic

(v c) *Je ne crois pas / que / personne réussisse.*
H K V K J N V
Sj V J Sj V

(v d) *Je trouve / en moi / quelque chose de confus / ou / de diffus.*
H V P R I N de N

(vi) *I saw the man, who came in.*
R V T N Q V
Sj V Od Co

(vi a) *Ich halte ihn / für einen sehr schlauen Mann.*
H V R P T D A N
Sj V Od Co

(vi b) *J'ai recontré récemment quelqu'un / qui collectionne les ouvrages /*
H Y E D N G V T N
Sj V D Od Sj V Od

que caractérisent ce / que / l'on a appelé le 'modern style'.
G V I J H Y E T A N
Sj V Od J Sj V Od

(vi c) *Je fais ce / que me plaît.*
H V I G R V
Sj V Od Sj Oi V

Some clauses are Prepositional Clauses, because they start with a Preposition – *in der Tür stehen, au pas*; others begin with a Conjunction – *aber sie kam nicht an, ou de diffus*, still others start with both Conjunction and Preposition – *außer zu ihn*. More about the Sentence and the Clauses the reader can find in the respective literature. The above succinct description was meant only as a reminder of what the sentence really is, before we start to parse it.

2 Parsing of the Sentence

There is no Text Processing (verification of the grammatical correctness of the Sentence, Machine Translation, Information Retrieval, etc.) without parsing.

The reader can find a definition of a Parse in Gazdar and Mellish (1989: 149), McEnery (1992: 80). In principle, Parsing is synonymous with identifying the grammatical and syntactical structure of the sentence. In Text Processing the outstanding problem is **what** structure, **how** and with what rate of success. There are different views and approaches; we have chosen the practical approach, the one that yields competitive results. In this section we will provide parsing examples, in several languages, to cover all possible varieties of Parts of the Sentence.

2.1 Subject

The most important element of the Sentence is the Subject (the doer) and then comes the Verb (the Predicate denoting action). For example:

(i) *Ann comes.* (English)
R V
Sj V

(i a) **Иван приехал.** (Russian)
R V
Sj V

(i b) *Theres kommt.* (German)
N V
Sj V

(i c) *Il marche.* (French)
R V
Sj V

2.2 Verb

The Verb (used in the Sentence as Verbal Tense) describes what the Subject does (did, or will do). We will discuss in greater detail the Verbal Tenses further below.

2.3 Object

Third in importance is the Object – Object Direct (Od) and Object Indirect (Oi) – the object of the action. Then the Subject and the Object (of the action) are placed in a relationship, described by a Verb (Verbal Tense). For example:

(ii) *Peter asked Mary.*
R V N
Sj V Od

(ii a) *Peter fragte Mary.*
N V N
Sj V Od

(ii b) *Je n'ai pas de voiture.*
R Y K T N
Sj V Od

(iii) *Mary has bought a book.*
N Y E T N
Sj V Od

(iii a) *Mary hat ein Buch gekauft.*
N Y T N E
Sj V Od

(iii b) *Je vais vendre cette voiture.*
R V V I N
Sj V Od

In order to find the Direct Object one asks such questions as: asked **whom** (*Mary*); bought **what** (*a book*), send **what** (*le formulaire*).

(iii c) *Le pape envoie le formulaire / tel / qu'on lui demandait.*
T N V T N G H R V
Sj V Od Sj Sj Oi V

In German grammar books the Object Direct is called Accusative Object (Akkusativobjekt) or Dative Object (Dativobjekt), if it follows a Verb that requires a Dative (*antworten, begegnen, gleichen*, etc.) or Genitive Object (Genitivobjekt), if it follows a Verb that requires a Genitive (*harren, gedenken, bedürfen*, etc.) – see Schwarz, A. (1978: 199–202). For example, in the sentence:

John hilft dem Vater.
N V T N
Sj V Od

dem Vater will be a Dative Object, which we prefer to call Object Direct. There are two varieties of Objects – Direct (Od) and Indirect (Oi). Examples (ii) and (iii) above are for a Direct Object. This means that the connection, or the relationship between the Sj and the Od is direct. There is nothing to intervene (to stand) in between. The Indirect Object (Oi) intervenes between the Sj and the Od and can be found by asking the question **to whom** (iv). For example:

(iv) *Mary gave him a book.*
N V R T N
Sj V Oi Od

(iv a) *Mary gab mir das Buch.*
N V R T N
Sj V Oi Od

(iv b) *Peter lehrte uns viele neue Lieder.*
N V R I A N
Sj V Oi Od

(iv c) *Er brachte den Menschen das Feuer.*
R V T N T N
Sj V Oi Od

(iv d) *Ich erinnerte mich des Vorfalls.*
R V S T N
Sj V Oi Od

(iv e) *Sie beschuldigten Peter Smith des Verrats.*
R V N N des N
Sj V Od PAC

(iv f) *Jeanne m' a promis son aide.*
N R Y E O N
Sj Oi V Od

According to Schwarz, A. (1978: 200–205) the examples (iv a) and (iv b) shown above have two Accusative Objects: *mir* and *das Buch* (iv a), *uns* and *viele neue Lieder* (iv b), example (iv c) has two Dative objects, (iv d) is an example of Genitive Object (*des Vorfalls*) and example (iv e) has two Objects (Accusative and Genitive). This is, no doubt, a difference of terminology, not of interpretation.

2.4 *Complement*

All other elements (or parts) of the Sentence are Complements (or modifiers) either to the Subject or to the Verb or to the Object Direct. The Complement explains, clarifies or brings additional information. Below we will discuss the complements one by one.

2.4.1 *Complement to the Subject (Cs)*

The Complement Subject can assume two positions in the sentence.

a) To follow after a Linking (v a, v b, v c) Verb, an Auxiliary Verb from the English **be** paradigm (v), the French **être** paradigm (v d), the German **sein** paradigm (v e, v f) or after a Modal Verb used with **sein** (v g, v h).

(v) *Mary is a nice woman.*

Mary	is	a	nice	woman.
N	X	T	A	N
Sj	V	Cs		

(v a) *J'aurais parfaitement pu **devenir** avocat.*

J'	aurais	parfaitement	pu	devenir	avocat.
R	Y	D	E	V	N
	Sj	V		V	Cs
	Sj	V			Od

(v b) *Elle **semble** inquiète.*

Elle	semble	inquiète.
R	V	A
Sj	V	Cs
Sj	V	Od

(v c) *Mary became a nice woman.*

Mary	became	a	nice	woman.
N	X	T	A	N
Sj	V			Cs

(v d) *Sa maison est belle.*

Sa	maison	est	belle.
I	N	X	A
Sj		V	Cs

(v e) *Mary ist eine Hausfrau.*

Mary	ist	eine	Hausfrau.
N	V	T	N
Sj	V	Cs	

(v f) *Das Mädchen auf dem Stuhl ist meine Schwester.*

Das	Mädchen	auf	dem	Stuhl	ist	meine	Schwester.
T	N	P	T	N	X	O	N
Sj		PAC			V	Cs	

(v g) *Sie muß eine Frau sein.*

Sie	muß	eine	Frau	sein.
R	U	T	N	X
Sj	V	Cs		

(v h) *Sie wird eine Frau sein.*

Sie	wird	eine	Frau	sein.
R	x	T	N	X
Sj	V	Cs		

b) To follow immediately after the Sj (vi) as part of an abridged Relative Clause (vi a, vi b, vi c). For example:

(vi) *The boy sitting in the bus comes from London.*

The	boy	sitting	in	the	bus	comes	from	London.
T	N	G	P	T	N	V	P	N
	Sj	Cs						

(vi a) *Der Mann, der den Kuchen ißt, ist hungrig.*
T N G T N V X D
Sj Cs V Cs

(vi b) *Tel qui rit vendredi, dimanche pleurera.*
I G V N N V
Sj Sj V D Sj V

(vi c) *Vous qui avez beaucoup voyagé, vous avez acquis une large expérience de la vie.*
R G Y D E H Y E T A N
Sj Sj V Sj V Od de T N

2.4.2 Complement to the Object (Co)

The Complement Object in most languages follows immediately after the Object Direct. For example:

(vii) *He called John a liar.*
R V N T N
Sj V Od Co

(vii a) *Sie nannte ihn einen Lügner.*
R V R T N
Sj V Od Co

(vii b) *Nous avions quitté le monde des conventions rassurantes.*
R Y E T N de N A
Sj V Od Co

The Infinitive can also be used as a Complement Object. Compare:

(viii) *I give them much space to swim.*
R V M I N B V
Sj V Oi Od Co

2.4.3 Complementing of the Verb

The Adverb, the adverbial phrase, the Prepositional Adverbial Clause and the Infinitival Complement are used to elucidate the meaning of the Verb. For example:

(ix) *We will go to the town by car.*
R V PAC PAC
Sj V

Wir fuhren in die Stadt mit dem Auto.
R V PAC PAC
Sj V

Je discute souvent avec lui bien que nous ayons des opinions différentes.
R V D PAC J H Y T N A
Sj V Od J Sj V Od Co

The Prepositional Adverbial Clauses in (ix) explain further the meaning of the Verb (the action denoted by the Verb) – towards what location and by what instrument or means – and play the role of a Prepositional Object.

Some authors (Graver, 1971: 146) point out that the Infinitive can also be used as an Object to the Verb (ix a, ix b). Compare:

(ix a) *Ich gebe meinen Leuten viel Freiheit zu schwimmen.*
R V O N I N B V
Sj V Oi Od Ic

(ix b) *Vous n'avez nul besoin de téléphone.*
R Y A N B V
Sj V Od Ic

However, we will call the Infinitive in this and in other cases an Infinitival Complement (Ic) because of its varied use (ix c, ix d). For example:

(ix c) *Sie bat ihn darum, zu warten.*
R V R D to v
Sj V Od Ic
Sj V Od Co

(ix d) *Votre ami a eu le tort de partir trop tôt.*
O N Y E T N B V D
Sj V Od Ic
Sj V Od Co

In (ix c, ix d) the Subject of the Infinitive is also the Object of the Main Verb, the Infinitive playing the role of a Co. In (ix e, ix f, ix g) the Subject of the Infinitive is a Cs, the Infinitive is also a Cs.

(ix e) *Er war der erste Mann zu gehen.*
R X T A N B V
Sj V Cs Ic
Sj V Cs Cs

(ix f) *C'est qu'il fallait recommencer à vivre.*
I X H V V B V
Sj V Sj V Ic
Sj V Cs Cs

(ix g) *Le roi ne sait que c'est d'honorer à demi.*
T N K V J I X B V P N
Sj V Sj V Ic PAC
Sj V Sj V Cs

In (ix h) the Ic plays the role of Cs.

(ix h) *Il est facile d'avoir.*
R X A B Y
Sj V Cs Ic
Cs

(ix i) *Je n'ai jamais pu découvrir laquelle.*
RKY D E V J
Sj V Ic

In the above example (ix i) the Conjunction *laquelle* acts as a Complement of the Verb and could be regarded also as Od.

3 Verbal Tenses

In the present analysis we use the following types of Verbs: (i) Auxiliary; (ii) Main Verb or Verb Proper (Present form); (iii) The Verb in its Past form; (iv) The Verb in its Participle form, as part of a Compound Tense.

The Auxiliary Verbs and the Verbs Proper including their Past and Participle forms are presented in the Dictionary of Wordforms (coded respectively). It is not possible to present the Verbal Tenses in the Dictionary of Wordforms. The recognition of the Verbal Tenses is done by the same software program, that does the parsing of the sentence and of the text. How this program recognizes the Verbal Tenses we will explain later. Now we will simply list the Verbal Tenses. Unlike the other Parts of the Sentence, which are fairly universal, the Verbal Tenses are quite unique and therefore need not necessarily have equivalents in other languages. For example, in English, there are around 36 Verbal Tenses used to express different Moods, and two Voices. In Russian there are only three Verbal Tenses (Past, Present and Future). Therefore, it is not easy to make comparisons. This does not mean, however, that what can be expressed with so many Tenses in English cannot be expressed in Russian. Every language has its own means of expression; in Russian this is the context.

English Verbal Tenses:

I. ACTIVE VOICE

1.0 Infinitive. For example: *to go*
1.1 Present Simple Tense. For example: *bring*
1.2 Past Simple Tense. For example: *worked, went*
1.3 Future Simple Tense. For example: *will go*
1.4 Future in the Past. For example: *should stay*
1.5 Present Continuous Tense. For example: *are reading*
1.6 Past Continuous Tense. For example: *was singing*
1.7 Future Continuous Tense. For example: *shall be working*
1.8 Future Continuous in the Past. For example: *should be playing*
1.9 Present Perfect Tense. For example: *has arrived*
1.10 Past Perfect Tense. For example: *had brought*
1.11 Future Perfect Tense. For example: *will have taken*
1.12 Future Perfect in the Past. For example: *would have believed*
1.13 Present Perfect Continuous. For example: *have been reading*
1.14 Past Perfect Continuous. For example: *had been studying*
1.15 Future Perfect Continuous. For example: *will have been playing*
1.16 Future Perfect Continuous in the Past. For example: *should have been resting.*

II. PASSIVE VOICE

2.17 Present Tense. For example: *am asked*
2.18 Past Tense. For example: *was taken*
2.19 Future Tense. For example: *shall be asked*
2.20 Future in the Past. For example: *should be asked*
2.21 Present Continuous. For example: *are being piled*
2.22 Past Continuous. For example: *was being driven*
2.23 Present Perfect. For example: *have been given*

2.24 Past Perfect. For example: *had been asked*
2.25 Future Perfect. For example: *shall have been gone*
2.26 Future Perfect in the Past. For example: *should have been asked*
2.27 Infinitive. For example: *to be asked*

III. MOOD
3.28 Present Conditional. For example: *should ask*
3.29 Perfect Conditional. For example: *should have slept*
SUBJUNCTIVE
3.30 Present Subjunctive. For example: *may come*
3.31 Past Subjunctive. For example: *could have stayed*
3.32 Perfect Infinitive. For example: *must have found*
3.33 When Subjunctive is used in a Conditional Sentence. For example: *If I were ...,*

IV. IMPERATIVE.
4.34 For example: *do be seated*

Note that *Syntparse* (Georgiev, 1993) does not differentiate the other forms of the Imperative – in the Active and the Passive Voice. The program displays the corresponding Verbal Tense instead of the Imperative. All interrogative forms of the above mentioned Verbal Tenses are also analysed correctly and displayed by the program. The German version of *Syntparse* (Satzzerlegung), Georgiev (1996a), displays the following German verbal tenses:

1. Präsens: *glaube*
   Präsens Passiv: *wird gekauft*
2. Futur: *werde kaufen*
   Futur Passiv: *wird gelobt werden*
   Futur II: *werde gesehen haben*
   Futur II Passiv: *werde gelobt worden sein*
3. Perfekt: *habe gemacht*
   Perfekt Passiv: *ist gelobt worden*
4. Plusquamperfekt: *hatte gesehen*
   Plusquamperfekt Passiv: *wäre gelobt worden*
5. Imperfekt: *kam, glaubte*
   Imperfekt Passiv: *würde gelobt, wurde gelobt*

In most cases the German Verbal Tenses are split apart within the Sentence, therefore other specifications in the program are needed to recognize them automatically. For example:

(i) *Mit dem regierungsrätlichen Entscheid ist die Buslinie abgeltungsberechtigt.*
PAC X T N E

Perfekt: *ist abgeltungsberechtigt.*

(ii) *Allerdings sind diese Früchte meistens nicht biologisch gezogen.*
J X I N D k D E

A similar problem affects the so called German separable Verbs:

Die Diskussionen regen zudem die Forschung an.
T N V P T N an

The split Verb is *regen an*, equivalent to *anregen*.

The French version of *Syntparse* (Analyse), Georgiev (1997) displays the following French verbal tenses:

1. Présent (indicatif): *avons, sommes, placions, payons*, etc.
   Présent (subjonctif): *ayons, soyons, finissions*, etc.
   Présent (conditionel): *aurions, serions, erions, finirions*, etc.
2. Futur (indicatif): *aurons, serons, placerai, payerai*, etc.
   Futur antérieur (indicatif): *aurons eu, aurons été, aurons aimé, aurons fini*, etc.
3. Passé simple (indicatif): *aimâmes, finîmes*, etc.
   Passé antérieur (indicatif): *eûmes aimé, eûmes fini*, etc.
   Passé composé (indicatif): *avons aimé, avons fini*, etc.
   Passé (subjonctif): *ayons aimé, ayons fini*, etc.
   Passé 1re forme (conditionel): *aurions aimé, aurions fini*, etc.
   Passé 2e forme (conditionel): *eussions aimé, eussions fini*, etc.
4. Plus-que-parfait (indicatif): *avions aimé, avions fini*, etc.
   Plus-que-parfait (subjonctif): *eussions aimé, eussions fini*, etc.
5. Imparfait (indicatif): *avions, étions, finissions*, etc.
   Imparfait (subjonctif): *eussions, fussions, aimassions, finissions*, etc.

The Verbal Tenses are Simple (consisting of only one word) and Compound (consisting of two or more words). The English, German and French versions of *Syntparse*, Georgiev (1993–7) recognize correctly the above-mentioned English, German and French Verbal Tenses when met in the sentence or in a text.

4 Parsing instructions programmed in C (C++)

To begin with, we would like to mention that the text to be parsed should be grammatically correct, meaningful and unambiguous. The punctuation marks should be used accurately and always where needed. This is expected, in any case, from anybody who writes, and it will help reduce the parsing errors. However careful we are, we cannot avoid the existing ambiguities in the sentence, therefore we will mention some of them before we proceed further. For instance, let's consider the following examples:

(i) *Sie nannte ihn einen Lügner.*

R	V	R	T	N
Sj	V	Oi		Od
Sj	V	Od		Co

This is a parsing ambiguity between Oi/Od and Od/Co (German).
In this case we have to tell the parsing software program that *nannte* differs from the other Verbs: that it takes Direct Object only, therefore the Noun following after the Direct Object is a Complement (in this case – Complement Object).

(i a) *C'est qu'il fallait recommencer à vivre.*

I	X	H	V	V	B	V
Sj	V	Sj		V		Ic
Sj	V		Cs			Cs

This is a parsing ambiguity between Sj/Cs, where the second subject has a double role: it is a subject of the new clause, but a complement to the first subject (French).

Some German verbs can be used both with and without Prepositions, or Adverbial Adjuncts (*an, auf, um*, etc.), as part of a separable Verb, and the computer program would not know if the

Preposition is used with the Verb, or if it belongs to the Adverbial Clause that follows next. The following sentence is an example of this type of ambiguity:

Ein Familienunternehmen kann auch schnell durch die eigenen
T N U D D an T O
T N U D D P T O
Familienmitglieder ruiniert werden.
N V x
N

because ***kann durch*** can be interpreted as one of the present forms of ***durchkönnen*** or ***durch*** can be a Preposition starting a Prepositional Clause. If we have two consecutive Prepositions, this can be an indication that the first Preposition is part of a Verb (if there is a separable Verb to the left), and the second Preposition can be part of a Prepositional Adverbial Clause.

In French:
d'aller.
P N
B V

can be a noun in the sentence
Billet d'aller et de retour.
N P N C T N
Sj Cs

or a verb in another sentence
J'ai envie d'aller au cinéma.
R Y E B V P N
Sj V Ic Od (PAC)

Other factors that may affect the overall parsing performance of the computer software program are the choice of the programming language and the experience and ingenuity of the programmer.

The parsing instructions are based on the programing work described in the previous chapters: the program should 'know' what is a Noun, what is a Verb, etc. and what grammatical, syntactical or semantical information is attached to them. Also, the parsing instructions work on the assumption that the ambiguity on word (Part of Speech) level is resolved.

In the English version of *Syntparse* (Georgiev, 1993) we have differentiated the following Parts of the Sentence:

ADVERB, ADVERBIAL PHRASE for Time, SUBJECT, VERB (Including Verbal Tense), COMPLEMENT, COMPLEMENT SUBJECT, COMPLEMENT to Previous NOUN, OBJECT, OBJECT DIRECT, OBJECT INDIRECT, PREDICATIVE and ADVERB, CONJUNCTION, COMPLEMENT OBJECT, INFINITIVE, INFINITIVAL COMPLEMENT, INFINITIVAL COMPLEMENT and COMPLEMENT OBJECT, INFINITIVAL COMPLEMENT and COMPLEMENT SUBJECT, INTERROGATIVE PRONOUN, PREDICATIVE, PREPOSITIONAL ADVERBIAL CLAUSE, RELATIVE CLAUSE, RELATIVE CLAUSE and ..., RELATIVE CLAUSE and COMPLEMENT, RELATIVE CLAUSE and COMPLEMENT SUBJECT, RELATIVE PRONOUN, RELATIVE PRONOUN and SUBJECT, RELATIVE PRONOUN and CONJUNCTION, DEPENDENT CLAUSE (SUBORDINATE CLAUSE).

In the German version of *Syntparse* (Georgiev, 1996a) we have differentiated the following Parts of the Sentence:

> SUBJEKT, VERBUM (incl. Verbal Tense), ADVERB, ADVERBIAL AUSDRUCK für Zeit, OBJEKTATTRIBUT, SUBJEKTATTRIBUT, ATTRIBUT vor SUBSTANTIV, NÄHERES OBJEKT, ENTFERNTERES OBJEKT, PRÄDIKAT und ADVERB, KONJUNKTION, INFINITIV, INFINITIVATTRIBUT, INFINITIVATTRIBUT und OBJEKTATTRIBUT, INFINITIVATTRIBUT und SUBJEKTATTRIBUT, PRÄDIKAT, PRÄPOSITIONALPHRASE, RELATIVSATZ, RELATIVSATZ und ATTRIBUT, RELATIVSATZ und SUBJEKTATTRIBUT, RELATIVPRONOMEN, RELATIVPRONOMEN und SUBJEKT, RELATIVPRONOMEN und KONJUNKTION, NEBENSATZ, ABHÄNGIGER SATZ.

In the French version of *Syntparse* (Georgiev, 1997) we have differentiated the following Parts of the Sentence:

> LE SUJET, l'ATTRIBUT DU SUJET, LE VERBE, LE COMPLÉMENT DIRECT, LE COMPLÉMENT INDIRECT, l'ADVERBE, COMPLÉMENT CIRCONSTANCIEL de TEMPS, COMPLÉMENT d'OBJET, l'ATTRIBUT de NOM PRÉCÉDENT, MOT qui PRÉDIT et l'ADVERBE, LA CONJONCTION, 'INFINITIF, COMPLÉMENT INFINITIF, COMPLÉMENT INFINITIF et COMPLÉMENT d'OBJET, COMPLÉMENT INFINITIF et l'ATTRIBUT DU SUJET, PRONOM INTERROGATIF, MOT qui PRÉDIT, LE COMPLÉMENT CIRCONSTANCIEL, LA PROPOSITION RELATIVE, LA PROPOSITION RELATIVE et COMPLÉMENT, LA PROPOSITION RELATIVE et l'ATTRIBUT DU SUJET, PRONOM RELATIF, PRONOM RELATIF et LE SUJET, PRONOM RELATIF et LA CONJONCTION, PROPOSITION SUBORDONÉE.

Below we provide identification procedures, written in C (C++), only for the major Parts of the Sentence (Subject, Object, Complement and some of the Verbal Tenses). In order to identify the Parts of the Sentence, we have to create a file called "segment.c" (or "segment.cpp") and another file called "segment.h". In the file "segment.c(pp)" we will write our identification instruction. The file "segment.h" will contain the additional specification related to this instruction, namely the specification of the context in which the Part of the Sentence can be found.

The beginning of the "segment.c(pp)" file looks like this:

```
#include <ctype.h>
#include <stdio.h>
#include <conio.h>
// .... etc. standard include files
#define MAX_SEGS 66
// define directive with a macro name MAX_SEGS and expansion 66
// where MAX_SEGS is a code name for maximum segments
extern BMENU    *meng;
extern SEGMENT *s;
extern struct QUE *tr_que[];
// etc. external declarations
int seg_parse(struct QUE *que[], int type, int i, SEGMENT *s);
void wrque(struct QUE *que[]);
DLIM *enque_dlm(struct QUE *que[], char syn, char ssyn);
WORD *enque_word(struct QUE *que[], char syn, char *word);

#include "segment.h"
// own include file
char *Sj = "\n SUBJECT: "; // for English
char *V = "\n VERB: ";
```

```
// char *Sj = "\n SUBJEKT: "; // for German
// char *V  = "\n VERBUM: ";
   // char *Sj = "\n LE SUJET: "; // for French
   // char *V  = "\n LE VERBE: ";
/* ... etc., listing all Parts of the English, German or French Sentence, as enumerated above.
This means that when we use the abbreviation Sj, the program prints out SUBJECT (in English),
SUBJEKT (in German), etc. For the other Parts of the Sentence see the Index to the Abbreviations
at the end of the book. */
void replace(SEGMENT s[],SEGMENT seg, int pos1, int pos2);
int insert_seg(SEGMENT s[], SEGMENT seg, int pos, int nseg);
int segcmp(SEGMENT seg[], int i, char *inst);
int buildseg(struct QUE *que[], SEGMENT s[]);
int restore_sentence(struct QUE *que[], SEGMENT s[], int nseg);
void wrsegs(SEGMENT s[], int nseg);
void verbtype(int vtype);
extern int fl_out;
extern int hout;
// .... etc.
// a void function follows next
void seg_parser1(struct QUE *que[], int type)
{
int nseg;
register i, j;
int last, next_i, sp;
struct T1_SEGM *psg;
SEGMENT seg;
WORD *w, *pre, *wrd, *w1, *w2;
char *cw;
char sn;
   if (type == '?') {
// if the sentence is interrogative
        wnprintfl("\nInterrogative\n");
// print 'Interrogative'
//   wnprintfl("\nFragesatz\n"); // print interrogative in German
// etc., depending on the language
   wnprintfl("---------------------");
   }
   for ( i = 0; i < nseg - 1; i++ ) {
   for ( psg = SEGM; psg->istr; psg++) {
   if ((last = segcmp(s, i, psg->istr)) )
   {
     switch (psg->cond)
     {

       case 1:          /* Start a case for each Part of the Sentence */
/* ... etc. cases, see below (4.1, 4.2, etc.) the case for each Part of the Sentence we have decided
to consider in this book. */
```

The respective "segment.h" file begins as follows:

```
struct T1_SEGM {
  char *istr;
  int cond;
};
struct T1_SEGM SEGM[] =
```

```
{
```
/* Below (in 4.1, 4.2, etc.) are listed the instructions related to the No of the case from the "segment.c(pp)" file. Each case relates to one particular Part of the Sentence. */

4.1 *Finding the Subject of the Sentence*

The subject is one of the most important parts of the sentence, because the subject is the performer of the action denoted by the verb. The subject usually starts the sentence. Case 1 is designed to detect the PPNC used as a subject.

```
      case 1:            /* R, Personal Pronoun Nominal Case, as a Sj */
       w1 = (WORD *) s[i].que[0];
// specifies the position of the running word w1
       if ( w1) {
/* if the Personal Pronoun Nominal Case is the first word (w1) in the sequence, as listed in the "segment.h" file */
       wnprintfl(Sj);
/* here the program prints out: SUBJECT (etc., as written in the respective language) */
       while ( w1 ) {
        wnprintfw("%s ", w1->inword);
// print the input (text) word w1
        w1 = w1->next;
       }
       }
       break;
```

Continuation of the above instruction in the "segment.h" file:

```
{"SR",     1},  // The Indicative Pronoun (S) is a Subject when followed by R.
{"R",        1},  // R (PPNC) is a subject
```

For example case 1 will parse the following sentences:

He knows that well
Elle est protégée par un cordon
Wir verzichteten auf das Thema

and will print that 'he' (Elle, wir) is a Subject.
The Personal Pronoun Nominal Case is a Subject, regardless of context, if there are no ambiguous personal pronouns like 'you' in English. Compare: *You came back home. I gave you the book*, where 'you' can be a subject or an object.

```
      case 2:
/* Noun Phrase, used as Sj or Od, depending on the Verb */
       if (s[i-1].syn == 'N' || s[i-1].syn == 'P' ||
        s[i-1].syn == 'G' || s[i].type == 'O') break;
// exit the case if ..., or if ...
       w = (WORD *) s[i-1].que[1];
// defines the position of the word s[i-1] in the sequence
       w1 = (WORD *) s[i].que[0];
// defines the position of the word s[i] in the sequence
       if ( w1) {
// if this particular (w1) defined word-position
```

```
      if (s[i-1].syn == 'V' && w->e.V.control == 0)
/* if on position s[i-1] there is a Verb and the control information of the word as a verb is 0 (negative) */
        wnprintfl(Od);        /* Print:  OBJECT DIRECT  */
/* Print: NÄHERES OBJEKT for German and LE COMPLÉMENT DIRECT for French */
      else                   // otherwise
        wnprintfl(Sj);       /* Print: SUBJECT */
      while ( w1 ) {
       wnprintfw("%s ", w1->inword);
// print the word w1 (word from the text)
       w1 = w1->next;
      }
      s[i].type = 'S';                    /* SUBJECT */
      }
      break;
```

Continuation of the above instruction in the "segment.h" file:

```
{"[NW#?ASIHO]<KkDdB>[VEhUXxY]",      2},
```

where [NW#?ASIHAO] is the first (w1) part of the sequence of parts of speech in the Sentence, consisting of either a Noun only [N], or Possessive Pronoun and Noun [ON], or Adjective and Noun [AN], or Indicative Pronoun, Numeral and Noun [SHN], etc. – combinations forming a Nominal Phrase. The middle part <KkDBb> specifies the optional Parts of Speech that can stand between the Nominal Phrase and the Verb. These are: negation <Kk>, Adverb <Dd> and the verbal Particle <B>. Note that the optional parts of speech separating the nominal phrase and the verb (verbal phrase) are language dependent. The final part [VEhUXxY] enumerates the Verbs that can follow: Verb Proper [VEh], Auxiliary Verb [UXxY].

Prior to taking a decision, case 2 controls the Verb to see whether the Verb following after the Nominal Phrase is a stand-alone Verb or a Verb used in a Compound Verbal Tense. In German, the Compound Verbal Tense is often split by a Nominal Phrase. For example:

Der Gouverneursrat der Internationalen Atomenergie
T N der N N

hat einen Revisionsentwurf angenommen .
Y T N E
Y Od

```
     case 3:            /* Nominal Phrase followed by Complement */
      w1 = (WORD *) s[i+1].que[0];
// specifies the position of the running word w1
      if ( w1) {
// if it is word (w1) in the sequence, as listed in the "segment.h" file
      wnprintfl(Sj); /* Print: SUBJECT */
      while ( w1 ) {
       wnprintfw("%s ", w1->inword);
// print the word w1 (word from the text)
       w1 = w1->next;
      }
      s[i+1].type = 'S';
      }
      break;
```

Continuation of the above instruction in the "segment.h" file, listing the surroundings of a Sj:

```
/* The Nominal Phrase must be positioned */
   {"[,|j*][NW#?SIH]<PD>[EFG]",    3},
/* between comma, Auxiliary Word, full stop and a Particple or Complement */
   {"*[NW#?SIH][PpsN,Llrm]",      3},    /* after full stop, Sj (i+1) */
   {"C[NW#?SIH][Llrs]",          3},  /* between Auxiliary Words */
   {"J[NW#?SIH],",             3},  /* between Auxiliary Word and a comma */
```

Case 3, in the *.h file above, lists four instances where the Nominal Phrase is a Sj. In one particular case the Verb can be also a Subject, that is when it is preceded by the verbal particle and only when the verbal particle starts the sentence. In order to be able to deal efficiently with this special situation, we have to rename the Verb, in this context, using the following case from "parser.c(pp)":

```
      case 14:
       if (wrdm->numb == 0){
/* if the word marked with V is in Singular*/
         wrdm->syn = 'N';
/* then V plays the role of a Noun  */
         copysyn(que, wp);
         i = wcount; continue;
       }
       break;
```

Continuation the above rule in the respective *.h file:

```
{"[bB]V<PTAOHINw?#>[,C]<dDK>Z", ".V$.$V", 14},    /* V = Noun */
```

On the basis of case 14 above, the sequence *to V …* in English (*zu V* in German, *le*, *de*, etc. plus V in French) at the start of the sentence becomes Nominal, and as such it will be considered to be a Subject.

There are many more cases relating to the recognition of the Subject, depending on the context in which the subject can be found. We will omit them from our description. For example, using the above mentioned cases, the computer, after processing

Peter asked Ann.

will 'understand' that Peter is the subject of this sentence and that he asked Ann and not vice-versa (Ann him). We will omit from our discussion such examples as

Peter was asked by Ann.

where according to our parsing *Peter* will be a subject and *by Ann* will be PAC; however here, it is, in fact, *Ann* who has asked *Peter*! This is important to note because in a question-answering software program it must be clear who has asked whom. Compare the difference between:

Has Peter asked Ann? – Yes, Peter has asked her to marry him.
Was Peter asked by Ann? – Yes, Ann asked him to marry her.

4.2 *Finding the Object of the Sentence*

The object is the next most important part of the sentence, after the subject and the verb. There are many cases to find the Object, depending on context and language. We will consider several

(47, 48, 49, 9), as an example.

```
      case 47:          /* VNN */
/* When the nominal phrase following after the verb contains indirect and direct object. */
      w1 = (WORD *) s[i+1].que[0];  // define the position of word w1
      w2 = (WORD *) s[last].que[0]; // define the position of word w2
      w = (WORD *) s[last].que[1];  // define the position of word w
      if (w1 && w2) {
// if w1 and w2 are as defined
       if (w->e.N.time)        // if the word w denotes time
         wnprintfl(Od);       // Print: OBJECT DIRECT
      else                    // otherwise
         wnprintfl(Oi);       // Print: OBJECT INDIRECT
      while ( w1 ) {
         wnprintfw("%s ", w1->inword); // Print word w1
         w1 = w1->next;
      }
       if (w->e.N.time)       // if the word w denotes time
         wnprintfl(ATime); // Print: ADVERBIAL PHRASE for Time
       else
         wnprintfl(Od);      // Print: OBJECT DIRECT
       while ( w2 ) {
         wnprintfw("%s ", w2->inword);  // Print word w2
         w2 = w2->next;
       }
       i = last;
       }
       break; // end
```

Continuation of the above instruction in the "segment.h" file:

```
{"[Vvz][Mm#N][SN]",  47},                /** Oi-Od **/
```

The nominal part following after the verb [Vvz] is Object Indirect [Mm#N] and Object Direct [SN].
For example, if we parse the following sentences with case 47:

He gave me two books.
Sie nannte ihn einen Lügner.

the program will print that *me* is Indirect Object, that *ihn* is 'Entfernteres Objekt', that '*two books*' is a Direct Object and '*einen Lügner*' is 'Näheres Objekt'. Case 48 below needs no analysis to find the Object.

```
      case 48:          /* Object Direct */
        wnprintfl(Od);  // Print: OBJECT DIRECT
// Print: NÄHERES OBJEKT
// Print: LE COMPLÉMENT DIRECT
      for (j = i+1; j <= last; j++){
        w1 = (WORD *) s[j].que[0]; // define the position of word w1
       if(w1) {
        while ( w1 ) {
         wnprintfw("%s ", w1->inword);  // Print word w1
         w1 = w1->next;
        }
```

```
  }
  }
  i = last;
  goto eol;
```

The specification given in the file “segment.h” is enough to state that the word w1 is Od.

Continuation of the above instruction in the “segment.h” file:

```
{"VMCm",      48},           /* Od  - English*/
```

The case is the same, but some instructions in the *.h file are language specific:

```
// {"VRCS",      48},          /* Od - German, French */
// {"VTMN",      48},          /* Od - French */
// etc.
```

Case 48 will parse the following French sentence:

J'avais apporté la copie de deux de mes articles.

and will print that *la copie de deux de mes articles* is ‘le Complément Direct’. Note that the instruction in the *.h file is language specific. It depends on which parts of speech, as a direct object, can follow the verb. Case 49 below analyses the meaning of the phrase to see whether it denotes time, before a decision is taken.

```
    case 49:          /* Sequence: VN~[N] */
      w2 = (WORD *) s[last-1].que[0]; // define the position of word w2
// word in a Nominal Phrase
     w1 = (WORD *) s[last-1].que[1]; // define the position of word w1
// another word in a Nominal Phrase (Noun)
     if ( w2) {
// if word w2 is considered
     if (w1->e.N.time)
// If the Noun, word w1, is denoting "time"
       wnprintfl(ATime); // Print: ADVERBIAL PHRASE for Time
     else
       wnprintfl(Od);      // Print: OBJECT DIRECT
     while ( w2 ) {
      wnprintfw("%s ", w2->inword); // print input word w2
      w2 = w2->next;
     }
     s[last-1].type = 'O';
     }
     break;
```

Continuation of the above instruction in the “segment.h” file:

```
{"[UVYvE]<PAD>N~[UVYX]",      49},  /* Od or Adverb for Time */
{"[UVY]<m>[WS#?IH]~[UVYX]",  49},
{"[vV]M~[AN]",       49},              /*  Od */
{"zN~N",             49},           /* Od */
```

The nominal part following after the Verb is Adverbial Phrase for Time, if the noun denotes time, otherwise it is Object Direct. Some cases (case 9, below) are language specific (German, French):

```
case 9:          /* Object: Direct or Indirect */
 w1 = (WORD *) s[i].que[0];
 if (s[i-1].syn == 'V')  // If the first word of the sequence is a Verb
 wnprintfl(Od);  // Print: NÄHERES OBJEKT
// Print: LE COMPLÉMENT DIRECT
 else
 wnprintfl(Oi); // Print: ENTFERNTERES OBJEKT
// Print: LE COMPLÉMENT INDIRECT
 if (w1) {
 wnprintfw("%s ", w1->inword);
 }
 break;  // end
```

Continuation of the above instruction in the "segment.h" file:

```
{"[Sm]",        9},          /* Od, Oi */
```

For example, if the computer software program, containing the above instructions, processes the sentence

Peter gave Ann an apple.

the computer will 'know' that 'an apple' is a direct object and 'Ann' is an indirect object. This means a lot in human-computer communication, because it is clear what was given to whom. In the chapters 'Lexical Semantics' and 'Question Answering' we will understand better how we can use the knowledge that the *apple* is a *fruit*, and that *fruit* is *food* to make the computer assume that, perhaps, *Ann is hungry*, *Ann will eat the apple*, etc., provided that there are no other specifications or restrictions in the sentence. For example:

Peter gave Ann an apple for her child.

whereby it will be clear that the apple will be for Ann's child, not for Ann. Ann's child, he or she, boy or girl will probably eat the apple.

4.3 Finding the Complement of the Sentence

The complement has a secondary importance in the sentence, but nevertheless plays a decisive differentiating role in understanding the meaning of the sentence on a computer in greater detail. For example, compare: *Peter bought a car, a jaguar*. By 'knowing' that *jaguar* is a Complement Object, the computer will be able to know that *jaguar*, in this context, is a *car* (a vehicle) and that Peter has not bought, for example, a Ford or another car make. It will be also clear, that *jaguar* is not a predator (an animal) – another example of word sense disambiguation due to parsing. This information is very valuable when constructing natural-language-understanding dialogue systems.

The complement, in a sentence, can be found using Case 10 and Case 12, as stated below.

```
case 10:         /* Complement Object */
 wnprintfl(Co);     // Print: COMPLEMENT  OBJECT
// Print: OBJEKTATTRIBUT
// Print: COMPLÉMENT d'OBJET
 for (j = i; j < nseg-1; j++){
 w1 = (WORD *) s[j].que[0];
// define the position of word w1
```

```
      if(w1) {
// if word w1 is considered
        while ( w1 ) {
          wnprintfw("%s ", w1->inword); // print input word w1
          w1 = w1->next;
        }
      }
      }
      break;
```

Continuation of the above instruction in the "segment.h" file:

```
  {"XQ<$>[*=,J]",        10},          /* Relative Clause as Co  */
```

For example, if we type in the sentence:

I saw a man who bought a newspaper.

and process it with the program containing case 10, the computer will 'know' that *who bought a newspaper* is a relative clause and complement object (Georgiev, 1993).

```
      case 12:          /** Complement: Subject or Object **/
      w2 = (WORD *) s[last].que[0];
// define the position of word w2
      if ( w2) {        // if the 2nd word is considered
      if (s[i].type == 'S')  // if the word is preceded by Subject
        wnprintfl(Cs);    // Print: COMPLEMENT  SUBJECT
// Print: SUBJEKTATTRIBUT
// Print: l'ATTRIBUT DU SUJET
      else // otherwise
        wnprintfl(Co);    // Print: COMPLEMENT  OBJECT
// Print: OBJEKTATTRIBUT
// Print: COMPLÉMENT d'OBJET
      while ( w2 ) {
        wnprintfw("%s ", w2->inword);  // print input word w2
        w2 = w2->next;
      }
      }
      i = last;
     break;
```

Continuation of the above instruction in the "segment.h" file:

```
{"N<,C>[AE]",  12},           /**Cs/Co */
// {"o<,C>[IAN]",  12},        /* additional for German or French */
// etc.
```

For example, if we parse the following French sentence with case 12:

Nous avions quitté le monde des conventions rassurantes.

the program will print that *le monde des conventions* is 'le Complément Direct' and that *rassurantes* is 'le Complément d'Objet'.

4.4 Recognition of the Verb

The verb, as the action in the sentence, is a very important part of the sentence, because with the verb we know what the subject has done, what the subject has done to the object (when there is one) and when the subject has done it, will do it or is doing it, with the knowledge of the verbal tense. The verb is very important also because it can stand alone in imperative sentences, while the object cannot. The subject can stand alone, but it doesn't make much sense. Compare:

Come in!

The subject is missing, but is implicitly understood, while

Ann.

The word is present (Subject or Object), but it is not understood why it is used. Below we will present two cases for recognition of the verb proper in a sentence.

```
     case 34:            /* Recognition of the Verb */
      wnprintfl(V); // Print: VERB (no recognition  needed)
// Print: VERBUM
// Print: LE VERBE
      w = (WORD *) s[i].que[0]; // define the position of 'word' w
      verbtype(w->tcase); // type of verb
      for (j = i; j <= last; j++){
       w1 = (WORD *) s[j].que[0];
// define the position of word w1
       if(w1) {       // if the first word w1 is analysed
        while ( w1 ) {
         wnprintfw("%s ", w1->inword);  // print input word w1
         w1 = w1->next;
        }
       }
      }
      s[last].type = 'z';
      if (s[last].syn == 'y')
      i = last-1;
      else
      i = last;
      break;
```

Continuation of the above instruction in the "segment.h" file:

```
   {"[UY]BV",        34},
/* Subjunctive, Auxiliary Verb followed by Infinitive */
   {"VBv",         34},         /* Main Verb followed by Infinitive */
   {"U<KkDw>[yYXV]",    34},
/* Subjunctive followed by Infinitive or an auxiliary verb */
```

The code <KkDw> means that a negation (Kk) or an Adverb (D), or an Adverbial Phrase (Dw) can intervene between the two Auxiliary Verbs (as defined), or between the Auxiliary Verb (U) and the Main Verb (V). The intervening parts of speech are language dependent. The structure itself is also language dependent; for example, in German, the auxiliary verb often follows the main verb and is usually positioned at the end of the sentence, without intervening parts of speech:

... *dass wir uns aus Europa <u>ausklicken können</u>.*

```
      case 35:          /* Verb - not included in a structure */
       if (s[i].type == 'z' || s[i-1].syn == 'y')
        break;  // exclude these possibilities
       w1 = (WORD *) s[i].que[0];   // define the position of word w1
// state, below, the condition in which this case is valid
       if (w1->syn == 'X' && !stricmp(w1->inword, "were") &&
       (s[i-1].syn == 'R' || s[i-1].syn == 'N')) {
/* if word w1 is an auxiliary verb from the 'be' (sein, être) paradigm and if this is 'were' (for
English, the corresponding word for another language) and if the
preceding word is PPNC or a noun */
        w = (WORD *) s[i-1].que[0];   // define the position of word w
        if (w && w1) {    // if both words follow one another
          while ( w ) {
           if (w->syn == s[i-1].syn)
            break;
           w = w->next;
          }
          if (w->numb == 0) // if word w is in singular
          wnprintfl("\nSUBJUNCTIVE: ");
// Print: Subjunctive
        else {    // otherwise (if not)
          wnprintfl(Vp);  // Print: Verb - ( and its Verbal Tense )
          verbtype(w1->tcase);
           }
          wnprintfw("%s ", w1->inword);
// print the word w1
         }
        }
    else
       if (w1) {
       wnprintfl(Vp);     // Print: Verb - ( and its Verbal Tense )
       verbtype(w1->tcase);
       while ( w1 ) {
        if (w1->syn == 'D' || w1->syn == 'K' || w1->syn == 'k') {
// ignore the intervening parts of speech in this word position
          w1 = w1->next;
          continue;
        }
        wnprintfw("%s ", w1->inword);
// print the input word w1
        w1 = w1->next;
       }
       }
       break;
```

Continuation of the above instruction in the "segment.h" file:

```
{"[yYXV]",    35},          /* not included in a structure */
```

Case 34 and 35 demonstrate only two possibilities. There is a case for each of the many possibilities to be a Verb in a context.

4.4.1 Recognition of the Verbal Tense

Having recognized the Verb, the next step will be to recognize its Tense, if we want to be more specific in our analysis. For this aim we need to do the following programming:

a) To name the existing Verbal Tenses in a *.c(pp) file, for example "tense.c" or "tense.cpp". For every language there will be its own tense.c(pp) file, because most of the verbal tenses are not identical. It is preferable to name the verbal tenses as they are called in their respective language. This file will begin with the following introduction (here we will use one file for the English, German and French tenses):

```
#include <ctype.h>
#include <stdio.h>
#include <conio.h>
#include <alloc.h>
#include <dir.h>
// etc. standard include files
#include "segment.h"
// include our own *.h file
SEGMENT *s;
extern struct QUE *tr_que[];
int rel_parse(struct QUE *que[], int type, int i, SEGMENT *s);
void wrque(struct QUE *que[]);
DLIM *enque_dlm(struct QUE *que[], char syn, char ssyn);
WORD *enque_word(struct QUE *que[], char syn, char *word);
extern const char *PIC;
char segstr[MAX_SEGS + 2];
// etc.
void verbtype(int vtype)    // Verbtype here means Verbal Tense
{
   switch(vtype)
   {          // start the enumeration of the cases:
/* Note: the verbal tenses are language specific. We will write the verbal tense for German and French, only when they coincide with the respective verbal tense in English. When they do not coincide, we will show the same case, for the respective language, closed for the compiler. We will do likewise when the tenses coincide, but the number of the case is different. */

   case 1:
    wnprintfl("Present Simple Tense: ");
        // wnprintfl("PRÄSENS: "); /* German */
    break;
//        case 1:
//         wnprintfl("Le Temps: ");    /* French */
// No specification of the Verbal Tense.
// Usually means: Present Tense.
//        break;

   case 2:
    wnprintfl("Past Simple Tense: ");
       // wnprintfl("Passé Simple): ");
    break;
//  case 2:
//   wnprintfl("PRÄTERITUM (IMPERFEKT): ");
//   break;
```

```
    case 3:
     wnprintfl("Future Simple Tense: ");
        // wnprintfl("FUTUR: ");
     break;
//  case 3: /* wir werden kaufen */
//   wnprintfl("FUTUR: ");
//   break;
//        case 3:
//         wnprintfl("Le Temps: ");
// the Verbal Tense is not specified or the Present Tense is meant
//         break;
    case 4:
     wnprintfl("Future in the Past Tense or Present Conditional: ");
     break;
//  case 4: /* er wurde gekauft */
//   wnprintfl("PRÄTERITUM (IMPERFEKT), Passiv: ");
//   break;
//        case 4:
//         wnprintfl("Conditionel, Passé 2e Forme \n");
//         wnprintfl("ou Plus-que-parfait \n");
//         wnprintfl("ou Imparfait: ");
// the Verbal Tense cannot be defined exactly, there are 3 possibilities
//         break;

// etc.
//  case 9:  /* German */
/* hat zu kaufen, gestopft werden sollen, werden kann */
//   wnprintfl("FUTUR: ");
//   break;
// etc.
//       case 11:  /* French */
//        wnprintfl("Imparfait: ");
//        break;
// etc.
//      case 13: /* French */
//       wnprintfl("Futur: ");
//       break;
//      case 14: /* French */
//       wnprintfl("Conditionnel Présent: ");
//       break;
// etc.
//     case 17: /* gesehen würde - German */
// wnprintfl("PASSIV: ");
// break;
// etc.
      case 61:
    wnprintfl("Present Perfect, Passive: ");
    break;
     case 62:
      wnprintfl("Past Perfect, Passive: ");
      break;
// etc. Verbal tenses for the respective language
    default :
     wnprintfl("........... ");
```

```
// If the Verbal Tense is not listed, print sequence of dots.
      break;
    }
}
```

This means, that when the program meets the specified Verbal Tense it prints its name, as shown above. Then the program prints the Verb or Verbs forming this Tense.

b) Specification and identification of the Verbal Tenses. This specification and identification can be done in one of the *.c(pp) files, for example "parser.c" or "parser.cpp". The "parser.*" files (*.c(pp) and *.h) are the most important files for the analysis of the text and its parsing. The "parser.c(pp)" file begins as follows:

```
#include <ctype.h>
#include <stdio.h>
#include <conio.h>
#include <alloc.h>
#include <dir.h>
// etc. standard include files
#include "dicgram.h"
#include "grammar.h"
#include "parser.h"
// etc. own include files
extern int wcount;
extern char synstr[MAXWORDS + 3];
int copysyn(struct QUE *que[], WORD *wp[]);
// etc.
WORD *wrd, *wrdm, *wrdp, *w;
// etc.
for (ptb = PART; ptb->inst; ptb++) {
   for ( i = 0; i < wcount - 1; i++ ) {
      if ( (mpos= piccmp(wp, i, ptb->inst)) ) {
        wrd = wp[i]; // define the position of the word 'wrd'
        wrdm = wp[mpos]; // define the position of the word 'wrdm'
        wrdp = wp[mpos-1]; // define the position of the word 'wrdp'
       switch (ptb->cond) {
      case 1 :          /* Start the cases */
```

(Note: the cases that follow are for English, German and French languages. The cases for the German and French languages are closed for the compiler to stress the fact that they belong to the respective German or French *.c(pp) and *.h files. All cases are language specific. For example, to identify the verbal tense in French we have needed to specify the French Auxiliary Verb or the verbal endings for the respective verbal tense. For English that was not needed.)

Then starts the enumeration of the cases, which specify the Verbal Tenses.

```
/***
      case 2 :          /* RE -> V , French */
       if (!stricmp(wrdm->inword, "avaient") ||
             !stricmp(wrdm->inword, "avait") ||
             !stricmp(wrdm->inword, "aviez") ||
// if these verbs match
// etc. Auxiliary Verbs in second position (wrdm)
          !stricmp(wrdm->inword, "suis")) {
          i = mpos; continue; // exclude the listed Auxiliary Verbs
        }
      if (isflex(wrdm->inword, wrdm->wl, "raient") ||
```

```
        isflex(wrdm->inword, wrdm->wl, "rait") ||
        isflex(wrdm->inword, wrdm->wl, "riez") ||
// if the verb has one of the above listed endings
// etc. verbal endings of the Verb in second position (wrdm)
        isflex(wrdm->inword, wrdm->wl, "vons")) {
        i = mpos; continue;
// exclude the Verbs with the listed verbal endings
      }
      if (wrdm->cflag == 'n') {
        i = mpos; continue; // exclude the Verbs bearing this code
      }
      if (isflex(wrdm->inword, wrdm->wl, "ais") ||
      isflex(wrdm->inword, wrdm->wl, "ait") ||
      isflex(wrdm->inword, wrdm->wl, "uat") ||
      isflex(wrdm->inword, wrdm->wl, "vaient") ||
      isflex(wrdm->inword, wrdm->wl, "viez") ||
      isflex(wrdm->inword, wrdm->wl, "vions") ||
      isflex(wrdm->inword, wrdm->wl, "saient") ||
      isflex(wrdm->inword, wrdm->wl, "siez") ||
      isflex(wrdm->inword, wrdm->wl, "sions") ||
      isflex(wrdm->inword, wrdm->wl, "sse") ||
      isflex(wrdm->inword, wrdm->wl, "sses") ||
// if the verb has one of the above listed endings
// etc. verbal endings
      isflex(wrdm->inword, wrdm->wl, "vais"))
// If the Verb has the above listed endings, its Tense is
      wrdm->tcase = 11;
//  Tense specified in case 11 in the French tense.c(pp) file
       else // otherwise
      wrdm->tcase = 2;
//  Tense specified in case 2 in the French tense.c(pp) file
      break;    // end the case   ***/
```

Continuation of the above French instruction in the "parser.h" file:

```
// {"[*RmN]<dD?#>[Ee]", "@$V", 2},       /* cases 2, 11, Past, French */
```

Case 2 for the French language will parse the following sentence:

La vaste gamme de services assurés par la Ville ...

and will print that *assurés* is Passé Simple (see case 2 in a) above

```
/***      case 9:        /* Passiv, German */
      if (wrd->person == 3){
/* If 1st Verb is Personal Form (3rd person) */
        i = mpos; continue;     /* Exit this case */
      }
      if (wrd->tense == T_PAST)
// If the first word is the Past (Participle) form
// of the Verb, The Verbal Tense is case 17
         wrd->tcase = 17;
//  Tense specified in case 17 in the German tense.c(pp) file
      break;     ***/
```

Continuation of the above German instruction in the "parser.h" file:

```
//  {"[Ee]<kDHITAONPw>x",        "V$v",  9},   /*  (case 17) German */
//  {"VX",                       "Vv",  9},    /*  (case 17) German */
//  {"[Ee]<kDHITAONPw>xX",        "V$vv", 9},  /*  (case 17) German */
//  {"[Ee]<kDHITAONPw>'worden'X",   "V$vv", 9},  /*  (case 17) German */
//  {"[Ee]<kDHITAONPw>X",        "V$v",  9},   /*  (case 17) German */
```

Case 9 for the German language will parse the following Verbal Tense in context:

... gelobt worden ist ...

and will print that *gelobt worden ist* is a Verb – Passive (wrd->tcase = 17), as specified in case 17 in a) above. Note that the part-of-speech codes enclosed in < > are language specific. Usually, in German, the auxiliary verb follows immediately after the past participle. However, often the past participle and the auxiliary verb are separated by intervening parts of speech: negation, adverb [kD], determiners [HI], entire nominal group [TAON] starting with the article and ending with a noun, entire prepositional adverbial clause [Pw].

```
        case 10:          /* do, does, did + V - English */
         if (wrd->inword[0] != 'd' && wrd->inword[0] != 'D'){
           i = mpos; continue;
/* Exclude all Auxiliary Verbs marked with X, except those that begin with "d" or "D". In the
DW we have marked 'do', 'does', 'did' with the code X. */
         }
         if (wrd->tense == 1)
// If the tense of the word is marked [<] for Past
           wrd->tcase = 2;
// Tense specified in case 2 in the English tense.c(pp) file
          else
           wrd->tcase = 1;
// Tense specified in case 1 in the English tense.c(pp) file
         break;                // end the case
```

Continuation of the above English instruction in the "parser.h" file:

```
   {"X<KdDRS\'\">'do'",   "V$v", 10},   /* do, does, did + do  - English */
   {"X<KdD\'\">[ZVueY]",   "V$v", 10},
/*  do, does, did + Main Verb or "have" paradigm - English */
   {"X<KdD\'\">'like'",  "V$v", 10},  /*  do, does, did + like - English */
```

Case 10 for the English language will parse the following sentences:

He does not like apples.
He did not like apples.

and will print that 'does not like' is Present Simple Tense (wrd->tcase = 1) and that 'did not like' is Past Simple Tense (wrd->tcase = 2).

```
/***      case 11:
/* PRÄTERITUM (IMPERFEKT), Passive or Future - German */
         if (wrdm->person == 3){
/* If the 2nd Verb is Personal Form (3rd person) */
           i = mpos; continue;       /* Exit this case */
         }
         if (wrd->tense == T_PAST)
// If the first word is the Past (Participle) form
```

```
// of the Verb, The Verbal Tense is case 4
          wrd->tcase = 4;
// Tense specified in case 4 in the German tense.c(pp) file
        else          // otherwise
          wrd->tcase = 3;
// The Verbal Tense is case 3 (Future Tense)
// Tense specified in case 3 in the German tense.c(pp) file
        break;  ***/
```

Continuation of the above German instruction in the "parser.h" file:

```
// {"x<CkD\'\"HITAONPw>'haben'", "V$v", 11}, /* German cases (3) (4) */
// {"x<CkD\'\"HITAONPw>X",   "X$v", 11},  /* German cases (3) (4) */
// {"x<CkD\'\"HITAONPw>V",   "X$v", 11},  /* German cases (3) (4) */
// {"x<TN>V",              "X$v", 11},  /* German cases (3) (4) */
// {"x<MN>V",              "X$v", 11},  /* German cases (3) (4) */
// {"V<kDHITAONPw>x",      "V$v", 11},  /* German cases (3) (4) */
```

Case 11 for the German language will parse the following Verbal Tense in context:

... es wurde gekauft ...

and will print that *es wurde gekauft* is Präteritum (Imperfekt), Passiv.

```
/***
      case 11:          /* Conditionel, Passé 2e Forme, etc. - French */
        if (wrdm->person == 3) {
/* If the 2nd Verb is Personal Form (3d person) */
          i = mpos; continue;     /* Exit this case */
        }
        if (wrd->tense == T_PAST)
// If the first word is the Past (Participle) form
          wrd->tcase = 4;
// of the Verb, The Verbal Tense is case 4
// Tense specified in case 4 in the French tense.c(pp) file
        else          // otherwise
          wrd->tcase = 3;
// Tense specified in case 3 in the French tense.c(pp) file,
// or rather, in this case, the Verbal Tense is not specified.
        break;  // end the case  ***/
```

Continuation of the above French instruction in the "parser.h" file:

```
// {"'fusse'<CKkdD\'\"RSTAONPw>[Ee]","V$v", 11}, /* (11) 2me - French*/
// {"'fussent'<CKkdD\'\"RSTAONPw>[Ee]", "V$v", 11}, /* (11) 2me - French*/
// {"'fusses'<CKkdD\'\"RSTAONPw>[Ee]", "V$v", 11}, /* (11) 2me - French */
// {"'fussiez'<CKkdD\'\"RSTAONPw>[Ee]", "V$v", 11}, /* (11) 2me - French */
// {"'fussions'<CKkdD\'\"RSTAONPw>[Ee]", "V$v", 11}, /* (11) 2me - French */
// {"'fût'<CKkdD\'\"RSTAONPw>[Ee]", "V$v", 11}, /* (11) 2me - French */
// {"'eusse'<CKkdD\'\"RSTAONPw>[Ee]", "V$v", 11}, /* etc. French */
// {"'eusses'<CKkdD\'\"RSTAONPw>[Ee]", "V$v", 11},
// {"'eût'<CKkdD\'\"RSTAONPw>[Ee]", "V$v", 11},
// {"'eussions'<CKkdD\'\"RSTAONPw>[Ee]", "V$v", 11},
// {"'eussiez'<CKkdD\'\"RSTAONPw>[Ee]", "V$v", 11},
```

```
// {"'eussent'<CKkdD\'\"RSTAONPw>[Ee]", "V$v", 11},
// {"'eusse'<CKkdD\'\"RSTAONPw>'été'", "V$v", 11},
// {"'eusses'<CKkdD\'\"RSTAONPw>'été'", "V$v", 11},
// {"'eût'<CKkdD\'\"RSTAONPw>'été'", "V$v", 11},
// {"'eussions'<CKkdD\'\"RSTAONPw>'été'", "V$v", 11},
// {"'eussiez'<CKkdD\'\"RSTAONPw>'été'", "V$v", 11},
// {"'eussent'<CKkdD\'\"RSTAONPw>'été'", "V$v", 11},

      case 21:          /* English */
       if (wrd->tense == T_PAST)
// If the first word is the Past (Participle) form of the Verb, The Verbal Tense
// is case 62 in the English file "tense.c(pp)"
         wrd->tcase = 62; // Past Perfect, Passive
       else // otherwise
// The Verbal Tense is case 61 in the English file "tense.c(pp)"
         wrd->tcase = 61; // Present Perfect, Passive
       break;          // end the case
```

Continuation of the above English instruction in the "parser.h" file:

```
{"Y<KdD?\'\"RSTAONPw>'been'[Eue]",  "V$vv", 21},
/* English, specified in cases (61) (62) in "tense.c(pp)" */
```

Case 21 for the English language will parse the following Verbal Tense in context:

The problem has been resolved successfully.

and will print that '*has been resolved*' is Present Perfect – Passive.

The codes within the square brackets [ ] show obligatory alternatives, the codes enclosed within the arrows < > show non-obligatory alternatives, which can be positioned between any two verbs (depending on the language), as, for example, between the English Auxiliary Verb from the "have" (Y) paradigm and "been". One of these alternatives can be a Prepositional Adverbial Clause (Pw).

The sign $ marks the presence of a non-obligatory alternative(s). The codes vv (in "V$vv") mark the English sequence "been" followed by the Past or Participle form of the Verb ('been'[Eue]) and show that "been" and the Past or Participle form of the Verb are an integral part of an inseparable Compound Verbal Tense "V$vv". The important thing here, which deserves attention, is the use of the lower-case letter "v" to mark the Verbs included in the Compound Verbal Tense, which starts with an upper-case V. This means that Vv or Vvv are one Verbal Tense, consisting of two (Vv) or three (Vvv) different Verbs, which are sometimes separated ($).

We have described, in a similar manner, 34 English, 12 German and 15 French Verbal Tenses (Simple and Compound) and have enabled their successful recognition by the respective software programs, developed from this description (Georgiev, 1993, 1996a, 1997). The examples above show only one of the many possible ways this can be done. Note: The reader can see how we have done it, in practice, by opening our software program Syntparse and working with it (an evaluation version can be found and downloaded from the Internet).

Accepting the well-established view of the hierarchical structure of the sentence (Noun Phrases and Verbal Phrases on different hierarchical levels, down to the constituent words of the sentence), we have used the traditional, interpositioning, parsing method, because the hierarchical method cannot provide the same information as the interpositioning method. The hierarchical method has only two Parts of the Sentence: Noun Phrases and Verbal Phrases. There is no information about the actual role of these Noun Phrases and Verbal Phrases in the Sentence, except their hierarchical position and division into smaller units on the lower level.

There is no information about the Verbal Tenses in the Sentence, either. By using the notion of the Segment (Georgiev, 2006: 44–52) and the interpositioning of the words within the Segment and the Clauses within the Sentence, we have differentiated about 20 different Parts of the Sentence and 34 English Verbal Tenses and enabled *Syntparse* (Georgiev, 1993) to recognize them correctly.

Note that while the Parts of the Sentence are identical for all languages, their sequence within the sentence is language specific. For example, in Turkish the subject will normally be followed by direct object, which in turn can be followed by indirect object and then will follow the verb. Therefore, our parsing instructions must be language specific.

5 Parsing errors

Word ambiguity (syntactical or semantical) often leads to parsing errors. The main cause for a parsing error is the incorrect recognition of the Part of Speech of a running word. For example, let's consider the following German sentence:

> *Das war uns immerhin über Caroline bekannt, dass sie zwar rechtlich eindeutig verheiratet war ...*

Initially, when testing the program, the word *bekannt* was recognized as an Adverb (d) and its role in the sentence was not displayed. The program has yielded the following sequence of Parts of Speech:

S X o D P N d

In the DW the word *bekannt* was registered as an Adjective. An existing rule in the software program has converted all Adjectives, positioned at the end of a Sentence or a Clause, into Adverbs (d). We need this rule in the program for analysis, which is also very important, and we cannot change this specification. The program could not recognize that, in this context, the word *bekannt* plays the role of a Complement. Therefore, we have re-named the Adverb (d) into Participle (E), using the following statement for this particular context:

```
{"X<oDPN>d",      "V$E", },      /* re-naming */
```
in the respective *.h file.

Then, the word *bekannt* was correctly recognized as a Complement, because it ends a Sentence (Clause) and follows an Auxiliary Verb (X). The sequence <oDPN> intervenes between the Auxiliary Verb (X) and its Complement (*bekannt*). Compare:

> *Das war bekannt.*

Where *bekannt* is a Complement Subject.

Eventually, we have closed the rule

```
// {"X<oDPN>d",      "V$E", },      /* re-naming */
```

because we were not sure what the consequences will be. We can leave it operational, only when we test it thoroughly and when we are absolutely sure that it will not produce errors. Another possibility will be to enable this rule only for the word *bekannt*:

```
{"X<oDPN>'bekannt'",     "V$E", },
```

or write a case to include all adjectives and adverbs that end with '-t'. This is only speculation; how it will be in the end depends on the tests. Only by testing this rule can we say for sure whether it produces errors or not.

Sometimes, the Part of Speech is recognized correctly, but the role of this Part of Speech in the Sentence is not. For example, let us consider the following German sentence:

In zunehmendem Masse sahen sie in Sylvie eine Ledige, ...
(*More and more they saw in Sylvie an unmarried ...*)

Here, the Personal Pronoun Nominal Case *sie* is recognized correctly as R. The program has wrongly determined it to be Object Direct. In fact, in this context *sie* is a Subject. We can change the rule and make the program recognize it as a Subject, but we must test the program to make absolutely sure that in all similar contexts *sie* is always a Subject.

There is no parsing error that cannot be corrected. That means that there is no limit to improving a natural language parsing program. The trouble is that when we improve the parsing results, we make new rules, and sometimes a new rule can generate more parsing errors than the old one. Therefore, we have to test extensively each new rule to make sure that the rule works well and has no side effects. When making a new rule to correct a wrong parsing, we should name the ambiguous word rather then use its code. For example:

```
{"'correct'*",      "d", },
```

The English word *correct* at the end of the sentence (*) is used as an Adverb 'd'.

```
{"'prevention'N",   "A",  },
```

The word *prevention* used before a Noun (N) is an Adjective. The rule

```
{"NN",   "A",  },
```

stipulating that every Noun, used before another Noun, is an Adjective (A) is wrong and can lead to parsing errors, such as the wrong recognition of a subject and its complement or of an object and its complement.

```
{"'like'R<Dd>X",    "JR$X",  },
```

The English word *like*, used before the sequence Personal Pronoun Nominal Case (R), possible Adverb <Dd>, followed by an Auxiliary Verb from the paradigm *be* (X), is a Conjunction (J). Any change in the above rules will lead to parsing errors.

The parsing errors and consequently the efficiency of a Natural Language Parsing software program should be judged, first of all, on the basis of the parsing method upon which the program was made. It should be examined whether the parsing software program produces the same results, as defined in the method. The parsing method enumerates all known (to this method) Parts of the Sentence and defines in which case to what Part of the Sentence a particular word belongs to. When the software program fails to determine correctly the Part of the Sentence of a particular word in accordance with the pre-defined specifications, then that is an error. When it is said that the sentences to be parsed should be grammatically correct, meaningful and unambiguous, this does not mean one should attribute any human failure in this respect to the parsing program. All grammatically incorrect, meaningless and ambiguous sentences, parsed incorrectly, should not be considered as a parsing error. In every language there are ambiguous sentences, in English most of all. As far as ambiguous sentences are concerned, it will be a plus, if the program can provide two (or more, if needed) possible parsings of the same ambiguous sentence. So, if you are a software critic, do not test all your ambiguous sentences, which you have collected for years, on this program. Test the program on randomly chosen texts, at least half a page long each, and quote the source. Let the parsing results dictate the amount of negative criticism and positive evaluation. Otherwise your review will be prejudiced. This applies also to the spell-checking and machine translation software programs.

There are many parsing theories. It is wrong to judge the parsing results from the point of view of another parsing theory. The only basis to compare the different parsing methods and the parsing results they achieve is to compare how detailed and accurate is the information they provide about the sentence and its constituent elements. Therefore, we agree, in principle, that a parsing program should identify: parts of speech, parts of the sentence, internal clauses, sentence type (using correct punctuation), and tense and voice in the main and subordinate clauses. If the program identifies also the meaning(s) of each word in the sentence, that will be a plus.

Part two

SPHERES OF APPLICATION

4 Orthographical Rules

No one can write absolutely correctly. Even if one writes absolutely correctly, there are text editors who will take over, without being asked to do so. Therefore, we need to read the text carefully again and again and even ask a friend to read it for us. To automate this proof-reading process, we need to create a spell-checking program, or use one that is already made. Any modern spell-checking software program needs, first of all, orthographical rules in order to be able to recognize a misspelt word and, perhaps, to suggest a correction. Below, we will discuss the orthographical rules one by one.

To begin with, we need to make files named, for example, "rules.c" or "rules.cpp" and "rules.h", which will contain our orthographical and grammatical rules. This *.c(pp) file will begin as follows:

```
#include <ctype.h>
#include <stdio.h>
#include <conio.h>
#include <alloc.h>
#include <dir.h>
// etc. standard include files
#include "dicgram.h"
#include "grammar.h"
#include "rules.h"
// etc. files, created by us
/* Note that the compiler always needs some standard include files and some created by us.
Those created by us, are also in a way 'standard', because we use them in many of our programs:
parsing, spelling, or machine translation, etc. */
extern char synstr[MAXWORDS + 3];
int copysyn(struct QUE *que[], WORD *wp[]);
int transout(WORD *wp[], int i, char *p);
int transpic(WORD *wp[], int i, int mpos, char *inst, char *p);
int syncmp(WORD *wp[], int i, char *inst);
int piccmp(WORD *wp[], int i, char *inst);
// etc.
WORD *wrd, *wrdm, *wrdp, *w, *w1;
// etc.

/* In this file it is necessary to define again the codes for the Parts of Speech and the information
they contain, in the same way as in the file "grammar.c(pp)" earlier in this book. */

   switch (wrd->syn) {
```

// start the enumeration of the cases:

```
case 'V' : // Define the Verb
```

/* etc., containing all parts of speech and the information about them, as described in the first chapter. */
// Then start the loop:

```
for ( ver = VERB_P; ver->inst; ver++)
{
 for ( i = 0, next_i = 1; next_i && i < wcount - 1; i++ )
 {
 if ( (mpos = piccmp(wp, i, ver->inst)) )
 {
   wrd  = wp[i];           /* 1st word in a sequence */
   wrdm = wp[mpos];        /* 2nd word in a sequence */
   switch (ver->cond)
   {
```

// then we will have to state the orthographical rules, arranged in cases:

```
     case 1:
```

// etc., case after case, as follow further below.

1 Recognition of a misspelt word

A misspelt word is any word that is not registered in the Dictionary of Wordforms and therefore not recognized by the software program as legitimate. That does not mean, however, that this particular word is a misspelt word. It can be a personal name (we cannot register all personal names used in all languages). It can be a newly coined word. It can be a technical term (we cannot register all technical terms either). Therefore, the one who writes the text must decide if this particular word is a misspelt word or not. The recognition of a misspelt word is programmed in C (C++) in the following case:

```
    case 24:          /* unknown or misspelt word */
   if (wrd->inword[1] != '\0' && wrd->inword[1] != '\"' &&
      (wrd->syn == '#' ||
      wrd->syn == '?' || wrd->esyn == '?' ||
      wrd->esyn == '#')) {
```

/* Enumerates the conditions and the signs used to mark the unrecognized words. */

```
      wnprintfw("\n Please check SPELLING: \"%s\"", wrd->inword);
```

/* The program prints the above message. In more recent spell-checkers, the program underlines the misspelt word in red. */
/* wnprintfw("\n BITTE überprüfe die Rechtschreibung: \"%s\"", wrd->inword); */
/* wnprintfw("\n S'il vous plaît VÉRIFIEZ la correction: \"%s\"", wrd->inword); */
// the program prints the misspelt word after this message

```
   }
   i++; continue;
```

Continuation of the above rule in the rules.h file:

```
{"[?#]",        NULL, 24}, /* unrecognized, misspelt, word */
```

The codes ? and # mark the unrecognized words in a text. When an unrecognized word is found, the program prints out: 'Please, check the spelling of ...' (and prints the unrecognized word). At the same time, the program can collect all unrecognized or misspelt words in a file named, for example, "unknown.txt" using the following specifications:

```
int file_unknown();
char outnew[81] = "UNKNOWN.TXT";
int file_unknown()
{
int error = 0;
char errmsg[80];
if ((len < 4 && !strpbrk(inword, "-/")) || (dot = strchr(inword, '.')))
  {
   *pre = wrd;
   if (save_unknown) {
    if (wrd->eprefix[0]) {
     strcpy(word1, wrd->eprefix);
     strcat(word1, inword);
     save_new(word1);
    }
    else
     save_new(inword);
   }
return wrd->next;
  }
// etc.
```

The user can read the file "unknown.txt" and decide which words are misspelt or spelt correctly, but unknown to the program. The file 'unknown.txt' will be very helpful, if we process a text in a batch mode. This means that we can open a file for spell-checking and let the program check it, while we do something else. Later, we can open the file 'unknown.txt' and see which words were unknown to the program or misspelt.

a) Recognition of a Name (geographical, proper) spelt with a lower-case letter. Since all Names must be spelt with a capital letter, a Name spelt with a small letter will be recognized as an error by the following case:

```
        case 65:                          /* Capital letter for the Name */
        if (!wrd->esyn)  // If the word is not recognized
         {
                   wnprintfw("\n Wrong Spelling of \"%s\" ",
                                            wrd->inword);
   // Print: Wrong Spelling of ... (word).
   // etc. messages in other language
                                            bad_words++;
   //  register the word for the statistics of misspelt words
            continue;
        }
        if (wrd->e.N.name && islower(wrd->inword[0]))
         {
   /* If the word is registered in DW as a Name and if this word is written with a low-case
   letter in the text */
         wnprintfw("\n Wrong Spelling of \"%s\" ",
         wrd->inword);  // Print: Wrong Spelling of ... (word).
          wnprintfl("\n Use the Capital Letter (Upper case) for names");
   //             wnprintfl("\n ÜBERPRÜFE die Grossschreibung von");
```

```
//              wnprintfl("\n VÉRIFIEZ la majuscule de:");
                   wrd->inword[0] = toupper(wrd->inword[0]);
                      wnprintfw(" : \"%s\" \n", wrd->inword);
       }
       continue;
```

Continuation of the above rule in the rules.h file:

```
{"N",       NULL, 65},   /** Capital letter for Names **/
```

Since all names are nouns, we can code in the DW all nouns that are names with the code [N] like this:

london=N[N]

Since, in German, not only names but all nouns are written with a capital letter, case 65 is slightly different:

```
      case 65:     /* Capital letter for the German Noun */
     if (wrd->esyn == 'N' && islower(wrd->inword[0]))  // If this is a Noun
     {          // and if it is written with a small letter
       wnprintfl("\n ÜBERPRÜFE die Grossschreibung von");
// Print the above message
       wnprintfw(": \"%s\" \n", wrd->inword);   // Print the misspelt Noun
     }
     i = mpos; continue;
```

Continuation of the above rule in the rules.h file:

```
{"[Nn]",       NULL, 65},   /* Capital letter in German */
```

Here, we have included the plural nouns also (coded, in the DW, with a small 'n'). Note: the spell-checking program assumes that any Noun can be written, by mistake, with a small letter and therefore the ambiguity Noun or Verb, or Noun or Adjective, is actual and must be dealt with accordingly before the spell-checking rule comes into effect. If we think that someone will write an Adjective or a Verb with a capital letter we can devise a similar rule to say that it is an error:

```
      case 63:     /* Small letter for the Adjective, Verb or Adverb, etc. */
     if (wrd->esyn == 'V' && isupper(wrd->inword[0]))  // If this is a Verb
     {          // and if it is written with a capital letter
                    wnprintfl("\n Use low-case letter for:");
//     wnprintfl("\n ÜBERPRÜFE: "); // Print the message
       wnprintfw(": \"%s\" \n", wrd->inword);   // Print the misspelt Verb
     }
     i = mpos; continue;
```

Continuation of the above rule in the rules.h file:

```
{"V",       NULL, 63},   /* small letter for the Verb */
```

b) Misspelt Compound Names. Sometimes a word is used as a Name in Compound Names and therefore it must be written with a capital letter. In this case we have registered the whole phrase in the Dictionary of Wordforms like this:

united states of america=WFFPF
etc. English phrases

abseits pfeifen=WNV
ach und weh=WNCN
acht geben=WNV
acht haben=WNY
allgemeine deutsche=WNN
allgemeiner deutscher=WNN
allgemeiner studentenausschuss=WNN
etc. German phrases
acier argent=WNN
moyen âge=WNN
soviet union=WNN
etc. French phrases

and specified, in the English version of the program, that F is a name and that it is an error when it is written with a small letter. Case 18 below detects this type of error.

```
    case 18:      /* capital letter */
   if (wrd->syn == 'F' && islower(wrd->inword[0]))
// if the word is coded with F and is written with a small letter
     {
     wnprintfl("\n This word is written with a capital letter:");
//   wnprintfl("\n ÜBERPRÜFE die Grossschreibung von");
     wnprintfw(": \"%s\" \n", wrd->inword);
// print the word
     bad_gross++;
// collect this error for the statistics
   }
   i = mpos; continue;
```

Continuation of the above rule in the respective *.h file:

```
{"F",          NULL, 18}, /* Capital Letter */
```

The sign W, in the DW, introduces the phrase, and the sign F or FF indicates the Name(s) in this phrase. The search-and-find rule of the program ignores

united=A
and picks up
united states=WFF
or
united states of america=WFFPF

etc., used as Name(s) in this context.

In the German version of the program the sign N or NN indicates the Noun(s) in this phrase. The German case is identical with case 18 above; the only difference is that we had to tell the program that F in the source code of the program is equal to N in the DW when N is in a phrase, as shown below. The search-and-find rule of the program ignores

allgemein=A
and picks up
allgemeine deutsche=WNN
or
allgemeiner deutscher=WNN
etc., used as Noun(s) in this context.

c) Double letter. Some words are written with a double letter. For example:

English	**German**	**French**
across=P	Allheilmittel=N[UC]	abattement=N[M]
actress=N		
admittance=N		

etc.

When the English or French word is written with one 's' or one 't' (*actres, admitance, abaitement*), or the German word is written with one 'l' or one 't' (*Alheilmittel, Allheilmitel, Alheilmitel*), the software program will recognize it as a misspelt word (case 24), but will not be able to suggest a correction. The software program will suggest a correction only if we register the misspelt version(s) of this word in the DW and specify its correct form in brackets:

actres=N[i](actres->actress)
admitance=N[i](admitance->admittance)
etc. for the English language
Alheilmitel=N[i](Alheilmitel; Allheilmittel)
Alheilmittel=N[i](Allheilmitel; Allheilmittel)
Allheilmitel=N[i](Allheilmittel; Allheilmittel)
Allheilmittel=N[UC]
etc. for the German language
abaitement=N[Mi](abaitement; abaittement)
abaittement =N[M]
etc. for the French language

where [i] means "irregular" (in this case "misspelt").

To make the program read and, eventually, display the information in the brackets we can use the following code:

```
    if (*cw == '(') {
// when a parenthesis is opened
    wirr = wrd->irrform;
/* the correct or the irregular form of the word */
    while (*cw && *cw != ')')  /* is within the brackets  */
     *wirr++ = *cw++;
    *wirr++ = *cw++;
    *wirr = '\0';
    }
```

Then we have to write the following case in 'rules.c(pp)':

```
     case 32:      /* irregular form */
    if (wrd->irrform[0] != '(') {
/* exclude those words which are not enclosed in brackets in the DW */
    i = mpos; continue;
    }
    if (wrd->syn == 'N' && wrd->numb &&
      wrd->e.N.singular_only) {  // If a singular-only Noun is used in plural
       wnprintfw("\"%s\"", wrd->inword);  // print the word
       wnprintfw("\n \"%s\" - Incorrect Form of:",  // print this message
       wrd->inword);  // print the word
       wnprintfw("\"%s\"",wrd->inbase);
```

```
        if (wrd->irrform[0] == '(')  // If this is irregular form, print the
          wnprintfw("\nCORRECT: %s", wrd->irrform);
// correct form
       bad_usage++;   // message for the statistics
    }
    else
    if (stricmp(wrd->inword, wrd->inbase) && wrd->gflag == 'i' &&
       wrd->person != 3) {
/* If the initial part of the word is identical and if this is irregular form */
       wnprintfl("\n");
      wnprintfw("\"%s\"", wrd->inword);
      wnprintfw(" - Incorrect Form of: \"%s\"", wrd->inbase);
// print the misspelt word
      wnprintfw("\nCORRECT: %s", wrd->irrform);
// print the correct form
    }
    i++; continue;
```

Continuation of the above rule in the rules.h file:

```
{"[NAVE]",       NULL, 32},              /* irregular forms */
```

The above case is used also to recognize the irregular form of a word when it is misspelt and can be used, with slight modifications, for all languages. For example, if we have registered in the DW:

addendum = N[Si](addendum->addenda)
hôpital=N[MSi](hôpital->hôpitaux)

pointing out that the word is singular and irregular [i] and, if we write in the text

addendums
hôpitals

the program (using the above case) will recognize this as an error and will suggest the correct forms:

addendum->addenda	(for English)
Allopath; Allopathen	(for German)
hôpital->hôpitaux	(for French)

The spell-checking program deals similarly with all irregular wordforms, for example:

alewife = N[Si](alewife->alewives)
alveolus = N[Si](alveolus->alveoli)
etc. English
alpinarium=N[USi](Alpinarium; Alpinarien)
korb=N[MSi](Korb; Körbe)
etc. German
jazzman=N[MSi](jazzman->jazzmen)
kouros=M[MSi](kouros->kouroi->couroi)
etc. French

There is yet another way to make the software program recognize the need of a double letter in German. For example, all German Feminine Nouns denoting a human being and ending in *-in* double the *-n-* in Plural. Compare:

Abonnentin - Abonnentinnen
Afghanin - Afghaninnen

In case someone writes the Plural Form of such a word with one *-n-*, we can use the following case to detect the error:

```
 case 75:      /* German Fem. pl. with double -nn- */
if (wrd->e.N.neuter == 1 ||wrd->e.N.masculin == 1 ||
  wrd->numb == 1 ||wrd->esyn == 'Z') {
i = mpos; continue;
}
// exclude the Neuter, the Masculine, the Plural and the ambiguous Nouns
}
if (isflex(wrd->inword, wrd->wl, "nnen")) {
i = mpos; continue;
// exclude the words that end in -nnen (they are correct)
}
if (stricmp(wrd->inword, wrd->inbase) &&
// if a word from the text matches the initial part of a word in the DW
   isflex(wrd->inword, wrd->wl, "erinen") &&
// and if the word from the text ends in -erinen
   !isflex(wrd->inword, wrd->wl, "nnen")) {
// and not in -nnen
  wnprintfw("\n UNGÜLTIGE Rechtschreibung: \"%s\" ",
  wrd->inword);
// print the above text and the misspelt word
  wnprintfw("\n \"%s\" soll enden mit '-nnen'",
  wrd->inbase);
// print the above text and the misspelt word
  bad_words++; // right this error for the statistics
}
i = mpos; continue;
```

Continuation of the above rule in the respective *.h file:

```
{"[N]",    NULL, 75},   /* German Fem. pl. -nnen */
```

d) More than two identical letters in a sequence. It is also possible to write three or more identical consecutive letters by mistake. For example:

ambasssador (English), *Amtsblättter* (German), *lancettte* (French).

In order to deal with this type of error we have used the following case:

```
 case 64:                /* trebled letter */
if (wrd->stat < 2)
// If the word has more than 2 identical consecutive letters
{
  wnprintfw("\n UNKNOWN word: \"%s\" ",
//     wnprintfw("\n UNGÜLTIGE Rechtschreibung: \"%s\" ",
//      wnprintfw("\n S'il vous plaît VÉRIFIEZ la correction: \"%s\" ",
  wrd->inword); // print the above message and the word
```

```
    }
    continue;
```

Continuation of the above rule in the rules.h file:

```
{"[vNA]",      NULL, 64},  /* English only */
// {"v",       NULL, 64},  /* German and French */
```

In cases where the letter has to be trebled, because the new, reformed German spelling requires it, we have registered the correct wordform in the DW:

allliebend=A
balllokal=N[U]
grammmol=N[U]
etc., to tell the program that this is a legitimate spelling.

e) The New German Spelling. We have specified the New German Spelling in the DW as follows:
gemse=N[FSLq]<Gemse; Gämse>

indicating that the word is a Noun (N), Feminine, Singular [FS] and that it now has a new spelling [Lq]. Then we have registered the old and the new spelling: <Gemse; Gämse>. In the appropriate file of the program we will also have to define the arrows between which to insert the New German Spelling, so that the program can recognize what this means:

```
    if (*cw == ,<') {    // if a backward arrow is opened,
    wirr = wrd->reform;  // containing the new spelling for the word,
    while (*cw && *cw != '>')   // before it is closed
      *wirr++ = *cw++;
    *wirr++ = *cw++;
    *wirr = '\0';
}
```

So, when we use the old spelling, the program will react and tell us that we should use the new spelling instead. To do this, the spell-checking software program uses the following case:

```
     case 67: /* Old and New spelling */
    if (wrd->irrform[0] == '(') {
      i = mpos; continue;
    }
// exclude the words in (   ), because they have nothing to do with the new
// spelling
    if (wrd->e.N.compound || wrd->e.V.newspell == 1 ||
       wrd->e.A.recht) {
// the codes 'newspell' and 'recht' are used for the new spelling
// if the above conditions are met (if the word has a new spelling)
       wnprintfl("\n");
       wnprintfw("\"%s\"", wrd->inword);
       wnprintfw(" - ALTE Schreibform: \"%s\"",
       wrd->inword);  // print the old spelling
       wnprintfw("\nDIE NEUE Schreibform ist: %s", wrd->reform);
// print the new spelling
       bad_neue++;  // write this in the statistics
```

```
    }
    else
    if (stricmp(wrd->inword, wrd->inbase) && wrd->gflag == 'q'
      && wrd->reform[0] == '<') {
// If the initial part of the word coincides and bears the new spelling code
      wnprintfw("\nDIE NEUE Schreibform ist: %s", wrd->reform);
// print the new spelling
      bad_neue++; // write this in the statistics
    }
    i = mpos; continue;
```

Continuation of the above rule in the rules.h file:

```
{"[NVvAED]",      NULL,  67},   /* New spelling */
```

In the square brackets [ ] we enumerate the Parts of Speech that are affected by the new spelling.

The reader can find out how effectively all the above mentioned orthographical rules work in Georgiev, 1993a and 1996–7.

5 Grammatical Rules

Any language needs words, and rules to arrange them, to form a correct sentence. These words and rules are language specific. There are other rules, also language specific, that are designed to detect the errors in the sentence and we will show how that is done in C(C++).

How does one define an error? So far as orthographical errors are concerned, there are spelling dictionaries. These dictionaries set the norm as to how the words should be spelt. However, when it comes to grammatical rules, we derive our knowledge from grammar books or from our teachers at school. Unfortunately, grammar books may not list all exceptions to a certain rule if they are written for a specific level of learning. Both spelling dictionaries and grammar books only list and describe what is considered to be correct, but do not tell us what is an error. And this is right. No one can predict and list all the possible errors people can make. After all, grammatical errors are also language dependent, they depend on the difference between our mother tongue and foreign languages, as any experienced language teacher knows. So, an alternative way to obtain information for our error checking rules is to list typical errors made by students.

The syntactical rules were evidenced in the construction and parsing of the sentence. In this chapter we will discuss individually the error-detecting grammatical rules that check the right word sequence, the agreement in Number, Person, Case and Gender and show how these rules are programed in C(C++). Since the error-detecting grammatical rules are language specific, we will describe them separately for the English and German languages. We will give some examples from French and Italian grammar as well to show that this programming method can be applied to other languages with slight modification, depending on the grammatical endings for number and gender. Though the rules are language specific, the programming method is applicable to all languages that have the same grammatical features. To do this we need to continue the "rules.c(pp)" and "rules.h" files. (Note: we will discuss error detecting rules only.)

1 Transfer of grammatical information

In many languages certain parts of speech do not have a grammatical feature (gender, number, case, etc.) and have to take the grammatical feature of another part of speech in order to agree with it. For example, in many languages (German, Russian, Bulgarian, etc.) the adjective does not have its own gender. The adjective takes the gender of the noun, when it precedes it, and assumes the respective endings for gender.

The following case (12) in a *.c(pp) file shows how the noun transfers its gender to the preceding adjective. When the adjective follows the noun, as in French, case 12 can be adapted to suit this situation.

```
          case 12:
/* transfer of gender from noun to a preceding adjective */
                    if (wrdm->syn == N_SYN &&
                wrdm->E.W.mgender == 1)
// if the 2nd word is a noun masculine gender
                    wrd->E.W.mgender = 1;
// the adjective, the 1st word, is also masculine gender
          else
                    if (wrdm->syn == N_SYN &&
                wrdm->E.W.fgender == 1)
// if the 2nd word is a noun feminine gender
                    wrd->E.W.fgender = 1;
// the adjective, the 1st word, is also feminine gender
          else
                    if (wrdm->syn == N_SYN &&
                wrdm->E.W.ngender == 1)
// if the 2nd word is a noun neuter gender
                    wrd->E.W.ngender = 1;
// the adjective, the 1st word, is also neuter gender
          else
                    if (wrdm->syn == N_SYN &&
                wrdm->E.W.qgender == 1)
// etc. as above, depending on gender
// 'qgender' is a German sub-gender, because of its ending
                    wrd->E.W.qgender = 1;
          else
                    if (wrdm->syn == N_SYN &&
                wrdm->E.W.ogender == 1)
// 'ogender' is another sub-gender, because of its ending
                    wrd->E.W.ogender = 1;
          else
                    if (wrdm->syn == N_SYN &&
               wrdm->E.W.hgender == 1)
                    wrd->E.W.hgender = 1;
// 'hgender' is a German sub-gender, because of its ending
          else
                    if (wrdm->syn == N_SYN &&
               wrdm->E.W.ygender == 1)
                    wrd->E.W.ygender = 1;
// 'ygender' is yet another sub-gender, because of its ending
             CopySyn();
                    i = mpos; continue;
```

Continuation of the above rule in the respective *.h file:

```
{"A<Dd>N", NULL, 12},
```

This rule is language independent and it can be applied successfully to assign the same gender or any other grammatical feature to the part of speech that needs it in a specified context. When the grammatical feature is assigned using Case 12, there are other cases that check whether this feature is used correctly in writing.

Below, we will discuss the error-detecting rules in each case for four languages: English, German, French and Italian. For all other languages, the reader can make the necessary parallels and adapt the rules to suit the language.

2 English grammatical rules

2.1 Impossible combination of two words

The impossible combination of two words is one of the grammatical rules that govern the word sequence. Case 10, case 13 and case 53 below show how this rule works.

```
     case 10:
/* impossible combination of  PPNC and the Auxiliary Verb am */
      if (!stricmp(wrd->inword, "i")) {
      i = mpos; continue;
      }
/* exclude the PPNC 1st person singular (I), because this combination is correct */
       wnprintfl("\n");
       wnprintfw(" CHECK if the Verb \"%s\"", wrdm->inword);
// print the above message and the 2nd word
       wnprintfw(" can be used after \"%s\"", wrd->inword);
// print the above message and the 1st word
       bad_usage++; // register this error for the statistics
          i = mpos; continue;
```

Continuation of the above rule in the rules.h file:

```
{"R<KkDd>'am'",            NULL, 10},  /* wrong word sequence  */
```

A Particle for Negation or an Adverb <KkDd> can stand between the two words under consideration.

Case 10 is an example with limited coverage: only when the PPNC (with the exception of I) is followed by the Auxiliary Verb *am*. For example *He am here* will be wrong. There are other impossible combinations between PPNC and an Auxiliary Verb, such as *you is*, *she are*, etc. In order to cover all these other combinations, we have to devise similar cases, or unify them in one case, which will monitor any disagreement in Number and Person between two words.

```
   case 13:               /* impossible combination of Auxiliary Verbs */
// without any exceptions
       wnprintfl("\n");
       wnprintfw(" CHECK if the Verb \"%s\"", wrdm->inword);
// print the above message and the 2nd word
       wnprintfw(" can be used after \"%s\"", wrd->inword);
// print the above message and the 1st word
       bad_usage++; // register this error for the statistics
       i = mpos; continue;
```

Continuation of the above rule in the rules.h file:

```
   {"'did'<KkDd>[XUx]",       NULL, 13},  /* impossible combination */
   {"[xY]<KkDd>[UX]",       NULL, 13},
   {"U<KkDd>x",         NULL, 13},
   {"X<KkDd>[vx]",   NULL, 13},
```

A Particle for Negation or an Adverb <KkDd> can stand between the two Auxiliary Verbs under consideration. Case 13 covers many possible errors: all impossible combinations between the Auxiliary Verb *did* and the Auxiliary Verbs from the paradigms of *be*, *can* and *will*, between the Auxiliary Verbs from the paradigms of *will*, *have* and the paradigms of *can*, *be*, between the Auxiliary Verbs from the paradigm of *can* and the paradigm of *will*, between the Auxiliary Verbs from the paradigm of *be* and the paradigm of *will* (including the impossible combination between the Auxiliary Verbs from the paradigm of *be* and 3rd person singular, Present Tense of the Verb (v)). We can add other impossible combinations to the above case, for example:

```
{"U<KkDd>'has'",     NULL, 13},
```

the impossible combination between the Auxiliary Verbs from the paradigm of *can* and the Auxiliary Verb *has*.

When we cannot deal with groups of words, because we cannot make a group, we have to deal with individual words instead. Case 53 below shows how to deal with the impossible combination of two individual words:

```
      case 53:
/* impossible combination between two individual words */
       wnprintfw("\n Wrong VERB: %s", wrd->inword);
// print the above message and the 1st word
       wnprintfw("\n or Wrong VERB: %s", wp[mpos-1]->inword);
// print the above message and the 2nd word
       bad_agree++;   // register this error for the statistics
       i = mpos; continue;
```

Continuation of the above rule in the rules.h file:

```
  {"'may'<KkDd>'has'~[&C]",  NULL, 53},
  {"'could'<KkDd>'has'~[&C]",  NULL, 53},
  {"'must'<KkDd>'has'~[&C]",  NULL, 53},
  {"'did'<KkDd>'has'~[&C]",  NULL, 53},
  {"'does'<KkDd>'has'~[&C]",  NULL, 53},
etc.
```

Case 53 will detect the error in the sentence

He does has a horse

and will print out the above warning messages. The same rule can be applied to any combination of two words, one has only to alter the error message(s) and the list of parts of speech that can intervene between these two words.

2.2 *Wrong use of -ly when making an Adverb from an Adjective*

Most English Adjectives can be turned into Adverbs by adding *-ly* at the end of the word. There are, however, exceptions. Case 14 detects these exceptions and prints out a warning error message:

```
      case 14:          /* Adj. ending in -ly - errors */
       if ((wrd->esyn == '?' || wrd->mood == 1) &&
          wrd->cflag == 'd') {
/* if the above conditions are met, in other words, if the word is unknown or the
Adjective is marked as an exception (wrd->mood == 1) and if we have used it
as an Adverb by adding -ly to it (wrd->cflag == 'd') */
```

```
        wnprintfw("\n Wrong Use of \"-ly\" or Wrong Spelling \"%s\" : ",
        wrd->inword);
// print the above message and the word
        wnprintfl(wrd->inbase);
        bad_words++; // register this error for the statistics
        }
    else
        if (wrd->esyn == 'E' && wrd->cflag == 'd' && wrd->mood) {
/* if the above conditions are met, in other words, if the word is Past Participle (many Past
Participles are also Adjectives) and if we have used it as an Adverb by adding -ly to it (wrd-
>cflag) and the Adjective is marked as an exception (wrd->mood) */
        wnprintfw("\n Wrong Use of \"-ly\" \"%s\" : ",
        wrd->inword);
// print the above message and the word
        wnprintfl(wrd->inbase);
        bad_words++; // register this error for the statistics
        }
    else
// finally if
        if (wrd->cflag == 'd' && wrd->mood) {
/* if we have used it as an Adverb by adding -ly to it (wrd->cflag == 'd') and
if the Adjective is marked as an exception (wrd->mood == 1) */
        wnprintfw("\n Wrong Use of \"-ly\" \"%s\" : ",
        wrd->inword);
// print the above message and the word
        wnprintfl(wrd->inbase);
        bad_words++; // register this error for the statistics
        }
        i++; continue;
```

Continuation of the above rule in the rules.h file:

```
{"D",          NULL, 14},        /* wrong use of -ly to form an Adverb */
```

In case 14 above D denotes an Adverb. We cannot use case 14 unless we mark all exceptions in the DW. For example, the marking can be done in the following way:

fathomable=A[M-]
fax=Z/N/A[M-]

etc., where [M-] marks the impossibility (cflag, mood) of adding -ly to this word. Following the specifications of this rule, it will be wrong to write *fathomably, faxly*. If, by any chance, we do, the program will react and consider this as an error.

2.3 *Wrong Use of a Degree*

In English Adjectives have a Degree: Comparative (*higher, warmer*, etc.) and Superlative (*highest, warmest*, etc.). A large number of Adjectives form their Comparative and Superlative Degree Form in an "irregular" way, as an exception to a general rule.

2.3.1 *Double Use of a Degree*

The Degree is usually formed by joining together such Adverbial quantifiers as *more, less,* etc. with an Adjective to form a Comparative Degree (*more beautiful*), or *most, least,* etc. with an Adjective to form a Superlative Degree (*least possible*). It will be wrong to double the Degree, for example to write *more higher* or *most highest* (*most higher*). In order to deal with this type of error, we have developed case 15:

```
case 15:        /* double use of Degree */
 if (wrdm->e.A.e_form || wrdm->cflag == 'a') {
/* if the 2nd word is registered in the DW with its Degree Form (wrdm->e.A.e_form) or a Degree Form is added to an Adjective (wrdm->cflag == 'a') */
 wnprintfw("\n Double Use of Degree: \"%s ", wrd->inword);
// print the above message and the 1st word
 wnprintfw(" %s\"", wrdm->inword);
// print the 2nd word
 bad_agree++; // register this error for the statistics
 }
 i = mpos; continue;
```

Continuation of the above rule in the rules.h file:

```
{"'more'A",      NULL, 15},
{"'most'A",      NULL, 15},
```

In the DW the adjective that already has a degree and the adjective that is without its degree will be registered as follows:

higher=A[e]
strong=A[a]

where [e] is 'e.A.e_form' and [a] says that this adjective can have a degree form. This rule enables the software program to print an error message when we write *more higher* or *most strongest.*

2.3.2 *Impossible Degree Form*

Some Adjectives can have a post-positioned Degree Form as a grammatical ending, as in *strong – stronger, strongest, cool – cooler, coolest*, etc. A large number of English Adjectives cannot have a Degree form attached at the end of the word (*difficult, impossible, beautiful*, etc.) and therefore it will be wrong to add to them *-er* to form the Comparative Degree, or *-est* to form the Superlative Degree. Case 33 below detects this type of error and deals with it.

```
case 33:        /* wrong use of Degree */
 if (wrd->e.A.all) {
 i = mpos; continue;
 }
// exclude the words that can have a Degree Form as word ending
 if (wrd->cflag == 'a' && wrd->tense && wrd->e.A.more_most) {
/* if a Degree Form is added to an Adjective (wrdm->cflag == 'a') and the Adjective ends in -er or -est (wrd->tense) and the Adjective is marked as one that cannot have a Degree as word ending (wrd->e.A.more_most) */
 if (wrd->tense == 1) {
```

```
// then, if the Adjective ends in -er (wrd->tense == 1)
        wnprintfw("\n \"%s\" Cannot Add '-er'",
        wrd->inbase);
// print the above message and the Adjective
        bad_words++; // register this error for the statistics
      }
      else
      if (wrd->tense == 2) {
// otherwise, if the Adjective ends in -est (wrd->tense == 2)
        wnprintfw("\n \"%s\" Cannot Add '-est'",
        wrd->inbase);
// print the above message and the word
        bad_words++; // register this error for the statistics
      }
      }
      i++; continue;
```

Continuation of the above rule in the rules.h file:

```
{"[Ad]",        NULL, 33},                /* wrong use of Degree */
```

Note that in the first chapter, when we defined case A, we said that if the Adjective can have a degree form (cflag) and ends in *-er*, its 'tense' is 1, when it ends in *-st* its 'tense' is 2. Here is a short reminder of how we defined the Adjective:

```
case 'A' :
 l = strlen(mor->mflex);
 wrd->cflag = 'a'; // can have a degree form
 if (mor->mflex[l - 2] == 'e' && mor->mflex[l - 1] == 'r')
 wrd->tense = 1;
else
 if (mor->mflex[l - 2] == 's' && mor->mflex[l - 1] == 't')
 wrd->tense = 2;
```

Case 33 will work only if the adjectives are differentiated and registered in the DW as follows:

a) An Adjective that can have *-er*, *-est* Degree Forms as a word ending is coded like this:

apt = A[a]

where [a] in the DW is equal to 'wrd->e.A.all' in the source code of the program.

b) An Adjective that cannot have *-er*, *-est* Degree Forms as a word ending is coded like this:

aquirable = A[M]

where [M] in the DW is equal to (wrd->e.A.more_most) in the source code of the program. In other words, this adjective can be used with *more, most*, but we cannot add *-er, -est* to it.

2.4 *Wrong use of the Article*

The Article (Definite or Indefinite) cannot be used before certain words. Case 19 below detects such contexts and alerts the user.

```
case 19:         /* Wrong use of the Article */
 if (!stricmp(wrdm->inword, "she") ||
  !stricmp(wrdm->inword, "he")) {
 i = mpos; continue;
 }
// exclude she and he as 2nd word
 if (!stricmp(wrdm->inword, "one") ||
  !stricmp(wrdm->inword, "other")) {
 i = mpos; continue;
 }
// exclude the above mentioned words, used after the Article
 wnprintfl("\n Strange grammar!: ");
 wnprintfw("%s ", wrd->inword);
// print the above message and the 1st word
 wnprintfw("%s ", wrdm->inword);
// print the 2nd word
 wnprintfl("\n ARTICLE cannot be used in this case ! ");
// print the above message
 bad_usage++;  // register this error for the statistics
 i = mpos;  continue;
```

Continuation of the above rule in the rules.h file:

```
{"T[TRSMOom,;:()*]",   NULL, 19}, /* Wrong use of the Article */
```

(Note: T denotes the Article, the codes listed in square brackets denote the Parts of Speech that cannot be preceded by an Article (the exceptions are excluded in the very beginning of the rule).) Case 19 will detect such errors as: ... *the this* ..., ... *a those* ..., ... *the me* ..., etc.

2.4.1 *Wrong use of an Indefinite Article with a Plural Noun*

The Indefinite Article (*a, an*) cannot be used with a Plural Noun. Case 25 below detects this type of usage and prints out a warning message.

```
case 25:
 if ((!stricmp(wrd->inword, "a") ||
  !stricmp(wrd->inword, "an")) && wrdm->numb) {
/* if the first word is a or an and the 2nd word (the Noun) is in Plural */
 wnprintfw("\n The ARTICLE doesn't match the noun in number: %s ",
 wrd->inword);
// print the above message and the first word
 wnprintfw("<==> %s", wrdm->inword);
// print <==> and the 2nd word
 bad_agree++;  // register this error for the statistics
 }
 i = mpos; continue;
```

Continuation of the above rule in the rules.h file:

```
{"T<AO>N",      NULL, 25},
```

Note that the Article and the Noun can often be separated by an Adjective or a Possessive Pronoun <AO>. Note also that T denotes both Definite and Indefinite Article. We have excluded the Definite Article by specifying the Indefinite Article as a condition for this rule:

```
(!stricmp(wrd->inword, "a") || !stricmp(wrd->inword, "an").
```

According to case 25, the phrase *an apples* will be wrong.

2.4.2 *Improper matching of the Indefinite Article with the first letter (Consonant or Vowel) of the next word*

In English, the Indefinite Article *a* is used only with words (Adjectives, Adverbs, Nouns) that start with a Consonant (*a house, a big house*, etc.). The Indefinite Article *an* is used only with words (Adjectives, Adverbs, Nouns) that start with a Vowel (*an apple, an American friend*, etc.). When this rule is not observed, case 27 below will find the error.

```
const char *glas = "aeiouAEIOU";
/* lists the Vowels (low case, upper case), declared at the beginning of the *.c(pp) file */
void parse2(struct QUE *que[])
{
// etc. , then start the cases.
      case 27: /* Improper matching of the article */
       if (wrdm->inword[0] == 'h') {
       i = mpos; continue;
       }
// exclude all 2nd words that start with the letter h
       if (!stricmp(wrdm->inword, "useful")) {
       i = mpos; continue;
       }
// exclude useful if used as 2nd word
       if (!stricmp(wrd->inword, "a") &&
       strchr(glas, wrdm->inword[0])){
// If the 1st word is the Indefinite Article a
// and the 1st letter of the 2nd word is a Vowel
       wnprintfw("\n USE article 'an' instead of 'a': \"%s",
       wrd->inword);
// print the above message and the first word
       wnprintfw(" %s\"", wrdm->inword);
// print the 2nd word
       }
      else
       if (!stricmp(wrd->inword, "an") &&
       !strchr(glas, wrdm->inword[0])){
// If the 1st word is the Indefinite Article an
// and the 1st letter of the 2nd word is not a Vowel
       wnprintfw("\n USE article 'a' instead of 'an': \"%s",
       wrd->inword);
// print the above message and the first word
       wnprintfw(" %s\"", wrdm->inword);
// print the 2nd word
       bad_words++; // register this error for the statistics
       }
       i = mpos; continue;
```

Continuation of the above rule in the rules.h file:

```
{"T[AODdN#?]",     NULL, 27}, /* wrong use of the article */
```

Case 27 will detect such errors as *a apple, an friend* and will display an error message.

2.5 Disagreement in Number or Person

Certain pairs of words must agree in Number. For example, we write: *many people, two women, several big boxes, one man*, etc. It is wrong to write: *three man, two big house*, etc. Case 26 below detects such errors.

```
    case 26:          /* Disagreement in Number/Person */
      if (wp[mpos+1]->syn == 'N') wrdm = wp[mpos+1];
// define the position of the word
      if (!stricmp(wrdm->inword, "percent")) {
       i = mpos; continue;
      }
      if (!stricmp(wrdm->inword, "may")) {
       i = mpos; continue;
      }
// exclude the above listed words, used as 2nd word
      if (wrdm->e.N.constant) {
       i = mpos; continue;
      }
// exclude the Nouns that can be used both in Singular and in Plural
      if (wrdm->e.N.plural_only) {
       i = mpos; continue;
      } // exclude the Nouns that are in Plural
      if (!wrdm->numb) {
// if the 2nd word (the Noun) is not in Plural
       wnprintfw("\n Wrong NUMBER/PERSON: %s", wrdm->inword);
// print the above message and the 2nd word
       bad_usage++;  // register this error for the statistics
      }
      i = mpos; continue;
```

Continuation of the above rule in the rules.h file:

```
  {"I<wPAOD?#\"H{}>N", NULL, 26},
```

The code I is used to mark all words and phrases expressing countable quantity. To make the rule more precise we can add the code H (all numbers) to it:

```
  {"[IH]<wPAOD?#\"H{}>N", NULL, 26},
```

These words and phrases are registered in the DW in the following way:

few=I
a few=WIw
many=I
etc.

There is an agreement in Number also between a Noun and the following Main or Auxiliary Verb. For example: *the people are ..., the car is ..., apples ripe*, etc. Case 23 below verifies the agreement between a plural Noun and an Auxiliary Verb from the *be* paradigm that follows it.

```
case 23:            /* NX */
    if (wp[mpos+1]->syn == 'N') wrdm = wp[mpos+1];
// specify the position of the word
    if (wrd->e.N.constant) {
    i = mpos; continue;
    }
// exclude the Nouns that can be both in Singular and in Plural
    if (wrd->e.N.time) {
    i = mpos; continue;
    } // exclude the Nouns denoting time
    if (wrd->e.N.plural_only && !wrdm->numb) {
// if the 1st word is used in Plural and the 2nd word is not in Plural
    wnprintfw("\n Wrong NUMBER/PERSON: %s", wrdm->inword);
// print the above message and the 2nd word
    bad_usage++; // register this error for the statistics
    }
    i = mpos; continue;
```

Continuation of the above rule in the rules.h file:

```
{"N<DdKk(?#)\">X",   NULL, 23},
```

where X denotes the paradigm of the Auxiliary Verb *be*.
According to case 23 such phrases as *the people is ..., the car are ...*, etc. will be wrong. We can also write a similar case to cover such errors as *the people has ..., the girl have ...*, etc. However, we should exclude such correct contexts as *both the mother and the girl have.*

2.6 *Wrong use of the Particle to before a Modal Verb*

One can say in English *to have, to be,* but one cannot say *to can, to must, to ought, to is, to was,* etc. Case 28 below deals efficiently with this type of error.

```
case 28: /* Infinitival Particle before a Modal Verb */
    wnprintfl("\nWrong USAGE of \"to\" before Modal Verb");
// print the above message
    bad_usage++; // register this error for the statistics
    i = mpos; continue;
```

Continuation of the above rule in the rules.h file:

```
{"BU",       NULL, 28},
```

We can use the same case for the *be* paradigm

```
{"BX",       NULL, 28},
```

but, then, we have to exclude *be* from this rule at the beginning of case 28:

```
    if (!stricmp(wrdm->inword, "be")) {
    i = mpos; continue;
    }
```

The link between the Particle *to* and the Modal Verb must be direct, no other word is allowed to intervene.

One cannot say *to has* either. Note also, that the Infinitival Particle *to* cannot be used after a Modal Verb, with the exception of *ought*, *is*, *was*, *were*, *have* (*ought (is, was, were, have) to*). One cannot write ... *can to* ..., ... *must to* .... The Particle *to* cannot be used after some other Auxiliary Verbs, for example: *shall to*, *will to*, etc. To cover these types of errors we will have to design similar rules. However, we must be careful because *to* can be a preposition and start a prepositional adverbial clause:

He will to the best of my knowledge go to this meeting.

Therefore, the proper use of punctuation marks is always recommended:

He will, to the best of my knowledge, go to this meeting.

2.7 *Incorrect Verbal Form*

The correct Verbal Form can be either 3rd Person Singular, Present Tense of the Verb or the Basic form of the Verb, or the Past Participle Form of the Verb. All depends on the context. When one does not use the correct Verbal Form, the software program pin-points the error.

2.7.1 *Incorrect use of the Basic Form of the Verb instead of 3rd Person Singular, Present Tense*

One can write *Peter comes today*, *She goes anyway*, etc., but one cannot write *Peter come today*, *She go anyway*, etc., unless one uses a comma after *Peter* and an exclamation mark after *today*. The name *Peter* is a Noun and we normally will regard him as *he* (*He comes today*). This will be third person singular of the Noun or of the Personal Pronoun Nominal Case (PPNC). The Noun or the PPNC must agree in Number and Person with the Verb following it. If not, case 130 will deal with the error.

```
    case 130:        /* [RS]V  agreement */
     if (type == '?') break;
/* exit if the sentence is interrogative */
     wrd = (WORD *) s[i].que[0];
     wrdm = (WORD *) s[last].que[0];
// define the position of the word
// down below follow many exclusions
     if (wrd->numb == 0 && wrdm->tcase == 8)
     break;
/* exit if the 1st word is in singular and if the 2nd word is marked as
special (wrdm->tcase == 8) */
     if (wrdm->esyn == 'E' || wrdm->esyn == 'e' || wrdm->esyn == 'h' ||
     wrdm->esyn == 'x' || wrdm->esyn == 'U' || wrdm->tense == T_FUTURE)
     break;
// exclude past, future and some auxiliary verbs as 2nd word
     if (wrdm->tense == T_PAST && wrd->numb == wrdm->numb)
     break;
// when the 1st word is in plural and the 2nd is a past form, exclude them
          if (!stricmp(wrdm->inword, "did") || !stricmp(wrdm->inword,
"had"))
     break;
// exclude 'did' and 'had' as 2nd words
     if (wrd->person == 1 && (wrdm->person == 0 || wrdm->person == 1))
```

```
        break;
// etc. exclusions below
        if (wrd->numb && wrdm->person == 0)
        break;
        if (!wrd->numb && !wrdm->numb && wrd->person ==
          wrdm->person)
        break;          /*Exclude: I am, he is/was/has/V-es */
        if (wrd && wrdm) {      /* if both words */
        if (wrdm->esyn == 'X' || wrdm->esyn == 'V') {
          if (wrd->numb && wrdm->numb)    /* we are (were) */
          break; // exclude the words when they are in plural
        }
        if (wrdm->esyn == 'Y') {
// when the 2nd word is from the 'have' paradigm
          if (wrd->person == 1 && !wrd->numb && !wrdm->person)
          break;  /* Exclude: I have */
          if (wrd->person == 3 && !wrd->numb && wrdm->person)
          break;                              /* Exclude: he has */
          if (wrd->numb && !wrdm->person)
          break;  /* Exclude: we have */
        }
// after making all necessary exclusions, shown above proceed further
        if (wrd->numb == 0) { // if 1st word is in singular
          if (wrd->person == 1 && wrdm->person == 3) {
// if the 1st word is 1st person and the 2nd word is 3rd person
  wnprintfw("\n Use Basic or PAST Form of the VERB: %s",
  wrdm->inword);
// print the above message and the 2nd word
          bad_agree++; // register this error for the statistics
          break;
          }
          if (wrdm->esyn == 'X' && !wrdm->tense &&
          wrdm->inword[0] != 'd' && wrdm->inword[0] != 'D' &&
          wrd->person != wrdm->person) {
/* if the 2nd word does not start with the letter D(d)
and if the two words do not agree in Person */
          wnprintfw("\n \"%s\" - Incorrect Personal Form",
          wrdm->inword);
// print the above message and the 2nd word
          wnprintfl(" of Auxil. Verb \"be\" (am, is)");
// print the above message
          bad_agree++; // register this error for the statistics
          }
          else
          {
                wnprintfw("\n Wrong VERB form of: %s",
                wrdm->inword);
// print the above message and the 2nd word
        wnprintfl("\nUse \"-s\" or PAST Form of the VERB");
// print the above message
          bad_agree++; // register this error for the statistics
          }
          }
        else
```

```
            {
             wnprintfw("\n Wrong VERB form of: %s", wrdm->inword);
// print the above message and the 2nd word
            bad_agree++; // register this error for the statistics
        }
        }
        break;
```

Continuation of the above rule in the rules.h file:

```
{"[RSN]<D>V",     130},
```

According to case 130, the sentence *The girl stand still* will be wrong and the program will issue the warning message as shown above.

2.7.2 *Incorrect use of a Plural Noun with 3rd Person Singular, Present Tense of the Verb*

For example: *men comes* instead of *men come*, is detected by case 131 and case 61 below.

```
      case 131:
        if (type == '?') break;
/* if the sentence is interrogative, exit the case */
        wrd = (WORD *) s[i].que[0];
        wrdm = (WORD *) s[last].que[0];
// define the position of the word
        if (wrd->numb == 0 && wrdm->tcase == 8)
        break;
/* If the 1st word is singular and the 2nd word is marked as special */
        if (wrdm->esyn == 'E' || wrdm->esyn == 'e' || wrdm->esyn == 'h' ||
        wrdm->esyn == 'x' || wrdm->esyn == 'U' || wrdm->tense == T_FUTURE)
        break;
// exclude past, future and some auxiliary verbs as 2nd word
        if (wrdm->tense == T_PAST && wrd->numb == wrdm->numb)
        break;
/* if the 1st and the 2nd words have the same number and the 2nd is a past form, exit the case */
            if (!stricmp(wrdm->inword, "did") || !stricmp(wrdm->inword,
"had"))
        break;
// exclude 'did' and 'had' as 2nd words
// etc. exclusions below
        if (wrd->person == 1 && (wrdm->person == 0 || wrdm->person == 1))
        break;
        if (wrd->numb && wrdm->person == 0)
        break;
              if (!wrd->numb && !wrdm->numb && wrd->person ==
          wrdm->person)
        break; /* Exclude: I am, he is/was/has/V-es */
        if (wrd && wrdm) {          /* if both words */
         if (wrdm->esyn == 'X' || wrdm->esyn == 'V') {
          if (wrd->numb && wrdm->numb)
          break;
// Exit when both words are in plural (we are (were))
```

```
        }
// after making all necessary exclusions, shown above, proceed further
        if (wrd->numb == 1 && wrdm->person == 3) {
// if the 1st word is in plural and the 2nd word is 3rd person singular
                wnprintfl("\nCheck for Agreement between these words: ");
            wnprintfl("\"");
            wnprintfl(wrd->inword); wnprintfl(" ... ");
            wnprintfl(wrdm->inword);
            wnprintfl("\"");
                    wnprintfl("\nWrong VERB form of: ");
            wnprintfw("\"%s\"", wrdm->inword);
// print the above messages and words
            bad_agree++; // register this error for the statistics
            break;
        }
        }
        break;
```

Continuation of the above rule in the rules.h file:

```
{"N<D>V",       131},
```

Or, we can use case 61 instead (a different approach to the same problem).

```
      case 61:          /* noun plural + verb 3d person */
       if (isflex(wrdm->inword, wrdm->wl, "ss")) {
       i = mpos; continue;
       }
// when the 2nd word ends in -ss exclude it
// exclude other words that end in -s but are not in plural
        if (wrd->numb && isflex(wrdm->inword, wrdm->wl, "s")) {
// if the 1st word is in Plural and the 2nd word ends in -s
      wnprintfw("\n Check the agreement between: %s", wrd->inword);
// print the above message and the 1st word
        wnprintfw(" <==> %s", wrdm->inword);
// print <==> and the 2nd word
        wnprintfw("\n Wrong Use of \"-s\" or Wrong Spelling \"%s\" : ",
        wrdm->inword);
        wnprintfl(wrdm->inbase);
// print the above message and the 2nd word
        bad_agree++;   // register this error for the statistics
        }
        i++; continue;
```

Continuation of the above rule in the rules.h file:

```
{"[RN][Vv]",       NULL, 61},
```

According to case 61 the sentence *The girls breaks the glass* will be wrong and the program will issue the above warning messages.

2.7.3 *Erroneous Verbal Form after Auxiliary Verb plus* be

The Past Participle or Gerund is required after a Modal Verb, followed by the Auxiliary Verb *be*: *can be taken (taking)*. When the Basic Form of the Verb is used instead, case 30 below will consider that as an error, for example, *can be take.*

```
      case 30:
       if (!stricmp(wp[i+1]->inword, "be")) {
/* if the 2nd word (the one between the Modal Verb and the Main Verb) is "be" */
         wnprintfw("\nIncorrect Verb Form; USE '-ed' or '-ing' Form of :
\"%s\"", wrdm->inword);
// print the above message and the last word
        bad_verbs++;  // register this error for the statistics
       }
       i = mpos; continue;
```

Continuation of the above rule in the rules.h file:

```
   {"'will'vV",      NULL, 30},           /* will be ask */
   {"'could'vV",      NULL, 30},          /* could be ask */
// etc.
```

2.7.4 *Wrong Verbal Form after an Auxiliary Verb from the* be *paradigm*

After an Auxiliary Verb from the *be* paradigm one should use the Past Participle *(is decided, was taken)* or Gerund (*is deciding, was taking*). When a basic form of the Verb is used instead (*is decide, was take*), case 31 below will find and point out the error.

```
      case 31:         /* XV */
       if (wrd->esyn == 'x') {
       i = mpos; continue;
       }
// exclude 'shall' and its paradigm as 1st word
       if (wrdm->esyn == 'Z' ||wrdm->esyn == 'A' ||wrdm->esyn == 'e') {
       i = mpos; continue;
       }
// make the necessary exclusions of Parts of Speech, as shown above
       if (wp[i+1]->tense != 2 ||wp[i+1]->esyn == 'X') {
// if the above conditions are met
        wnprintfw("\nIncorrect Verb Form; USE_ '-ed' or '-ing' Form of :
\"%s\"", wrdm->inword);
// print the above message and the last word
        bad_verbs++;  // register this error for the statistics
       }
       i = mpos; continue;
```

Continuation of the above rule in the rules.h file:

```
{"~[srqLi][Xv]<KkDd>V",   NULL, 31},
```

2.7.5 *Incorrect use of the Participle after a Modal Verb or an Auxiliary Verb from the* shall *paradigm*

After a Modal Verb or an Auxiliary Verb from the *shall* paradigm, or after *did*, *does*, one should use the basic form of the Verb (*shall decide*). If the Past or Participle form of the Verb is used instead (*shall decided, shall deciding*), this will be an error, which case 34 or case 41 below will detect.

```
    case 34:        /* x[EG] */
      wnprintfw("\nIncorrect \"%s\"", wrdm->inword);
// print the above message and the last word
      wnprintfl("\n Use Basic Form of the Verb");
// print the above message
      wrd->cflag = 'r';                    /* registered */
      bad_verbs++;  // register this error for the statistics
      i = mpos; continue;
```

Continuation of the above rule in the rules.h file:

```
{"x<KkDd>[EG]",     NULL, 34},
    case 41:        /* U[Eh] */
      if (wrdm->e.V.alltense == 1) {
       i = mpos; continue;
      }
/* Exclude all verbs with identical present and past forms, such as 'burst', 'cut', 'put', etc.
These verbs were marked with the code [?] and named 'alltense' */
      if (wrdm->person || wrdm->tense == T_PAST) {
// if the 2nd word, the verb, is 3d person or in the past
      wnprintfl("\nIncorrect:");
      wnprintfl(wrdm->inword);
      wnprintfw("\n After Modal Verb use
        Basic Form of the Verb");
// print the above message
      bad_verbs++;  // register this error for the statistics
      }
      i = mpos; continue;
```

Continuation of the above rule in the rules.h file:

```
  {"U<KkDdw>[vVX]", NULL, 41},
```

Because case 34 and case 41 deal with the same type of error we can merge them into one single case.

2.7.6 *Incorrect use of the Basic Form of the Verb instead of the Participle Form*

After an Auxiliary Verb from the *have* paradigm one should use the Participle Form of the Verb (*have wanted*). When the Basic Form of the Verb is used instead (*have want*), case 39 below will detect this error.

```
    case 39:        /* YV */
      wnprintfl("\n Strange grammar: ");
// print the above message
      wnprintfw("%s ", wrd->inword);
// print the 1st word
      wnprintfw("%s ", wrdm->inword);
// print the 2nd word
      wnprintfw("\nUse corresponding Participle Form of \"%s\"",
      wrdm->inword);
// print the above message
      bad_verbs++;  // register this error for the statistics
      i = mpos; continue;
```

Continuation of the above rule in the rules.h file:

```
{"Y<KkDd>V",     NULL, 39},
```

2.7.7 *Wrong use of 3rd Person Singular, Present Tense, after the Verbal Particle* to

After the Verbal Particle *to* one should always use the Basic Form of the Verb (*to consider*). If one uses 3rd Person Singular (*to considers*) Present Tense (case 43) or Participle (case 44), one will make a grammatical error (*to considered*).

```
    case 43:          /* PV */
     if (wrd->esyn == 'B' && wrdm->person ) {
/* if the first word is the Verbal Particle "to"
and the 2nd word is 3d Person Singular, Present Tense */
     wnprintfl("\nIncorrect:");
// print the above message
     wnprintfl(wrdm->inword);
// print the 2nd word
     wnprintfw("\n After Particle 'to' use Basic Form of the Verb");
// print the above message
     bad_verbs++; // register this error for the statistics
     }
     i = mpos; continue;
```

Continuation of the above rule in the rules.h file:

```
{"'to'[vVXY]",     NULL, 43},               /* BV */
```

```
    case 44:
     if (wrd->esyn == 'B') {
// if the code of the 1st word is B
     wnprintfl("\nIncorrect:");
// print the above message
     wnprintfl(wp[i+1]->inword);
// print the 2nd word
     wnprintfw("\n After Particle 'to' use Basic Form of the Verb");
// print the above message
     bad_verbs++; // register this error for the statistics
     }
     i = mpos; continue;
```

Continuation of the above rule in the rules.h file:

```
{"'to'ET",         NULL, 44},      /* BE */
```

2.8 *Wrong use of the Verbal Particle* to *after a Modal Verb or an Auxiliary Verb from the* shall *paradigm or* did, does, done

The Particle *to* can be used after an Auxiliary Verb from the *be* paradigm (with the exception of *be*). For example: *was to come*. The Particle *to* cannot be used after most other Auxiliary Verbs (*shall to come, can to come*, etc.), with the exception of *ought, have, has*. Case 46 below deals with this type of error.

```
    case 46:        /* [Ux]B */
     if (!stricmp(wrd->inword, "ought")) {
     i = mpos; continue;
     }
// If the first word is "ought", skip it, because "ought to" is correct.
     wnprintfl("\n Wrong USE of: ");
// print the above message
     wnprintfl(wrdm->inword);
// print the 2nd word
     bad_verbs++; // register this error for the statistics
     i = mpos; continue;
```

Continuation of the above rule in the rules.h file:

```
{"[Ux]<KkDd>B",     NULL, 46},
```

2.9 *Unrecognized irregular form of a Verb*

There are around 160 English verbs that form their Past and Participle Forms in an 'irregular' way. The linguists call them 'irregular' because there is no governing rule to describe this phenomenon. All dictionaries mark this exception by listing all forms of the Verb. We have done the same, marking these exceptions with [i] and then listing the correct forms within brackets (...; ...). Then we have made a rule (a **case**, case 32 below) to tell the program that if someone attempts to write the Past or Participle form of these Verbs in the regular way (with *-ed* at the end of the Verb), he or she is making an error and the person must be informed about it.

```
    case 32:        /* error with the irregular Verbs */
     if (wrd->irrform[0] != '(') {
      i = mpos; continue;
     }   // if the word is not marked as "irregular", skip it
     if (wrd->syn == 'V' && wrd->person == 3 && (wrd->esyn == 'E' ||
      wrd->esyn == 'h' || wrd->esyn == 'F')) {
/* if the above conditions are met (Verb, 3d Person and Past or Participle Form */
     wnprintfw("\"%s\"", wrd->inword);
// print the word
     if (wrd->gflag == 'i' && wrd->irrform[0] == '(')
/* if the word is marked as "irregular" and its forms are provided in brackets */
        wnprintfw("\nCorrect Forms: %s", wrd->irrform);
// print the correct forms of the word
     bad_usage++; // register this error for the statistics
     }
    else
     if (stricmp(wrd->inword, wrd->inbase) && wrd->gflag == 'i' &&
      wrd->person != 3) {
/* if the above conditions are met (if the word from the text matches the initial part of the word in the DW and if the word in the DW is marked as "irregular" and it is not 3d person) */
     wnprintfw("\"%s\"", wrd->inword);
// print the word
     wnprintfw(" - Incorrect Form of: \"%s\"",
            wrd->inbase);
     wnprintfw("\nCORRECT: %s", wrd->irrform);
// print the correct forms of the word
```

```
bad_usage++; // register this error for the statistics
}
i++; continue;
```

Continuation of the above rule in the rules.h file:

```
{"[EhV]",        NULL, 32},                /* error with the irregular Verbs */
```

For example, the Verb *arise* is registered in the DW as follows:
arise = V[i](arise; arose; arisen)

If someone writes *arised*, *arosed* or *aroses*, the above rule will be triggered on and case 32 will issue the warning message.

2.10 *Unrecognized irregular form of a Noun*

Many English Nouns do not form their Plural Form in the 'regular' way (by adding *-s* at the end of the Noun). There is no underlining rule to describe how these Nouns get their Plural Forms. Therefore each such Noun must be registered individually with its irregular plural form. Case 122 below checks whether these Nouns are written incorrectly.

```
case 122:        /* error with the irregular Nouns */
 if (wrd->irrform[0] != '(') {
 i = mpos; continue;
 } // if the word is not marked as "irregular", skip it
 if (wrd->syn == 'N' && wrd->numb &&
   wrd->e.N.singular_only) {
/* if the word is a Noun and if it is used in Plural, but it is marked as a Noun which can be used only in Singular (as registered) */
 wnprintfw("\"%s\"", wrd->inword);
// print the word
 wnprintfw("\n \"%s\" - Incorrect Form of:",
 wrd->inword);
 wnprintfw("\"%s\"",wrd->inbase);
// print the above message and the word
 if (wrd->irrform[0] == '(')
// if the word is marked as "irregular",
    wnprintfw("\nCORRECT: %s", wrd->irrform);
/* print the above message and the correct form(s) of the word */
 bad_usage++; // register this error for the statistics
 }
 i++; continue;
```

Continuation of the above rule in the rules.h file:

```
{"N",        NULL, 122},                /* error with the irregular Nouns */
```

For example, the word *bacillus* is registered in the DW as follows:

bacillus=N[%i](bacillus->bacilli)

If someone writes *bacilluses*, case 122 will detect the error and issue a warning, providing the correct Plural Form. Similarly, one can write such a rule for any other irregular Part of Speech.

2.11 *Wrong use of* which *and* who

The pronouns *which* and *who* refer to the previous noun, and the use of one or the other depends on whether this noun is animate (a person) or inanimate. In the DW we have coded all nouns denoting a human being with its respective code in square brackets and made the following rule: it is an error to use '*which*' after a noun denoting a human being (case 36) and *who*, *whose*, '*whom*' after a non-animate noun (case 38).

```
    case 36:        /* man which */
      if (wrd->e.N.human) {
// if the 1st word denotes a human being
      wnprintfw("\n Check the Correctness of \"%s\" + ",
      wrd->inword);
      wnprintfw("\"%s\"", wrdm->inword);
      wnprintfw("\nIncorrect \"%s\"", wrdm->inword);
      wnprintfl("\n Use \"who\"");
// print the above messages and words
      wrd->cflag = 'r';
      bad_agree++; // register this error for the statistics
      }
      i = mpos; continue;
```

Continuation of the above rule in the rules.h file:

```
  {"N<,B>'which'",    NULL, 36},
    case 38:        /* a door who */
      if (!wrd->e.N.human) {
// if the 1st word does not denote a human being
      wnprintfw("\n Check the Correctness of \"%s\" + ",
      wrd->inword);
      wnprintfw("\"%s\"", wrdm->inword);
      wnprintfw("\nIncorrect \"%s\"", wrdm->inword);
      wnprintfl("\n If the Noun is non-animate, use \"which or that\"");
// print the above messages and words
      wrd->cflag = 'r';
      bad_agree++; // register this error for the statistics
      }
      i = mpos; continue;
```

Continuation of the above rule in the rules.h file:

```
  {"N<,>'who'",       NULL, 38},
  {"N<,>'whose'",     NULL, 38},
  {"N<,B>'whom'",     NULL, 38},
```

2.12 *Wrong use of a Preposition*

Certain prepositions are used only with certain words. There are many grammar books on this, including one on English prepositions by J. B. Heaton (1965). There are also words used with only one preposition. This is easy to program, since there is no other choice of preposition. However, most words are used with two, three and more prepositions, depending on context. More prepositions used with a particular word means greater programming difficulty to find out in what context(s) they are used. In our spell-checking software program for the English language (Georgiev, 1993a) we have coded only those words that are used with one, two and three prepositions. When a word is used with more than one preposition, we have not specified the context(s) in which they are used, not because this is impossible, but because the amount of work to do it is enormous. Case 71 shows how to program the use of a preposition with a particular word or words.

```
case 71:          /* [NVA] -> P */
  if (!stricmp(wrdm->inword, "from")) {
  i = mpos; continue;
  }
/* If the 2nd word, the preposition, is 'from', exit the case. */
/* This means, that it is correct to use 'from' with this word. */
  if (wrd->xflag) {
// if the 1st word is used with the preposition 'from' (xflag)
   if (!wrdm->xflag) {
// and if the 2nd word is any other preposition
   wnprintfl("\n THIS WORD is used with the following
     Preposition:\n");
   wnprintfl(wrd->inword);
   wnprintfl(" from ");
   wnprintfl("\n");
   wnprintfw("CHECK if the Preposition \"%s\"",
    wrdm->inword);
   wnprintfw(" can be used after \"%s\"",
    wrd->inword);
// print the above messages
   bad_neue++; // register this error for the statistics
   }
  }
  i = mpos; continue;
```

Continuation of the above rule in the rules.h file:

```
{"N<Ddk>P",         NULL, 71},
{"[EeVF]<DdMmSkO>P",  NULL, 71},
```

For example, in English one says *alienated from*, *alight from*, *arise from*, etc. If we use another preposition, case 71 will detect our error, issue a warning and register the error for the statistics 'wrong use of a preposition'. In the DW we have coded the above-mentioned words as follows:

alienated=E[D]
alight=Z[D]/A[M-]
arise=V[Di](arise; arose; arisen)

where [D] codes the use of this particular word with the preposition *from*. When the word is used with more than one preposition, we have simply enumerated them, without going into further detail (case 86).

```
case 86:          /* [NVA] -> P */
  if (!stricmp(wrdm->inword, "to")) {
  i = mpos; continue;
  }
// exclude preposition 'to'
```

```
if (!stricmp(wrdm->inword, "of")) {
i = mpos; continue;
}
// exclude preposition 'of'
if (!stricmp(wrdm->inword, "with")) {
i = mpos; continue;
}
/* If the 2nd word, the preposition, is 'to', 'of' or 'with', exit the case. */
if (wrd->uflag) {
// if the 1st word is used only with these prepositions (uflag)
 if (!wrdm->uflag) {
// if the 2nd word cannot be used with these prepositions
 wnprintfl("\n THIS WORD is used with the
  following Prepositions:\n");
 wnprintfl(wrd->inword);
 wnprintfl(" with, to ");
 wnprintfl("\n");
 wnprintfw("CHECK if the Preposition \"%s\"",
  wrdm->inword);
 wnprintfw(" can be used after \"%s\"",
  wrd->inword);
// print the above messages
 bad_neue++; // register this error for the statistics
 }
}
i = mpos; continue;
```

Continuation of the above rule in the rules.h file:

```
{"N<Ddk>P",        NULL, 86}, /* to, with */
{"[EeVF]<DdkMm>P",   NULL, 86}, /* to, with */
```

For example, in English one says *conformity to*, *conformity with*, *correlate to*, *correlate with*, *married to*, etc. In the DW we have coded the above-mentioned words as follows:

conformity=N[x]
correlate=Z[x]/A[M-]
correlated=E[x]
etc.

where [x] codes the use of this word with the prepositions *to* and *with* and the code word used in the program to refer to [x] is 'uflag'. Any other preposition, used with these words, will be regarded as an error. For example, *married with* is a typical error many Germans make.

In case this instruction is wrong, in the opinion of an expert, we have tried to be on the safe side by printing the message: 'CHECK if the Preposition ... can be used after ...'. (Note: C++ interfaces have other ways to display the above messages.)

3 German grammatical rules

3.1 Wrong grammatical ending

Some Nouns cannot have certain grammatical endings, while other Nouns can have them. For example, German Feminine Nouns cannot end in *-s* (with some exceptions, excluding also all those ending in *-ss*), while the Masculine and Neuter Nouns can. Therefore, we can write the following case in the rules.c(pp) file (or its German equivalent) and specify that the ending '*-s*' cannot be used with the Feminine Nouns:

```
     case 13:          /* N[F] ending in -'s' */
    if (wrdm->e.N.masculin || wrdm->e.N.neuter ||
          wrdm->uflag == 1) {
    i = mpos; continue;
    }
// exclude the Masculine and Neuter Nouns from consideration
    if (wrdm->e.N.name) {
    i = mpos; continue;
    }
// exclude the Names
    if (wrdm->e.N.constant == 1 || wrdm->uflag == 1) {
    i = mpos; continue;
    }
// exclude the ambiguous Nouns
    if (!stricmp(wrdm->inword, "praxis") ||
          !stricmp(wrdm->inword, "gastritis")) {
    i = mpos; continue;
    }
// exclude the words praxis and gastritis
    if (!stricmp(wrdm->inword, "maus") ||
          !stricmp(wrdm->inword, "preis")) {
    i = mpos; continue;
    }
// exclude the words maus and preis
// if this list of exceptions is too big, use a code for all these exceptions
    if (isflex(wrdm->inword, wrdm->wl, "nis") ||
          isflex(wrdm->inword, wrdm->wl, "maus")) {
    i = mpos; continue;
    }
// exclude the words that end in -nis or -maus
    if (isflex(wrdm->inword, wrdm->wl, "asis")
          || isflex(wrdm->inword, wrdm->wl, "mus")) {
    i = mpos; continue;
    }
// exclude the words that end in -asis or -mus
    if (isflex(wrdm->inword, wrdm->wl, "ss")) {
    i = mpos; continue;
    }
// exclude the words that end in -ss
    if (wrdm->numb || wrdm->e.N.plural_only) {
    i = mpos; continue;
    }
// exclude the plural Nouns
    if (isflex(wrdm->inword, wrdm->wl, "s")) {
// if the word ends in -s
       wnprintfw("\nPRÜFE Übereinstimmung: %s ",
       wrd->inword);
// print the above message and the first word
       wnprintfw("<==> %s", wrdm->inword); // print the second word
       wnprintfw("\n \"%s\" - braucht kein '-s'",
```

```
        wrdm->inbase);
// print the second word and the above message
     }
     i++; continue;
```

Continuation of the above rule in the rules.h file:

```
{"[PTS]<Aäö>[NÛ]",      NULL, 13},       /** N[F] -'s' **/
```

If someone writes *die Fraus* instead of *die Frau*, case 13 will detect the error and issue a warning. Note that we have re-named the Noun. The Noun, when used after a Preposition, is no longer N, it is Û. This is why, here, we use two different codes for the noun. We have re-named the Noun in the "parse.h" file:

```
{"PT<A>N",          "@@$Û",   }, /* re-naming of the Noun */
{"P<TÛ>TAN",         "@$TAÛ",  }, /* re-naming of the Noun */
```

We will explain why this was necessary later.

Case 13 deals only with the Feminine Nouns used after a Preposition, Article or Determiner. Another, similar case, can be designed to apply to all Feminine Nouns regardless of context. Similarly, we can deal with other grammatical endings. All Masculine and Neuter Nouns can take the Case or Plural ending *-s*, but not all of them take *-es*. For example:

Schluck, Schluckes, Schlucks	(takes both *-s* and *-es*)
Schmelz, Schmelzes	(takes only *-es*, cannot take *-s*)
Schlummer, Schlummers	(takes only *-s*, cannot take *-es*)

Following the example of case 13, we can write another case to tell the software program that *Schmelzs* and *Schlummeres* are wrong Case Forms of the respective Nouns. Before we write such a case we have to do some research. Firstly we have to see if there are exceptions, and then, we have to decide how to make the rule:

a) on the basis of how the Noun ends (*-z*, *-er*, etc.) or
b) on the basis of which sub-group the Noun belongs to.

If we choose b), we have to mark all words belonging to the sub-group with a sign enclosed in square brackets or to re-name the Noun by giving it another sign, valid only in a particular context.

Yet another possibility to deal with the wrong grammatical ending is to declare all such Nouns irregular and to specify the correct grammatical endings. The correct grammatical endings are specified in the DW as follows:

frau=N[FSiH](Frau; Frauen)
frauen=n[FH]

Using case 32 (see, in the previous chapter, 'Recognition of a misspelt word') the software program will consider the plural ending *-e* of the word *Frau* as wrong. However, case 32 will not recognize the ending *-er* as wrong, because *-er* is not declared to be a Plural ending. We will have to write a special case for that, similar to case 13 above. Also, when we want to use such a rule, we must exclude the respective grammatical ending. The exclusion is done in the file 'degram.h' by closing the ending. If we do not close the ending, we will have a problem treating it as irregular, because the rule applies to all words belonging to a particular Part of Speech, including the irregular ones. Also, the closure of the ending means that the program will no longer recognize the wordform having this ending, unless we register the wordform in the DW.

3.2 Wrong agreement between two words in Gender

This type of agreement is often seen between an Article and a Noun. Unlike English, some Articles are used only with Neuter Nouns, others are used only with Masculine Nouns, and still others only with Feminine Nouns. The use of a particular Article with a particular Noun depends not only on the Gender of the Noun, but also on the Number and Case of this Noun. It is inconvenient to make one rule (one case) for all, therefore we will consider these dependences one by one. For example, we can make the following case (66) for the wrong agreement between a Neuter Article and a Feminine or Masculine Noun:

```
    case 66:
/* Article - Noun agreement in Gender "das -> N[F] or N[M]" */
    if (wrdm->e.N.constant || wrdm->uflag == 1) {
       i = mpos; continue; // exclude the ambiguous Nouns
    }
// it will be wise to exclude the Neuter Nouns as well
    if (wp[mpos+1]->syn == 'N') wrdm = wp[mpos+1];
// fix the position of the Noun
    if (wrdm->e.N.fem == 1) {
// if the Gender of the Noun is Feminine
       wnprintfw("\nPRÜFE Übereinstimmung: %s ",
       wrd->inword);
 // print the above message and the Article (first word)
       wnprintfw("<==> %s", wrdm->inword);
// print the sign <==> and the second word
       bad_agree++;    // write this for the error statistics
    }
    else
    if (wrdm->e.N.masculin == 1) {
// if the Gender of the Noun is Masculine
       wnprintfw("\nPRÜFE Übereinstimmung: %s ",
       wrd->inword);
// print the above message and the Article (first word)
       wnprintfw("<==> %s", wrdm->inword);
// print the sign <==> and the second word
       bad_agree++;      // write this for the error statistics
    }
    else
    if (wrdm->numb) {
// if the Noun (the 2nd word) is in Plural
       wnprintfw("\nPRÜFE Übereinstimmung: %s ",
       wrd->inword);
// print the above message and the Article (the first word)
       wnprintfw("<==> %s", wrdm->inword);
// print the sign <==> and the 2nd word
       wnprintfl("\nbenutze den Artikel 'die'");
// print the above message
       bad_agree++;      // write this for the error statistics
    }
    i = mpos; continue;
```

The second part of case 66 declares the agreement between the specified Article(s) and the Noun and suggests the Article *die* as the correct Article to be used when the Noun is in Plural.

Continuation of the above rule in the rules.h file:

```
{"'das'<AöO>N",   NULL, 66}, /* das - F or M */
{"'ans'<AöO>N",   NULL, 66},
{"'ums'<AöO>N",   NULL, 66},
{"'aufs'<AöO>N",   NULL, 66},
{"'durchs'<AöO>N",   NULL, 66},
{"'ebendas'<AöO>N",   NULL, 66},
{"'ebendasselbe'<AöO>N",   NULL, 66},
{"'eueres'<AöO>N",   NULL, 66},
{"'eures'<AöO>N",   NULL, 66},
{"'fürs'<AöO>N",   NULL, 66},
{"'hinters'<AöO>N",   NULL, 66},
{"'ins'<AöO>N",   NULL, 66},
{"'irgendein'<AöO>N",   NULL, 66},
{"'irgendeines'<AöO>N",   NULL, 66},
{"'jenes'<AöO>N",   NULL, 66},
{"'keines'<AöO>N",   NULL, 66},
{"'keins'<AöO>N",   NULL, 66},
{"'übers'<AöO>N",   NULL, 66},
{"'unters'<AöO>N",   NULL, 66},
{"'vors'<AöO>N",   NULL, 66},
```

Note that we have listed the Preposition and the Neuter Article, written as one word, as is usually done in German, as for example *fürs = für das*. We have to list the words individually unless we include them in a group and code the group. The codes enclosed between the arrows < > show the alternative Parts of Speech that can separate the Neuter Article from the Noun. According to case 66, the expression *das Frau* will be wrong. The expression *das Frauen* will be also wrong and the program will suggest the Article *die* instead of *das*.

We deal similarly with other Articles by writing a case for each Article – Noun agreement in Gender. When we write the case, we specify which Articles cannot agree with a particular Gender. For example, the Articles (or a Preposition and an Article) or the Pronouns *ein, des, dem, am, beim, im, vom, zum, dieses, jedes, diesem, alles*, etc. cannot agree in Gender with the Feminine Nouns and with the Plural of the Nouns.

3.3 Wrong agreement between two words in Number

The Plural of the German Noun can be expressed in three different ways:

- with a grammatical ending *-e, en, -er* or Umlaut, as in *Halte, Frauen, Kinder, Häfen*;
- with a preceding word, without specific grammatical ending, as in *zwei, alle, beide*, etc.;
- with a preceding figure (2, 12, 386, etc.).

The word denoting Plural (usually without specific grammatical ending) must agree in Number with the Noun following it. Compare: *alle Männer, beide Frauen, 2 Kinder*, etc. If it does not, then it is wrong; for example, it is wrong to write *beide Frau*. The following case uses a rule to detect such grammatical errors:

```
 case 26:                              /* [HI]N */
if (wp[mpos+1]->syn == 'N')  wrdm = wp[mpos+1];
// determine the position of the noun
if (!stricmp(wrdm->inword, "Prozent")) {
i = mpos; continue;
```

```
// exclude the Noun Prozent (as 2nd word)
    }
    if (isflex(wrdm->inword, wrdm->wl, "n")) {
    i = mpos; continue;
// exclude the Nouns ending in -n (as 2nd word)
    }
    if (wrdm->e.N.time || wrdm->e.N.plural_only ||
    wrdm->e.N.constant) {
    i = mpos; continue;
    }
// exclude the Nouns denoting "time", the Nouns in Plural, the ambiguous Nouns
    if (wrdm->numb == 1) {
    i = mpos; continue;    // exclude the Plural Nouns
    }
    if (!wrdm->numb) {
// if the 2nd word (2nd Noun) is not in Plural
     wnprintfw("\n PRÜFE \"%s\" + ",
     wrd->inword);
 // print this message and the 1st word
     wnprintfw("\"%s\"", wrdm->inword); // print the 2nd word
     wnprintfw("\n FALSCHE Anzahl/Person: %s", wrdm->inword);
// print this message and the 2nd word
     bad_agree++;        // write this error for the statistics
    }
    i = mpos; continue;
```

Continuation of the above rule in the rules.h file:

```
  {"I<wPAäöOD?#\"H{}>N", NULL, 26},    /* wrong agreement in Number */
  {"H<AOD(?#)\">N",   NULL, 26},
```

The two words, which must agree in Number, can be separated by a number of other words (enclosed between < >).

According to case 26, the expressions *zwei Frau*, *3 Stunde*, etc. will be wrong. The program will not suggest the correct plural form at this stage. It must be done anyway when we have to translate into German and it needs some more programming effort. There are also other ways to express the agreement in Number (case 29 and 90):

```
     case 29:        /* agreement between a  Pronoun and a Noun */
    if (wp[mpos+1]->syn == 'N')  wrdm = wp[mpos+1];
// fix the position of the words
    if (wrd->gflag != 's' && wrd->numb == 0) {
    i = mpos; continue;
    }
// exclude some Singular words used as 1st word
    if (!stricmp(wrd->inword, "viel") ||
     !stricmp(wrd->inword, "viele")) {
    i = mpos; continue;
    }
// exclude viel and viele as 1st word
    if (wrdm->e.N.time || wrdm->e.N.constant) {
    i = mpos; continue;
    }
// exclude the ambiguous Nouns and the Nouns denoting 'time'
```

```
    if (!wrdm->e.N.singular_only && wrd->numb && wrdm->numb) {
    i = mpos; continue;
    }
// cancel the case when both words are in Plural
    if (wrd->numb != wrdm->numb) {
// if the two words do not agree in Number
       wnprintfw("\n FALSCHE Anzahl: %s", wrd->inword);
// print the above message and the 1st word
       wnprintfw("\n oder falsche Anzahl: %s", wrdm->inword);
// print the above message and the 2nd word
       bad_usage++;    // write this error for the statistics
    }
    i = mpos; continue;
```

Continuation of the above rule in the rules.h file:

```
{"[OS]<Aäö>N",      NULL, 29},    /* agreement in Number */
```

According to case 29, the expression *mein Kinder* will be wrong. The correct form is *meine(n) Kinder* or *meiner Kinder* (Genitive). The program can suggest the correct alternatives, if needed. The program can also suggest the only correct alternative if we can make it recognize the Case in which it is used.

```
     case 90:  /* Adj. - Noun agreement in Case and Number */
    if (wrdm->e.N.constant || wrdm->uflag == 1 ||
     isflex(wrd->inword, wrd->wl, "er") ||
     isflex(wrd->inword, wrd->wl, "e") ||
        isflex(wrd->inword, wrd->wl, "n") ||
     wrdm->numb == 0) {
    i = mpos; continue;
    }
/* exclude the ambiguous Nouns, Adjectives with a particular ending or Nouns in Singular
*/
    if (isupper(wrd->inword[0])) {
    i = mpos; continue;
    }
// exclude those Adjectives that are written with a capital letter
    if (wrdm->numb == 1) {
// if the 2nd word (the Noun) is used in Plural
      if (!isflex(wrd->inword, wrd->wl, "n") ||
      !isflex(wrd->inword, wrd->wl, "er")) {
// and if the 1st word (the Adjective) does not end in -n or in -er
      wnprintfw("\nPRÜFE Übereinstimmung: %s ",
      wrd->inword); // print the above message and the 1st word
      wnprintfw("<==> %s", wrdm->inword);
// print the sign <==> and the 2nd word
      wnprintfw("\n \"%s\" soll enden mit '-(e)n'",
      wrd->inbase);    // print the above message and the 1st word
      bad_agree++;  // write the error for the statistics
      }
     }
    i = mpos; continue;
```

Note that the above rule has two conditions: 'if', and then 'if ...' Sometimes there are more than two conditions, before the rule can take effect. Continuation of the above rule in the rules.h file:

```
{"[AN]N",    NULL, 90},  /* Adj. - Noun agreement in Case and Number */
```

According to the above rule *gutem Weinbrände* will be wrong. The Adjective *gutem* does not have the right plural ending. The program will suggest the ending *-e(n)* for *gutem* (i.e., *gute(n) Weinbrände* or *guter Weinbrände* (Genitive)).

3.4 Wrong agreement between two words in Person

The agreement in Person is best illustrated by the agreement between the personal Pronoun Nominal Case (*ich, du, er, wir*, etc.) and the Verb that follows it. The regular Verb must have a particular grammatical ending, required by the Person. If it does not, that is considered to be an error. Case 17 below finds these errors using the following rule:

```
      case 17:        /* R -> V-ending */
     if (wrdm->esyn == 'X' ||wrdm->esyn == 'x' ||
      wrdm->esyn == 'U') {
     i = mpos; continue;
     }    // exclude the Auxiliary Verbs, as 2nd word
    if (!stricmp(wrdm->inword, "lass") ||!stricmp(wrdm->inword, "miss"))
{
     i = mpos; continue;
     }
       if  (!stricmp(wrdm->inword,  "mass")  ||  !stricmp(wrdm->inword,
"schmilzt")) {
     i = mpos; continue;
     }
     if (!stricmp(wrdm->inword, "bleib")) {
     i = mpos; continue;
     }
// exclude the above mentioned Verbs (the list is not complete), as 2nd word
     if (wrdm->person ||wrdm->esyn == 'V' ||wrdm->esyn == 'E') {
// if in respect of the person or the Verb (Present or Past form) of the 2nd word
         if (!stricmp(wrd->inword, "ich") &&
          !isflex(wrdm->inword, wrdm->wl, "e")) {
/* then, if the first word is 'ich' and the 2nd word (the Verb) does not end in -e */
          wnprintfw("\nPRÜFE Übereinstimmung: %s ",
          wrd->inword);
// print the above message and the 1st word
          wnprintfw("<==> %s", wrdm->inword);
// print the sign <==> and the 2nd word
          wnprintfw("\n \"%s\" soll enden mit '-e'",
          wrdm->inbase);
// print the above message and the 2nd word
          bad_agree++;  // write the error for the statistics
         }
         if (!stricmp(wrd->inword, "du") &&
          !isflex(wrdm->inword, wrdm->wl, "st")) {
/* then, if the first word is 'du' and the 2nd word (the Verb) does not end in -st */
// the above explanations apply to the rules below as well
          wnprintfw("\nPRÜFE Übereinstimmung: %s ",
```

```
      wrd->inword);
      wnprintfw("<==> %s", wrdm->inword);
      wnprintfw("\n \"%s\" soll enden mit '-st'",
      wrdm->inbase);
      bad_agree++; // send the error for the statistics
    }
    if (!stricmp(wrd->inword, "er") &&
      isflex(wrdm->inword, wrdm->wl, "n")) {
      wnprintfw("\nPRÜFE Übereinstimmung: %s ",
      wrd->inword);
      wnprintfw("<==> %s", wrdm->inword);
      wnprintfw("\n \"%s\" soll enden mit '-e, -t(e)'",
      wrdm->inbase);
      bad_agree++; // send the error for the statistics
    }
    if (!stricmp(wrd->inword, "es") &&
      isflex(wrdm->inword, wrdm->wl, "st")) {
      wnprintfw("\nPRÜFE Übereinstimmung: %s ",
      wrd->inword);
      wnprintfw("<==> %s", wrdm->inword);
      wnprintfw("\n \"%s\" soll enden mit '-t, -e'",
      wrdm->inbase);
      bad_agree++; // send the error for the statistics
    }
    if (!stricmp(wrd->inword, "er") &&
      isflex(wrdm->inword, wrdm->wl, "st")) {
      wnprintfw("\nPRÜFE Übereinstimmung: %s ",
      wrd->inword);
      wnprintfw("<==> %s", wrdm->inword);
      wnprintfw("\n \"%s\" soll enden mit '-t, -e'",
      wrdm->inbase);
      bad_agree++; // send the error for the statistics
    }
    if (!stricmp(wrd->inword, "es") &&
      isflex(wrdm->inword, wrdm->wl, "n")) {
      wnprintfw("\nPRÜFE Übereinstimmung: %s ",
      wrd->inword);
      wnprintfw("<==> %s", wrdm->inword);
      wnprintfw("\n \"%s\" soll enden mit '-t, -e'",
      wrdm->inbase);
      bad_agree++;   // send the error for the statistics
    }
    if (!stricmp(wrd->inword, "wir") &&
      !isflex(wrdm->inword, wrdm->wl, "n")) {
      wnprintfw("\nPRÜFE Übereinstimmung: %s ",
      wrd->inword);
      wnprintfw("<==> %s", wrdm->inword);
      wnprintfw("\n \"%s\" soll enden mit '-(e)n'",
      wrdm->inbase);
      bad_agree++;   // send the error for the statistics
    }
}
i++; continue;
```

(Note: extreme care should be taken to exclude all those Verbs that are exceptions to the above rule.)

Continuation of the above rule in the rules.h file:

```
{"R[çvY]",        NULL, 17},        /* for R -> V agreement */
```

According to the above rule *du glauben* will be wrong and the program will suggest the ending *-st* for *glauben* (i.e., *du glaubst*).

If we define the ending and the Person in the file "de_gram.c(pp)" or code the number and the person in the DW, we can shorten the above case by writing only

```
if (wrd->person != wrdm->person) {
```

// if the two words do not agree in Person
without having to name again the PPNC and the verbal ending that goes with it.

3.5 Wrong agreement between two words in Case

We had to deal with the Case in a number of cases above (29, 90), including the wrong Case ending *-s* for Feminine Nouns (case 13 above). A typical example for agreement in Case is the agreement between the Article *des* (used in Genitive) and the Masculine or Neuter Nouns following it. The Masculine or Neuter Nouns following it must end in *-s* to express 'possessiveness'. If they do not end in *-s*, case 25 below states that this is an error:

```
case 25:  /* des -> N[M] or N[U] */
 if (wrdm->e.N.masculin && isflex(wrdm->inword, wrdm->wl, "en")) {
 i = mpos; continue;
 } // exclude the Masculine Nouns ending in -en as 2nd word
 if (isflex(wrdm->inword, wrdm->wl, "x")) {
 i = mpos; continue;
 }  // exclude the Nouns ending in -x as 2nd word
 if (wrdm->e.N.fem || wrdm->numb == 1 || wrdm->uflag == 1) {
 i = mpos; continue;
 }
/* Exclude the Feminine Nouns, the Nouns in Plural and
the ambiguous Nouns (uflag) as 2nd word. */
// Note: ambiguous as far as the Gender is concerned.
 if (!stricmp(wrdm->inword, "ok")) {
 i = mpos; continue;
 }  // exclude the word ok as 2nd word
 if (wrdm->e.N.time || wrdm->e.N.name) {
 i = mpos; continue;
 }
/* Exclude the names and the Nouns denoting "time". This does not mean that they cannot
be subjected to this rule. We simply do not want to look for exceptions among them, therefore
we decide to get rid of them, just in case there are exceptions. */
 if (!isflex(wrdm->inword, wrdm->wl, "s")) {
// if the Noun, as 2nd word, does not end in -s
    wnprintfw("\nPRÜFE Übereinstimmung: %s ",
    wrd->inword);
// print the above message and the 1st word
    wnprintfw("<==> %s", wrdm->inword);
```

```
// print the sign <==> and the 2nd word
        wnprintfw("\n \"%s\" soll enden mit '-s'",
        wrdm->inbase);
// print the 2nd word and the above message
        bad_agree++;      // write the error for the statistics
    }
    i++; continue;
```

Continuation of the above rule in the rules.h file:

```
{"'des'<AO>N",          NULL, 25},  /* Genitive -s */
```

Note that we have named the Article *des*. By doing so, we have excluded the other Articles (in fact, all other words) from consideration. Using the above rule, the program will find out that *Wort* is wrongly used in the sentence *Der Grapefruitkern ist im wahrsten Sinn des Wort in aller Munde* and will suggest *-s* at the end of *Wort* (i.e., *Wortes*).

3.6 *Wrong agreement between Adjective and Noun in Case, Number and Gender*

In German the Adjectives are inflected only when they are used attributively. The attributive Adjectives have two declensions: strong (when no determinative word precedes the Adjective) and weak (when a determinative word precedes the Adjective). Determinative words are the Article, the Indicative or Possessive Pronoun, etc. The determinative words indicate the Gender, Number and Case of the Noun. Case 33 (below) does not take into consideration the type of declension (strong or weak), but concentrates on the Case ending of the Adjective and on the Gender and the Number of the Noun.

```
     case 33:         /* Adj - Noun agreement */
    if (wrdm->e.N.constant == 1 || wrdm->uflag == 1) {
    i = mpos; continue;
    }
// exclude those Nouns that can be both in Singular and in Plural
    if (wrd->esyn == 'ö' || wrd->syn == 'ö') {
    i = mpos; continue;
    } // exclude the "weak" Adjectives
    if (isupper(wrd->inword[0])) {
    i = mpos; continue;
    } // exclude those Adjectives that are used as a Noun
    if (isflex(wrd->inword, wrd->wl, "es") && (wrdm->e.N.fem ||
        wrdm->e.N.masculin || wrdm->numb == 1)) {
/* if the Adjective ends in -es and the Noun is Feminine, Masculine or Plural */
        wnprintfw("\nPRÜFE Übereinstimmung: %s ",
        wrd->inword);
        wnprintfw("<==> %s", wrdm->inword);
// print the above message and both the Adjective and the Noun
        bad_agree++;    // write the error for the statistics
    }
    else            // otherwise
    if (isflex(wrd->inword, wrd->wl, "er") &&
        wrdm->e.N.neuter && wrdm->numb == 0) {
// if the Adjective ends in -er and the Noun is Neuter and Singular
        wnprintfw("\nPRÜFE Übereinstimmung: %s ",
        wrd->inword);
```

```
        wnprintfw("<==> %s", wrdm->inword);
// print the above message and both the Adjective and the Noun
        wnprintfl("\n für ");
        wnprintfw("\n \"%s\" Möglicherweise ist zu benützen: '-e(n)'",
        wrd->inbase);
// print the above message and the Adjective
        bad_agree++;     // write the error for the statistics
    }
else
    if (isflex(wrd->inword, wrd->wl, "em") &&
        (wrdm->e.N.fem && wrdm->numb == 0)) {
// if the Adjective ends in -em and the Noun is Feminine, Singular
        wnprintfw("\nPRÜFE Übereinstimmung: %s ",
        wrd->inword);
        wnprintfw("<==> %s", wrdm->inword);
// print the above message and both the Adjective and the Noun
        wnprintfl("\n für ");
        wnprintfw("\n \"%s\" Möglicherweise ist zu benützen: '-e'",
        wrd->inbase);
// print the above message and the Adjective
        bad_agree++;    // write the error for the statistics
    }
    i++; continue;
```

Continuation of the above rule in the rules.h file:

```
{"A<A>N",         NULL, 33},                /* Adj (strong or weak) + N[ ] */
```

According to case 33, such phrases as *gutes Mensch*, *gutem Frau*, etc. will be wrong. Case 34 presents a rule that takes into account the weak declension of the Adjectives. In order to enable this rule, we had to re-name the Adjective used with a determiner. Re-naming means giving another sign. In this particular case we have renamed the Adjective *ö*.

```
     case 34:         /* Adj - Noun agreement, weak declension */
    if (isupper(wrd->inword[0])) {
    i = mpos; continue;
    }      // exclude those Adjectives that are used as a Noun
    if (isflex(wrd->inword, wrd->wl, "es")) {
// if the Adjective ends in -es
        wnprintfw("\nPRÜFE Übereinstimmung: %s ",
        wrd->inword);
        wnprintfw("<==> %s", wrdm->inword);
// print the above message and both the Adjective and the Noun
        wnprintfw("\n \"%s\" Möglicherweise ist zu benützen: '-e(n)'",
        wrd->inbase);
// print the above message and the Adjective
        bad_agree++;    // write the error for the statistics
    }
    else          // otherwise
    if (isflex(wrd->inword, wrd->wl, "em")) {
// if the Adjective ends in -em
        wnprintfw("\nPRÜFE Übereinstimmung: %s ",
        wrd->inword);
        wnprintfw("<==> %s", wrdm->inword);
```

```
// print the above message and both the Adjective and the Noun
        wnprintfl("\n für ");
        wnprintfw("\n \"%s\" Möglicherweise ist zu benützen: '-e(n)'",
        wrd->inbase);
// print the above message and the Adjective
        bad_agree++;    // write the error for the statistics
    }
    else
// etc. with the other case endings
    if (isflex(wrd->inword, wrd->wl, "er")) {
        wnprintfw("\nPRÜFE Übereinstimmung: %s ",
        wrd->inword);
        wnprintfw("<==> %s", wrdm->inword);
        wnprintfl("\n für ");
        wnprintfw("\n \"%s\" Möglicherweise ist zu benützen: '-e(n)'",
        wrd->inbase);
        bad_agree++;
    }
    i++; continue;
```

Continuation of the above rule in the rules.h file:

```
{"öN",        NULL, 34}, /* Determiner + week A + Noun */
```

In weak declension the Adjective can end only in *-e(n)*. All other Case endings are wrong, as specified by case 34. No differentiation is made when the ending is *-e* and when it is *-en*, because that involves correct recognition of the Case and needs further programming to do it. However, for Machine Translation, it has to be done.

3.7 *Wrong use of* haben *and its paradigm with a Past Participle*

Some Participles are used only with the Auxiliary Verb *sein*, others are used only with the Auxiliary Verb *haben* and still others are used both with *sein* and *haben*. Most dictionaries mark this usage and some grammar books provide a short list (Hammer's, 1995: 239–246). Below, we provide a rule to detect the wrong use of the Auxiliary Verb *haben* (instead of *sein*) with a Past Participle:

```
     case 20:          /* E <-> haben */
    if (wrd->esyn == 'E' && wrd->e.V.sein == 1) {
/* if the Past Participle (the 1st word) is used only with "sein" and marked so */
       wnprintfw("\nPRÜFE Übereinstimmung: %s ",
       wrd->inword); // print the above message and the 1st word
       wnprintfw("<==> %s", wrdm->inword);
// print the sign <==> and the 2nd word
       wnprintfl("\nMöglicherweise ist zu benützen die richtige
           Form des Verbes: sein");
// print the above message
       bad_verbs++;        // write this error for the statistics
    }
    break;
```

Continuation of the above rule in the rules.h file:

```
{"EY",   NULL, 20},   /* wrong use of haben with a Past Participle */
```

According to case 20, the expression *geblieben hat* will be wrong. The correct usage will be *geblieben ist* (or any other Verb from the *sein* paradigm). Note that the Past Participle and the Auxiliary Verb *haben* are linked directly, there is nothing to stand between them. This was the case when the Auxiliary Verb *haben* was positioned after the Past Participle. Now, we will consider the case when the Auxiliary Verb *haben* is used before the Past Participle:

```
    case 21:        /* Y<-> E */
   if (wrdm->esyn == 'E' && wrdm->e.V.sein) {
/* if the Past Participle (the 2nd word) is used only with "sein" and marked so */
      wnprintfw("\nPRÜFE Übereinstimmung: %s ",
      wrd->inword);
// print the above message and the 1st word
      wnprintfw("<==> %s", wrdm->inword);
// print the sign <==> and the 2nd word
      wnprintfl("\n Möglicherweise ist zu benützen die richtige
         Form des Verbes: \"sein\"");
// print the above message
      bad_agree++;        // write this error for the statistics
   }
   i = mpos; continue;
```

Continuation of the above rule in the rules.h file:

```
{"Y<TPAäöN>E",      NULL, 21},         /* wrong agreement */
```

Note the alternative Parts of Speech < > that can stand between the Auxiliary Verb *haben* and the Past Participle. According to case 21, the expression *hat erloschen* will be wrong. The correct way to say that will be *ist erloschen*. Cases 20 and 21 will work provided that we have marked in the DW the Past Participles that are only used with *sein*: E[s].

3.8 *Wrong use of* sein *and its paradigm with a Past Participle*

Those Past Participles that are used only with *haben* (and its paradigm) are marked as: E[h]. When such a Participle is used with the Auxiliary Verb *sein* (or its paradigm) the following cases (19, 37) will detect the error.

```
    case 19:        /* E <-> sein */
   if (wrdm->esyn == 'X' && wrd->e.V.haben == 1) {
/* if the 2nd word is "sein" or a Verb from its paradigm and the Past Participle (the 1st word)
is used only with "haben" and marked so */
      wnprintfw("\nPRÜFE Übereinstimmung: %s ",
      wrd->inword);     // print the above message and the 1st word
      wnprintfw("<==> %s", wrdm->inword);
// print the sign <==> and the 2nd word
      wnprintfl("\nMöglicherweise ist zu benützen die richtige
         Form des Verbes: haben");
// print the above message
      bad_verbs++;      // write this error for the statistics
   }
   break;
```

Continuation of the above rule in the rules.h file:

```
{"[Ee]X",   NULL, 19},   /* wrong use of "sein" with a Past Participle */
```

Note that the Past Participle and the Auxiliary Verb *sein* are linked directly, there is nothing to stand between them and the Auxiliary Verb *sein* follows after the Past Participle. According to case 19, the expression *gefressen ist* will be wrong. The correct form is *gefressen hat*. This was the case when the Auxiliary Verb *sein* was positioned after the Past Participle. Now, we will consider the case when the Auxiliary Verb *sein* is used before the Past Participle:

```
    case 37:                          /* X<->E[h] */
   if ((wrdm->esyn == 'E' && wrdm->e.V.haben) {
/* if the Past Participle (the 2nd word) is used only with "haben" and marked so */
      wnprintfw("\nPRÜFE Übereinstimmung: %s ",
      wrd->inword);  // print the above message and the 1st word
      wnprintfw("<==> %s", wrdm->inword);
// print the sign <==> and the 2nd word
      wnprintfl("\n Möglicherweise ist zu benützen die richtige
          Form des Verbes: \"haben\"");
// print the above message
      bad_agree++;        // write this error for the statistics
   }
   i = mpos; continue;
```

Continuation of the above rule in the rules.h file:

```
{"X<TPAäöN>E",       NULL, 37},        /* agreement */
```

Note the alternative Parts of Speech < > that can stand between the Auxiliary Verb '*sein*' and the Past Participle.

According to case 37, the expression *ist gegolten* will be wrong. The correct form is *hat gegolten*. That is on the understanding that the Past Participles, used only with *haben*, are marked respectively in the DW. The Past Participles used both with *haben* and *sein* are problematic, because analysis of the context is needed to determine when the same Participle is used with *haben* and when with *sein*. It is possible to separate those contexts where such a Participle is used either only with *haben* or only with *sein*, but there will be exceptions, and, consequently, program errors if we cannot deal efficiently with the exceptions.

3.9 *Wrong use of* zu *with forms of the Main Verb*

The Verbal Particle *zu* can only be used with the Main Form of the Verb (1st and 3rd person Plural). The use of the Verbal Particle *zu* with the other Forms of the Main Verb or with the Past Participle, is wrong. Case 43 presents a rule specifying that the use of *zu* with 3rd person singular of the Verb is wrong:

```
    case 43:         /* zu + 3d person Singular of the Verb */
   if (wrd->esyn == 'B' && wrdm->person) {
/* if "zu" is used as Infinitival Particle and if the main Verb is 3d Person Singular */
      wnprintfl("\nFALSCH: "); // print this message
      wnprintfl(wrdm->inword); // print the Verb
      wnprintfw("\n gebrauche Grundform des Verbes");
// print the above message
      bad_verbs++; // send the error for the statistics
```

```
}
i = mpos; continue;
```

Continuation of the above rule in the rules.h file:

```
{"'zu'[vVXY]",      NULL, 43},              /** BV **/
```

According to case 43 the phrase *zu kauft* is wrong. Cases 44 and 88 present a rule specifying that the use of *zu*, with the Past Participle, is wrong:

```
      case 44:          /* use of "zu" with Past Participle */
    if (wrd->esyn == 'B') {
// if "zu" is used as Infinitival Particle
       wnprintfl("\nFALSCH: "); // print this message
       wnprintfl(wp[i+1]->inword); // print the Participle
       wnprintfw("\n gebrauche Grundform des Verbes");
// print the above message
       bad_verbs++;  // write this error for the statistics
    }
    i = mpos; continue;
```

Continuation of the above rule in the rules.h file:

```
{"'zu'ET",          NULL, 44},      /* wrong use of "zu"  */
```

According to case 44 the phrase *zu gekauft* is wrong. Case 88 below is slightly different because it prints the irregular forms of the verb.

```
      case 88:          /* zu E */
    if (wrdm->syn == 'E'
      && wrdm->gflag == 'i') {
// if the 2nd word is Past Participle and if it is marked as irregular
      wnprintfl("\n");
      wnprintfw("GEBRAUCHE die Grundform
           des Verbes von \"%s\"", wrdm->inbase);
// print the above message and the Past Participle
      wnprintfw("\nFormen des Verbes sind: \"%s\"",
              wrdm->inbase);
      wnprintfw("\n %s", wrdm->irrform);
// print the above message and the irregular forms of the Past Participle
      bad_usage++;    // write this error for the statistics
    }
   else
    if (wrdm->syn == 'E') {
      wnprintfl("\n");
      wnprintfw("GEBRAUCHE die Grundform
              des Verbes von \"%s\"", wrdm->inbase);
// print the above message and the Past Participle
      bad_usage++;    // write this error for the statistics
    }
    break;
```

Continuation of the above rule in the rules.h file:

```
{"'zu'E",      NULL, 88},
```

According to case 88 the phrase *zu gemacht* is wrong. The program will print out all irregular forms of the Verb and will suggest the Basic Form (Present Tense, 1st person Plural – *machen*).

3.10 Wrong use of a Relative Pronoun or Article after a Transitive or Dative Verb

Certain Articles (*des, deren*, etc.) and Relative Pronouns (*jemandes, niemandes*, etc.) cannot be used after Transitive and Dative Verbs. Case 53 introduces this rule:

```
    case 53:          /* wrong use of V + Article or Pronoun */
   if (wrd->e.V.transit && wrd->e.V.dativ) {
// if the Verb is marked both as Transitive and Dative
     wnprintfw("\nVERB stimmt nicht mit dem Artikel überein: %s ",
     wrd->inword);
// print the above message and the Verb
     wnprintfw("<==> %s", wrdm->inword);
// print the Article or the Pronoun
     wnprintfw("\nFALSCH \"%s\"", wrdm->inword);
// print the above message and the Article or the Pronoun
        wnprintfl("\n gebrauche: \"den, die, das, ein, eine, einen,
etc.\"");
// print the above message
     wrd->cflag = 'r';                  /* registered */
     bad_agree++;     // write this error for the statistics
   }
   i = mpos; continue;
```

Continuation of the above rule in the rules.h file:

```
  {"ë'des'",       NULL, 53},
  {"ë'dessen'",      NULL, 53},
  {"ë'jemandes'",      NULL, 53},
  {"ë'jemands'",     NULL, 53},
  {"ë'niemands'",      NULL, 53},
  {"ë'niemandes'",      NULL, 53},
  {"ë'deren'",     NULL, 53},
// etc., naming each individual word
```

According to rule 53, the phrase *abraten des* ... will be wrong. Note that we have re-named the Verbs that are both Transitive and Dative in order to differentiate them in this particular context. The re-naming of a particular Part of Speech for particular purpose and context is exemplified by case 36 in the file "parser.c(pp)":

```
     case 36: /* re-naming of the Verb for a specific role */
     if (wrd->e.V.transit == 1 && wrd->e.V.dativ == 1)
/*if the Verb (the 1st of two words, in sequence) is both Transitive and Dative */
      wrd->syn = 'ë';  // its sign is  ë
     else  // if not,
      wrd->syn = 'V';     // its sign remains V
      continue;
```

Continuation of the above rule in the rules.h file:

```
{"[ZVe]'des'",      NULL, 36},            /* [at] des */
{"[ZVe]'jemandes'",      NULL, 36},      /* [at] jemandes */
```

etc. Articles or Pronouns, where [at] is the Dictionary information about the verb (transitive or dative).

Note that the re-naming of the Verb is valid only in this particular context (only when followed by the specified word(s)).

3.11 *Impossible combination of two words*

Often, for various grammatical or semantical reasons, two specific words cannot be used one after the other in a context. When they are, case 55 monitors this usage and declares it wrong:

```
      case 55:    /* impossible combination of two consecutive words */
       wnprintfw("\nFALSCHE Übereinstimmung: %s ",
       wrd->inword);  // print the above message and the first word
       wnprintfw("<==> %s", wp[mpos-1]->inword);
// print <==> and the second word
       wnprintfw("\n oder falsche : %s", wp[mpos-1]->inword);
// print the above message and the second word
       bad_agree++;     // write this error for the statistics
       i = mpos; continue;
```

Continuation of the above rule in the rules.h file:

```
{"'bis''des'~[&C]", NULL, 55}, /* Prep. + Gen/Nom/Dat */
{"'ab''des'~[&C]", NULL, 55}, /* Prep. + Nom/Gen. */
{"'an''meines'~[&C]", NULL, 55}, /* Prep. + Nom/Gen. */
// etc. word combinations
```

According to case 55, the Prepositions *bis des* cannot be used consecutively. Note that case 55 is valid only for two consecutive words, without intervening words between them. Case 55 can only be used for individual words, which we cannot include in a group and mark the whole group with a sign. When we have many such impossible combinations of two words, it is better to invent a code and mark these words in the DW and then make a case to cover them all, without specifying the individual words in the program.

3.12 *Wrong use of the Reflexive Pronoun*

The Reflexive Pronoun *sich* cannot be used with non-reflexive Verbs. For example, one cannot write *gurren sich*. Most Dictionaries mark the Verb when it is Reflexive. Cases 108 and 109 below demonstrate a rule, according to which it is an error to use a non-reflexive Verb with the Reflexive Pronoun *sich* used after (108) or before (109) the verb.

```
    case 108:       /* V[z] + sich following the Verb */
  if (wrd->e.V.dativ == 1)
  break;        // exclude the Dative Verbs
  if (wrd->e.V.reflexiv == 1)
  break;       // exclude the Reflexive Verbs
```

```
    if (!stricmp(wrd->inword, "sorgen") ||
         !stricmp(wrd->inword, "bezeichnen"))
    break;
```
// exclude the above mentioned Verbs, as exceptions to this rule
```
    if (wrd->e.V.intransit == 1) {
```
/* if the 1st word (the Verb) is Intransitive and, it goes without saying, non-reflexive, because all Reflexive Verbs are excluded from consideration */
```
      wnprintfw("\nNACH: \"%s\"", wrd->inword);
```
// print the above message and the first word
```
      wnprintfl("\n 'sich' ist unmöglich.");
```
// print the above message
```
      bad_agree++;    // write this error for the statistics
    }
    break;
```

Continuation of the above rule in the rules.h file:

```
{"v'<R>sich'",        NULL, 108},
```

Case 108 covers all contexts when the Reflexive Pronoun *sich* follows immediately after the non-reflexive Verb. Case 109 below covers all contexts when the Reflexive Pronoun *sich* precedes the non-reflexive Verb:

```
     case 109:       /* sich + V[z] */
    if (wrdm->e.V.dativ == 1)
    break;          // exclude the Dative Verbs
    if (wrdm->e.V.reflexiv == 1)
    break;          // exclude the Reflexive Verbs
      if (!stricmp(wrdm->inword, "sorgen") || !stricmp(wrdm->inword,
"bezeichnen"))
    break;  // exclude the above mentioned Verbs, as exceptions to this rule
    if (wrdm->e.V.intransit == 1) {
// if the 2nd word (the Verb) is Intransitive and, it goes without saying, non-reflexive, because
// all Reflexive Verbs are excluded from consideration
       wnprintfw("\nBEVOR: \"%s\"", wrdm->inword);
// print the above message and the second word
       wnprintfl("\n 'sich' ist unmöglich.");
// print the above message
       bad_agree++;  // write this error for the statistics
    }
    break;
```

Continuation of the above rule in the rules.h file:

```
{"'sich'<TSN>v",      NULL, 109},
```

The Reflexive Pronoun *sich* can be separated from the Verb by an Article, Pronoun or Noun (included between the arrows). Note that the Verb 'V' is re-named to 'v' to cover the contexts for this particular Case. In the DW, the reflexive and non-reflexive verbs are marked as follows:

allianzieren=V[r]
arbeiten=Z[r]/N[FC]
ablauten=V[z]

abwassern=Z[z]/N[US]
etc.

where [r] codes the reflexive, [z] codes the non-reflexive verbs.

3.13 Wrong use of Article in Genitive (between two Nouns)

Certain German Articles and Pronouns, depending on their Case, cannot be used between two Nouns to express possessiveness (Genitive). Case 71 detects this error:

```
     case 71:          /* N von N  Genitive */
    if (wrd->esyn == 'N' && wrdm->esyn == 'N') {
// when we have two Nouns, first and last
       wnprintfw("\nPRÜFE den richtigen Artikel zwischen: %s ",
       wrd->inword);   // print the above message and the first Noun
       wnprintfw("<==> %s", wrdm->inword);
// print <==> and the second Noun
       wnprintfl("\n gebrauche eventuell:
           \"des, dem, den, der, von, eines, einer, etc.\"");
// print the above message
       wrd->cflag = 'r';                     /* registered */
       bad_agree++;          // write this error for the statistics
    }
    i = mpos; continue;
```

Continuation of the above rule in the rules.h file:

```
   {"N'diese'N",    NULL, 71},    /* N diese N Genitive and Dative  */
   {"N'mein'N",     NULL, 71},    /* N mein N Genitive and Dative  */
// etc. Pronouns or Articles
```

According to case 71, the sentence:

Die ***Frau diese Mann*** *ist gross.*

will be wrong and the program will suggest alternatives.

3.14 Wrong reference of a Relative Pronoun

The Pronominal Reference is a major issue in spell-checking and Machine Translation. This is a huge problem to resolve satisfactorily because the Pronoun can be far away from the Noun it refers to. The reference-checking rules are not straight forward as often there is more than one Noun as a possible referent of the Pronoun. In those cases where the Pronoun has more than one meaning (more than one possible translation into another language) the difficulty to find its referent is even greater, as in *sie*. The Personal Pronoun Nominal Case *sie* (*Sie*) can mean *she, it, them, her* (*sie ist eine Frau, er sah sie, sie ist es, sie sind es*) and *they* (*sie sind hier*). When it is written with a capital letter it means *you* or *she* (*Sind Sie schon lange hier?, Es ist eine Sie*). This means that in order to translate the Pronoun correctly we must find first its referent. We will discuss the Pronominal Reference again in the chapter 'Machine Translation'. Here, we will consider only one type of reference: that of a Relative Pronoun to a preceding Noun. Case 82 introduces a procedure to detect the wrong reference of a Relative Pronoun denoting place (*wohin, woher*, etc.) to a Noun denoting a 'human being':

```
  case 82:           /* human being + Pronoun for non-human being */
 if (wrd->e.N.human) {
// if the first word (the Noun) denotes a "human being"
    wnprintfw("\n PRÜFE: \"%s\" + ",
    wrd->inword); // print the above message and the first word (the Noun)
    wnprintfw("\nFALSCHE: \"%s\"", wrdm->inword);
// print the above message and the second word (the Pronoun)
    wnprintfl("\n GEBRAUCHE: \"wer, (wem, wen, der, die, das)\"");
// print the above message
    wrd->cflag = 'r';                    /* registered */
    bad_agree++;         // write this error for the statistics
 }
 i = mpos; continue;
```

Continuation of the above rule in the rules.h file:

```
{"N<,>'wohin'",     NULL, 82},      /* wrong reference */
{"N<,>'woher'",     NULL, 82},      /* wrong reference */
```

According to case 82, the sentence ***Er ist der Mann, wohin ich habe*** ... will be wrong. Case 83 introduces a procedure to detect the wrong reference of a Relative Pronoun denoting 'human being' (***wem, wen, wer***, etc.) to a Noun that is not denoting a 'human being':

```
  case 83:           /* non-human being + Pronoun for human being */
 if (!wrd->e.N.human) {
// if the first word (the Noun) does not denote a "human being"
    wnprintfw("\n PRÜFE belebtes Substantiv von:\"%s\" + ",
    wrd->inword);
// print the above message and the first word (the Noun)
    wnprintfw("\nevt. FALSCH: \"%s\"", wrdm->inword);
// print the above message and the second word (the Pronoun)
    wnprintfl("\n GEBRAUCHE sonst: \"welche(r,s)\"");
// print the above message
    wrd->cflag = 'r';                    /* registered */
    bad_agree++;  // write this error for the statistics
 }
 i = mpos; continue;
```

Continuation of the above rule in the rules.h file:

```
{"N<,>'wer'",     NULL, 83},        /* wrong reference */
{"N<,>'wem'",     NULL, 83},        /* wrong reference */
{"N<,>'wen'",     NULL, 83},        /* wrong reference */
```

According to case 83, the sentence ***Der Tag, wer*** ... will be wrong. The correct form is *Der Tag, wo* ....

3.15 Wrong use of a Preposition

In German certain Adjectives are used with a particular Preposition (Prepositional Construction). The use of another Preposition in this context will be wrong. For example: *abhängig von* (dependent on), *aufmerksam auf* (aware of), *berechtigt zu* (justified in), *bezeichnend für* (characteristic of), etc., is the correct usage. We have devised a case for each Preposition, when it is the only Preposition used with certain words (Adjectives and Nouns). Case 99 below checks for the correct use of the Preposition *für*:

```
 case 99:        /* A -> P */
if (!stricmp(wrdm->inword, "für")) {
i = mpos; continue;
}
// exclude the Preposition für from consideration (when you meet it)
/* Note: here we can exclude also other Prepositions, if some of the words from the set of
words are used with other Prepositions as well. */
if (wrd->fflag) {
/* if the first word (the Adjective, in this case) has the code 'fflag'
   this means that it can be used with the Preposition für */
  if (!wrdm->fflag) {
// and only then, if the second word (the Preposition) has not the code 'fflag'
     wnprintfl("\n DIE RICHTIGE Wörter sind:\n");
     wnprintfl(wrd->inword);
// print the above message and the first word (the Adjective)
     wnprintfl(" für "); // print: für
     wnprintfl("\n");    // start a new line
     wnprintfw(" PRÜFE wenn \"%s\"", wrdm->inword);
// print the above message and the second word (the Preposition)
     wnprintfw(" kann nach \"%s\"", wrd->inword);
// print the above message and the first word (the Adjective)
     wnprintfl(" benützt werden.\n");
// print the above message and start a new line
     bad_agree++;    // write this error for the statistics
  }
}
i = mpos; continue;
```

Continuation of the above rule in the rules.h file:

```
{"AP",       NULL, 99}, /* Prep. für used with a specific Adjective */
```

In the DW those words that can be used with the Preposition *für* will be coded as follows

charakteristisch=A[X]
fuer=P[XZ]

where [X] is equivalent to *fflag* in the program.

According to case 99, such phrases as *charakteristisch von* (characteristic of), *empfänglich zu* (susceptible to), *bezeichnend von* (characteristic of), *typisch von* (typical of), etc. will be wrong and displayed for correction, suggesting the correct Preposition *für* instead.

Similar cases can be developed for any Preposition and any Part of Speech, when we are absolutely sure that this Preposition is used only with these particular words and no other Prepositions can be used with them. If there is another Preposition that can be used with some of the words, we can exclude it at the very beginning of the case. However, if there are several or many Prepositions that can be used with this particular set of the words, then we have to exclude these words, otherwise our rule will be useless.

4 French grammatical rules

All source code used above for the English and German languages can be successfully modified for the French error-detecting grammatical rules: wrong agreement between two words in Gender, Number and Person, wrong use of the Reflexive Pronoun, etc. Below, we provide a few cases to illustrate the similarity of the procedures. Case 13 verifies the agreement in number and person between a noun and an auxiliary verb.

```
case 13:
 if (wrd->numb != wrdm->numb ||
    wrd->person != wrdm->person) {
// if the two words do not agree in number or person
   wnprintfw("\nESSAYEZ la concordance: %s ",
   wrd->inword);
   wnprintfw("<==> %s", wrdm->inword);
   wnprintfw("\n FAUX nombre/personne de: %s",
   wrdm->inword);
// print the above message
   bad_usage++; // count the error
 }
 i = mpos; continue; // exit the case
```

Continuation of the above rule in the French rules.h file:

```
{"N[YXxU]",      NULL, 13},
```

Case 13 will detect the error in: *Les femmes été ....*
Case 69 below checks for agreement between an article or pronoun and the following noun.

```
case 69: /* Article, Pronoun - Noun agreement in Gender */
 if (wp[mpos+1]->syn == 'N') wrdm = wp[mpos+1];
// fix the position of the word
 if (wrdm->e.N.masculin ||wrdm->e.N.neuter ||
   wrdm->uflag == 1) {
 i = mpos; continue;
 }
// exclude all masculine and neuter nouns used as 2nd word
 if (!stricmp(wrdm->inword, "débat")) {
 i = mpos; continue;
 }
// exclude the above word used as 2nd word
 if ((wrdm->e.N.fem) || (wrdm->numb)) {
// if the 2nd word is feminine or plural
 wnprintfw("\nESSAYEZ la concordance: %s ",
 wrd->inword);
 wnprintfw("<==> %s", wrdm->inword);
// print the above message and the words
 bad_agree++; // count the error
 }
 i = mpos; continue;
```

Continuation of the above rule in the French rules.h file:

```
{"'le'<AO>N",  NULL, 69},
```

```
{"'un'<AO>N",   NULL, 69},
{"'d'un'<AO>N",   NULL, 69},
{"'du'<AO>N",   NULL, 69},
{"'au'<AO>N",   NULL, 69},
{"'quel'<AO>N",   NULL, 69},
{"'ce'<AO>N",   NULL, 69},
{"'cet'<AO>N",   NULL, 69},
```

Case 69 will detect the error in: *Le femme ....*

5 Italian grammatical rules

Italian grammatical features do not differ from French. The only difference is in the actual grammatical endings, the actual words or wordforms. The rules establishing the incorrect agreement are the same and we can write the warning messages in Italian instead of English. Case 69 below looks for wrong agreement in gender.

```
    case 69:   /* agreement in Gender */
      if (wp[mpos+1]->syn == 'N') wrdm = wp[mpos+1];
// define the position of the word
      if (wrdm->e.N.masculin || wrdm->uflag == 1) {
      i = mpos; continue;
      }
// exclude masculine nouns
      if ((wrdm->e.N.fem) || wrdm->e.N.neuter
        || (wrdm->numb)) {
// if the 2nd word is feminine or neuter or plural
      wnprintfw("\nCHECK the agreement: %s ",
      wrd->inword);
      wnprintfw("<==> %s", wrdm->inword);
// print the above message and the words
      bad_agree++; // count the error
      }
      i = mpos; continue;
```

Continuation of the above rule in the Italian rules.h file:

```
{"'il'<A>N",    NULL, 69},
{"'un'<A>N",    NULL, 69},
{"'dello'<A>N",   NULL, 69},
```

In other words, *il*, *un* and *dello* can be used only with masculine nouns. It is an error when they are used with feminine, neuter or plural nouns.

To sum up, the languages are different, but the programming procedures are very similar, often identical for the agreement. German grammar is much more complicated to describe for the computer, because the agreement in number and gender depends on the case. French and Italian have no case, only gender. English grammar is unproblematic for the computer compared with the other three languages since we only have to consider agreement in number.

There is no grammatical error that we cannot detect by means of a rule. The more general the rule, the more the exceptions and, we must therefore take special care to exclude all exceptions. All rules are language specific, we cannot make an error-checking software program for the English language and use the same software program to detect errors in German or another language.

6 Lexical Semantics

There can be satisfactory parsing and grammatical spell-checking without lexical semantics, but there cannot be good Machine Translation, Question Answering, Text Attribution, Information Retrieval, etc. without it. In this chapter we will describe our practical experience in lexical and computational semantics – namely, how we have structured it for use in our Question Answering (Georgiev, *Dialogue*, 2003) and *Word and Text Attribution* (Georgiev, 2003a) software programs, which we will describe later in this book.

1 Thesauri – *Softhesaurus, Linguaterm and Geoatlas*

The software programs *Softhesaurus*, *Linguaterm* and *Geoatlas* (Georgiev, 1993b, 1994–94a) were primarily constructed as Computer Assisted Vocabulary Learning tools and later adapted for the purposes of automatic content recognition. These thesauri present an alternative method for description of lexical semantics that can be used both by humans and computers. They contain a database that can be used for summarized recognition of the meaning of the sentence.

The Artificial Language for Semantic Description, upon which the thesauri were built, answers the need for standardization and stratification of lexical semantics for the purposes of Text Processing, natural language based Artificial Intelligence and teaching and learning foreign language vocabularies, including terminology and lexical semantics.

2 Introduction

The Artificial Language for Semantic Description (ALSD), proposed in this study, combines all methods hitherto known in lexicography, namely:

a) arranging the words in sets, for each Part of Speech separately, as synonyms;
b) arranging the words in sets as synonyms, according to a common meaning – irrespective of Part of Speech (thesaurus);
c) grouping together words that belong to the same subject field;
d) selection of the diverse meanings ingredient in a word using componential analysis and single language dictionaries;
e) comparing and contrasting the word meanings in various ways, including the contrast known as 'antonymical'.

In short, ALSD is a classification of knowledge about the objective and subjective reality contained in the meaning of words.

Meaning is a complex phenomenon, stretching simultaneously in two different – syntagmatical (contextual) and paradigmatical (inherent) – directions, and no single method is capable of depicting it fully. Besides, all methods used in lexicography have controversial points.

ALSD specifies the relevant meaning or meanings of the word and codes those meanings for computer use. Since there are no exact guide-lines as to what is the most accurate presentation of lexical meaning, it must be stressed that ALSD is a model of the lexico-semantical system of the language. The adequacy of this model can be tested only when it is used in a computer software program for understanding the meaning of the sentence and that of the text as a whole. ALSD is a meta language that is applicable to any other natural language. The standardized word meanings are translated into this meta language and the computer uses the meta language – not the natural language – to understand the meaning of the word, irrespective of natural language. The meta language consists of codes representing meanings and relationships between different meanings.

3 Purpose and scope

The aim of this lexical study was:

a) to describe lexical semantics in greater detail and precision than was previously done and to study word meaning in its relationship to the meaning(s) of other words, looked at from different angles;
b) to describe lexical semantics for the computer and thus to create an electronic dictionary capable of explaining the meaning of the word to the artificial mind of the computer, a dictionary that can serve as a basis for the construction of an artificial intellect based on Natural Language. The artificial intellect is seen as a subjective computer model of the outer reality, expressed in meta language;
c) to provide ample descriptive material for text (sentence) analysis and synthesis and for computer aided language learning and translation;
d) to provide an alternative way for learning and teaching word meanings, concepts and terminology. The object of analysis was the word, as presented in the existing thesauri, synonymical, thematical and single language dictionaries. The scope was restricted to about 23,000 English word entries of current use, including some terminology (12,000 English, German, French and Spanish linguistic terms) and about 4,000 place names in English, German, French and Italian. This vocabulary forms our database for the construction of the meta language used by the computer for understanding the meaning of the word.

4 Presentation

In order to study the lexical meaning of the words linguists often compare or relate them by assembling them in groups of words. Depending on the selection criteria there are several different approaches to grouping words together: as synonyms or antonyms, thematical (subject field), thesaurus (starting with the thesaurus of Roget (1852)), and according to a common componential meaning (Trier, 1931, 1934a, 1934b; Fodor and Katz, 1964, etc.). What all these approaches have in common is the fact that the words are gathered in a group according to a particular meaning they all share. All these approaches are faced with the same difficulty: to choose which words are eligible to enter a particular group and to justify the criteria of selection. In our study we have also accepted the fundamental truth that words have meanings and that there can be as many word groups as there are meanings in the whole vocabulary. With this in mind, as a guideline we started grouping the words together, using the selection criteria described below.

4.1 Syntagmatical synonyms

This is an unstructured, non-hierarchical relationship between two or more words, whereby one word (or more) can substitute all other words from the same semantic group, context permitting, without changing the meaning of the sentence but simply making its meaning less specific. For example, the words: *assert, claim, allege, insist, mention, maintain, note, utter, mumble, reveal, state, announce, repeat, disclose, allude, hint, imply, observe, concede, suggest, emphasize*, etc., can be replaced, context permitting (because some have other meanings as well, and for a particular meaning there are restrictions governing its use), by the word ***say***, without altering the meaning of the sentence. For example:

He claims that he is innocent.
*He **says** that he is innocent.*
She suggested that we should go home.
*She **said** that we should go home.*
He mentioned that he is going today.
*He **said** that he is going today.*
We insisted repeatedly that we must go.
*We **said** repeatedly that we must go.*

Each of the above mentioned words relates only to the word *say* and does not relate, in this instance, to any other word from the set of words. In practical terms this type of relationship between *say* and the other words from the set means that we don't have to explain to the computer the meaning of all those words. It suffices to say that in a specified context each one of them is equivalent to *say*. However, there are contexts, in which we cannot replace the words from this particular group with *say*, directly, for example:

He mentioned him in his report.
He insisted upon his innocence.

unless we specify that in this context *mentioned* must be replaced by *said something about* and *insisted upon his* must be replaced by *said that he is*. In the latter example, *insisted upon* can be replaced by words belonging to other groups, such as *believed in, knew about*.

For computer use only, in the above mentioned software programs we have replaced the natural language words with artificial codes. In this case the words: *admit, point out, allege*, etc. are coded with the artificial sign DC. The word *say* bears the code DC' to distinguish it from all other words in this set and to let the computer program 'know' that *say* acts as a substitute to all other words bearing the code DC. Below the reader will find listed most words that can act as substitutes (syntagmatical synonyms) of other words in English.
(Note: This is also a list of the most important words (head words) in language teaching. The words listed below should be learnt first when teaching English as a foreign language, because then the students can have an earlier opportunity to express themselves in English correctly using fewer words. The later stages of learning English vocabulary will gradually include all the words from the group.) List of head words that can substitute all other words in their group:

agree(ment)	aim	allow
area	ask	begin (ning)
big	brief(ly)	capture
cemetery	change	chief
clean	clergyman	coloured
come	command	constant(ly)
control	cut	decrease
dirt	disagree(ment)	disconnect
eat	educate education	educated

encircle	end	enter
fail	find	fly
free(dom)	gather	get
give	govern	grave
hate	have	hell
hide	hit	increase
job	keep	kill (-er)
know (-ledge)	leadership	lie (-er)
like	link	live
look	love	make
man	management	meaning
meet	move	need
needless	next of kin	nice
often	open	paradise
place	place	plan
power	put	rare(ly)
regulate	restrain	rule
say	secret	see
send	show	song
stop	strength	study
take	talk	tell
terrorist	think	thought
travel	try	understand
uneducated	unite	use
vehicle	vessel	villain
want	weak	wish
woman	work	write (-ing)

List of the entire group of words under the 'head word' (in bold):

say, pass on info	**end, ending,** finish	**begin**(ning), initial, **start**	**get**(ting)
admit	abolish, abolition	activate	accrue
advocate	abrogate	arise	accruing
allege	abut	break out	acquire(ment)
allude	accomplish	commence	acquisition
announce	annul	embark	attain
articulate	be done with	embryonic	capture
be of the opinion	be over	emerge(nce)	earn
boast	be through with	engender	gain
confirm	bring to an end	genesis	inherit
declare	bring to rest	give rise	obtain
disclose	cancel	give the go ahead	procure
divulge	cease, cessation	inception	receive
emphasize	close, closure	initiate	retrieve
emphasize	close, closure	initiate	seize, seizure
express a view	come to a close	initiation	take hold of
express an opinion	come to an end	launch	
hold the view	complete (-ion)	lay the foundations	
imply	conclude	milestone	
indicate	conclusion	nascency, nascent	
indicate	deactivate	offset	
insinuate	discontinue	onset	
insist	discontinuation	open	

let be known	do away	origin(ate) (-ion)	
maintain	do with	outset	
make a statement	draw to a close	put into effect	
mean	elapse	recommence	
mention	eradicate	resume	
mumble	expire	root	
mutter	final(e), finalize	set(-out)	
note(d)	give a final touch	source	
observe	halt	take effect	
persist	interrupt (-ion)	trigger	
phrase	nip in the bud	undertake	
postulate	nullify		
reiterate	outcome		
repeat	phase out		
speak	put an end		
spell out	suspend		
stipulate	terminal		
suggest	terminate		
swear	termination		
tell	terminus		
testify	thistle out		
utter	ultimate		
	verge		
	wind up		
etc.	etc.	etc.	etc.

Note that there is no strict guideline as to which words to include or exclude from the above lists, which of them are synonymous or near synonymous and which not. The inclusion of every new synonym leads us to believe that its synonyms should also be included in the group. Therefore this word relationship can easily transform itself into another type of word relationship, described in 4.3. Below is a list of linguistic terms that can act as 'head words' in their own group of terms:

acoustics	action
adaptation	agglutinative language
agreement	alliteration
alphabet	analytic language
analysis	anaphora
aorist	apposition
area	arrangement
article	artificial language
aspect	aspiration
assimilation	assonance
attraction	attribute
augment	auxiliary word
baltic languages	beginning
bond	boundary
case	category
celtic languages	class
classification	clause
compound	coherence
computer editors	compound word
conditional	computer language
consonant	conjugation
constraint	constituent

contact
continuous
correlation
degree
derivation
dictionary
diphthongization
distinctive feature
ending
euphony
expression
extension
flexion
formation
function
glide
gradation
grammar
grammatical unit
hierarchy
homonym
hypotaxis
image
infinitive
intonation
inversion
item
language
length
linguistic categories
macrolinguistics
marker
member
metaplasm
method
model
monologue
morpheme
morphology
mutation
norm
order
part
part of the sentence
pause
phases of articulation
phonology
phraseological unit
plural
position
principal parts
punctuation mark
question
relation

construction
content
contraction
definition
deixis
dialect
diphthong
disassimilation
dual
epithet
exaggeration
expressivity
field
form
fricative
german languages
government
grade
grammatical category
graphical sign
higher units of language
homonym(y)
idiom
indian language group
inflexion
intonation
iranian language group
juncture
law
level
linguistics
mark
meaning
metaphor
metathesis
modality
modification
mood
morphologization
motivation
neutralization
opposition
pair
part of speech
passive
perfect
phonetics
phrase
pitch
polysemy
priming
prosody
quantifier
reference

rhythm	rhyme
root	roman languages
semantics	school
slavonic languages	sentence
speech	smallest unit
stanza	sound group
stress	speech organ
study of language	stem
study of language	structural unit
stylistics	style
subordination	subjunctive
substitution	substitute
syllable	suprasegmental
synonym	synecdoche
syntactical hierarchy	synonymy
syntagm	syntactical unit
synthetic languages	syntax
tagging	system
theory	tense
timbre	thinking
transition	transcription
transposition	translation
unit	type of sentence
unit of meaning	unit of expression
unit of speech	unit of sound
unit of time	unit of measure
use	unity
variant	utterance
variation	variant of a language
versification	verse
voice	vocabulary
word	vowel
word-group	word-combination
etc.	

For example, the head word 'Part(s) of Speech' can substitute all the words from the group, listed below, context permitting, in the following three languages:

English	**German**	**French**
Parts of Speech	**Redeteile**	**Parties du discours**
noun	Substantiv	nom
verb	Verbum	verbe
adjective	Adjektiv	adjectif
numeral	Zahlwort	numéral
etc.		

As you see from the above example, the spelling of these terms is language specific, but the meaning is the same. In order to let the computer 'know' what type of word relationship the code designates, we have used a number placed before the two-letter code. The syntagmatical synonyms are marked with 1: 1DC; 1RG; 1RD, etc. When learning a language, especially learning to speak (not to understand!) with a limited vocabulary, it is essential to learn the words listed above first, because they can substitute all those words in one's native language that mean the same, but for which the speaker does not know the English equivalent.

In conclusion, it should be stressed that this type of word relationship is similar to, but nevertheless, distinct from the relationship between two synonyms, one of which has a narrower meaning and the other a broader meaning. This is also a relationship between a whole set of words (similar in meaning, but not necessarily synonymous) and one (or more) pre-chosen word(s) that can substitute the entire set. For example:

claim
declare
utter
etc.
SAY (so called 'head word')

Note that *claim* etc. have the meaning 'say' only in specified contexts, not in all contexts. The word *claim* in another context can mean 'want'. In *Softhesaurus* (Georgiev, 1993b) we have differentiated 127 groups marked as syntagmatical synonyms.

4.2 *Word Class*

This type of word relationship is well known in the literature, but never fully studied. The word class is a structured set of words and can be divided into subclasses. For example, the words: *pharmacy, chemistry, drug store*, etc., *clinic, hospital, infirmary*, etc., *warehouse, storehouse, depot*, etc., *fortress, castle*, etc., *consulate, embassy, mission*, etc., *church, cathedral, monastery*, etc., *hut, cottage, house*, etc., *theatre, cinema*, etc., *jail, prison*, etc., *stable, barn*, etc., *bar, pub, restaurant* and so on, can be readily substituted, in all contexts, by the words: *edifice, construction, structure, erection* and ***building***. In this case, we have chosen the word ***building*** as a general representative and substitute of all words from this class. This set of words can be divided into subclasses and each subclass can have its own representative word(s). For example, *hospital* can be chosen to represent the rest of that subclass because of its more general use. For computer (program) use only, and for the construction of the meta language, in *Softhesaurus* we have assigned the code AB to *building* etc., AB-A to *hospital* etc., AB-C to *church* etc. and so on, thus explaining to the computer (and in this case to the student) the division of that set of words into sub-sets. The sub-set is separated with a dash from the main set of words.

An important rule through which we could easily recognize a class of words was the formula: A is always B but B is not necessarily A, which means that, for example, *clinic* is a *building*, but a *building* is not necessarily a *clinic* (it can be a *church*, a *mansion*, etc.). Another way to differentiate the sub-classes of a class of words is by putting them in context. For example:

People eat in restaurant(s)
canteen(s)
pizza shop(s)
Mcdonald's

People live in houses
villas
palaces
jurtes
huts
etc.

Thus, the word class is a structured and hierarchically organized set of words. The word class can be of two types:

a) when the words forming the subclasses are synonymous and word substitution is context sensitive (depends on the context) as in relationship 4.1, where some of the word groups mentioned can be presented as word classes as well. For example, let's consider again *say* and the words it can substitute. The words: *assert, claim, allege, insist, maintain,* etc. are synonymous and as such they can form a subset. The words: *hint, allude, imply,* etc. are also synonymous and therefore they can form another subset of words having the same 'head word' or word substitute – ***say***. These two subsets stand on the same hierarchical level, but they are distinct from one another. This distinction is coded respectively.
b) when the words forming the subclasses are not synonymous and word substitution does not depend on the context (for example word class AB – *building*). A distinctive feature of type (b) is that the words forming the entire class (not only the subclasses) are not synonyms. Often their relationship is very remote, because it is based on a particular peculiarity or feature (concept) that distinguishes one subclass from another. For example in the case of 'quadruped animals' (*sheep, cow*), or 'carnivorous animals' (*fox, cat*), etc., it can be said that the distinctive component (*quadruped, carnivorous,* etc.) represents the componential meaning of that word.

The word class, unlike the syntagmatical synonyms and many other types of word groups, is structured. Every word constituting the class has an exact location and defined hierarchical relationship (close, remote, upwards, downwards) with every other word from the same class. Other examples of word relationship 4.2 type (a) and (b) can be found in such classes as: *tool(s), food, army rank(s), school(s), groups* (of people), etc. A list of 'word class' head words used in *Softhesaurus* (Georgiev, 1993b) is provided below.

administrative group	adulthood
age	aim
ammunition	animal
artificial language	assembled group (of people)
atrocity	bank
bare necessities of life	basic arithmetic operation
be excited	bedding
behaviour	bird
blemish	book
book	boundary
boy(girl)hood	building
calculate	capital
capture	celestial being
celestial body	cemetery
charge	chemical (substance)
chief	child
clean	clever
cloth	clothes
colour	combustibles
command	commodities
coniferous	constellation
construction material	container
continent	correspondence
country	craft(sman)
crime	criminal group
culture	currency
dance	detergent
device	dirt
disable(-ility)	document
drug	eat(ing)

educated
element
energy
establishment
extrasensory perception
family
feel(ing)
fighter
fish
flower
footwear
foreigner
fuel
furniture
game
gather
give
grass
greeting word
hear
herb
hobby
human character
ill(ness)
income
information source
instrument
intuition
jewellery
language
lifetime
line
live
luggage
machine
martial art
means
medicine
metal
military rank
mineral
money, monetary unit
move(ment)
music
musical instrument
national resistance group
noise
occupational group
offspring
opening
orchestra
packet of cigarettes
parasite
Part of Speech

education
end
equipment
explosive
faith
family
feel(ing)
fire
flora
food
force
fruit
fund
game
gas
generation
grandparent
grave
group of things
help
hit
holiday
ignorance
implement
information
insect
intellectual
invalid
juridical group
leave
light
liquid
loan
machine
make
meal
measure
merchandise
microorganism
mind
misfortune
mountain
munitions
musical group
musician
nationality
nut
official
one's
operate
organisation
paper
parent
particle

party
pay(ment)
peak
perceive
perception
person
philosophy
piece
plan
planet
plant
poison
political group
poor
powder
produce
product
profit
property
public utilities
publishers
punctuation mark
punish
purchase
put
race
regulation(s)
relative
religious group
research group
rest
rich
river
room
route
royal family
ruler
run
school
schooling method
school subject
seat
secret service
seed
sense
senses
separate
set
settlement
shape
shop
sin
sing
skill(ful)
smell
social class
social system
society
soldier
somebody
song
sound
spacecraft
spices
sport
sportsman
stop
strength
strong
student
stupid
swimming stroke
take
taste
tax
teacher
temporarily
terrorist
terrorist group
thing
throw
time
title
toilet
tool
trace
transport
travel
treasure
tree
trouble spot
uneducated
uninteresting
unit
vehicle
voice
walk
weapon
winds
wood
worker
world power
worm
wound
writer
writing
zodiac
etc. (the list shown above is not complete).

Below is an example of the hierarchically structured class of words 'musical instrument' from *Softhesaurus*:

musical instrument

string instrument	**wind instrument**	**percussion instrument**		
banjo	bagpipe	drum	organ	accordion
cello	clarinet	organ	piano	harmonica
contrabass	fife	tabor	pianino	
double-bass	flute	tambour		
fiddle	oboe	tambourin(e)		
guitar	organ	timbal		
harp	piccolo	timpano		
lute	saxophone			
lyre	trumpet			
mandolin				
samisen				
stradivarius				
viola				
violin				
violoncello				

Some words can enter in to more than one sub-group. For example 'organ' is both 'wind instrument' (supplied with wind by bellows) and 'percussion instrument', because it is sounded by keys. That is why we have put it under three sub-groups, because it is similar to 'piano'. Below is an example of the hierarchically structured linguistic term *case* used in *Linguaterm* (Georgiev, 1994).

2AC' case	2AC-A ablative case
2AC-B abessive case	2AC-C absolutive case
2AC-D essive case	2AC-E adessive case
2AC-G aditive case	2AC-H accusative case
2AC-I actum case	2AC-J vocative case
2AC-JB adversive case	2AC-JC lative case
2AC-JC translative case	2AC-K dative case
2AC-L delative case	2AC-M destinative case
2AC-N discriminative case	2AC-P illative case
2AC-Q nominative case	2AC-R caritive case
2AC-S comitative case	2AC-U limitative case
2AC-V locative case	2AC-W mediative case
2AC-X inactive case, oblique case	2AC-Y genitive case
2AC-Z instrumental case	etc.

The word 'case' can have also other meanings, we have enumerated only the meanings when it is used as a grammatical term. This type of word relationship, when applied to place names, will look as follows:

Major city in Britain	**European Union country**
Edinburgh	Britain
London	France
Manchester	Germany
etc.	etc.

Similarly, the geographical term 'pole' can be subdivided into 'North Pole' and 'South Pole'. (Note: Each letter after the dash (–) represents a particular sub-class.)

Using the above classification and division into hierarchical sub-groups will unable us to explain to the computer that 'panther' is a subclass of 'predator' and in turn 'predator' is a subclass of **animal**, therefore 'panther' is an animal. The word relationship 'Class of Words' is marked with the number 2, placed before the code.

The head words of the 'class' (those words that stand at the top of the hierarchical tree are important words in the language – they represent fundamental concepts, valid for all natural languages, and like the 'head words' in relationship 4.1 should be learned before the words they represent if the student wants to make earlier attempts to speak the language.

The 'head words' from group 4.1 and group 4.2 are only about 500 in number (excluding the terms and the place names), easy to learn and they will allow the student to cover all important aspects of communication and thus to express in a conversation all important ideas the speaker wants to convey to the listener. Here, it is important to note that we have in mind a student who has already mastered his (her) mother tongue and can easily translate the English words into the corresponding words in her (his) native language. For example, *Bibel* (German) is a ***book***, *Buch* (German), *livre* (French), *libro* (Italian), ***kitab*** (Turkish), *книга* (Russian, Bulgarian), etc.; *Prospekt, Heft* (German), *brochure* (French, English), *prospetto* (Italian), *брошюра* (Russian, Bulgarian), etc. is also a **book** (booklet). As for young children making their first steps in building up their vocabulary, word learning seems to start at the opposite end (this is well documented in the literature) – from the words at the bottom of the hierarchical tree, from what they see and touch, gradually moving upwards towards more general concepts and ideas: *cat, dog*, etc. -> *pet* (domestic animal) -> *quadruped* -> *carnivorous* -> **animal.**

In *Softhesaurus* (Georgiev, 1993b) we have differentiated 357 word classes. Next, we will describe one more type of word relationship that will help broaden the list of important head words.

4.3 Substitute word

This type of word relationship is very similar to that described as syntagmatical synonymy 4.1; the only difference is that while the syntagmatical synonyms, as a group, are close in meaning when compared with one another, the substitute word can substitute words unrelated to one another in meaning. The other difference is that while substitution in 4.1 depends on the context, substitution in 4.3 can be carried out in any context when we want to generalise the meaning. Some of the word groups defined in 4.1 can take in more words, unrelated in meaning to the main body of words constituting the group. In this case relationship 4.1 can transform itself into relationship 4.3. Words such as '**make**', '**take**', '**get**' and '**do**' can substitute a narrower body of words, as defined in 4.1, as in 'get > receive' or 'do > perform', and a larger body of words as defined in 4.3, such as: *construct* (**make**) an airplane, *build* (**make**) a bridge, *produce* (**make**) steel; *drink* (**take**) two spoonfuls before meal; *conquer* (**take**) the city, etc. Or, sometimes we say *Please, give me this **thing** there*, or *Let's visit that **place** again*, without naming the object or the place. In this case the word '**thing**' (item, etc.) can stand for all objects and the word '**place**' can substitute all places. For example *Please, give me that **thing** (chair, spoon, bottle,* etc.*) there*, or *Let's visit that **place** (river, mountain, town*, etc.*) again.*

The 'substitute word' is also similar to the word class 4.2 (b), because the words constituting a group are not synonymous. The difference is that the word class 4.2 is hierarchically structured, while the word group 'substitute word' is not.

Another characteristic feature of this type of word relationship is the fluctuation of the words in some of the word groups. For example, we can call anyone a *demagogue*, depending on our judgement. All these people will form a group, which the word *demagogue* can replace in any context. The names of some of our own politicians or world leaders will always stay in this group for most people. However, the word entries of this group will vary from person to person.

Below, we provide a short list of generalized substitutes of type 4.3 used in our thesauri (Georgiev, 1993b, 1994, 1994a). This type of word relationship is marked with the figure 3 placed before the two-letter code (3BA, etc.). (Note: The codes mentioned in this chapter are thesaurus specific, but the coding itself is outside the scope of this book because it is not related to the programming code used here.) This type of word set is not structured. Below we will list some non-terminological 'head words':

be on holiday	change	chemical
countryside	culture	deterrent
disapprove	evidence	field
'flu	get	have 'flu
help	hostilities	land
living	make	material
nervous breakdown	object	operate
place	plain	process
protest	rest	substance
take	thing	vice
work	etc.	

and some linguistic terms used as 'head words' in *Linguaterm* (Georgiev, 1994)

group	letter	phoneme
sign	sound	process

Similarly, we can list under 'mountain' all the mountains in the world, under 'river' all the rivers in the world, under 'ocean' all oceans, etc. When the place names are viewed linearly, they form a group with the meaning 'stretch'. Thus, we can form a group of countries bordering, for example, the river Danube. In *Softhesaurus* (Georgiev, 1993b) we have 37 word groups of this type.

4.4 *Part of*

This is a relationship between two individual words (or a group of words and another group of words, or a group of words and an individual word), where one of the words means that it is an integral part of the other. This is a well-known relationship in linguistic literature. We would like to stress the importance of this type of relationship for the computer if we intend to teach the computer to understand natural language. For example, 'spike' is part of a 'fence', 'room' is part of a 'building' (AB), 'peak' is part of a 'mountain', etc. This type of word relationship is marked with the sign þ, as in: *engine* þ *vehicle*. There are two more similar types of word relationships: 'member of' (marked with þ') and 'belongs to' (marked with þ"). Here are some more examples: *junction* þ *road*; *sand* þ *beach*; *ash* þ *fire*; *skin* þ *body*; *member* þ' *group*; *star* þ" *sky*; *eye* þ *head*; *head* þ *body*, etc. Of course, for the polysemical words there is a coded specification as to which meaning is meant exactly (for example, 'star' is also part of a Mercedes or of something else, or 'star' can mean a human being). Most things that enter into a 'part of' relationship (respectively 'belongs to' and 'member of') are part of a sequence of mutual inclusion. For example, 'retina' is part of the 'eye' and the 'eye' is part of the 'head', etc., or a 'distributor' is part of an 'engine' and an 'engine' is part of a 'motor vehicle'. For computer use it is necessary to point out only the next constituent, not the entire sequence. The sequence can be traced easily with a program via which the computer will immediately 'know' that 'retina' is part of a larger unit called 'body', or that the 'distributor' is part of a 'motor vehicle', and not a human being. This program will be one of the modules that provide the associative 'thinking' of the computer. The above-mentioned relationship is common to thousands of words and requires a separate study.

One can make full use of word relationship 4.2 (class of words) when specifying relationship 4.4. For example, it suffices to say to the computer that AB (building) is part of CH (populated area, settlement), without going into further details (without mentioning each individual word denoting 'building'). Many buildings in one place make a populated area (*village, town, city*, etc.). The computer program will trace immediately what we mean by that and therefore there will be no need to specify individually all the words contained in AB and all those contained in CH ('house' is part of a 'village' (town, city), etc.) This is yet another module that will extend the associative 'thinking' of the computer and bring many words under a single rule.

4.4.1 Located in

This is a relationship between two individual words, or groups of words to a group of words, or group of words to an individual word (as in 4.4), where one of the words (group of words) is marked as being positioned (located) in the other. For example a 'vehicle' (FY) can be found on the road (*street, motorway, car park, garage*, etc.). All those words that enter into relationship 4.4 enter also into relationship 4.4.1. For example, it can also be said that the engine is located in a motor vehicle. As such, relationship 4.4.1 is far more general in meaning and a much greater number of words are involved than in 4.4. In our study this type of word relationship was marked with the sign &. Here are some more examples of this type of word (group) relationship: punctuation mark (CQ) & text; Moscow & Russia; Great Britain & Europe; sand & beach (dune, desert, etc.); dune & desert, etc. Everything else that was said for 4.4 applies also to 4.4.1.

4.5 Narrower meaning – broader meaning

This is a relationship between two individual words, whereas one of the words has a broader meaning than the other. For example 'thing' has a broader meaning than 'object' and 'item'; 'worker' has a broader meaning than 'proletarian', etc. In our study this type of word relationship was marked with the sign " placed between the words, as in *edition " publication*; *issue " publication*, etc. As we have already said in the previous sections, one should not forget to specify (to mark accordingly) the exact meaning involved, because words usually have more than one meaning.

4.6 One – many (things, or beings constituting a group)

This is a relationship between one individual word (or group of words) and another, where one of the words means an unspecified sum of the other. This relationship is similar to the relationship between the singular of the Noun and its plural, but it is not identical to it. This type of word relationship is well known in the respective literature, but it is much neglected in language teaching and in the Dictionaries. We bring it up again because it is indispensable for that part of computer science that deals with natural language. For this reason we provide a comprehensive list below. Please note that this type of relationship is marked with the sign :

airplane : wing
apple (cherry, plum, etc.) : fruit
article (paper, book, etc.) : bibliography (references)
bee : (bee) hive, swarm
bird : flock, swarm
book (novel, etc.) : literature
bracelet (ring, necklace, etc.) : jewellery
chair (table, etc.) : furniture

cherry (apple, plum, etc.) : orchard
chicken (turkey, etc.) : poultry
chip(s) (apple, cake, bread, cheese, meat, etc.) : food
coin (bank note) : money
corpse (dead body) : casualties (victims, death toll)
delegate (envoy) : delegation (deputation)
dish : menu
dollar (pound, frank, etc.) : money (cash, currency)
drop : pool (dew, rain, ocean, sea, etc.)
feather : plumage
fish : school
flock : population
flower : flowerbed (wreath, bouquet)
food, meal : cuisine
footmark (footprint, etc.) : trail (track)
goose (duck, etc.) : (water) fowl
human being : community (nation, population, people, etc.)
human being : species
insect (animal, bird) : population
island : archipelago
leader : leadership
leaf : book (notebook)
leaf : foliage
member : group
national : ethnic group (state)
plant : verdure (vegetation, greenery)
player : team
poem (short story, etc.) : book
poem : poetry (poesy, verse)
priest (bishop, etc.) : clergy
province : country
room : building
settlement : province
settler : colony
sheep (cattle) : herd
ship (boat) : flotilla (fleet)
short story (novel, etc.) : prose (belles-lettres, fiction)
singer : chorus
soldier : army (armed forces)
song : repertoire
species : organic matter
star (planet) : planetary system (galaxy)
tank : armoured vehicle
tree : wood (forest)
vehicle : traffic jam
wolf : pack (of wolves)
word : phrase (sentence, text, vocabulary, dictionary, lexicon)
worker : staff (personnel),
worker : work force

etc.

This method of description of word meanings is a computer way of saying 'worker : personnel', code 'personnel' as 'group of people' and then relate "personnel" to other words or groups of words, instead of saying 'Body of persons engaged in some public service or in a factory, office', etc. (Fowler and Fowler, 1973: 907), which is a description of lexical meanings solely designed for the human frame of mind and needs language proficiency to understand it.

The relationship *one : many* constitutes yet another program module, by means of which the computer can improve its knowledge of word meanings and of the outer reality. For example, if the computer program, when analysing the text, meets the word 'dollar(s)', the computer will immediately 'know' that this is also 'cash', 'hard currency', 'currency', 'money', used in the United States and Australia, that it is in a hierarchical relationship with the head word 'monetary unit', etc.

4.7 Smaller – bigger

This is a relationship between two individual words (or a group of words and another group of words; a group of words to an individual word and vice versa), where one (the first) of the words denotes something smaller than the other. These words denote both perceptible and imagined objects and beings. The words (groups of words) thus compared can belong to:

a) the same semantic group;
b) different semantic groups.
In the thesauri, mentioned above, this type of word relationship was marked with the sign <. For example: *sea* < *ocean; brook* < *river*, etc. (the same semantic group), or *insect* (LH) < *building* (AB); *vessel* (FX) < *sea* (words or a group of words from different semantic groups).
As in the previous relationships, we only need to show the immediate link (the next thing that is slightly bigger than the previous one) and the computer program (the module) will connect the links into a sequence, which will bring the computer further knowledge. For example, since 'vessel' (FX) is smaller than 'sea', the computer will automatically assume that 'vessel' (FX) is also smaller than 'ocean' , since 'sea' is smaller than 'ocean', etc.

This sign (<) is used also to denote two other types of relationship – 'more intensive than', as between *cry* < *scream* and 'later in time than', as between *morning* < *afternoon*, *Cheops pyramid* < *american president*, *young* < *old*. etc.; the latter pair of words are also in antonymical relationship.

4.8 Synonyms and thesaurus

The synonyms and the thesauri are well presented in the literature, therefore we will not dwell on this subject. Words that are very similar in meaning (there is no measurement for similarity, some authors impose a number of syntactic / contextual restrictions) and belong to the same Part of Speech are synonymous.Words that are synonymous and are gathered together from all Parts of Speech to form a group are a thesaurus set of words. For example: *It was* ***announced****, that* ... = *It was* ***proclaimed****, that* ... = *The* ***announcer*** *said, that* ... = *The* ***announcement*** *was about* ... = *The* ***proclamation*** ..., etc. We are well aware of the limitations and uncertainties that arise using such a general rule. Therefore, *proclaim, announce, declare*, etc. form a synonymical set of words. When we add *announcer, announcement, proclamation*, etc., we form a thesaurus set of words. In the above example it was shown that the words are interchangeable and the meaning of the sentence is (hopefully) preserved. The thesaurus set of words can be:

a) complete, when all major parts of speech are presented, as in:

compact	concentrate	concentration
concise	condensation	condense
condenser	**dense**	densely
shrink	shrinking;	succinct
succinctly		density

compete	**competition**	competitioner
competitive	competitively	competitor
contest	contestant	emulation
tournament	match	

and

b) incomplete (not all parts of speech can belong to this group), as in: *beautiful, beautify, beauty, comely, handsome, lovely, pretty, winsome*, where the Adverb ‘handsomely’ is missing, because it means ‘considerably’.

In *Softhesaurus* (Georgiev, 1993b) we have used a three-letter code to mark the thesaurus groups, and 5 stands before the code to designate the thesaurus-type of word relationship. Here are some examples:

5EAJ = endorse(ment), sign, approbate, approve, give one’s consent, etc.;
5EAL = except(ion), with the exception (of), with the exclusion (of), without, excluding, etc.;
5EAN = at the back of one’s mind, subconscious(ly), etc.

The hyphen (-) indicates the beginning of a sub-class. For example: difficult = 5CGU-A, 5CGU-B, where we have marked ‘tense’ = A and ‘adverse’ = B, because these two words were considered to be less related to the main body of words denoting *difficult*, and to be dissimilar in meaning. In the example above, the word ‘match’ can also be separated with a dash from the rest of the group because of its restricted use: ‘match’ is a special type of **competition** (compare: *football match, boxing match, tennis tournament*, etc.). (Note: All words in the thesaurus set are equal – they equally represent the lexical-semantical meaning of the set.

In *Softhesaurus* (Georgiev, 1993b) we have differentiated 1280 thesaurus-type word groups. The thesaurus of Roget (1852) has 1000 word groups.

4.9 Subject field (topic, thematical group of words)

Words used in a particular scientific or other special sphere of communication are related to each other in meaning, because they belong to one and the same subject field, topic, theme or sphere of discourse. This type of word relationship is well known in the literature and there are many thematical dictionaries available on the market. We will not dwell on the principles of selection of words for those dictionaries – they are discussed elsewhere and we agree with them, in principle. However, we should emphasize the need of a code to accompany each thematical word in the electronic dictionary for computer use. In *Softhesaurus* (Georgiev, 1993b) we have used a two-letter code preceded by the number 4 to mark the thematical type of word relationship. Here are some examples:

LJ	= industry	SA’	= internal conflicts
SA-A	= human rights	SA-B	= violent internal conflict
SA-BA	= civil war	SA-C	= terrorism
SA-D	= social conflicts	SA-DA	= communal violence
SA-DB	= industrial action	SA-DC	= drug abuse
SA-DD	= industrial crises	SB’	= international conflict(s)

SC'	= politics	SC-A	= diplomacy
SC-C	= democracy	SC-CA	= western democracy
SC-CB	= swiss democracy	SC-B	= election
SD'	= police	SE'	= agriculture
SF'	= climate & weather	SG'	= finance
SH'	= trade	SI'	= space exploration
SJ'	= sport	SK'	= amusements
SL'	= occult	SM'	= medicine
SN'	= aviation	SO'	= religion
SP	= mythology	SQ '	= law
SR'	= hygiene	SS'	= cosmetics
ST'	= smoke	SU'	= kitchen
SV'	= military	SW'	= transport
SX'	= literature	SY'	= correspondence
SZ'	= journalism	YY-A	= domestic (household) work

etc.

The hyphen marks the 'head word' – the word used to represent the theme. The 'head word' can substitute other words as in 4.1, 4.2 and 4.3. For example, the head word 'industrial action' (SA-DB') represents the theme expressed by such words as*: strike, walk-out, sit-in, picket, picketing, work-to-rule, stage a walk-out, industrial unrest*, etc., all bearing the same code. The subject field can also be structured and hierarchically organized ('internal conflicts' = SA; 'industrial action' = SA-DB, etc.), but the structuring of the constituent words is very subjective. To overcome this subjectivity, we have to create many different groups and sub-groups within a subject field to suit all possible interpretations of it. Consider how vast Linguistics is alone, even without the border disciplines.

In *Softhesaurus* (Georgiev, 1993b) we have differentiated 26 subject fields. The list is not complete.

4.10 Modal sem

This is one of the most abstract and far-fetching meanings of all, because it can unite, in a group, hundreds, even thousands of words that are very dissimilar in meaning. For example, the words: *correct, free, fluent, forgive, excellent, beautiful, praise, witty, bliss, good, healthy*, etc. have a '**positive**' meaning. On the other hand words such as: *ugly, infamous, erroneous, incipient, bad, menace, rotten, fool, sad*, etc. have a '**negative**' meaning. The modal sem can be present in all groups and sub-groups of a word class, such as '**time**' (present, past, future) or '**animal**'. As in some of the previous word groups, we have used a two-letter code to mark the meaning of the modal sem, the number 6 to underline the type of relationship 'modal sem', and the 'head word' was marked with a hyphen to represent the set. Here are some examples:

TA'	= positive	TB'	= negative
TC'	= speech and communication	TD'	= thought
TE'	= group	TF'	= school and education
TG'	= time	TG-A	= present time
TG-B	= future time	TG-C	= past time
TH'	= conflict	TI'	= control
TJ'	= immobile	TK'	= mobile
TL'	= flora	TM'	= fauna
TN'	= concrete	TP'	= abstract
TQ'	= subjective	TR'	= objective
TS'	= negate(ion)	TT'	= below standard

TU'	= direction	TW'	= velocity
TX'	= shine	TY'	= measure
TZ'	= disapprove	UA'	= hard object
UB'	= thing with a smell	UB-A	= pleasant smell
UB-B	= unpleasant smell	UC'	= thing without a smell
UD'	= temperature	UE'	= peace
UF'	= impair the integrity of an object	UH'	= species
UI'	= hidden	UJ'	= full charged
UK'	= empty	UL'	= cut
UM	= illegal activity	UN	= antique
UO	= science	UP	= perceived by ear or emitting sound
UQ	= perceived by eye	UR	= inorganic
US	= organic	UT	= non-standard
UU	= impossible	UV	= possible
VA'	= psychic activity	VA-A	= intellectual process
VA-B	= emotion	VA-B	= emotion

etc. Note that some of the above 'head words' can be used also as subject fields or as substitute words in word relationships 4.1, 4.2 and 4.3. Also, this type of word relationship describes quantifiers such as: *all, a few, several, some, many, any, lots of, a lot, a number, a couple (of), less, much, more, most, far more, none, every, few, so little, all the, almost all the, a great deal, great many, a good deal, all of R, so many, large number(s) (of), certain, much more, each, each one (of), a great many, tens of thousands, other, another, a few more, quite a lot (of), any other, far too much, half the, half a(n), the whole lot, very few, very many, tens, thousands, hundreds, dozens, millions, score, none, half, 1/2, 1/3, 1/4, 1/5*, etc. In *Softhesaurus* (Georgiev, 1993b) we have differentiated 54 modal sems. The list is not complete.

4.11 Links

This type of relationship marks the links (the connections) that exist or might be possible between objects, things or living beings. For example, the computer is usually connected (or can be connected) to *a printer, modem, external CD-ROM*, etc., forming a group of words that can be linked to a computer. Human beings have to do, for example, with buildings because they either live in them, work in them or use them for some other activity (sport, religion, etc.). Human beings are also connected to tools, because they use them in their work. Drinks can be linked to (assigned to, attributed to) human beings, because people drink water, alcohol, tea, etc. There will be exceptions: muslims drink no alcohol. Animals drink only water. So, buildings, tools, instruments, drinks, etc. are groups of words that can be linked to human beings. We can divide the links into *concrete* (for example, the links of our computer through cables, radio waves) and *abstract* (for example, the links of living beings with their environment, where there is no obvious, material, connection). Another good example of concrete links are the rail, road, etc. networks linking populated areas (settlements). These links are already computerised, there are commercial software programs that will lead your vehicle to the chosen location. All the links and the exceptions form a complex net of relationships, which we will need when we start to construct an artificial intellect.

4.12 Other types of relationships in the ALSD

a) **Antonymical relationship.** This relationship can be of two kinds: between individual words and between groups of words (to be more precise – between meanings). We have marked this type of relationship with the sign ^. Examples of antonymical relationship between individual words can be found in all antonymical dictionaries. The new element here that deserves attention is the antonymical relationship between groups of words. For example: TA > TB (positive – negative); DH > DF (agree – disagree); DL > DM (need – needless); HB > HD (rare – often); HC > HA (brief – constant), etc. This is an antonymical relationship between selected meanings present in many words, not between individual words. The individual words in the above examples are the 'head words' that represent the meaning, and, in fact, these words enter into an antonymical relationship as individual words. The words within such a group do not enter into a specified individual relationship; for example the negative word *ugly* is not related to the negative word *criminal*, though a criminal action is an ugly action while an ugly action is not necessarily a criminal action.

The constituent words of the antonymical groups do not enter into an individual antonymical relationship; for example *ugly* is not an antonym of *successful*.

b) **Sequence.** Many words are part of a sequence. For example, the Numerals or certain words denoting 'time' such as: *morning, afternoon, evening, night; January, February*, etc., the Egyptian pharaohs, the American presidents, etc. In *Softhesaurus* (Georgiev, 1993b) we have coded the sequence respectively with 1, 2, 3, etc. at the end of the code.

c) **Equal to.** When one word is not simply a synonym, but is identical or equivalent to another word. The equality is marked with the sign =. For example:

AD=after Christ
abaft=behind
ablaze=on fire
etc.

d) **Similar to.** When one word (or group of words) is similar (but not identical) to another word (group of words), the similarity is marked with the sign # in *Softhesaurus* (Georgiev, 1993b). For example:

abscissa#line
alder#birch
etc.

e) **In opposition to.** This is a relationship between two individual words and is characteristic of linguistic terminology. In *Linguaterm* (Georgiev, 1994) we have marked it with the sign > placed before the word. For example:

analysis > synthesis
animate > inanimate
apheresis > elision
arsis > thesis
assimilation > dissimilation
cacophonic > euphonic
cacophony > euphony
co-ordination > subordination
compact > diffuse
conclusive > durative
connotation > denotation
consonant > vowel
etc.

f) **Variant of a word.** This is another type of relationship between two individual words and is characteristic of linguistic terminology. In *Linguaterm* (Georgiev, 1994) it is marked with the sign (placed before the word. For example:

allograph (grapheme
allolex (word
allolog (word
allonym (proper name
allophone (phoneme
allophrase (phrase
alloseme (sem
etc.

g) **Used for** or **made for** or **purpose served.** Many words denoting things can form a group depending on their use or purpose. These groups of words are best seen through the action of the verb(s) describing their use. For example, the clothes are to be worn, they are to be washed and ironed, kept or stored. The (fire) wood, coal, etc. is to be burned. The weapons are used to kill. Some of the features related to these groups are secondary; for example, washing, drying, ironing and keeping the clothes in the wardrobe has to do with their **maintenance** and location when they are not on us, but the main purpose they serve is to be worn. Besides, it is not only the clothes that we wash and iron, a larger body of words such as curtains, embroidery, bedding, etc., must be washed and ironed as well, as part of the sub-field **household work.** As for keeping them in the wardrobe, we take it for granted that people keep clothes and nothing else in their wardrobes.

The actions performed with the clothes have a logical sequence. They must be bought or acquired, worn, washed, dried, ironed, worn again or stored. Whereas washed and dried is an obligatory sequence, ironing is not a must, because some clothes need no ironing (note the sub-division within this group!). We can store them after buying and later wear them, or wash them first.

All these groups of words and knowledge about them is needed for the construction of our artificial intellect, especially for the question-answering (dialogue) software programs. For example, if someone asks *Where are Peter's trousers*? the computer may want to know whether they are washed and ironed, before answering the question.

One can find other types of relationships between individual words or group of words. For example, **'made of'** (wood, stone, metal, plastic, etc.). We do not claim to have listed all.

5 Discussion

Word relationships, groups (sets) of words and their relationships, the codes marking those relationships and the codes marking the meanings, as presented briefly above, form a meta-language for description of lexical semantics. This meta-language is valid for all languages and is a model of the lexico-semantical system of any natural language.

Every individual natural-language word or phrase from the vocabulary, depending on the number of meanings, can be a member of more than one group of words and can enter into more than one type of relationship with other individual words (incl. phrases) or word groups. The actual words met in the groups are language specific. For example, the word 'church' has the following meanings: a religious institution (GR-E) in a sentence such as *The Church of England*, which is distinct from other institutions and establishments (the banks, firms, ministries); a religious site (AB-C), where it is in the same group with such words as *mosque, shrine, monastery, chapel*, etc. and is in contrast to the other subsets of AB (building), which, in turn, is in contrast to all other word groups.

Or, for example, the word 'father' has the following meanings, marked respectively: human being, male, living being (UH); family member (RX), as part of the word class 'family'; parent (ET), as part of the word class 'parents'; relative (EV-BC), as part of the word class listing the relatives; older generation (EY), as part of the word set 'generation' (younger / older generation and the words constituting them); clergyman (OU), where it is on a par with such words as: *priest, curate, pastor*, etc.; 'father' bears the code SO, because of its presence in the thematical group 'religion'; 'father' can mean also 'god', etc.

In many languages the word 'father' will lack the meanings OU and SO and will not be present in these groups. Via its programmed associative 'thinking', based on the above description, the computer will immediately 'know' that:

a) 'father' is a 'parent' (on a higher hierarchical level within the word class 'parents') and that 'father' requires a 'mother' (on the same hierarchical level) to form the class of 'parents';
b) that 'father' together with 'mother' are 'parents' to 'children' (on the lower hierarchical level), that the children are 'son(s)' and 'daughter(s)' (on a still lower level) and that they all together form a 'family';
c) that 'father' is a 'close relative' to the persons located on the same level (mother), to 'grandmother – grandfather' (located on the next upper level) and to 'children' (located on the lower level), and more distant relative to 'grandchildren', etc., within the class 'relatives';
d) that 'father' belongs to the 'older generation', if we divide the family or the relatives into older and younger generation;
e) since the words associated with 'father', within the word groups described above, do not belong to the subject field 'religion' (SO), the computer will be programmed to be aware of the second meaning of 'father', associated with 'religion' and 'god'.

The table below presents the types of word relationships and the presence (+) or absence (-) of a particular characteristic feature.

Table 1

No	Structured	Unstructured	Individual	Group	Head word(s)
1 syntagm	-	+	-	+	+
2 class	+	-	-	+	+
3 substitute	-	+	-	+	+
4 subj. field	-	+	-	+	-
5 thesaurus	-	+	-	+	-
6 modal sem	-	+	-	+	-
part of	-	+	+	+	-
located in	-	+	+	+	-
narrow - broad	-	-	+	-	-
one - many	-	-	+	-	-
small - big	-	+	+	+	-
links	-	-	+	-	-
antonym	-	-	+	+	-
sequence	-	-	+	-	-
equal	-	-	+	-	-
similar	-	-	+	+	-
opposition	-	-	+	-	-
variant	-	-	+	-	-
used for	-	-	+	+	-
made of	-	-	+	+	-

Softhesaurus (Georgiev, 1993b) uses 16 types of word, and word-group relationships to explain the lexical meanings of the words and has approximately 1800 word groups without the terminological word groups (linguistic, industrial, etc.).This means that we need at least 1800 different codes to code the meaning of the words in the dictionary. In our C (C++)

programming examples, in the previous and in the following chapters, we use a one-letter code for one meaning. This means that the Latin, Cyrillic and Greek alphabets, taken together, do not have enough letters to code all the meanings and relationships in the language.

Of course, we can use two-letter, of three-letter codes to code a single meaning or relationship, but we will have a very heavy programming task and a problem to overcome. The problem is that [a], used as an individual code for one particular meaning, must be different from [a] used in [ab] and in [abc], used also as individual codes for other meanings, not connected with the meaning of [a]. In other words, the meaning coded with [a] has nothing to do with the meaning coded with [ab], which is no longer the meanings of [a] and [b]. An alternative way to overcome this problem is to enclose the additional information about the word once in [ ] using all possible letters in all alphabets, then to enclose more information about the word within ( ) using all possible letters in all alphabets, and when that is not enough, to enclose more additional information within { } or within < >. We have explained how that can be done in paragraph 2.5.1 b).

7 Representation of knowledge

In a recent publication (Georgiev, 2006: 231–6) we have shown how a pre-defined sequence of Parts of Speech, called a 'segment', can be replaced (substituted) with a pre-defined sequence of meanings called a 'thought pattern'. The thought patterns are sequences of coded meanings and represent truthful statements about external reality. For example,

People live in houses.
1HE 2NE in 2AB-D

where '1HE' substitutes all human beings, 2NE substitutes all synonyms of 'live' (*dwell, inhabit, lodge, reside*, etc.), 'in' is a natural language word (not a code) – the preposition 'in', starting an adverbial phrase for location – and 2AB-D is a sub-group of 'buildings', denoting living quarters (*block of flats, bungalow, palace, residence, skyscraper, villa*, etc.). Since many houses, in one place, make a 'settlement' (populated area) relationship – 'one – many' described previously – the computer can be programmed to make the logical inference that 'people live in populated areas'

1HE 2NE 2CH

where 2CH codes all words denoting a 'populated area' (*town, city, village*, etc.), without having to register the thought pattern

1HE 2NE 2CH

in the computer's memory.

On the other hand, if we go downwards, towards the smaller constituent groups of this hierarchy, the computer will also know that people live in *rooms*, since the *rooms* are a constituent part of a building (relationship *room : building*). Let us consider another example:

People like flowers.
1HE 1RB 2QL-AB

where 1RB codes such words as 'admire', 'are fond of', 'love', etc. and 2QL-AB codes all kinds of flowers, as a sub-group of vegetation (2QL). Though this statement is generally speaking truthful, we are not sure whether all people like flowers or bouquets (relationship *flower : bouquet*) or vegetation. Therefore, we can exclude all those people who do not like *carnations*, if we know who are they. Similarly, we can say that all people eat food, but we cannot say that all people eat meat (*meat* is *food*). We have to exclude the vegetarians, and when it comes to eating pork (*pork* is a kind of *meat*), we have to exclude the muslims, since they eat meat but not pork. Therefore, when we describe different national cuisines, we will need to vary our meat menu. Later in this book, when we come to programming natural language understanding and question answering, we will see how the program can be made to say 'Yes', when we ask *Does Peter eat pork*? and *No, he doesn't*, when we ask *Does Sadam eat pork*?.

All human beings (1HE) drink (5GAQ) drinks (2LM). This knowledge can be represented with the thought pattern

1HE 5GAQ 2LM

Animals, when we exclude human beings, also drink, but only water, though some of them drink milk, mainly when young. Pets like milk irrespective of age. The varieties of drinks people can possibly drink is huge. There are many sub-groups and sub-groups of sub-groups. For example, the drinks can be sub-divided into 'alcoholic drinks' and 'non-alcoholic drinks', 'aerated' and 'non-aerated', etc.

When we make a rule to tell the computer that all people drink drinks, we must exclude the muslims when we come to the alcoholic drinks. Likewise, we must exclude the alcoholic drinks when we come to listing what can be bought in a shop in a muslim country. Of course, there are always exceptions, certain individuals in the muslim world perhaps drink alcohol, and when we come to the exclusions, we must exclude them by naming them.

To sum up, we repeat that the meaning of a word group has properties that put this word group in a deterministic, syntactic relationship with the meanings of other word groups in the text. For example, **humans** can *eat, drink, walk, sleep, work, live*, etc. Humans can eat *food*, drink *drinks*, live in *populated areas* (towns, villages, etc) or in *houses* (villas, huts, etc.), work in *offices* (enterprises, companies, organisations, factories, etc), etc. These properties do not apply to all human beings, since, as we said earlier, vegetarians do not eat meat and muslims do not drink alcohol. The properties people can have, the things, people can do, do not apply to all living beings. The animals drink water only (some of them drink milk when young), and only some of them (cows, oxen, horses) work in the field. A **door** (entrance, window, etc.) can be opened, closed, or passed through. **Food** can be *eaten, stored, frozen, transported*, etc. A **room, building,** hence a **populated area,** can be *entered, cleaned, renovated, populated, (re)built*, etc. The syntagmatic representation of the relationships among meanings form the so-called thought patterns, mentioned in this chapter. (Note: the abbreviations for the semantic groups, used above, are taken from *Softhesaurus* (Georgiev 1993b). Note also that when programming in C(C++) we use different abbreviations for the semantic groups: we use only one letter code for one meaning and place this code in square brackets.)

8 Machine Translation

In this chapter we will present the most important linguistic and programming tasks needed to know when developing a machine-translation software program.

1 Construction of the bilingual dictionary

The construction of the bilingual dictionary is the same as the construction of the Dictionary of Wordforms discussed earlier in this book. There is, however, a need to add more information in order, firstly to make the program translate and, secondly, to translate correctly. We have to add this additional information, simultaneously in several places:

a) After the source (input) language word (English) we have to add its translation or translations into the foreign language (German):

    accounts=schätzt;buchführung
    accumulate=anhäufen;stauen;summieren
    accurate=exakt;richtiggehend;genau
    act=verfahren;vorspielen;akt;aufzug;gesetz
    aim=zielen;anlegen;ziel;absicht
    american=amerikaner;amerikanisch
    child=kind
    woman=frau

   We have good reason not to write the German Nouns *Buchführung, Kind, Frau* with a capital letter. We will explain why later. Also, vice-versa (German–English):

    abbeizen=pickle;stain wood
    abbeißen=bite off
    abbeißen von=bite from
    abbeißt=bites off
    abbeißte=bit off
    abbekaeme=got
    abbekam=got
    abbekommen=get
    abberief=recalled
    abberufen=recall
    abberufung=cancellation
    abberufung von=cancellation of

abberufung von amt=sacking
abberufungsschreibe=recall notice
abberufungsschreiben=recall notice
abberufungsurkunde=recall notice
abbestellen=cancel
abbestellung=cancellation
abbetteln=implore
abbezahlen=pay
abbgebeten=excused
etc.

When the word has more than one translation the words are separated using a semicolon. Note that often the German translations of a single English word belong to different Parts of Speech (*schätzt* – Verb, *Buchführung* – Noun; *Amerikaner* – Noun, *amerikanisch* – Adjective). Moreover, those translations that belong to the same Part of Speech often cannot be used in the same context (*anhäufen, stauen, summieren*). The English translations of a single German word can also belong to different Parts of Speech.

abbeizen=pickle;stain wood
abbitte=apologize;apology
abbitten=apologize;apologies

b) The next thing to do is to create a sign for the Part of Speech of the output (input) word. Then, the English–German bilingual dictionary will look like this:

accounts=Z schätztNbuchführung
accumulate=V anhäufen;stauen;summieren
accurate=A exakt;richtiggehendDgenau
act=Z verfahren;vorspielenNakt;aufzug;gesetz
aim=Z zielen;anlegenNziel;absicht
alternate=Z wechseln;abwechselnAabwechselnd
american=N amerikanerAamerikanisch
etc.

The German-English bilingual dictionary will look like this:

abbeizen=V pickle;stain wood
abbeißen=V bite off
abbeißen von=V bite from
abbeißt=v bite off
abbeißte=h bit off
abbekaeme=h got
abbekam=h got
abbekommen=V get
abberief=h recalled
abberufen=V recall
abberufung=N cancellation
abberufung von=N cancellation of
abberufung von amt=N sacking
abberufungsschreibe=N recall notice
abberufungsschreiben=N recall notice
abberufungsurkunde=N[F-P]recall notice
abbestellen=V cancel
abbestellung=N[F]cancellation

abbetteln=V implore
abbezahlen=V pay
abbgebeten=E excused
deutschland=N[N]germany
etc.

Note that we do not write the target German Nouns with a capital letter. This is necessary for two reasons: because we can make a general rule, to tell the program that all German nouns are written with a capital letter, and because we need the capital letters for codes, which is more important. We have marked the Noun with the capital letter N, the Verb with the capital letter V, the past forms of the verb with the letter 'h' (past) or E (past or participle), the Adjective with the letter A and the Adverb with the letter D. Note that we can use small letters for codes as well, but we must leave a space after such a code (see 'h' and 'v' above) to tell the program that the small-letter code after = is not a translation. For clarity, we can leave a space after the capital-letter code and tell the program what that means with an appropriate instruction.

We have used the letter Z and not the letter V to tell the program that we are dealing with an ambiguity Verb or Noun (sometimes Verb or Adjective, Verb or Noun or Adjective). If we don't alert the program

act=V verfahren;vorspielenNakt;aufzug;gesetz
or
abbitten=V[FP]excuse;apologizeNapology

and code this ambiguity as shown above, we will have programming problems, because not all Verbs can be Nouns as well. The sign Z is used only for those Verbs that can also be Nouns or Adjectives. The sign Z alerts the program of the existing ambiguity and says that the first translation is a Verb. Therefore, the correct coding will be:

act=Z verfahren;vorspielenNakt;aufzug;gesetz
or
abbitten=Z[FP]excuse;apologizeNapology

c) The coding of the Bilingual Dictionary (BD) is not complete without proper grammatical, syntactical and semantical information about the input (source) and the output (target) word. This information we can place in square brackets [ ]. Within the square brackets [ ] we will have to add the gender (masculine, feminine, neuter or no-gender) of the source (input) language word and the gender (masculine, feminine, neuter or no-gender) of the target (output) language word. When German is the source language (the language from which we will have to translate), the gender information is not needed, because the English words do not have to agree in gender. Only when we have to refer a Pronoun to a Noun, will we need to specify the English gender and the gender of the target language – in our case, the German Gender. For example:

John met Janet. She gave him a flower.
John traft Janet. Sie gab ihm eine Blume.

We will not be able to tell the program that *she* or Sie refer to *Janet* and *him* or *ihm* refer to *John*, unless we code the gender of *Janet, she,* Sie, *John, him, ihm*.

When we have to translate from German or English into French or from English into German, the gender information about the target language word (French, German) is absolutely needed. We put the gender information inside square brackets like this:

accounts=Z[F]schätztNbuchführung
accumulator=N[M]sammler

accusation=N[F]anklage
alternative=N[F]alternativeAalternativ
ankle=N[U]fußgelenk;knöchel
wirklichkeit=N[F]réalité
wirrsal=N[UF]confusion
etc.

The Verb and Adjective in German do not have a gender, the Adjective takes the gender of the Noun in context. The gender coded above belongs to the Noun. The M code marks the masculine gender, the F code marks the feminine gender and the U code marks the neutral gender. We cannot use the same code to mark the gender of the source language word and that of the target language word if we need both genders, because often the genders of the source and target words do not coincide. Therefore, if we want to mark the German and the French genders within these same square brackets [UF] for 'wirrsal', we must ensure that the U code is only used to mark neuter in German, and F is only used to mark feminine in French. For the French Neuter and for the German Feminine we must use other codes.

d) When a word has more than one translation within the same Part of Speech and these translations are not close synonyms, we have to mark them separately, in order to be able to specify in what context each translation will be correct. For example:

apologize=V[R]abbitten;abbitte leistenFentschuldigen

or

abgebildet=E depictedAportrayed

or (Bulgarian - English)

път=N roadYtime

or (Russian - English)

мир=N peaceYworld

The code R, in square brackets, means that the Verb is Reflexive. When *apologize* is used with a Reflexive Pronoun (*apologize oneself*), the German translation must be ***entschuldigen*** and not ***abbitten*** as in other contexts. That is why we have to give to ***entschuldigen*** its own code (F), activated only in the specified context. Since many other verbs have different translations depending on whether they are used as reflexive or not, we can use the F code for all of them.

In the above example, the software program will always translate either ***entschuldigen*** or ***abbitten*** and never ***abbitten leisten***, because ***abbitten leisten*** is not differentiated, it does not have its own code to mark a specific context. Which English translation will be chosen for the German wordform 'abgebildet' depends on whether 'abgebildet' is used as a Participle or an Adjective.

Similarly, the translations of the Bulgarian word ***път*** as 'time', and of the Russian word ***мир*** as 'world', into English will depend on such contexts as:

за първи път (for the first time)
весь мир ((the) entire world)

The preceding context must be entered in the appropriate *.h file in the following way

```
{"'първи''път'",   "@Y",  },
{"'весь''мир'",   "@Y",  },
```

to tell the program which translation to choose in which context. Which English translation will be recorded first – *road* or *time*, *peace* or *world* – depends on the programmer or the person who makes the bilingual dictionary. However, it is better to record as the first word the word that is used most often.

e) The final English–German Bilingual Dictionary of Wordforms (BDW), with all the codes and translations, will look like this:

accounts=Z[F]schätztNbuchführung
accumulate=V anhäufen;stauen;summieren
accumulator=N[M]sammler
accurate=A exakt;richtiggehendDgenau
accusation=N[F]anklage
act=Z verfahren;vorspielenNakt;aufzug;gesetz
aim=Z zielen;anlegenNziel;absicht
alternate=Z wechseln;abwechselnAabwechselnd
alternative=N[F]alternativeAalternativ
american=N amerikanerAamerikanisch
ankle=N[U]fußgelenk;knöchel
apologize=V[R]abbitten;abbitte leistenFentschuldigen
child=N[U]kind
she=R[3FSø]sie;die;ihrAweiblich
woman=N[F]frau
etc.

Note that the sign ø in

she=R[3FSø]sie;die;ihrAweiblich

denotes the Feminine Gender of the English Personal Pronoun Nominal Case *she*. It is distinct from the sign F denoting the Feminine Gender of the German Pronouns: *sie, die, ihr*. The program will not recognize what ø means, unless we define it in the source code presented in the chapter Dictionary of Wordforms, paragraph 1.2, or in the section below.

The BDW consists not only of words and wordforms, but also a large number of phrases. When we list the phrases and their translation, we save much programming effort and obtain an accurate translation. For example, we can list these phrases in the respective BDW

за първи път=f for the first time
весь мир=f the entire world

and skip the instruction in the *.h file, shown above.

2 Source code used to define the information about the word

The source code presented below, written in a file named, for example, "transgram.cpp", is an alternative way (to that described in the first part of the book) to define the grammatical, syntactical and semantical information contained in the word as registered in the BDW:

```
#include "_spsyst.h"
// a file containing includes of standard (compiler) *.h files
#include "_spengna.h"
/* a file containing includes of *.h files written by the programmer
one of the included *.h files in "_spengna.h" will be "dcgram.h" */
#include "grammset.inl"
#endif
/* below follows coded description of the information contained in the word regardless of part
of speech */
_ENGINEENTRY char * _EXPFUNC get_semantics(char *c, SEMANTICS *S)
{
```

```
 return get_sem(c, S);
}
char *get_sem(char *c, SEMANTICS *s)
{
 for(; *c && *c != ']' && *c != '\\' ; c++)
 {
  switch (*c)
  {
   case '@':
    s->B.anim = 1;   // the word denotes a living being
   break;

   case 'T':
    s->B.time = 1;   // the word denotes time
   break;

   case 'A':
    s->B.place= 1;   // the word denotes place
   break;

   case 'C':
    s->B.color = 1;  // the word denotes colour
   break;

   case 'Q':
    s->B.quality= 1;  // the word denotes quality
   break;

   case 'Z':
    s->B.size = 1;  // the word denotes size
   break;

   case 'N':
    s->B.name = 1;  // the word denotes a personal name
   break;

   case 'n':
    s->B.number = 1;  // the word denotes a number
   break;

   case 'J':
    s->B.measure= 1;  // the word denotes measure
   break;

   case 'G':
    s->B.geo = 1;   // the word denotes a geographical name
   break;

   case 'L':
    s->B.lang = 1;  // the word denotes a language
   break;

   case (uchar)',':
    s->B.akk = 1;  // the word is in Accusative
```

```
    break;
// etc.
   } // end switch
}
 return c;
}
```

The code of the case (@, T, C, etc.) is to be used only within square brackets to code the information about the word. Note that here we have separated the geographical names from the personal names. Continuation of the file "transgram.cpp" describing the information about the word for each part of speech separately:

```
_ENGINEENTRY char * _EXPFUNC get_rgramc(char *c, char *Rsyn, GRAMINFO *G,
SEMANTICS *S, char syn, char *sem)
{
short neg = 0;
short par;
   for  (; *c && *c != ']' && *c != '\\' ;c++)
   {
    switch (*c)
    {
       case '%':
         c = get_sem(++c, S);
         break;
// etc.
     default:
       switch (syn)
       {
/* below follows the case for the Noun (singular, plural, ambiguous Noun, Noun not in the
BDW) etc. possibilities connected with the Noun */

          case 'N': case 'n': case '#': case 'z':
          case '‰': case (uchar)'"': case (uchar)'"':
// define all types of Nouns
                         *Rsyn = syn;
                         switch (*c)
                         {
// start defining the information about the Noun
                          case 'P': // defines the Plural of the Noun
                                         if (neg) {
                         G->W.singular = G->W.singular_only = 1;
                                         neg = 0;
                                         }
                         else
                         G->W.plural = 1;
                         break;

                         case 'S': // defines the Singular of the Noun
                         if (neg) {
                         G->W.plural = G->W.plural_only = 1;
                                         neg = 0;
                                         }
                         else
                         G->W.singular = 1;
```

```
                    break;

                    case 'M': // defines Masculine Gender
        G->W.mgender = 1;
                    break;

                    case 'F': // defines Feminine Gender
        G->W.fgender = 1;
                    break;

                    case (uchar)',': G->W.tcase |= C_AKK; break;

        case 'U': // defines Neuter Gender
        G->W.uncountable = 1;
        G->W.ngender = 1;
                    break;

                    case 'B': // defines a Countable Noun
        G->W.countable = 1;
                    break;
                    case 'V': // defines a Collective Noun
        G->W.collective = 1;
                    break;

                    case 'H': // defines a living being
        G->W.animated = 1;
                    break;
      // etc. information about the Noun
        } /* end switch */
      break;
// etc. cases for each Part of Speech: Verb, Adjective, etc.
      } /* end switch */
      break;
   }
   if (!*c || *c == ,]' || *c == ,\\') break;
  } /* end for */
  if (*c) c++;
  return c;
}
```

Another necessary file called "grammset.inl", will contain the following piece of source code concerning the above-mentioned information about the word:

```
_ENGINEENTRY char * _EXPFUNC set_semantics(char *c, SEMANTICS *S)
{
 return set_sems(S, c);
}
char *set_sems(SEMANTICS *s, char *c)
{
 if (s && s->L != 0L)
 {
  *c++ = ,%';
  if (s->B.anim)   *c++ = 'H';
  if (s->B.name)   *c++ = 'N';
```

```
  if (s->B.time)     *c++ = 'T';
  if (s->B.place)    *c++ = 'E';
  if (s->B.quality)  *c++ = 'Q';
  if (s->B.number)   *c++ = 'n';
  if (s->B.size)     *c++ = 'Z';
  if (s->B.color)    *c++ = 'C';
  if (s->B.measure)  *c++ = 'J';
  if (s->B.geo)      *c++ = 'G';
  if (s->B.lang)     *c++ = 'L';
  if (s->B.akk)      *c++ = ',';
// etc.
}
 return c;
}
```

To substantiate (confirm) the codes used in the file "transgram.cpp", the file "dcgram.h" will contain the following source code:

```
typedef struct
{
struct T_COMMONPART word;
unsigned        mgender     : 1;   /*  masculine gender  */
unsigned        fgender     : 1;   /*  feminine gender  */
unsigned        ngender     : 1;   /*  neuter gender*/
unsigned        singular    : 1;   /*  singular only  */
unsigned        plural      : 1;   /*  plural  */
unsigned        person      : 2;   /*  human being  */
unsigned        countable   : 1;   /*  countable  */
// etc. grammatical, syntactical and semantical information about the word
} NOUN; // end the description of the noun

// etc. for the other Parts of Speech
```

(Note: the file "dcgram.h" is included in the file "transgram.cpp".)

The source code presented above does not duplicate the source code presented in the chapter Dictionary of Wordforms, paragraph 1.2. It shows only an alternative way to present the same grammatical, syntactical and semantical information about the word. The codes used to code this information are also different in most cases.

3 Choosing the right meaning depending on context

When a word has several possible translations and these translations are not close synonyms (cannot be substituted with one another in every possible context), we will have to give a distinguishing sign (a code, a label) to each translation. For example:

please=Z gefallen;freuen;freude machen;behagen;erfreuenDbitte

The English Verb *please* can be translated into German as a Verb (Z) or as an Adverb (D), depending on the context. The context is defined in the respective *.h file.

Here, we have not differentiated (labelled) the other possible translations, *freuen, freude machen, behagen, erfreuen* of 'please' used as a Verb, and the software program will never give one of them as an actual translation of 'please'. We have differentiated only the translation *bitte*, when 'please' is used as an Adverb (D). The English verb 'please' will be translated always as 'gefallen', if we do not intervene to say in which context it must be translated as ‘bitte’. The following simple instructions, written in an included file named, for example, “grammar0.h” will be enough to choose the correct translation of ‘please’ when used as an Adverb in the following contexts:

```
struct T_BEGT {
  char *inst;
  char *outst;
  int cond;
}
  BEGT[] =
{
  {"'please'*",        "D",  },
// please before full-stop is an Adverb
  {",'please'[,\]",   "@D",  },
// please between commas is an Adverb
  {"o'please'",       "@D",  },
// please after a Pronoun (Possessive, Relative), PPOC, is an Adverb
  {"'please'V",    "D",  },
// please before Verb is an Adverb
// etc.
{NULL,      NULL, 0}
};
```

In all other contexts the word *please* will be translated as *gefallen*, unless defined otherwise. Let us take the following example from BDW of a German–English machine translation software program:

von=P[]from;Tout of;’on;Oof (the)Alasting

where, in the bilingual dictionary, P marks the first meaning, as a Preposition, always given as a translation, if not specified otherwise, and T, ’, O and A mark other meanings of the same word, depending on context. Programmed in the respective *.h file, the choice of the correct translation in specified contexts looks like this:

```
{"'viel''von'", "@O",  }, /* 1 */
{"[AD]'von'M",  "@O",  },  /* 2 */
{"N'von'[NMë]",    "@O",  },  /* 3 */
{"[IH]'von'[IH]",   "@T",  }, /* 4 */
{"'geschwindigkeit''von'[HI]",  "@T",   }, /* 5 */
{"'von'[IH]'stunden'", "A",  },  /* 6 */
```

This means that after *viel* (1), after an Adjective or Adverb and before a Pronoun (2), after a Noun and before a Noun or Pronoun (3) *von* assumes the sign ‘O’ and the English translation of *von* will be *of (the)*. When *von* is used after and before a Numeral (4), after ‘geschwindigkeit’ and before a Numeral (5), its sign becomes T and its English translation will be *out of*. Finally, when *von* is used before a Numeral and this Numeral is followed by ‘stunden’ (6), its code becomes A and its translation into English will be ‘lasting’. Note that *von* can have other translations in English as well, such as ‘on’ marked with the sign ’. Similarly, we can translate any word from any language that has more than one possible translation. All we have to do is to specify the context(s) for each translation, as we have done above.

Often, in order to choose the correct translation of a word, we need the information about the word registered in the BDW in square brackets []. Because we cannot present this information in the rule, in the *.h file, we need to make a special case, in a *.c(pp) file and to define the context(s) in the respective *.h file. For example, if in the BDW we have choke=Z[FR]erwürgtNdrosselspule;chokesFverschluckt

where [FR] denotes Feminine Noun, Reflexive Verb, the capital F before *verschluckt* singles out the translation *verschluckt* and the capital N points to the German translation (*drosselspule*) of 'choke' as a Noun.

We have to tell the program when to translate *choke* as *verschluckt*. In order to do this, we have to make the following case (123) and specify, that when we have a Reflexive Verb and a translation marked with the sign F, the program must choose the translation marked with F:

```
        case 123: /* [R] -> F */
      if (wrd->E.W.reflexive_only ||wrd->E.W.reflexive)
// if the 1st word (the verb) is reflexive
                  wrd->syn = F_SYN;
// its sign is F
            else  // otherwise
         wrd->syn = V_SYN;
// its sign is V
            CopySyn();
      i = mpos; continue;
```

Specification of the context for the above case in the respective *.h file:

```
{"[VEZeF]<DdKkTN>m", NULL, 123},
```

The Reflexive Verb [VEZeF] and the Reflexive Pronoun (m) can be separated by an Adverb, Negation, Article or Noun <DdKkTN>. Here, we introduce yet another condition: the Reflexive Verb must be followed by a Reflexive Pronoun (m). If the Reflexive Verb is not followed by a Reflexive Pronoun, the translation will be *erwürgt* (V_SYN). The translation of 'choke' as a Noun is determined by the following general rule in the *.h file:

```
{"[PTS]<A>[Zz]*",   "@$N",  },
```

where [PTS] is a Preposition or an Article or Indicative Pronoun, <A> is a possible Adjective and [Zz] marks the ambiguity Noun or Verb. In other words, if *choke* is preceded by a Preposition, Article or Indicative Pronoun it is a Noun and its translation will be *drosselspule*. The same applies when we translate from French into English. For example:

bois=Z[M]drink;swallow;pocketNwood;forest

We will use the same rule

```
{"[PTS]<A>[Zz]*",   "@$N",  },
```

to determine whether the program should translate *'bois'* as a Verb (*drink*) or as a Noun (*wood*). Let us now take as an example the English words 'miss' and 'mister', which have more than one possible translation in German. In the BDW these words will be entered for translation as follows:

miss=Z[M]verfehlen;vermissen;danebengehen;fehlenNfehlschußMfräulein
mister=N[M]misterMherrDsie da

In order to decide when *miss* is *Fräulein* and when *mister* is *Herr*, we need a case to be made specially for these two words.

```
case 111:  /* miss, mister */
    if (wrdm->numb == 1) break;
```
// exit if the 2nd word is in plural
```
        if (wrdm->syn == NAME ||
    wrdm->syn == '#' ||
      isupper(wrdm->inword[0]) ||
    wrdm->syn == '?')
```
/* if the 2nd word is a name or unknown (not registered in the BDW) or is written with a capital letter */
/** The rule will be more accurate, if the capital letter for the unknown word is a condition: (isupper(wrdm->inword[0]) && (wrdm->syn == '#' |
wrdm->syn == '?')) **/
```
                wrd->syn = M_SYN;
```
// the sign of the 1st word is M
```
        else // otherwise
                wrd->esyn = V_SYN;
```
// it is a verb
```
        CopySyn();
        i = mpos; continue;
```
Specification of the context for the above rule in the *.h file:

```
{"'miss'[N#?]", NULL, 111},
{"'mister'[N#?]", NULL, 111},
```

For the last translation of *mister* as *sie da*, we need only a specification of the context:

```
{"'heigh''mister'*", "@D", },
```

This rule means that after 'heigh', 'mister', used before a full stop or exclamation mark takes the sign D and is translated in German as 'sie da'.
Note how we have resolved the semantic ambiguity of ***път*** and ***мир*** earlier in this chapter. We can do the same with 'heigh mister': register it in the BDW as a phrase and provide a translation.

4 Choosing the correct grammatical ending for the translated word

The grammatical information (Number, Gender, Case) contained in the input word must be reflected in the ending of the translated word. Usually, it is the ending of the word that carries the grammatical information in European languages. This applies especially to the languages that have many different grammatical endings, such as French, German, Russian, etc. There are two major types of grammatical information:

a) Fixed (determined, known beforehand). This type of grammatical information is contained in the wordform itself, like the Number of the Noun, or the Present, Past or Participle Form of the Verb. This grammatical information can be translated in the BDW, by listing all the wordforms of the word and their translation. For example, (English–German):

    association=N[F]verbindung;gemeinschaft;assoziation;bund
    associations=N[P]bünde;umgänge;verbände

   When the input (English) word is Plural, the translation of the word is also Plural. However, this is not always the case. Sometimes the input word is in Singular, but we must translate it as Plural and vice versa:

salvage work=N bergungsarbeiten

or

bergungsarbeiten=N salvage work

In another German–English example

bruder=N[MH]brother
brueder=n[MH]brother

the input (German) word *brueder* is Plural, so its translation must also be Plural. In this case, the sign *n* marks the Plural form of the Noun and the program is instructed to add automatically the ending -s to the English output word, to make it *brothers*. An alternative way to code the Plural will be

brueder=N[MHP]brothers

where the sign N marks the Noun (Singular), the Plural is marked separately, in the square brackets with the sign P and the translation of the word is Plural (*brothers*). In this case, the program does not have to add the English Plural ending *-s*, but knows that the input German word and its English translation are Plural, which is why we have used the sign [P] as a marker. The same applies to the translation of 'associations' in the example above, where the German word *bund* forms its plural irregularly. By marking the plural with the sign [P] and providing the translation *bünde* we save ourselves programming effort.

However, we do not have to list in the BDW all the regular plural forms of the source language, especially when their translation in the target language is also regular, i.e. they can be defined by a general rule. But when not listed, we have to make a rule for them. This rule will recognize that the word is in plural. For example, if we have listed

adjustement=N[F]regulierung

we do not have to list

adjustements=N[FP]regulierungen

The following piece of source code does the job:

```
.................................., etc. C(C++) source code
{
// a case for the Noun (singular, plural, unrecognized) regardless of language
   case 'N': case 'n': case '#':
// exclude all possible exceptions first (all other Parts of Speech)
if (g->W.singular_only) wrd->numb = 0;
/* If the noun is marked as 'singular_only', the noun is in singular. This means also that the
noun cannot have a plural form. */
// When the Noun is singular, its number is zero
// or we can give a more detailed specification below.
// Instructions for English as a source language follow below.
else if (isflex(wrd->inword, wrd->wl, "'s")) wrd->numb = 0;
// when the English Noun ends in -'s, its number is zero (singular)
    else if (isflex(wrd->inword, wrd->wl, "ss")) wrd->numb = 0;
// when the English Noun ends in -ss, its number is zero (singular)
    else if (isflex(wrd->inword, wrd->wl, "s")) wrd->numb = 1;
// in all other cases, when the English Noun ends in -s, it is in Plural
// end of the instructions for English
```

```
/* Instructions for German as a source language follow below in another
such *.c(pp) file for the German language only. */
//   else if (g->W.mgender && isflex(wrd->inword,
// wrd->wl, "ss")) wrd->numb = 0;
/* which will mean that only the Masculine Nouns that end in -ss are in Singular (etc. for
the other Genders) */
//   else if (g->W.mgender && isflex(wrd->inword, wrd->wl, "e"))
// wrd->numb = 1;
//   else if (g->W.ngender && isflex(wrd->inword, wrd->wl, "e"))
// wrd->numb = 1;
/* when the German Masculine or Neuter Nouns end in -e ,
they are in Plural */
/* Note: the above rule does not exclude the irregular Nouns, it applies to all Masculine and
Neuter Nouns. */
// end of the instructions for German
// etc. for the Noun in other languages
}
  break;
```

In the case above we specify that when the English Noun ends in *-s*, it is Plural, but we make the necessary exclusions first. Similarly, we specify the plural endings for the German noun or the noun in any other language, in another *.c(pp) file. There is no rule for the irregular nouns in the German–English machine translation and we must list all the irregular nouns, both source and target, in the BDW. For example:

kind=N[U]child
kinder=N[UP]children
frau=N[F]woman
frauen=N[FP]women

where both *kinder* and *children* are irregular, *frauen* is regular but *women* is irregular, etc.

The same considerations apply when we translate the Verbs: regular and irregular, source and target. The irregular Verbs must be registered and translated in the BDW because we cannot make a rule for them in the program. Note that we make a rule only when there is sufficient number of words that can be subjected to the same rule. The programmer alone decides if the number is sufficient.

In another *.cpp file, for a German–English machine translation, called for example "add_en_gram.cpp", we will have the following source code, which will add the correct verbal ending to the translated English Verb when the verb is regular:

```
case 'V' : case 'v' :
// a case for the Verb only, excludes all other Parts of Speech
   if (w->syn == 'V' || w->syn == ,G' &&
      w->syn != 'X' && w->numb != 1)
// specifiy what codes of the Verb are applicable
// and exclude the unapplicable (X) and the Plural Verbs
      {
                   wcw = w->cw;
      xfer = 1;
       for(cw = wcw; *cw && !isdigit(*cw); cw++); *cw = 0;
      if (xfer)
                   {
                   l = strlen(w->cw);
                   if (w->cw[l - 1] == 'a')
```

```
                {
                w->cw[l - 1] = 0;
                }
      else
      if (w->tense == 0 && w->numb == 0 && w->person == 3 &&
                                              w->tflag == 0)
/* If this is the Basic Form of the Verb (Present Tense, Singular) and the Verb is used in 3rd
Person and is not 'flagged' (i.e. marked for something else). */
/* Note, that the Person is being recognized syntactically when the preceding Noun or
Personal Pronoun Nominal Case is taken into consideration. */
                {
                l = strlen(w->cw);
      if (w->cw[l - 1] == 'y' &&
// if the last letter of the Verb is -y and
                                              w->cw[l - 2] != 'a' &&
                                              w->cw[l - 2] != 'e' &&
                                              w->cw[l - 2] != 'o' )
// the last but one letter is not -a, -e, -o
                                              {
                                              w->cw[l - 1] = 0;
                                              strcat(w->cw, "ies");
// transform the ending from -y into -ies
/* In other words, if the translation of the source Verb, into English, is carry, and the Verb is
used in 3rd Person Singular the above rule will transform carry into carries. */
                                              }
                else
// further on, when the Verb is in 3d Person Singular
                if (w->cw[l - 1] == 'x' ||
                                              w->cw[l - 1] == 's' ||
                                              w->cw[l - 1] == 'o' ||
                                              isflex(w->cw, l, "zz") ||
                                              isflex(w->cw, l, "sh") ||
                                              isflex(w->cw, l, "ch")  )
// and has one of the above listed endings
                strcat(w->cw, "es");
// add -es after this ending
                                              else // otherwise


strcat(w->cw, "s");
// add -s
       }
      else // otherwise
// further on
      if (w->tense == T_PAST && w->npar != -1) {
/* if the Verb is used in the Past and is not an exception where "wrd->npar = flx->sclass;"
*/
                                              l = strlen(w->cw);
          if (w->cw[l - 1] == 'd' &&
            w->cw[l - 2] == 'e')
// and it already has the Past ending -ed
                                              strcat(w->cw, "");
// leave it, as it is (add nothing)
                                              else
                if (w->cw[l - 1] == 'e')
```

```
// if the Verb ends in -e
                    strcat(w->cw, "d");
// add -d to make it Past
                                        else
// otherwise
                                        {
                    if (w->cw[l - 1] == 'y' &&
                  w->cw[l - 2] != 'a' &&
                                          w->cw[l - 2] != 'e' &&
                  w->cw[l - 2] != 'o' )
// if the Verb ends in -y
// and the last but one letter is not -a, -e, or -o
                    {
                    w->cw[l - 1] = 0;
                    strcat(w->cw, "ied");
// transform -y into -ied to make it Past
// in our case, carry will become carried
                    }
                    else // otherwise
                                        {
                                        if (w->cw[l - 1] == '-') {
// if the word ends with a dash
                                        w->cw[l - 1] = 0; l--;
// it is the last letter of the word
                                        }
                                        else

GenWw(w->cw, l);

strcat(w->cw, "ed");
// in all other cases
// add -ed to make it Past
                              }
                         }
                        }
                    }
                    break;
// end of rule
```

The fixed (determined) grammatical information is of two types: regular (the grammatical ending for Gender, Number or Tense is the same for most words, such as *-s* for the English Plural Nouns or *-ed* for Past or Participle form of the Verb) and irregular (certain words have their own, special, grammatical ending for Number, Case or Gender). When we make the English–German machine translation, there is no rule for the irregular grammatical information and we must list all the wordforms in the BDW that have it. For example:

child=N[U]kind
children=n[U]kind*er*
gave=h gab;eingab;angab;nachgab
woman=N[F]frau
women=n[F]frauen

Often, the source (input) language word is regular, but the target (output) language word is irregular. In this case we have to list in the BDW all such regular input words too. There is no rule for them. For example, the German translation of the English word *hits* as a regular plural noun, in the English–German machine translation will be:

hits=Z[MP]schlägtNanschläge;schläge;knüller;schlager;treffer

compare

hit=Z[MR]schlagen;stossenNschlag;anschlagSgeschlagen;gestossen;getroffenEtrafFanhauen

Note the difference between *schlag* (singular) and *anschläge* (plural).

The same considerations apply when we translate the English Verbs, regular or irregular, into another foreign language. We can assign an ending to the regular Verbs, in the program, depending on the Tense, Number and Person, without having to register all verbal wordforms in the BDW. The irregular Verbs must be registered and translated in the BDW, because there is no rule for them. Note in the above example, the German translations of the English irregular verb *hit* when used in the Present Tense plural or infinitive (*schlagen*), when used as a Participle (*geschlagen*) and when used in the Past Tense (*traf*), each translation bearing its own code, which is activated in a particular context. The *.h file specifies the context(s).

b) Undetermined, depending on context or syntax. This type of grammatical information cannot be registered in the BDW together with the translation of the word. We have to find out ourselves what the correct grammatical ending of the translated word is and program it in a rule. There are two types of undetermined grammatical information, both depend on the role of the word within the Sentence:

- One depends on agreement (concord); in many languages the Pronoun (also the Article) and particularly the Adjective must agree in Number and Gender with the Noun.
- The other depends on syntax (on the position of the word in the sentence, such as whether it is before or after the Verb), an example for this is the Case.

The translation of the Adjective *beautiful* will be recorded in the English–German BDW as follows:

beautiful=A schön;wunderschön

The German translation *schön* must agree in Gender and Case with the Noun it precedes and take various grammatical endings, depending on the Case and the Gender of the Noun (*schöne, schönem, schönen, schöner, schönes*). We cannot record this information in the BDW because it depends on the context. We can only record the basic form *schön*. For example, in German, the Adjective, when not preceded by an Article or Indicative or Possessive Pronoun and used before a Neuter, Singular Noun, ends in *-es*, when used before a Feminine, Singular Noun ends in *-e* or in Genitive Case in *-er*, etc. (depending on the Case). In order to find a solution, we have to give the Adjective the Gender of the Noun it precedes, by using the following case in the file “add_de_gram.cpp” for an English–German machine translation:

```
case 'A' :
/* ending of the Adjective depending on the Gender and Number of the next Noun */
   if (w->esyn == 'A' || w->syn == 'A')
// if the word is an Adjective
      w->inword[0] = islower(w->inword[0]);
// it is written with a small letter
      wcw = w->cw;
      xfer = 1;
```

```
        for(cw = wcw; *cw && !isdigit(*cw); cw++); *cw = 0;
        if (xfer) {
        if (w->next->numb == 0 && w->next->E.W.fgender)
// if the next word, the Noun, is in Singular and Feminine Gender
            {
            l = strlen(w->cw);
            if (w->cw[l - 1] == 'n' ||w->cw[l - 1] == 'ß'
              ||w->cw[l - 1] == 'g' ||w->cw[l - 1] == 'h'
              ||w->cw[l - 1] == 'd' ||w->cw[l - 1] == 't'
              ||w->cw[l - 1] == 'k' ||w->cw[l - 1] == 'u'
              ||w->cw[l - 1] == 'm' ||w->cw[l - 1] == 'i'
              ||w->cw[l - 1] == 'f' ||w->cw[l - 1] == 'b'
              ||w->cw[l - 1] == 'p' ||w->cw[l - 1] == 'z'
              ||w->cw[l - 1] == 'r' ||w->cw[l - 1] == 'l'
              ||w->cw[l - 1] == 's' ||w->cw[l - 1] == 'v')
            {
// if the last letter of the Adjective is one of those indicated above
                          strcat(w->cw, "e");
// add -e after the last letter
            }
        else
                          strcat(w->cw, "");
// else, add nothing
        }
        if (xfer) {
        if (w->next->numb == 0 && (w->next->E.W.mgender))
// if the next word, the Noun, is in Singular and Masculine Gender
                          {
            l = strlen(w->cw);
            if (w->cw[l - 1] == 'n' ||w->cw[l - 1] == 'ß'
              ||w->cw[l - 1] == 'g' ||w->cw[l - 1] == 'h'
              ||w->cw[l - 1] == 'd' ||w->cw[l - 1] == 't'
              ||w->cw[l - 1] == 'k' ||w->cw[l - 1] == 'u'
              ||w->cw[l - 1] == 'm' ||w->cw[l - 1] == 'i'
              ||w->cw[l - 1] == 'f' ||w->cw[l - 1] == 'b'
              ||w->cw[l - 1] == 'p' ||w->cw[l - 1] == 'z'
              ||w->cw[l - 1] == 'r' ||w->cw[l - 1] == 'l'
              ||w->cw[l - 1] == 's' ||w->cw[l - 1] == 'v')
            {
// if the last letter of the Adjective is one of those indicated above
                          strcat(w->cw, "er");
// add -er after the last letter
            }
        else
                          strcat(w->cw, " ");
// else, add nothing
        }
        }
        if (xfer) {
        if (w->next->numb == 0 && (w->next->E.W.ngender))
// if the next word, the Noun, is in Singular and Neuter Gender
                          {
            l = strlen(w->cw);
            if (w->cw[l - 1] == 'n' ||w->cw[l - 1] == 'ß'
```

```
        ||w->cw[l - 1] == 'g' ||w->cw[l - 1] == 'h'
        ||w->cw[l - 1] == 'd' ||w->cw[l - 1] == 't'
        ||w->cw[l - 1] == 'k' ||w->cw[l - 1] == 'u'
        ||w->cw[l - 1] == 'm' ||w->cw[l - 1] == 'i'
        ||w->cw[l - 1] == 'f' ||w->cw[l - 1] == 'b'
        ||w->cw[l - 1] == 'p' ||w->cw[l - 1] == 'z'
        ||w->cw[l - 1] == 'r' ||w->cw[l - 1] == 'l'
        ||w->cw[l - 1] == 's' ||w->cw[l - 1] == 'v')
       {
// if the last letter of the Adjective is one of those indicated above
                        strcat(w->cw, "es");
// add –es after the last letter
       }
     else
                        strcat(w->cw, " ");
// else, add nothing
     }
     }
     if (xfer) {
     if (w->next->R.W.plural_only ==1 ||
       w->next->numb == 1) {
// if the next word, the Noun, is in Plural
       l = strlen(w->cw);
       if (w->cw[l - 1] == 'n' ||w->cw[l - 1] == 'ß'
        ||w->cw[l - 1] == 'g' ||w->cw[l - 1] == 'h'
        ||w->cw[l - 1] == 'd' ||w->cw[l - 1] == 't'
        ||w->cw[l - 1] == 'k' ||w->cw[l - 1] == 'u'
        ||w->cw[l - 1] == 'm' ||w->cw[l - 1] == 'i'
        ||w->cw[l - 1] == 'f' ||w->cw[l - 1] == 'b'
        ||w->cw[l - 1] == 'p' ||w->cw[l - 1] == 'z'
        ||w->cw[l - 1] == 'r' ||w->cw[l - 1] == 'l'
        ||w->cw[l - 1] == 's' ||w->cw[l - 1] == 'v')
       {
// if the last letter of the Adjective is one of those indicated above
                        strcat(w->cw, "e");
// add –e after the last letter
       }
     else
                        strcat(w->cw, "");

// else, add nothing     }
                   }
     }
  if (w->gflag == (uchar)'í') {
     strcat(w->cw, w->rprefix);
     w->rprefix[0] = '\0';
  }
  break;   // end the rule
```

To deal with the ending of the Adjective when preceded by a Determiner, we have renamed the German Adjective for the English–German machine translation by specifying the context for this new code:

```
  {"'the'<Dd>A",      "@$Ä",  },
```

/* renaming of the Adjective from A into Ä after *the* */

```
{"'this'<Dd>A",        "@$Ä",  },
```

/* renaming of the Adjective from A into Ä after *this* */
// etc. determiners

With this rule we tell the program that the German Adjective when used after a Determiner differs from the other Adjectives (as far as its grammatical ending is concerned). Then, for the endings of the re-named Adjective Ä we will have other rules: the German Adjective Ä can end only in *-e* or *-en*. It cannot end in *-em*, *-er*, or *-es*. We make a case for Ä, in the file "add_de_gram. cpp", similar to the case for the German Adjective A shown above:

```
case 'Ä' :
/* ending of the Adjective, preceded by a Determiner,
depending on the Gender and Number of the next Noun */
   if (w->esyn == 'Ä' || w->syn == 'Ä')
// if the sign of the word is Ä (re-named Adjective)
// etc. as shown for case A above, then
      if (xfer) {
      if (w->next->numb == 0 && w->next->E.W.fgender)
         {
// if the next word (the Noun) is singular and feminine
         l = strlen(w->cw);
         if (w->cw[l - 1] == 'n' || w->cw[l - 1] == 'ß'
          || w->cw[l - 1] == 'g' || w->cw[l - 1] == 'h'
          || w->cw[l - 1] == 'k' || w->cw[l - 1] == 'u'
          || w->cw[l - 1] == 'm' || w->cw[l - 1] == 'i'
          || w->cw[l - 1] == 'f' || w->cw[l - 1] == 'b'
          || w->cw[l - 1] == 'p' || w->cw[l - 1] == 'z'
          || w->cw[l - 1] == 'd' || w->cw[l - 1] == 't'
          || w->cw[l - 1] == 'r' || w->cw[l - 1] == 'l'
          || w->cw[l - 1] == 's' || w->cw[l - 1] == 'v')
// if the ending of the Adjective is as shown above
         {
                     strcat(w->cw, "e");
// the ending of the Adjective is -e (place it)
         }
      else
```

// etc., for the other two genders and the plural, similar to case A above.

When we translate into German, for example, we must add the correct Case ending to the German Pronoun, Numeral, etc. Parts of Speech that have a Case ending. This is done in a similar way, preferably without re-naming, because re-naming has its disadvantages. A better way is 'flagging', exemplified in the case that attaches a possessive ending *–(e)s* to the Noun in a Possessive (Genitive) construction. Below is a case from the file "parser.c(pp)" that does the flagging.

```
         case 56:
/* flagging of the German Noun used later in 'add_de_gram.cpp' */
      if (wrdm->numb != 1 &&
            wrdm->numb == 0 && !wrdm->E.W.fgender)
// if the 2nd word is not in Plural and it is in Singular and it is not Feminine
                        wrdm->adj_flag = 1;
// the 2nd word is flagged with adj_flag
/*  Note: adj_flag is defined in the respective *.h file,
```

otherwise the program will not know what it means. */

```
                CopySyn();
                i = mpos; continue;
```

In 'parser.h' we define in what context the Noun is flagged as *adj_flag*:

```
  {"N<F>N",       NULL, 56},
```

The sign F is optional. It replaces the source-language Preposition used between two Nouns to express possessiveness, the second word is the second Noun. Then, in the file "add_de_gram. cpp ", for the English–German machine translation, in case N, we add the following source code for the ending of the German Nouns used in Genitive Case:

```
case 'N' :

   if (w->esyn == N_SYN || w->syn == 'N')
    w->inword[0] = toupper(w->inword[0]);
```

// This noun is written in German always with a capital letter.
/* The above rule is applicable only when we translate into German.
In the translation, it will write, with a capital letter
all German nouns written with a small letter in the BDW .*/

// etc.
// Genitive

```
   if (w->numb == 0 && !w->R.W.uncountable && !w->R.W.collective
      && !w->R.W.plural_only && w->cflag != '=' &&
      !w->R.W.singular)
```

/* set the necessary conditions for this rule */
/* if the Noun is in Singular and not collective, plural, Singular only, etc. */
/* Note the difference between Singular and Singular only: Singular can have a Plural, Singular only - not. */

```
      {
      wcw = strchr(w->cw, '3');
      if (wcw) {
         w->cw = ++wcw;
      }
     else {
         wcw = w->cw;
         xfer = 1;
      }
      for(cw = wcw; *cw && !isdigit(*cw); cw++); *cw = 0;
      }
      for(cw = wcw; *cw && !isdigit(*cw); cw++); *cw = 0;
      if (xfer && w->adj_flag == 1 && (w->E.W.fgender != 1
        || w->E.W.qgender != 1 || w->E.W.plural_only != 1))
```

/* This is a sub-condition: if the Noun is flagged with *adj_flag* and is not Feminine, Masculine (those German Masculine Nouns that end in *-en* in Plural) or Plural only. */

```
                  {
         l = strlen(w->cw);
         if (w->cw[l - 1] == 'n' || w->cw[l - 1] == 'w'
           || w->cw[l - 1] == 'g' || w->cw[l - 1] == 'h'
           || w->cw[l - 1] == 'd' || w->cw[l - 1] == 't'
           || w->cw[l - 1] == 'k' || w->cw[l - 1] == 'u'
```

```
            || w->cw[l - 1] == 'm' || w->cw[l - 1] == 'i'
            || w->cw[l - 1] == 'o' || w->cw[l - 1] == 'y'
            || w->cw[l - 1] == 'a' || w->cw[l - 1] == 'c'
            || w->cw[l - 1] == 'f' || w->cw[l - 1] == 'b'
            || w->cw[l - 1] == 'p' || w->cw[l - 1] == 'z'
            || w->cw[l - 1] == 'r' || w->cw[l - 1] == 'l'
            || w->cw[l - 1] == 'v')
// and if the Noun has one of the above shown endings
// (a sub-condition to the previous sub-condition)
          {
                      strcat(w->cw, "s");
// add –s after this ending
          }
       else
                      strcat(w->cw, "");
// else, don't add anything
       }
   }
   else
// end of Genitive
```

// etc., the case continues to deal with other endings for the translated Noun such as, for example, when to add the plural ending *-en* to ***regulierung*** (mentioned earlier in this chapter). Note that we have not said when the program must add –es. As shown above, it adds only –s.

5 Choosing of the right word sequence for the target language

Last but not least, the words in the target language must be arranged properly, if we do not want a word-for-word translation in which the words follow the sequence of the source language and the translated text makes little sense. We will take an example from the English-German-English Machine Translation. In particular we will consider the positioning of the Auxiliary Verb before or after the Past Participle of the Verb.

In German the Auxiliary Verb usually follows the Past Participle of the Verb. Often the sentence ends with an Auxiliary Verb. In English, the Auxiliary Verb always precedes the Past Participle of the Verb and the sentence almost never ends with an Auxiliary Verb. To resolve this translation problem we will have to write the following piece of source code in the file "grammar0.cpp" in order to obtain the correct verbal sequence for the target English or German Language, when we translate either from German or from English:

```
            case 20:  /* same case for German or English */
                      if ( (wrdp->mood & M_IMPER) == 0)
// If the above conditions are met (the Verb is not used in imperative)
            {
          change_wrd(wp, synstr, mpos-1, mpos);
// change the word sequence by substituting the places
// of the two adjacent words
                                          CopySyn();
            }
                      i = mpos; continue;
```

This rule will be continued in the file "grammar0.h" only for English as target language:

```
T_PARSE PSEG_DEEN[] =
{
{"[Ee]<'TSOAÜN>[XYxU]",                 NULL, 20},
/* when the source language word sequence is Past Participle of the Verb [Ee]
followed by an optional Nominal Word Group <'TSOAÜN> (Determiner,
Adjective, Noun) and then followed by Auxiliary Verb [XYxU],
substitute the places of the two adjacent words (exclude <'TSOAÜN> ) */
{NULL,        NULL, 0}
};
```

For example, the German sentence

... dass die meisten Tests durchgeführt wurden

where the auxiliary verb follows the participle, will be translated into English, using the above rule, as

... that the most tests were led through.

The accurate translation will be: ... *that the most tests were carried out*, although this is another matter. Thanks to case 20 the auxiliary verb has now moved before the participle. Case 20 repositions the compound Auxiliary Verbs with the same ease when they are registered in the BDW as a phrase (German–English)

werden koennte=U could be

For example

gebraucht werden koennte

will be translated *could be needed*. The translation of *werden koennte* has moved before the participle *gebraucht*, as required by the English word order.The same rule will be continued in the file "de_gram0.h" for German only as target language:

```
T_PARSE PSEG_DEEN[] =
{
{"[XYxU]<dDkK>E", NULL, 20},
/* when the source language word sequence is Auxiliary Verb [XYxU]
followed by an optional Adverb or negation <dDkK> and then followed by Past Participle of the
Verb [Ee], substitute the places of the two adjacent words (exclude <dDkK> ) */
{NULL,        NULL, 0}
};
```

This rule will change the input of the English-sequence auxiliary verb followed by a participle into a participle followed by an auxiliary verb in translation, if necessary, because this is not always the case in German. Case 20 can change the places of a Noun followed by a Verb to a Verb followed by a Noun if we change the rule in the *.h file:

```
{"NV",          NULL, 20},
```

Then, the German sentence

Ich solle Frau spielen

will not be translated into English word-by-word

I should woman play

but will be translated with the correct word sequence

I should play woman.

If there is a target language that requires a different word order for

Ich solle Frau spielen

such as, for example

I woman should play

case 28 below will substitute the places of *solle* and *Frau*.

```
    case 28: /* move word */
if (i > 1 && wp[i-1]->syn == K_SYN)
  x = i-1;
 else
  x = i;
  wcount = move_seg(que, wp, synstr, x, mpos-1, 1);
  i = mpos; continue;
```

Continuation of the above case in the respective *.h file:

```
{"U<KD>NV",        NULL, 28},
```

We should be extremely careful when we change the word order, because the word order may depend on the meaning of the words as well.

In another example we will show that the English separable compound verbs (Verb followed by a Nominal Word Group and then followed by an Adverbial Particle) can be translated correctly into German in the BDW (of course, a source code is needed to make the program read the rule shown below):

add <NP>'up'=@Vzusammenzählen\@ \

add precedes the intervening Noun Phrase <NP>, *up* is not translated and the German translation will be *zusammenzählen*. Otherwise, the translation of *add* (without *up*) is *hinzusetzen*. Without this rule, the German translation will follow the English word sequence: *hinzusetzen* – Noun Phrase – *ob* and the translation will make no sense. Similarly, we can translate correctly a Preposition and a Noun separated by an intervening phrase:

within <NP>'reach'=@Verreichbar für\@ \

within precedes the intervening phrase <NP>, let's say *ten miles*, *reach* follows it and the German translation will be *erreichbar für*, followed by the Nominal Phrase <NP>, instead of the wrong translation *innerhalb* <NP> *Reichweite* without this rule.

When we translate from German into English, we can use the same method. In German there are many separable verbs (the same verb is split into two parts by an intervening Nominal Phrase). For example:

achten <NP>'hoch'=@Vappreciate\@ \

The verb *achten* precedes the intervening Nominal Phrase <NP>, *hoch* will be found to justify the rule but will not be translated, and the translation will be *appreciate*. Otherwise, the translation of *achten* (without *hoch*) is *respect*. Without this rule, the translation will follow the German word sequence: *respect* – Nominal Phrase – *highly*, which is not quite usual for English. Similarly, we can translate correctly a Preposition and an Adjective separated by an intervening phrase:

ab <HN>'gültig'=@Vcoming into effect on\@ \

ab will precede the intervening phrase <HN>, where H is a number N is a Noun, *gültig* will follow it, and the English translation will be *coming into effect on*, followed by the phrase <HN>. The output word sequence can be also determined in the BDW, when we translate whole phrases or even whole sentences. For example:

within a few hours=f im laufe von wenigen stunden
within a radius of=P im umkreis von
within a week=f binnen acht tagen
within a year=f innerhalb jahresfrist;in jahresfrist

abgesichert sind=f are made safe
absolut nicht leiden=f absolutely dislike
abstand naehme=h gave up
ach du grune neune=f good heavens
alle acht tage=f once a week

etc.

Without translation of whole phrases, the word-by-word translation of *within a few hours* or *within a week*, etc. will be pure nonsense.

6 Blocking a word in the translation

Sometimes, to avoid word-to-word translation, we have to tell the program not to translate a certain word in a specified context. The following case (67) is an example of how this is done.

```
// const char BLANK = ' ';   // declared earlier in the program files

          case 67:  /* block word position */
// no conditions imposed
                                        wrd->syn = BLANK;
// block the 1st word (its translation will not be displayed)
                    CopySyn();
        i = mpos; continue;
```

Continuation of the above rule in the *.h file:

```
{"X<dKk>V", NULL, 67},                  /* X is blank */
```

If we have the sentence

We will come.

its German translation will be *Wir kommen*, *will* is suppressed and will not be translated.

7 Inserting a word in the translation

Sometimes, we need to insert a word in the translation to make it sound better. This word may not exist in the sentence to translate, but it must exist in our program for a specified context. Therefore, we have to define it first in a *.c(pp) file, called for example 'definitions. c(pp)':

```
const char *MUST_GER = "müßte";
```

Then we have to declare our code MUST_GER in the respective *.h file, here 'definitions.h':

```
extern const char *MUST_GER;
```

We have defined the German auxiliary verb '*müßte*' (must). In the English–German machine translation we can use case 9 below to block a word in a specified context, and at the same time to insert a word to make a correct German translation:

```
        case 9:     /* YB */
                         wrd->syn = U_SYN;
// the 1st word is an auxiliary verb from the U paradigm
                         wrdm->syn = BLANK;
// block the 2nd word (do not display it in the translation)
                         strcpy(wrd->cw, MUST_GER);
/* the 1st word assumes the translation as defined for  MUST_GER */
        CopySyn();
        i = mpos; continue;
```

Continuation of the above rule in the corresponding *.h file:

```
{"YB",    NULL, 9},
```

where Y is an auxiliary verb from the English Y paradigm.
For example, if we translate the English sentence:

He had to bring the clock.

without the above case the translation will be word-to-word:

Er hätte zu bringen die Uhr.

with the help of case 9, the translation will be correct:

Er müßte bringen die Uhr.

The verbal article *to*, as 2nd word, is not translated because it is suppressed (blocked), and the program displays *müßte* instead of *hätte*. There is an easier way to obtain a correct translation, by registering the phrase in the BDW:

had to=U müßte

However this leads to errors, because *to* is not always a verbal particle. Compare:

He had to my knowledge accepted the conditions.

An alternative way is to write the following case in the file "add_en_gram.cpp" for a Foreign language – English machine translation:

```
case 'X' :
/* For the translations of the auxiliary verbs 'do' and 'be', referred to 'do' and 'be' in the BDW irrespective of person and number. On the bases of the number and person of the target language word, the case below decides how to translate the English auxiliary verbs 'do' and 'be'. */
  if (!w->person && !w->numb) break;
// exit if the above conditions are not met
  if (w->cw[0] == 'd') {
// if the code is X and the first letter of the Auxiliary Verb is 'd'
  if (w->tense == T_PAST)
// if the target language word is in past tense
    strcpy(w->cw, "did");
// translate 'did'
  else {
  if (w->numb == 0 && w->person == 3)
// if the target language word is in singular, third person
    strcpy(w->cw, "does");
// translate 'does'
  else // otherwise
    strcpy(w->cw, "do");
// translate 'do'
     }
  break;
   }
   if (w->tense == T_PAST){
// if the target language word is in past tense
  if (w->numb)
// if it is in plural
    strcpy(w->cw, "were");
// translate 'were'
  else // otherwise
  strcpy(w->cw, "was");
// translate 'was'
   }
 else {
  if (w->numb)
// if the target language word is in plural
    strcpy(w->cw, "are");
// translate 'are'
  else if (w->person == 1)
// if the target language word is 1st person (meant - singular)
  strcpy(w->cw, "am");
// translate 'am'
  else if (w->person == 2)
// if the target language word is in 2nd person
  strcpy(w->cw, "are");
// translate 'are'
  else // otherwise
  strcpy(w->cw, "is");
// translate 'is'
   }
   break;
```

In the German–English BDW the translations of 'do' and 'be' will be registered as follows:

ist=X[3S]\be
tun=Z[]doNaction;doings
war=X[3S<]\be

Using the reference \ and providing the main form of the auxiliary verb, the correct translation is chosen on the basis of the information provided in square brackets [ ]: third person (3), singular (S), past (<), etc.

We find the above case unnecessary, because we can register the correct translation in the BDW

ist=X[3S]is
war=X[3S<]was

Delete the case above and omit the reference to 'be' in the BDW.

8 Known difficulties and problems

The difficulties and problems arise when dealing with two languages. Every language has its specifics and needs both programming specialists and language specialists. We will discuss some of the difficulties common to most languages.

a) Never make a general rule when there are exceptions from this rule. For example, don't make a list of all prefixes and tell the program that any of the input words in the BDW can have any of these prefixes. In German the prefixes are often prefixed words, and the translation obtained, due to such a general rule, either makes no sense or is misleading and incorrect. See the wrong translation of the following examples:

   Lebensgemeinschaft is translated as *life community* instead of *unregistered marriage* or *flat sharing*; *Leuchtspurgeschoss* is translated as *shining tracking storey* instead of *tracer bullet*. This list is almost endless. The solution is to list all the words and wordforms in the BDW and only then make a rule. Some languages, like German, are agglutinative – they occasionally allow unrestricted combination of words to form a compound word, and these newly formed compound words are not registered in any Dictionary. For example, the word *Sprachlernmittel* (language learning materials) is not registered in a dictionary, but someone may invent it. In this case, the software program may translate it as *language learning means*, not *materials*.

b) Specify the context of each meaning of every polysemous word and make the program choose the right meaning. The easiest way to do this is to list, in the BDW, the whole phrase in which a particular meaning of a polysemous word is used. For example, the German word *aalglatt* has the following translations into English: *dexterous, slippery, oily*. However, the translation of *aalglatt Reden* must be *smooth speech*. Therefore, list *aalglatt reden* in the BDW as a phrase:

   aalglatt reden=f smooth speech

   The list of phrases will be very long, and the longer it is the more accurate will be the translation. Compare the following German–English examples:

   ab=from;since
   ab sein=be far away;be broken

ab und zu=sometimes
abbau=dismantling;reduction;mining
abbau des lohnes=wage cuts
abgeblasst=waned;pale
abgeblasst redensart=complicated phrase
etc.

c) Last, but not least, don't forget the word sequence. Test extensively your Machine-Translation program before you bring it to the market and never claim that it translates perfectly. Above all, do not provide an example of a perfect translation on the box to attract the attention of the buyer. It is always wise to say that this Machine-Translation software program is not perfect and that the translated text needs post-editing. Otherwise, the Machine Translation will be discredited, and the customer disappointed, reducing the market for such programs, as is the case now. The programmer can correct any wrong translation, but never all, which is why programs have versions. Usually, the next version is better than the previous one. The improvement of a Machine-Translation software program is an ongoing process, but one must stop somewhere and say, so far so good for this version.

9 Question Answering

Dialogue systems have a long history. One can find a number of on-line question-answering software programs on the Internet. The immediate aim is to teach the computer, via a software program, to understand your question and to provide an answer to it. The longer aim is to communicate with the computer, as you communicate with a friend, or friends. This means that the computer can not only answer your question, but also ask you a question in return, so that you engage the computer in a real dialogue, keeping, at least for a while, the initial theme. Such software programs appeared in the early 1980s, but often the dialogue ended abruptly with the computer saying that you were stupid and did not understand. This is an easy way to play clever.

Dialogue systems, both via voice and text recognition, are making steady progress in various industrial fields, especially in the aviation and car industries (to make the aircraft, robot or vehicle turn left, turn right, switch off, switch on, etc.). On the Internet, the aim is to save time reading through all FAQs (frequently asked questions) by allowing you to ask your own question and immediately receive an answer to it. Search engines on the Internet are similar but elementary. Their aim is to provide a list of places on the Internet where you can find an answer to your query.

1 Dividing the knowledge about the word and the world into fields and groups

In the first chapter we showed how to place additional grammatical, semantical, etc. information for each word entry into square brackets. All information is relevant; the more information we have about the meaning of the wordform, the better will be the programmed result. Therefore, we had to classify the information needed by gathering the words into groups according to a particular relationship and meaning, as we explained in the chapter 'Lexical semantics' and demonstrated practically in Georgiev, 1979 and Georgiev and Raynova, 1989, *Softhesaurus* (Georgiev, 1993b), *Linguaterm* (Georgiev, 1994) and *Geoatlas* (Georgiev, 1994a), with a detailed semantic description in accordance with the subject field described. In our question-answering software programs *Dialogue* (Georgiev, 2003) and *Antwort* (Georgiev, 2006a), we have proven the applicability of our ALSD to content recognition. We have coded with a one-letter code the following word meanings in English and German:

code English	'head' **word(s)** German	**code** English	'head' **word(s)** German
# game (sport)	# Spiel	- sound, noise	- Lärm, tönen
/ grammatical feature	/ grammaticalisch	(month	(Monat
~ song (music)	~ Musik, Gesang, Lied	^ feeling	^ Gefühl

¨ object(s) in outer space, star, celestial body	¨ Stern, himmlisch
± negative	± negativ
§ speed(y)	§ Geschwindigkeit, Tempo
° continent	° Kontinent
¶ fish	¶ Fisch
¾ measure(ment)	¾ messen, Mass
Å clean(ing)	Å säubern, Reinigung
Æ desire	Æ wünschen, Wunsch
æ see, perception	æ sehen
B building	B Gebäude
C country (state)	C Land (Staat)
Ç think, thought	Ç denken, Gedanke
D medicine, medicament, drug	D Medizin, Droge, Arzneimittel
é book	é Buch
è drink	è trinken, Getränk
E education, schooling	E Ausbildung, Schulung
Ê EEC, European Union (countries)	Ê EU, Europäische Gemeinschaft
Ë island Ë Insel	È America
ê liquid ê Flüssigkeit	e end (finish)
É river	É Fluss
ë supernatural being	ë überirdisch
F feminine	F weiblich
f hit	*f* Schlag, schlagen
G group of people, crowd	G Trupp, Menge
	ì doctrine
H human being	H Mensch
I stone (mineral)	I Stein (Mineral)
K measuring instrument, tool, gauge	K Messinstrument
	î rich
L language	L Sprache
M masculine	M männlich
Ñ leave, departure	Ñ Abreise, abreisen
N name	N Name
ñ payment	ñ Zahlung
ó door, entrance, opening	ó Tür, Eingang
ø eat, eating	ø essen, Essen
Ô kill, killer, killing	Ô Tötung, Totschläger
ô lie, deceive, deceit	ô Lüge, betrügen, Betrug
ò nationality	ò Nationalität
O organization	O Vereinigung

' way, road, street	' Strasse
| colour	| Farbe
¦ jewellery	¦ Schmuck
´ crime, criminal, commit crime	´ Verbrechen, Verbrecher, kriminell
= construction	= Konstruktion
¢ written material, writing	¢ Schreiben
¬ jurisdiction	¬ Rechtsprechung
À (chemical) element	À chemisch
ã Africa	ã Afrika
á Asia	á Asien
Á Australia	Á Australien
ä bird	ä Vogel
Ã Europe	Ã Europa
a get, achieve, obtain	a bekommen
à metal	à Metall
Ä premises (room)	Ä Zimmer
b apparatus	b Gerät
c chemical substance	c Chemikalien
ç group of things	ç Gruppe
d mountain	d Berg
È Amerika	
e beenden, Ende	
f fruit or nut	f Frucht, Nuss
g gather	g sammeln
í damage	í beschädigen, Schaden
Í decrease	Í mindern, Abnahme
ì Doktrin (teaching)	
ï increase	ï steigen, Zunahme
Ì particle	Ì Partikel
Î poor	Î arm
î reich	
k clothes (incl. shoes and hats), clothe	k Kleidung, Kleider
m musical instrument	m Musikinstrument
Ö furniture	Ö Möbel
o holiday	
ö insect	ö Insekt
Õ part of body	Õ Körperglied
Ò populated area	Ò Stadt, Siedlung
õ tree	õ Baum
p sport	p Sport
q illness, disease	q Krankheit
r free	r befreien, frei

Ó	region, area, piece of land, place	Ó	Region, Gebiet, Standort
Ø	take, taking	Ø	nehmen, Einnahma
P	plural	P	Mehrzahl
R	religion	R	Religion
T	time	T	Zeit
Þ	agree(ment)	Þ	zustimmen, Abkommen
Ü	living being, animal	Ü	Tier
ú	material, fibre, fabric	ú	Stoff, Faser, Gewebe
U	military	U	Militär
Ú	positive	Ú	positiv
Ù	seed, grain	Ù	Korn, Samen
ù	vessel (boat, etc.)	ù	Schiff, Boot
V	vegetation, plants	V	Vegitation, Pflanze
W	weapon	W	Waffe
X	food	X	Nahrung
ÿ	attack	ÿ	Angriff, angreifen
Y	instrument, tool, implement	Y	Instrument, Werkzeug
Z	grammatical term	Z	Sprachlehre
s	science	s	Wissenschaft
ß	chief	ß	Häuptling
u	art	u	Kunst
ü	container	ü	Gefäss
û	gas(eous) substance	û	gas, gasig
Û	jem, precious (semiprecious) stone	Û	Edelstein
v	vehicle	v	Fahrzeug
w	worker	w	Arbeiter
x	next of kin (relative)	x	Verwandete
ý	create, make, creation, discover	ý	schaffen, Schöpfung
y	money	y	Geld
z	help	z	Helfen, Hilfe

Note that the same code codes the same meaning in both languages and that the meaning is language independent. The coded meanings can be found in all languages, but the words that represent these meanings are language specific. These codes are put in square brackets [ ] in the DW and explained in the source code of the program (see further below and the 1st chapter).

Of course, the above list is not complete. It can be expanded in all directions: grammatical, semantical, syntactical, pragmatical, as long as we find a unique code to mark a particular meaning and use it in the software program for content recognition. Worth noting is the fact that the ALSD is valid for all languages, because the external, objective, reality is the same for all people. How we visualize, interpret and explain objective reality is another matter and beyond the scope of this book.

2 Adding semantical, pragmatical, etc. information to each word in the DW and programming this information

In the DW the meaning of the words is coded within the square brackets like this:

English	German
academician=N[HE]	akademie=N[BGOE]
academy=N[BOE]	akademiemitglied=N[HE]
acajou=N[0]	akademiemitglieder=n[HE]
acanthi=n[V]	akademiemitgliedes=N[HE]
albatross=N[ä]	akademien=n[BGOE]
bat=Z[0]/N[ä]	akademiker=N[HE]
bird=N[ä]	akademikerin=N[HFE]
blackbird=N[ä]	akademikerinnen=n[HFE]
catfish=N	akademisch=A[E]
fish=Z[0]/N[¶X]	akademismus=N[E]

horse=N[Ü] blaetterfisch=N[¶]
petrol=N[ê] dunnbier=N[è]
etc.

where H is also Ü (a living being), a 'drink' [è] (*dunnbier*) is always 'liquid' [ê], but a liquid is not always a drink (for example, *petrol*). Therefore, we don't have to tell the computer that

dunnbier=N[êè]

(*beer*) is liquid, we can do it within the program when necessary. We can sub-categorize a major meaning, such as that of H (human being) by adding another meaning that goes with it. For example:

English	**German**
academician=N[HsE]	akademiker=N[HsE]

In the examples above we have added the code *s* (science) to create the meaning *scientist*. An academician is a scientist. Of course, we must tell the software program, with a piece of source code that the combination of H and s within the same square brackets no longer represents two separate meanings (a human being and science) but now one meaning, a *scientist*. Following the same logic, the combination of a *human being* [H] and a *musical instrument* [m] will make up the sub-group *musician*. Therefore,

pianist=N[Hm]

will be read by the program as a *musician*.
We can make any such combinations in order to create new meanings. However, with this approach we burden the software program by adding many conditions for each combination of meanings. It is better to stick to the rule, one meaning – one code.
(Note: the codes used above are not listed in the Index of Abbreviations, because they are part of the programming code.)
(Tip: When the semantical description of a word entry is complete, we will have more than one code within the square brackets [ ]. Many other word entries also have some of these codes. Therefore, we must make sure that we always arrange the codes in the same sequence within the square brackets [ ]. The sequence is not important for the software program to function, but it is important, when we have to edit the Dictionary of Wordforms and make changes. When the codes have the same sequence it is easy to find a particular sequence with the 'search' command of our text editor. For example, compare the difficulty to find the sequence [HMN] (human being, masculine, name), if it is written in one place like this [HNM] and in another place in the DW like this [NMH]).

In order to enable the computer software program to recognize and interpret our codes in the DW, we must write a piece of source code in the program itself and then compile it on a compiler.

Below, in a file called 'grammar.c(pp)', we define the above-listed semantical information carried by the Noun and presented in square brackets.

```
void get_engram(char *word, char *cw, WORD *wrd)
{
char *wdic;
char *wirr;
 if (!wrd->inbase ||wrd->inbase[0] == '\0')
   strcpy(wrd->inbase, word);          /* Source Form */
   strcpy(wrd->eprefix, cw);      /* Debug Info */
```

```
switch (wrd->syn)
{
case 'N' :   /* Noun Singular, basic Form */
   if (isdigit(*cw)) wrd->tflag = *cw++ - '0';
   if (isdigit(*cw)) wrd->tense = *cw++ - '0';
   if (isdigit(*cw)) wrd->gender = *cw++ - '0';
   if (*cw == '[') {
/* If there is a square bracket opened to enclose additional */
    while (*cw && *cw != ']') {     /* information about the Noun */

//       code            name of code
   if (*cw == 'N')   wrd->e.N.name = 1;
   if (*cw == 'ß')   wrd->e.N.chief = 1;
   if (*cw == 'H')   wrd->e.N.human = 1;
   if (*cw == 'T')   wrd->e.N.time = 1;
   if (*cw == '=')   wrd->e.N.constrct = 1;
   if (*cw == 'Õ')   wrd->e.N.body = 1;
   if (*cw == '±')   wrd->e.N.negative = 1;
   if (*cw == '¶')   wrd->e.N.fish = 1;
   if (*cw == '§')   wrd->e.N.speed = 1;
   if (*cw == 'Þ')   wrd->e.N.agree = 1;
   if (*cw == 'Ú')   wrd->e.N.positive = 1;
   if (*cw == '')    wrd->e.N.noise = 1;
   if (*cw == '¾')   wrd->e.N.measure = 1;
   if (*cw == 'õ')   wrd->e.N.tree = 1;
   if (*cw == 'm')   wrd->e.N.musicinst = 1;
   if (*cw == 'p')   wrd->e.N.sport = 1;
   if (*cw == 'Ü')   wrd->e.N.animal = 1;
   if (*cw == 'v')   wrd->e.N.vehicle = 1;
   if (*cw == 'ù')   wrd->e.N.boat = 1;
   if (*cw == 'À')   wrd->e.N.element = 1;
   if (*cw == 'Ö')   wrd->e.N.furniture = 1;
   if (*cw == 'ö')   wrd->e.N.insect = 1;
   if (*cw == 'Ò')   wrd->e.N.town = 1;
   if (*cw == 'ò')   wrd->e.N.nationality = 1;
   if (*cw == 'Ô')   wrd->e.N.kill_er = 1;
   if (*cw == 'ô')   wrd->e.N.lie = 1;
   if (*cw == 'Ó')   wrd->e.N.region = 1;
   if (*cw == 'ó')   wrd->e.N.entrance = 1;
   if (*cw == 'ú')   wrd->e.N.material = 1;
   if (*cw == 'Ù')   wrd->e.N.seed = 1;
   if (*cw == 'ü')   wrd->e.N.container = 1;
   if (*cw == 'Û')   wrd->e.N.jem = 1;
   if (*cw == 'û')   wrd->e.N.gas = 1;
   if (*cw == 'Ä')   wrd->e.N.room = 1;
   if (*cw == 'à')   wrd->e.N.metal = 1;
   if (*cw == 'è')   wrd->e.N.drink = 1;
   if (*cw == 'é')   wrd->e.N.book = 1;
   if (*cw == 'Ë')   wrd->e.N.island = 1;
   if (*cw == 'ã')   wrd->e.N.africa = 1;
   if (*cw == 'È')   wrd->e.N.america = 1;
// etc.,
/* We can use the same codes for German or any other language, we do not
have to translate them, because this is a programming code. */
```

```
      } /*end*/
     cw++;
    }
    cw++;
    }
}
   wrd->person = 3;
  break;
```

Definition of the semantical information carried by the Noun (presented in square brackets) in the file 'grammar.h'.

```
typedef struct {
//              name of code            code
unsigned        name        : 1;   /*    [N]    */
unsigned        human       : 1;   /*    [H]    */
unsigned        constrct    : 1;   /*    [=]    */
unsigned        chief       : 1;   /*    [ß]    */
unsigned        body        : 1;   /*    [Õ]    */
unsigned        negative    : 1;   /*    [±]    */
unsigned        fish        : 1;   /*    [¶]    */
unsigned        speed       : 1;   /*    [§]    */
unsigned        agree       : 1;   /*    [l]    */
unsigned        positive    : 1;   /*    [Ú]    */
unsigned        crime       : 1;   /*    [h]    */
unsigned        noise       : 1;   /*    [-]    */
unsigned        measure     : 1;   /*    [¾]    */
unsigned        tree        : 1;   /*    [õ]    */
unsigned        musicinst   : 1;   /*    [m]    */
unsigned        sport       : 1;   /*    [p]    */
// etc.

/* This is also a programming code and we do not have to translate it. */
} NOUN;
```

Note that *name of code* (human, measure, tree, etc.) is the name we use in the source code of the program to refer to the *code* used in the DW, in square brackets. Similarly, we define the information carried by the Verb, the Adjective, etc. Parts of Speech. For example, in a file called 'main.h' we have to declare, once again, what is a Noun, Verb, Adjective, etc.

```
typedef union {
 NOUN N;  // Noun singular form
 ADJ A;  // Adjective
 VERB V;  // Verb, basic form
 nOUN n;  // Noun plural
 aDJ a;  // Adjective, comparative or superlative form
 vERB v;  // Verb, third person singular
 PRON pron;  // Pronoun
 PREP prep;  // Preposition
 char z[5];  // etc.
} GRAMINFO;
```

and what information is contained in the WORD

```
typedef struct in_word
{
  struct in_word *next, *back;
  unsigned char syn;
  unsigned char ssyn;
  unsigned char type;
  char      cflag;
  char   inword[LMAX];
  char      esyn;
  GRAMINFO    e;
  char      rsyn;
  GRAMINFO    r;
  unsigned char numb; // Number
  unsigned char tense; // Tense
  unsigned char person; // Person (human being)
  unsigned char insect; // Insect
  unsigned char furniture; // furniture
// etc. Below, the words speak for themselves:
  unsigned char name;
  unsigned char chief;
  unsigned char human;
  unsigned char time;
  unsigned char constrct;
  unsigned char body;
  unsigned char negative;
  unsigned char fish;
  unsigned char speed;
  unsigned char agree;
  unsigned char positive;
  unsigned char noise;
  unsigned char measure;
  unsigned char tree;
  unsigned char musicinst;
  unsigned char sport;
  unsigned char animal;
  unsigned char vehicle;
  unsigned char boat;
  unsigned char element;
  unsigned char town;
  unsigned char nationality;
  unsigned char kill_er;
  unsigned char lie;
  unsigned char region;
  unsigned char entrance;
  unsigned char material;
  unsigned char seed;
  unsigned char container;
  unsigned char jem;
  unsigned char gas;
  unsigned char room;
  unsigned char metal;
  unsigned char drink;
  unsigned char book;
  unsigned char island;
```

```
unsigned char africa;
unsigned char america;
unsigned char asia;
unsigned char australia;
unsigned char europe;
unsigned char making;
unsigned char distance;
unsigned char deity;
unsigned char in_shop; // what one can buy in a shop
unsigned char eec; // European Union
unsigned char liquid;
unsigned char damage;
unsigned char decrease;
unsigned char increase;
unsigned char payment;
unsigned char bird;
unsigned char rich;
unsigned char poor;
unsigned char doctrine;
unsigned char seeing;
unsigned char see;
unsigned char thought;
unsigned char attack;
unsigned char eat;
unsigned char take;
unsigned char hit;
unsigned char clean;
unsigned char desire;
unsigned char leave;
unsigned char no_info;
unsigned char sound;
unsigned char feeling;
unsigned char writing;
unsigned char grammar;
unsigned char road;
unsigned char jewellery;
unsigned char colour;
unsigned char crime;
unsigned char star;
unsigned char song;
unsigned char month;
unsigned char game;
unsigned char continent;
unsigned char money;
unsigned char obtaining;
unsigned char apparatus;
unsigned char chemical;
unsigned char mountain;
unsigned char end;
unsigned char fruit;
unsigned char gather;
unsigned char mech_part;
unsigned char clothe;
unsigned char holiday;
```

```
  unsigned char illness;
  unsigned char free;
  unsigned char science;
  unsigned char art;
  unsigned char work_er;
  unsigned char next_of_kin;
  unsigned char help;
  unsigned char building;
  unsigned char country;
  unsigned char drug;
  unsigned char education;
  unsigned char crowd;
  unsigned char stone;
  unsigned char gauge;
  unsigned char language;
  unsigned char organization;
  unsigned char religion;
  unsigned char military;
  unsigned char vegetation;
  unsigned char weapon;
  unsigned char food;
  unsigned char tool;
  unsigned char longterm;
  unsigned char answer;
  unsigned char get;
// etc.
} WORD;
```

3 Making a list of all possible questions. Examples

Now we must define what questions can be asked to be sure that the program will find the question and the correct answer to it. Some of these questions we have listed in the DW alphabetically as normal word (phrase) entries, together with all other word entries:

can i find=Wlww
can it be that=Wqwww
can you compare=Wgww
can you make a comparison between=Wgwwww
do you know that=Wqwww
do you know=Wqww
how do i get rid of=Wöwwwww
how do people get rid of=Wöwwwww
how do you destroy=Wöwww
how do you eliminate=Wöwww
how do you get rid of=Wöwwwww
how does one chase away=Wöwwww
how does one get rid of=Wöwwwww
how far is ~ from=WKwwww
how many kilometers are there to=WKwwwww
how many miles are there to=WKwwwww
how much did ~ cost=Wbwwww
how much did ~ earn=Wbwwww
how much do ~ cost=Wbwwww

how much do ~ earn=Wbwwww
how much does ~ cost=Wbwwww
how much does ~ earn=Wbwwww
how much is per=Wbwww
how much is=Wbww
how much=Wcwwww
how the president of the=Wdwwww
how the president of=Wdwww
is it possible that=Wqwww
is there a comparison between=Wgwwww
what ~ think about=Wfwww
what costs=Wcw
what currency is used=WÜwww
what currency=WÜw
what do others think about=Wfwwww
what do you charge for=Wcwwww
what do you know about the=Wfwwwww
what do you know about=Wfwwww
what do you think about=Wfwwww
what is the capital of=Wäwwww
what is the charge for=Wcwwww
what is the cost of=Wcwwww
what is the currency=WÜwww
what is the difference between=Wüwwww
what is the distance between ~ and=WKwwwwww
what is the main city of=Wäwwww
what is the main town of=Wäwwww
what is the monetary unit=WÜwww
what is the name of the president=Wdwwwwww
what is the price=Wcwwww
what is the price of=Wcwwww
what is the price per=Wcwwww
what is your opinion about the=Wfwwwww
what is your opinion about=Wfwwww
what monetary unit is used=WÜwwww
what money is used=WÜwww
what money one needs=WÜwww
what the others think about=Wfwwww
what was the name of the president=Wdwwwwww
who is the president=Wdwww

etc. English questions

gibt es eine Vergleichung zwischen=Wgwwww
ist es möglich, dass=Wqwww
kann es sein, dass=Wqwww
kann ich finden=Wlww
können sie eine Vergleichung machen zwischen=Wgwwwww
können sie vergleichen=Wgww
was denken andere Leute über=Wfwwww
was denken die andere über=Wfwwww
was denken sie über=Wfwww
was für eine monetäre Einheit braucht man=WÜwwwwww
was für eine Währung braucht man=WÜwwwww

was für Geld braucht man=WÜwwww

etc. German questions for the German module of the program.

Note the following:

a) The above list presents only the initial part of the question – namely, how the question is asked and what is asked. The answer to the question is not provided.
b) We have tried to ask the same question in all possible ways by paraphrasing it. Every question has its own code (b, c, d, f, Ü, ö, etc.). If the question does not have its own code, the program will not be able to differentiate the questions.
c) The sign 'W' marks a phrase, the sign 'w' marks a constituent word in the phrase.
d) The sign ~ replaces a missing word. Any word can be placed here. We must be careful when we use this sign, because it can easily alter the meaning of the question.
e) The answer to the above questions is not ready made, it is programmed and depends on meaning and context.

4 Ready-made answer to a question, presented only in the DW. Examples

In contrast to the so-called programmable questions listed above, we also have ready made questions–answers. The answer to such a question accompanies the question and is presented also in the DW, alongside the question, in a way similar to the presentation of the source word and the target word in the BDW for the Machine-Translation program. Below are some examples of such questions.

are the ~ at home=N[1]-Yes.
are the ~ here=N[1]-Yes.
are the ~ hungry=N[1]-No.
could ~ come=N[1]-Yes.
could ~ imagine=N[1]-Yes.
could ~ see=N[1]-Yes.
did the ~ arrive=N[1]-No.
had the ~ known=N[1]-No doubt.
had the ~ taken=N[1]-I think so.
had the ~ thought=N[1]-I don't think so.
how can i look up the ~ address=N[1]-In the telephone book.
where is london=N[1]-In Great Britain.
etc. English questions.

German questions:

Sind die ~ zu Hause=N[1]-Ja.
Ist der ~ zu Hause=N[1]-Ja.
Ist die ~ zu Hause=N[1]-Ja.
Sind die ~ hier=N[1]-Ja.
Ist der ~ hier=N[1]-Ja.
Sind die ~ da=N[1]-Ja.
Ist der ~ da=N[1]-Ja.
Sind die ~ hungrig=N[1]-Nein.
ist der ~ hungrig=N[1]-Nein.
Könnten ~ kommen=N[1]-Ja.
Sollen die ~ hereinkommen=N[1]-Ja.
War der ~ zornig=N[1]-Sehr zornig.
Könnten ~ vorstellen=N[1]-Ja.

could ~ see=N[1]-Yes.
Könnten ~ sehen=N[1]-Ja.
Hat ~ gewusst=N[1]-Nein.
etc.

The sign ~ replaces a word that can take this position. The sign [1] marks the type of question: a question that has an immediate answer, provided after the question. Note that the above answers imply understanding: instead of 'Yes' (Ja) the answer can be 'No' (Nein). This is because we do not know what word was used for ~. The ready-made answers are programmed in a file called "questions.c(pp)" in the following way:

```
case 41:          /* direct answer */
 if (wrd->irrform[0] != '-') {
  i = mpos; continue;
/* excludes from consideration the questions that have no direct answer (code -) */
 }
 if (wrd->e.N.answer == 1) {
// if the word bears the code [1], a code for direct answer
  wnprintfw("\n %s", wrd->irrform);
// print what follows after -
 }
 i++; continue;
```

Case 41 is continued in the included file 'questions.h':

```
{"[Nw]",    NULL, 41},                /* direct answer */
```

where [Nw] means that a direct answer is given only to a question consisting of more than one word and coded in the DW with the sign N.
(Note: this procedure is similar to that used in the spell-checking software program in the chapter 'Grammatical rules: Unrecognized irregular form of a Noun', for wrd->irrform. The only difference is that here the program prints the answer to the question, instead of the correct form of the misspelt word.)

5 Programmed answer to a particular question. Examples

The programmed answer to a particular question needs a piece of source code, where we have *if* and *else*. This means that if certain conditions are fulfilled, the answer is such and such, or, if these conditions are not fulfilled, the answer is different or there is no answer. This is a much more accurate way for dealing with the questions and finding the correct answer than the ready-made answers to a question shown above. These procedures are programmed in the same file called "questions.c(pp)". For such standard questions as *What is ... ?*, *What means ... ?*, *Was ist ... ?*, *Was bedeutet ... ?* (German) we have made the following case:

```
case 14:          /* What is N? */
 if (wrdm->syn != 'N') {
  i = mpos; continue;
 }
// if the word sign is not N (Noun) continue without analysis
 if (type == '?' &&
    !stricmp(wrd->inword, "what")) {
// if this is a question (?) and if it starts with what
 if (wrdm->e.N.insect == 1 &&
```

```
         wrdm->insect == 1) {
// if the word (N) belongs to the group of insects
         wnprintfw("\n \%s\ means an insect.",
          wrdm->inword);
// we can print this message in another language, if we need to do that
//       wnprintfw("\n \%s\ bedeutet Insekt.",
//        wrdm->inword);
// print the word and the above message
      }
      else
      if (wrdm->e.N.sport == 1 &&
         wrdm->e.N.human != 1 &&
         wrdm->sport == 1) {
// else if the word (N) belongs to the sport group and is not a human being
         wnprintfw("\n \%s\ means a kind of sport.",
          wrdm->inword);
// print the word and the above message
      }
      else
      if (wrdm->e.N.sport == 1 &&
         wrdm->e.N.human == 1 &&
         wrdm->sport == 1 && wrdm->human == 1) {
// else if the word (N) belongs to the sport group and is a human being
         wnprintfw("\n \%s\ means a sports person.",
          wrdm->inword);
// print the word and the above message
/* Note that here we have combined two meanings (sport and human being) to make the
meaning sportsman. We have used 'sports person' to cover both genders.
Note also that we use && (and) to merge the two different meanings into one meaning. */
      }
      else
      if (wrdm->e.N.animal == 1 &&
         wrdm->animal == 1) {
/* Else, if the word (N) belongs to the group of animals (humans, insects, fish are excluded
from this group, because they are identified separately, and can be included to the group of
animals, where needed). In other words, here are the rest of the animals, not differentiated in
groups. */
         wnprintfw("\n \%s\ means a living being.",
          wrdm->inword);
// print the word and the above message
      }
      else
      if (wrdm->e.N.vehicle == 1 &&
         wrdm->vehicle == 1) {
// else if the word (N) belongs to the group of vehicles
         wnprintfw("\n \%s\ means a vehicle.",
          wrdm->inword);
// print the word and the above message
      }
      else
      if (wrdm->e.N.boat == 1 &&
         wrdm->boat == 1) {
// else if the word (N) belongs to the group of boats
         wnprintfw("\n \%s\ means a boat.",
```

```
        wrdm->inword);
```
// print the word and the above message
```
      }
      else
      if (wrdm->e.N.element == 1 &&
         wrdm->e.N.metal == 1 &&
         wrdm->element == 1 && wrdm->metal == 1) {
```
// else if the word (N) belongs to the group of metallic elements and metals
```
         wnprintfw("\n \%s\ means a metalic element.",
          wrdm->inword);
```
// print the word and the above message
```
      }
      else
      if (wrdm->e.N.element == 1 &&
         wrdm->element == 1) {
```
// else if the word (N) belongs to the group of elements
```
         wnprintfw("\n \%s\ means an element.",
          wrdm->inword);
```
// print the word and the above message
```
      }
      else
      if (wrdm->e.N.body == 1 &&
         wrdm->body == 1) {
```
// else if the word (N) means part of the body
```
         wnprintfw("\n \%s\ means part of a body.",
          wrdm->inword);
```
// print the word and the above message
```
      }
      else
      if (wrdm->e.N.tree == 1 &&
         wrdm->tree == 1) {
```
// else if the word (N) belongs to the group of trees
```
         wnprintfw("\n \%s\ means a tree.",
          wrdm->inword);
```
// print the word and the above message
```
      }
      else
      if (wrdm->e.N.human == 1 &&
          wrdm->human == 1) {
        if (wrdm->e.N.human == 1 &&
          wrdm->e.N.mgender == 1 &&
          wrdm->e.N.next_of_kin == 1 &&
           wrdm->human == 1 &&
           wrdm->mgender == 1 &&
         wrdm->next_of_kin == 1) {
```
// else if the word (N) belongs to the group of humans and is of masculine gender and is next
// of kin
```
         wnprintfw("\n \%s\ means a male human being,
           next of kin.", wrdm->inword);
```
// print the word and the above message
/*Note: here we have a combination of three meanings to make the meaning a *male relative* (next of kin) .*/
```
        }
      else
```

```
        if (wrdm->e.N.human == 1 &&
           wrdm->e.N.mgender == 1 &&
           wrdm->mgender == 1 &&
           wrdm->e.N.chief == 1 &&
           wrdm->human == 1 &&
           wrdm->chief == 1) {
// else if the word (N) belongs to the group of humans and is of masculine gender and is a chief
         wnprintfw("\n \%s\ means a man of power
          and authority.", wrdm->inword);
// print the word and the above message
        }
      else
        if (wrdm->e.N.human == 1 &&
           wrdm->e.N.mgender == 1 &&
           wrdm->human == 1 &&
           wrdm->mgender == 1) {
// else if the word (N) belongs to the group of humans and is of masculine gender
         wnprintfw("\n \%s\ means a male human being.",
          wrdm->inword);
// print the word and the above message
        }
      else
        if (wrdm->e.N.human == 1 &&
         wrdm->e.N.fgender == 1 &&
         wrdm->e.N.next_of_kin == 1 &&
         wrdm->human == 1 &&
         wrdm->fgender == 1 &&
         wrdm->next_of_kin == 1) {
// else if the word (N) belongs to the group of humans and is of feminine gender and is next of
// kin
         wnprintfw("\n \%s\ means a female human being,
          next of kin.", wrdm->inword);
// print the word and the above message
        }
      else
        if (wrdm->e.N.human == 1 &&
           wrdm->e.N.fgender == 1 &&
           wrdm->human == 1 && wrdm->fgender == 1) {
// else if the word (N) belongs to the group of humans and is of feminine gender
         wnprintfw("\n \%s\ means a female
          human being.", wrdm->inword);
// print the word and the above message
        }
      else
        if (wrdm->e.N.human == 1 &&
           wrdm->e.N.chief == 1 &&
           wrdm->human == 1 &&
           wrdm->chief == 1) {
// else if the word (N) belongs to the group of humans and is a chief
         wnprintfw("\n \%s\ means a human being,
          a chief.", wrdm->inword);
// print the word and the above message
        }
      else
```

```
        if (wrdm->e.N.human == 1 &&
           wrdm->e.N.language == 1 &&
           wrdm->human == 1 &&
            wrdm->language == 1) {
// else if the word (N) belongs to the group of humans and is a language as well
         wnprintfw("\n \%s\ means a nationality
          and a language.", wrdm->inword);
// print the word and the above message
        }
      else
        if (wrdm->e.N.human == 1 &&
           wrdm->e.N.kill_er == 1 &&
           wrdm->human == 1 &&
            wrdm->kill_er == 1) {
// else if the word (N) belongs to the group of humans and is a killer
         wnprintfw("\n \%s\ means a human being,
          a killer.", wrdm->inword);
// print the word and the above message
        }
      else
        if (wrdm->e.N.human == 1 &&
           wrdm->e.N.attack == 1 &&
           wrdm->human == 1 && wrdm->attack == 1) {
// else if the word (N) belongs to the group of humans and also means an attack
         wnprintfw("\n \%s\ means an aggressor.",
          wrdm->inword);
// print the word and the above message
        }
      else
        if (wrdm->e.N.human == 1 &&
           wrdm->e.N.crime == 1 &&
           wrdm->human == 1 && wrdm->crime == 1) {
// else if the word (N) belongs to the group of humans and also means a crime
         wnprintfw("\n \%s\ means a human being,
          a criminal.", wrdm->inword);
// print the word and the above message
        }
      else
        if (wrdm->e.N.human == 1 &&
           wrdm->e.N.doctrine == 1 &&
           wrdm->human == 1 &&
            wrdm->doctrine == 1) {
// else if the word (N) belongs to the group of humans and also means a doctrine
         wnprintfw("\n \%s\ means a follower of a
          doctrine.", wrdm->inword);
// print the word and the above message
        }
      else
        if (wrdm->e.N.human == 1 &&
           wrdm->e.N.military == 1 &&
           wrdm->human == 1 &&
            wrdm->military == 1) {
// else if the word (N) belongs to the group of humans and also means a military
         wnprintfw("\n \%s\ means a human being in
```

```
        the army.", wrdm->inword);
// print the word and the above message
        }
      else
        if (wrdm->e.N.human != 1 &&
            wrdm->e.N.language == 1 &&
           wrdm->language == 1) {
// else if the word (N) does not belong to the group of humans and means a language
         wnprintfw("\n \%s\ means a language.",
          wrdm->inword);
// print the word and the above message
        }
      else
        if (wrdm->e.N.human == 1 &&
           wrdm->e.N.fgender == 1 &&
           wrdm->e.N.work_er == 1 &&
           wrdm->human == 1 &&
           wrdm->fgender == 1 &&
          wrdm->work_er == 1) {
/* else if the word (N) belongs to the group of humans and is of feminine gender and is a worker
*/
         wnprintfw("\n \%s\ means a female human
          being, a worker.", wrdm->inword);
// print the word and the above message
        }
      else
        if (wrdm->e.N.human == 1 &&
           wrdm->e.N.musicinst == 1 &&
           wrdm->human == 1 &&
            wrdm->musicinst == 1) {
/* else if the word (N) belongs to the group of humans and to the group of musical instruments
*/
         wnprintfw("\n \%s\ means a musician.",
          wrdm->inword);
// print the word and the above message
        }
      else
        if (wrdm->e.N.human == 1 &&
           wrdm->e.N.mgender == 1 &&
           wrdm->e.N.work_er == 1 &&
           wrdm->human == 1 &&
           wrdm->mgender == 1 &&
          wrdm->work_er == 1) {
/* else if the word (N) belongs to the group of humans and is of masculine gender and is a
worker */
         wnprintfw("\n \%s\ means a male human being,
          a worker.", wrdm->inword);
// print the word and the above message
        }
      else
        if (wrdm->e.N.human == 1 &&
           wrdm->e.N.work_er == 1 &&
           wrdm->human == 1 &&
            wrdm->work_er == 1) {
```

```
// else if the word (N) belongs to the group of humans and is a worker
        wnprintfw("\n \%s\ means a human being,
         a worker.", wrdm->inword);
// print the word and the above message
        }
      else
        if (wrdm->e.N.human == 1 &&
           wrdm->e.N.science == 1 &&
           wrdm->human == 1 &&
            wrdm->science == 1) {
// else if the word (N) belongs to the group of humans and to the group of science
        wnprintfw("\n \%s\ means a human being,
         a scientist.", wrdm->inword);
// print the word and the above message
        }
      else
        if (wrdm->e.N.human == 1 &&
           wrdm->e.N.next_of_kin == 1 &&
           wrdm->human == 1 &&
            wrdm->next_of_kin == 1) {
// else if the word (N) belongs to the group of humans and to the group of relatives
        wnprintfw("\n \%s\ means a human being,
         next of kin.", wrdm->inword);
// print the word and the above message
        }
      else
        if (wrdm->e.N.human == 1 &&
            wrdm->e.N.rich == 1 &&
           wrdm->human == 1 &&
            wrdm->rich == 1) {
/* else if the word (N) belongs to the group of humans and to the group of rich people */
        wnprintfw("\n \%s\ means a rich person.",
         wrdm->inword);
// print the word and the above message
        }
      else
        if (wrdm->e.N.human == 1 &&
           wrdm->e.N.poor == 1 &&
           wrdm->human == 1 &&
            wrdm->poor == 1) {
/* else if the word (N) belongs to the group of humans and to the group of poor people */
        wnprintfw("\n \%s\ means a poor person.",
         wrdm->inword);
// print the word and the above message
        }
      else
        if (wrdm->e.N.human == 1 &&
          wrdm->human == 1 &&
          (wrdm->e.N.fgender != 1 ||
          wrdm->e.N.mgender != 1)) {
// else if the word (N) belongs to the group of humans, regardless of gender
        wnprintfw("\n \%s\ means a human being.",
         wrdm->inword);
// print the word and the above message
```

```
      }
// end the humans (of course, these procedures about humans can be extended)
      }
      else
      if (wrdm->e.N.attack == 1 &&
        wrdm->attack == 1) {
// else if the word (N) means an attack
        wnprintfw("\n \%s\ means an attack.",
         wrdm->inword);
// print the word and the above message
      }
      else
      if (wrdm->e.N.fish == 1 &&
        wrdm->fish == 1) {
// else if the word (N) belongs to the group of fish
        wnprintfw("\n \%s\ means a fish.",
         wrdm->inword);
// print the word and the above message
      }
      else
      if (wrdm->e.N.star == 1 && wrdm->star == 1) {
// else if the word (N) belongs to the group of stars
        wnprintfw("\n \%s\ means a celestial
        body.", wrdm->inword);
// print the word and the above message
      }
      else
      if (wrdm->e.N.vegetation == 1 &&
        wrdm->vegetation == 1 &&
       wrdm->e.N.tree != 1) {
// else if the word (N) belongs to the group of vegetation
// trees are excluded, because they are identified separately
        wnprintfw("\n \%s\ means a vegetation.",
         wrdm->inword);
// print the word and the above message
      }
      else
      if (wrdm->e.N.vegetation == 1 &&
        wrdm->vegetation == 1) {
// else if the word (N) belongs to the group of vegetation
        wnprintfw("\n \%s\ means a vegetation.",
         wrdm->inword);
// print the word and the above message
      }
      else
      if (wrdm->e.N.weapon == 1 &&
        wrdm->weapon == 1) {
// else if the word (N) belongs to the group of weapons
        wnprintfw("\n \%s\ means a weapon.",
         wrdm->inword);
// print the word and the above message
      }
      else
      if (wrdm->e.N.food == 1 &&
```

```
        wrdm->food == 1) {
// else if the word (N) belongs to the group of food
        wnprintfw("\n \%s\ means food.",
         wrdm->inword);
// print the word and the above message
      }
      else
      if (wrdm->e.N.constrct == 1 &&
         wrdm->constrct == 1) {
// else if the word (N) belongs to the group of constructions
// we have not put buildings into this group, we have separated them
        wnprintfw("\n \%s\ means a construction.",
         wrdm->inword);
// print the word and the above message
      }
      else
      if (wrdm->e.N.kill_er == 1 &&
        wrdm->kill_er == 1) {
// else if the word (N) belongs to the group of killing
// humans are excluded, in the DW
        wnprintfw("\n \%s\ means a killing.",
         wrdm->inword);
// print the word and the above message
      }
      else
      if (wrdm->e.N.time == 1 &&
        wrdm->e.N.month == 1 &&
        wrdm->time == 1 && wrdm->month == 1) {
// else if the word (N) belongs to the group of time and is a month
        wnprintfw("\n \%s\ means a month.",
         wrdm->inword);
// print the word and the above message
      }
      else
      if (wrdm->e.N.time == 1 &&
         wrdm->time == 1) {
// else if the word (N) belongs to the group of time
        wnprintfw("\n \%s\ denotes time.",
         wrdm->inword);
// print the word and the above message
      }
      else
      if (wrdm->e.N.crime == 1 &&
         wrdm->crime == 1) {
// else if the word (N) belongs to the group of crime
// humans are excluded, in the DW
        wnprintfw("\n \%s\ denotes crime.",
         wrdm->inword);
// print the word and the above message
      }
      else
      if (wrdm->e.N.lie == 1 &&
         wrdm->lie == 1) {
// else if the word (N) means a lie
```

```
        wnprintfw("\n \%s\ means a lie.",
         wrdm->inword);
// print the word and the above message
      }
      else
      if (wrdm->e.N.entrance == 1 &&
         wrdm->entrance == 1) {
// else if the word (N) means an entrance
        wnprintfw("\n \%s\ means an entrance.",
         wrdm->inword);
// print the word and the above message
      }
      else
      if (wrdm->e.N.region == 1 &&
        wrdm->region == 1) {
// else if the word (N) means a region, area
        wnprintfw("\n \%s\ means a region.",
         wrdm->inword);
// print the word and the above message
      }
      else
      if (wrdm->e.N.measure == 1 &&
        wrdm->measure == 1) {
// else if the word (N) means a measure
        wnprintfw("\n \%s\ means a measurement.",
         wrdm->inword);
// print the word and the above message
      }
      else
      if (wrdm->e.N.building == 1 &&
        wrdm->building == 1) {
// else if the word (N) belongs to the group of buildings
        wnprintfw("\n \%s\ means a building.",
         wrdm->inword);
// print the word and the above message
      }
      else
      if (wrdm->e.N.country == 1 &&
         wrdm->country == 1) {
// else if the word (N) is a country
        wnprintfw("\n \%s\ means a country.",
         wrdm->inword);
// print the word and the above message
      }
      else
      if (wrdm->e.N.drug == 1 &&
         wrdm->drug == 1) {
// else if the word (N) is a drug
        wnprintfw("\n \%s\ means a medicament.",
         wrdm->inword);
// print the word and the above message
      }
      else
      if (wrdm->e.N.town == 1 &&
```

```
        wrdm->e.N.name == 1 &&
        wrdm->town == 1 &&
        wrdm->name == 1) {
// else if the word (N) belongs to the group of towns and is a name
        wnprintfw("\n \%s\ is a town.",
        wrdm->inword);
// print the word and the above message
    }
    else
    if (wrdm->e.N.name == 1 &&
        wrdm->name == 1) {
// else if the word (N) is a name
        wnprintfw("\n \%s\ is a name.",
        wrdm->inword);
// print the word and the above message
    }
    else
    if (wrdm->e.N.desire == 1 &&
        wrdm->desire == 1) {
// else if the word (N) means a desire
        wnprintfw("\n \%s\ means a desire.",
        wrdm->inword);
// print the word and the above message
    }
// etc. answers to the question 'What is (means) ... ?'
    else
    if (wrdm->e.N.no_info == 1 &&
        wrdm->no_info == 1) {
// else if the word (N) has no specified meaning attached to it
        wnprintfw("\n I don't know the
        meaning of \%s\ .", wrdm->inword);
// print  the above message and the word
    }
    }
    i = mpos; continue;
// end the case
```

The case above does not include all semantic groups of the Noun.

This case is continued in an included file named, for example 'questions.h':

```
{"Q<XT>N",      NULL, 14},  /* what is ... */
```

where Q is an Interrogative Pronoun, N is a Noun, the Interrogative Pronoun and the Noun are separated by <XT> an Auxiliary Verb from the paradigm *be* (X) and an Article (T). Here < > we can define exactly what Parts of Speech can separate the question word and the Noun, depending on the question and on the language.

Note that we have not given a definition of the meaning of the word. Some question-answering software programs print the entire definition of the word as it is given in the word-to-word dictionary. We can also do this, but we do not think it is necessary. We have provided the meaning of the whole class, as, for example, when the question *is What is a* ***wasp***?, or *What is a* ***fly***?, the answers will be w*asp means* ***insect***, *fly means* ***insect***. To get a more detailed answer, to a question such as *What means* ***brother***?, we have to have several conditions met. The word must mean a human being, it must have masculine gender and it must belong to the group of words denoting relative (next of kin). Then the answer to this question will be *brother means a male human being, next of kin.* We provide the answer in the same way when we ask about the meaning of a Verb, or an Adjective, or other Part of Speech.

```
case 18:          /* What is V? */
 if (wrdm->esyn == 'N' ||wrdm->esyn == 'A' ||
 wrdm->syn == 'N') {
 i = mpos; continue;
 }
// exclude all other parts of speech except the verb
 if (type == '?' &&
   !stricmp(wrd->inword, "what")) {
// if this is a question and the 1st word of the question, is 'what'
 if (wrdm->e.V.increase == 1 &&
   wrdm->increase == 1) {
// if the 2nd word means 'increase'
   wnprintfw("\n \%s\ means to increase.",
    wrdm->inword);
// print the above message
   }
 else // otherwise
 if (wrdm->e.V.see == 1 && wrdm->see == 1) {
// if the 2nd word means 'see'
   wnprintfw("\n \%s\ means to see.",
    wrdm->inword);
// print the above message
   }
 else // otherwise
 if (wrdm->e.V.agree == 1 &&
   wrdm->agree == 1) {
// if the 2nd word means 'agree'
   wnprintfw("\n \%s\ means to agree.",
    wrdm->inword);
// print the above message
 }
// etc. meanings of verbal groups
 else
 if (wrdm->e.V.no_info == 1 &&
   wrdm->no_info == 1) {
// if the meaning of the verb was not coded
   wnprintfw("\n The meaning of \%s\ is
    unknown to me.", wrdm->inword);
// say that the meaning is not known
 }
 }
 i = mpos; continue;
```

Specification of the context for the above rule in the *.h file:

```
{"Q<XB>V",     NULL, 18}, /* what is V? */
```

In the English version of the program, we have allowed only two parts of speech between the question starting with a pronoun 'Q' and the verb 'V': an auxiliary verb from the paradigm 'be' (X) and the verbal particle *to* (B). For this context we have assigned to the verb *means* the code 'X' to enable 'understanding' of the *question What means to ...* ?

The user must ask a question and end the question with a Question Mark in order to get an answer. If the Interrogative Sentence does not end with a Question Mark, the program alerts the user. We will use the following case to do this (both for English and German):

```
    case 24:        /* no ? */
     if (type != '?') {
// if the sentence does not end with a Question Mark
     wnprintfl("\n This is not a question.
      A question ends with ?");
// print the above message
     }
     i = mpos; continue;
```

Continuation of the above rule in the included file named "questions.h":

```
{"N",      NULL, 24}, /* no ? */
```

Now we will give an example case for questions starting with *where*.

```
    case 16:        /* Where is N? */
     if (wrdm->syn != 'N') {
     i = mpos; continue;
     }
// if the word we ask about is not a Noun (N), exit the case
     if (type == '?' &&
        !stricmp(wrd->inword, "where")) {
// if the sentence ends with a question mark and starts with where
     if (wrdm->e.N.name == 1) {
// consider first the group of words marked as geographical names
      if (wrdm->e.N.asia == 1 &&
         wrdm->asia == 1) {
// if the word is marked as located in Asia
       wnprintfw("\n \%s\ is in Asia.",
        wrdm->inword);
// print the word and the above message
      }
     else
      if (wrdm->e.N.europe == 1 &&
         wrdm->europe == 1) {
// if the word is marked as located in Europe
       wnprintfw("\n \%s\ is in Europe.",
        wrdm->inword);
// print the word and the above message
      }
     else
      if (wrdm->e.N.america == 1 &&
         wrdm->america == 1) {
// if the word is marked as located in America
       wnprintfw("\n \%s\ is in America.",
        wrdm->inword);
// print the word and the above message
      }
// etc.
     else
       wnprintfw("\n I don't know where is \%s\.",
```

```
        wrdm->inword);
// if the name is not marked where it is located
// print  the above message and the word
      }
// start analysing other word groups
      if (wrdm->e.N.clothe == 1 &&
          wrdm->clothe == 1) {
// if the word belongs to the group of clothes
         wnprintfw("\nThe \%s\ can be in the wardrobe.",
          wrdm->inword);
/* Print the word and the above message.

Note that the words denoting clothes do not only mean those in the wardrobe. We can wear
them, or somebody else can wear them, or they can be in the washing machine, or drying, etc. We
can provide an exact answer to such a question if we develop a real dialogue system and analyse
the previous context. The same applies to the answers of the questions below. */

         }
      else
        if (wrdm->e.N.building == 1 &&
            wrdm->building == 1) {
// if the word belongs to the group of buildings
         wnprintfw("\nThe \%s\ can be in the populated
          area.", wrdm->inword);
/* Print the word and the above message.
Note that this is one of the reasons we have differentiated buildings and constructions, because
the constructions can also be located outside populated areas. */

      }
      else
        if (wrdm->e.N.human == 1 &&
            wrdm->e.N.work_er == 1 &&
           wrdm->human == 1 &&
            wrdm->work_er == 1) {
// if the word belongs to the group of humans and to the group of workers
         wnprintfw("\nThe \%s\ can be at work.",
          wrdm->inword);
// print the word and the above message
      }
      else
        if (wrdm->e.N.human == 1 &&
           (wrdm->e.N.crime == 1 ||
           wrdm->e.N.kill_er == 1) &&
            wrdm->human == 1 &&
             (wrdm->crime == 1 ||
           wrdm->kill_er == 1)) {
/* If the word belongs to the group of humans and to the group of crimes or to the group of
killers. */
/* We can vary the conditions depending on what location we want to choose. */
         wnprintfw("\nThe \%s\ can be in prison.",
          wrdm->inword);
// print the word and the above message
// that is the most likely place where such people can be in the end
      }
```

```
else
  if (wrdm->e.N.animal == 1 ||
     wrdm->e.N.insect == 1 ||
     wrdm->e.N.bird == 1 ||
      wrdm->animal == 1 ||
       wrdm->insect == 1 ||
     wrdm->bird == 1) {
// if the word belongs to the group of animals or insects or birds
    wnprintfw("\nThe \%s\ can be in the
     natural habitat.", wrdm->inword);
// print the word and the above message
}
else
  if (wrdm->e.N.human == 1 &&
      wrdm->e.N.science == 1 &&
      wrdm->human == 1 &&
       wrdm->science == 1) {
// if the word belongs to the group of humans and to the group of science
    wnprintfw("\nThe \%s\ can be at the
     University.", wrdm->inword);
// print the word and the above message
}
else
  if (wrdm->e.N.human == 1 &&
     wrdm->e.N.religion == 1 &&
     wrdm->human == 1 &&
      wrdm->religion == 1) {
/* if the word belongs to the group of humans and to the group of words denoting religion */
    wnprintfw("\nThe \%s\ can be in the
     church.", wrdm->inword);
// print the word and the above message
}
else
  if (wrdm->e.N.human == 1 &&
     wrdm->e.N.musicinst == 1 &&
     wrdm->human == 1 &&
      wrdm->musicinst == 1) {
/* if the word belongs to the group of humans and to the group of musical instruments */
    wnprintfw("\nThe \%s\ can be on a performance
     tour with the orchestra.", wrdm->inword);
// print the word and the above message
}
else
  if (wrdm->e.N.human == 1 &&
     wrdm->e.N.military == 1 &&
     wrdm->human == 1 &&
      wrdm->military == 1) {
/* if the word belongs to the group of humans and to the group of words connected with
anything that is military */
    wnprintfw("\nThe \%s\ can be in the army.",
     wrdm->inword);
// print the word and the above message
}
else
```

```
        if (wrdm->e.N.human == 1 &&
           wrdm->human == 1) {
/* if the word belongs to the group of humans without any other specification (without
additional meaning(s) */
         wnprintfw("\nThe \%s\ can be at home.",
          wrdm->inword);
// print the word and the above message
// at home is the most likely place
       }
       else
       if (wrdm->e.N.fish == 1 &&
          wrdm->e.N.food == 1 &&
         wrdm->fish == 1 &&
          wrdm->food == 1) {
// if the word belongs to the group of fish and to the group of food
         wnprintfw("\nThe \%s\ can be on the
          dinner table.", wrdm->inword);
// print the word and the above message
       }
       else
       if (wrdm->e.N.fish == 1 && wrdm->fish == 1) {
// if the word belongs to the group of fish
// no additional information
         wnprintfw("\nThe \%s\ can be in the sea.",
          wrdm->inword);
// print the word and the above message
       }
       else
       if (wrdm->e.N.vehicle == 1 &&
         wrdm->vehicle == 1) {
// if the word belongs to the group of vehicles
         wnprintfw("\nThe \%s\ can be parked in
          the garage.", wrdm->inword);
// print the word and the above message
// of course, when it is not driving at the moment
       }
       else
       if (wrdm->e.N.boat == 1 &&
          wrdm->boat == 1) {
// if the word belongs to the group of boats
         wnprintfw("\nThe \%s\ can be at sea.",
          wrdm->inword);
// print the word and the above message
       }
       else
       if (wrdm->e.N.furniture == 1 &&
          wrdm->furniture == 1) {
// if the word belongs to the group of furniture
         wnprintfw("\nThe \%s\ can be in the room.",
          wrdm->inword);
// print the word and the above message
       }
       else
       if (wrdm->e.N.room == 1 &&
```

```
        wrdm->room == 1) {
// if the word belongs to the group of premises
        wnprintfw("\nThe \%s\ can be in the
         building.", wrdm->inword);
/* print the word and the above message.
Not quite correct, because a room is always in a building! It is not mobile.
Note that we have used 'can be', to avoid singular or plural 'is in', 'are in'.
Singular or plural can be differentiated with ease, when needed. */
      }
      else
      if (wrdm->e.N.book == 1 &&
         wrdm->book == 1) {
// if the word belongs to the group of books
        wnprintfw("\nThe \%s\ can be in the
         library.", wrdm->inword);
// print the word and the above message
      }
      else
      if (wrdm->e.N.jewellery == 1 &&
         wrdm->jewellery == 1) {
// if the word belongs to the group of jewellery
        wnprintfw("\nThe \%s\ can be in the
         jewellery box.", wrdm->inword);
/* Print the word and the above message.
We can also vary the conditions to get a more accurate answer. */
      }
      else
      if (wrdm->e.N.star == 1 &&
         wrdm->star == 1) {
// if the word belongs to the group of celestial bodies
        wnprintfw("\nThe \%s\ can be in
         the sky.", wrdm->inword);
/* Print the word and the above message.
Here we can be very accurate and identify the exact planetary system. */
      }
      else
      if (wrdm->e.N.money == 1 &&
         wrdm->money == 1) {
// if the word belongs to the group of money (currency, etc.)
        wnprintfw("\nThe \%s\ can be in the
         bank.", wrdm->inword);
// print the word and the above message
      }
      else
      if (wrdm->e.N.tree == 1 &&
         wrdm->e.N.fruit == 1 &&
        wrdm->tree == 1 && wrdm->fruit == 1) {
// if the word belongs to the group of trees and is a fruit-bearing tree
        wnprintfw("\nThe \%s\ can be in the
         orchard.", wrdm->inword);
// print the word and the above message
      }
      else
      if (wrdm->e.N.tree == 1 && wrdm->tree == 1) {
```

```
// if the word belongs to the group of trees
// no other specification of meaning
        wnprintfw("\nThe \%s\ can be in the
         forest.", wrdm->inword);
// print the word and the above message
      }
      else
      if (wrdm->e.N.vegetation == 1 &&
        wrdm->vegetation == 1 &&
        wrdm->e.N.tree != 1) {
// if the word belongs to the group of vegetation and is not a tree
        wnprintfw("\nThe \%s\ can be in the field.",
         wrdm->inword);
// print the word and the above message
      }
      else
      if (wrdm->e.N.food == 1 ||
        wrdm->e.N.drink == 1 &&
        wrdm->food == 1 || wrdm->drink == 1) {
// if the word belongs to the group of food or drink
        wnprintfw("\nThe \%s\ can be on the
         dinner table.", wrdm->inword);
// print the word and the above message
      }
      else
/* Now we will deal not with groups of words but with individual words, which we need to
specify in the program. */
      if (!stricmp(wrdm->inword, 'sofia')) {
// if you match the word Sofia
      wnprintfl('\n In Bulgaria.');
// print the above message
// etc. individual words
      }
      else
      if (wrdm->e.N.no_info == 1 ||
        wrdm->no_info == 1 ||
        wrdm->e.N.name != 1) {
// else, if the meaning of the word was not specified in the DW
// or if the word is not a name
        wnprintfw("\n I don't know where can
         be the \%s\.", wrdm->inword);
// print  the above message and the word
      }
      }
      i = mpos; continue;
```

Continuation of the above rule in the included file named "questions.h":

```
{"Q<XSTAO>N",        NULL, 16},  /* Where is ... ? */
```

The words that can separate the Interrogative Pronoun *where* and the Noun (N) can be <XSTAO>, the paradigm of the Auxiliary Verb be (X), Indicative Pronoun (S), Article (T), Adjective (A) and/or Possessive Pronoun (O). Nothing else can be used unless defined and depending on the language. In the same way we can answer questions starting with the

Interrogative Pronouns *what, is, who, which*, etc., and with any of the Interrogative Phrases we have listed earlier in this chapter. We can also answer questions not just about the Noun (N), but also about all other Parts of Speech (Verb, Adjective, Adverb, etc.). Here is a case for asking if somebody is stupid:

```
      case 20:          /* N stupid */
       if (type == '?') {
// if this is an Interrogative Sentence
//      if (wrd->e.N.human == 1 && wrd->human == 1 &&
//        !stricmp(wrdm->inword, "stupid") ||
//        !stricmp(wrdm->inword, "foolish")) {
/* Note the position of the brackets above and below. The if statement above will compile successfully and give correct answers to some test questions, but it will also give incorrect answers to some other questions. When we put the brackets correctly, as shown below, the answers will be correct, as specified. */
        if (wrd->e.N.human == 1 && wrd->human == 1 &&
          (!stricmp(wrdm->inword, "stupid") ||
          !stricmp(wrdm->inword, "foolish"))) {
// if the first word denotes a human being
// and the second word is stupid or foolish
       wnprintfl("\n Perhaps. Most people are stupid.");
// print the above message
        }
       else
        if (wrd->e.N.human != 1 && wrd->human != 1) {
// if the first word does not denote a human being
        wnprintfl("\n I don't no.");
// print the above message
        }
        }
        i = mpos; continue;
```

Continuation of the above rule in the included file named "questions.h":

```
   {"N'foolish'",   NULL, 20},
   {"N'stupid'",    NULL, 20},
```

We can list all the synonyms of *stupid*, or group the synonyms and mark them with a sign. Here is an example with one of the interrogative phrases we have listed earlier in this chapter. This type of phrase was marked with the sign *f*.

```
       case 22:         /* what you think about = f */
        if (type == '?') {
// if this is an Interrogative Sentence
         if (wrdm->e.N.human == 1 &&
           wrdm->e.N.mgender == 1 &&
           wrdm->numb != 1) {
/* If the second word denotes a human being and is of masculine gender
and is not in plural. */
// Note: here we have differentiated singular and plural.
       wnprintfl('\n He is a nice chap.');
// print the above message
         }
        else
```

```
        if (wrdm->e.N.human == 1 &&
         wrdm->e.N.fgender == 1 &&
         wrdm->numb != 1) {
// if the second word denotes a human being and is of feminine gender
// and is not in plural
      wnprintfl('\n She is a nice person.');
// print the above message
        }
      else
        if (wrdm->e.N.human == 1 &&
         wrdm->numb == 1) {
// if the second word denotes a human being
// and is in plural
      wnprintfl('\n They are nice people.');
// print the above message
        }
      else
// now we will deal with individual words
        if (!stricmp(wrdm->inword, 'john')) {
/* If the second word is John.
Note that we have to exclude John in the very beginning of this case, or code it differently in the
DW, otherwise we will get two answers about John. */
      wnprintfl('\n He is a fascinating chap.');
// print the above message
/* We do not need to analyse 'John', we know that 'John' is a male human being, because of the
source code. In a real dialogue the program can ask us in return
Who you mean, your brother or the neighbour? */
        }
      else
        if (!stricmp(wrdm->inword, 'ann')) {
/* If the second word is Ann.
Note that the same above applies to 'Ann', or else we will get two answers. */
      wnprintfl('\n Ann is a very clever woman.');
// print the above message
        }
      else
// etc. for names of people, when we want more specific information about them.
        if (!stricmp(wrdm->inword, 'peter')) {
// if the second word is Peter
      wnprintfl('\n Not quite my liking.');
// print the above message
        }
      else
        if (wrd->e.N.human != 1) {
// if not a human being
// Note that we have asked about the 1st word, not the 2nd, this is not an error.
      wnprintfl('\n I do not know what to think.');
// print the above message
        }
      }
      i = mpos; continue;
```

Continuation of the above rule in the included file named "questions.h":

```
{"f<TAO>N",    NULL, 22},
```

where 'f' marks the phrases 'what do you think about', 'what people think about', 'what others think about', etc. alternatives. We can invent all sorts of questions and answers. For example, let's see how to get rid of something.

```
      case 25: /* how does one get rid of ... */
       if (wrd->type != 'W') {
       i = mpos; continue;
       }
// exit when the 1st word is not a phrase
       if (type == '?') {
// if this is a question
       if (wrdm->e.N.animal == 1 ||
          wrdm->e.N.human == 1) {
// if this is an animal or human being
      wnprintfl('\n By chasing away.');
       }
// print the above message
// Note that we have not gone into detail: 'it' or 'him', 'her'.
      else
       if (wrdm->e.N.food == 1) {
// if this is a kind of food
      wnprintfl('\n Eat it.');
// print the above message
       }
      else
       if (wrdm->e.N.building == 1) {
// if this is a building
      wnprintfl('\n Pull it down.');
// print the above message
       }
      else
       if (wrdm->e.N.vehicle == 1) {
// if this is a vehicle
      wnprintfl('\n Scrap it.');
// print the above message
       }
      else
// etc. things
      wnprintfl('\n I don't know.');
// print the above message
        }
       }
       i = mpos; continue;
```

Specification of the context for the above rule in the *.h file:

```
{"ö<TSAO>N",    NULL, 25}, /* get rid of */
```

In the DW, the question

how does one get rid of=öwww

and all its alternatives such as 'how does one dispose of', etc., in all languages (if needed), are coded with the sign 'ö'.

Now, we will give an example case for questions starting with *does*, *can*, *will* and their past and present alternatives. The question will be whether someone drinks (V) a drink (N). In order to avoid misinterpretation errors, within the program, we will isolate 'drink a drink' from all other verbs and nouns by renaming the codes in this particular context. We will change V into è and N into ê when these words mean 'drink', and we will apply that to all synonyms of 'drink' as a verb and to all words that mean a drink, as a noun, using the following two cases in the file 'parser.c(pp)':

```
      case 9 :          /* drink */
      if (wrd->e.V.drink == 1 && wrd->drink == 1 &&
        wrdm->e.N.drink == 1 && wrdm->drink == 1) {
// if the 1st word (the verb) and the 2nd word (the noun) mean 'drink'
        wrd->syn = 'è';
// the code of the verb will be è
        }
      else // if not
        wrd->syn = 'V';
// the code of the verb will stay as it is: V
      copysyn(que, wp);
      continue;
```

Continuation of the above rule in the respective *.h file:

```
   {"VN",    NULL, 9},  /* drink */
      case 18 :         /* drink */
      if (wrd->e.V.drink == 1 && wrd->drink == 1 &&
        wrdm->e.N.drink == 1 && wrdm->drink == 1) {
// if the 1st word (the verb) and the 2nd word (the noun) mean 'drink'
        wrdm->syn = 'ê';
// the code of the noun will be ê
        }
      else // otherwise
        wrdm->syn = 'N';
// the code of the noun will stay as it is: N
      copysyn(que, wp);
      continue;
```

Continuation of the above rule in the respective *.h file:

```
   {"[Vè]N",    NULL, 18}, /* drink */
```

With these two cases we have created new codes for all verbs that mean 'drink' and all nouns that mean 'drink'. Having done this, we can proceed without fear of being misunderstood by the program when we create the following question-answering case in the file 'questions.c(pp)':

```
      case 30:          /* drink */
       if (type == '?') {
// if this is a question
        if (wrd->e.N.human == 1 &&
         wrd->human == 1 && wrdm->syn == 'ê') {
/* if the 1st word denotes a human being and the 2nd word has the code ê for 'drink' */
        if (wrd->e.N.human == 1 && wrd->human == 1 &&
        wrdm->e.N.alcohol != 1 &&
```

```
        wrdm->alcohol != 1/*&& wrdm->syn == 'ê'*/) {
/* a sub-condition
if the 1st word is a human being and the 2nd word is non-alcoholic drink
(here we can omit the condition about the 2nd word because we have it above) */
        wnprintfl('\n -Yes, when thirsty.');
// print the above message
        }
        if (wrd->e.N.religion == 1 &&
         wrd->religion == 1 &&
         wrdm->alcohol == 1 &&
         wrdm->e.N.alcohol == 1
         /* && wrdm->syn == 'ê'*/) {
// if the 1st word is a priest, and the 2nd word is an alcoholic drink
        wnprintfl("\n -No. Never.");
// Print the above message.
        }
        if (wrd->e.N.human == 1 &&
         wrd->human == 1 &&
          wrd->e.N.religion != 1 &&
         wrd->religion != 1 &&
          wrdm->e.N.alcohol == 1 &&
         wrdm->alcohol == 1) {
/* if the 1st word is a human being, but not a priest, and the 2nd word is alcoholic drink */
        wnprintfl('\n -Yes, from time to time.');
// Print the above message.
        }
       }
      }
      i = mpos; continue;
```

Continuation of the above rule in the 'questions*.h' file:

```
{"N<è>ê",      NULL, 30}, /* drink liquid */
```

Note the new codes for drink. The verb is between the arrows <è>. The 1st word is N (denoting a human being), the 2nd word is ê (a noun denoting a drink). This rule applies to this particular context only. We have imposed semantical restrictions (only humans can drink), syntactical restrictions (a human drinks drinks, *humans drink a drink* is excluded here, but can be added) and code restrictions (è, ê). We have not imposed restrictions on how the question is being asked: *Does ... drink ... ?, Has ... drunk?, Will ... drink?*, etc. For a question such as

Does Peter drink whiskey?

the answer will be, -*Yes, from time to time*, if we know Peter personally and if we know for sure that he does not drink often. If we ask, *Does the bishop drink whiskey*?, the answer will be, -*No. Never*. On the other hand, if we ask, *Does Peter drink water*?, *Does the bishop drink tea*?, the answer will be, -*Yes, when thirsty*.

If some clergymen (abbots, abbesses, nuns, bishops, popes, priests, vicars, etc.) drink alcohol, and if we know who they are, we can exclude them from the above rule and say that they 'drink from time to time'. We can do likewise with muslims, because, as a rule, if they obey the Koran, they do not drink alcohol. If we include muslims in the above rule and ask, *Does Sadam drink whiskey*?, the answer will be, -*No. Never*. In *Dialogue* (Georgiev, 2003) and *Antwort* (Georgiev, 2006a) the reader will find practical implementation of the rules mentioned above, and much more.

(Note: This is a simulated, artificial intelligence. It is not a human intelligence. There is a long way ahead to making the computer more intelligent, which is why we are writing this book and sharing our experience with you, in the hope that you will do better where we have failed.)

10 Content Recognition and Text Attribution to a particular subject field

This is an old theme in computational linguistics with wide application in information retrieval. Present-day search engines on the Internet and on private networks operate using data banks with detailed classification of information. This information is our knowledge about the world expressed in words, sentences and texts. Since we produce new or different information, such as on the Internet, a need has arisen to process this information automatically, on a computer. The human effort is costly and cannot cope with this avalanche of information. Therefore, we have to teach the computer to recognize the content of a word, sentence and text and to classify this information into Subject Fields or themes of discourse. Below, we will discuss a way to do this.

1 How to use the meaning of the word-groups for text attribution

In the chapters Lexical Semantics and Question Answering we have grouped the words according to a particular meaning. Now, we can make larger groups, by grouping certain meanings together to form subject fields. For example we can group together *education, doctrine, book, written material, discover, science* to form a subject field called Education, Science and Technology.

We can group *weapon, military, army vehicle* (a sub-group of vehicles), *navy boat* (a sub-group of boats), *war, casualty*, etc. to form the group International Conflicts (a sub-group of conflict). These major groups, called Subject Fields, exist already in all library classifications and in the search engines on the Internet, and are quite standard. However, when we want to find something, we do not know how this classification is made. We look for particular information from our subjective point of view and this does not always match the standard classification. In reality, if we cannot find exactly what we want it means that the standard classification is not detailed enough. Therefore, new groups of words are needed, and new word relationships, to match any subjective classification of information more effectively.

If we want to extract more specific information from a text, we must divide and sub-divide our existing word groups. For example, the word group *Musical Instrument* can be sub-divided into *String Instrument* (violin, guitar, balalaika, etc.), *Percussion Instrument* (drum, tambourine, etc.), etc. The sub-divisions can be used as long as we can find a difference between, at least, two words belonging to the same sub-group.

2 Making a list of all possible subject fields. Example

Since this list is very long, we will cut it short by listing, as an example, the Subject Fields recognized by the software program *Word and Text Attribution* (Georgiev, H., 2003a):

Cloth
Container
Education, Science and Technology
Finances
Food and Vegetation
Health
Living Being
Military and Conflict
Place (location, area, region, etc.)
Sport
Transport and Road

Note that because the program is, basically, a DOS application (it runs well on all Windows versions), there were certain limitations to expanding this list. Therefore, this is a Platform limitation, not a theoretical one. The reader can find a more detailed list of subject fields in the chapter 'Lexical Semantics'.

3 Counting the occurrences of a particular meaning in a text for decision-making

This is a statistical count, within the software program that counts the occurrence of each meaning met in the text, when it belongs to a particular subject field from our pre-defined list. Note that one wordform has not just one meaning and that one meaning can belong to different subject fields. To suit this new purpose, we have to alter slightly the file called "questions.c(pp)". At the beginning of the file we will need to remind the program of our defined meanings:

```
extern long food;
extern long vegetation;
extern long fish;
extern long science;
extern long sport;
extern long transport;
extern long health;
extern long religion;
extern long military;
extern long region;
etc.
```

We also have to repeat the word meanings for each Part of Speech:

```
case 'N' : // for the Noun
 if (*cw == '[') {
  while (*cw && *cw != ']') {
   if (*cw == 'á')  wrd->e.N.chief = 1;
   if (*cw == 'N')  wrd->e.N.name = 1;
   if (*cw == 'H')  wrd->e.N.human = 1;
   if (*cw == 'M')  wrd->e.N.mgender = 1;
   if (*cw == 'F')  wrd->e.N.fgender = 1;
   if (*cw == 'T')  wrd->e.N.time = 1;
   if (*cw == '=')  wrd->e.N.constrct = 1;
   if (*cw == 'å')  wrd->e.N.body = 1;
   if (*cw == 'ñ')  wrd->e.N.negative = 1;
   if (*cw == 'ô')  wrd->e.N.fish = 1;
   if (*cw == 'õ')  wrd->e.N.speed = 1;
   if (*cw == 'è')  wrd->e.N.agree = 1;
// etc.
   cw++;
  }
  cw++;
```

```
    }
    if (*cw == '(') {
     wirr = wrd->irrform;
     while (*cw && *cw != ')')
      *wirr++ = *cw++;
     *wirr++ = *cw++;
     *wirr = '\0';
}
    wrd->person = 3;
    break;
```

We do not need to check if the text is a question. The only thing we need to know is whether a particular meaning is present in the text, using the following case:

```
      case 14:          /* collect meanings */
      if (wrd->syn == 'N' || wrd->esyn == 'N') {
// if the wordform is a noun
      if (wrd->e.N.sport == 1 && wrd->e.N.human != 1 &&
        wrd->sport == 1) {
// if the noun means a kind of sport, excluding the sportsmen
        wnprintfw("\n \%s\ => sport", wrd->inword);
// print that this word belongs to the word group 'sport'
      sport++;
// collect this meaning 'sport' for the statistics
      }
      else
      if (wrd->e.N.animal == 1 && wrd->animal == 1) {
// if the noun means a kind of animal
        wnprintfw("\n \%s\ => animal", wrd->inword);
// print that this word belongs to the word group 'animal (kingdom)'
      animal++;
// collect this meaning 'animal' for the statistics
      }
      else
      if (wrd->e.N.vehicle == 1 && wrd->vehicle == 1) {
// if the noun means a kind of vehicle
        wnprintfw("\n \%s\ => vehicle", wrd->inword);
// print that this word belongs to the word group 'vehicle'
      transport++;
// collect this meaning under 'transport' for the statistics
      }
      else
      if (wrd->e.N.boat == 1 && wrd->boat == 1) {
// if the noun means a kind of boat
        wnprintfw("\n \%s\ => boat", wrd->inword);
// print that this word belongs to the word group 'boat'
      transport++;
// collect this meaning under 'transport' for the statistics
      }
      else
      if (wrd->e.N.body == 1 && wrd->body == 1) {
// if the noun means part of body (of a human, animal)
        wnprintfw("\n \%s\ => organ", wrd->inword);
// print that this word belongs to the word group 'organ'
```

```
      health++;
// collect this meaning under 'health' for the statistics
      }
      else
      if (wrd->e.N.tree == 1 && wrd->tree == 1) {
// if the noun means a kind of tree
         wnprintfw("\n \%s\ => tree", wrd->inword);
// print that this word belongs to the word group 'tree'
      vegetation++;
// collect this meaning under 'vegetation' for the statistics
// etc. meanings
      }
      else
      if (wrd->e.N.no_info == 1 && wrd->no_info == 1) {
// if no meaning is coded for this word
         wnprintfw("\n \%s\ => unknown", wrd->inword);
// print that the program does not know this meaning
      }
      }
      i = mpos; continue;
```

The statistical count is placed just after the identification of the meaning:

```
sport++;  // for counting all words denoting sport
animal++;  // for living being (human, fish, insect, etc.)
transport++;  // for vehicle, boat, road, etc.
health++;  // for all words from the Subject field Health Service
vegetation++; // for tree, herb, daisy, etc.
etc.
```

Continuation of the above rule in the respective *.h file:

```
{"N",     NULL, 14}, /* count the meanings of the noun */
```

Similarly, we can count the meanings for any other part of speech. The counting here is similar to the counting of grammatical errors in a previous chapter, but the aim is different. To enable the count, we have to define the Subject Fields in a file named, for example, 'statistic.c(pp)':

```
// begins with a list of the include files, etc.
int wr_info(int opt)
{
char *ptime_string;
// ptime_string = asctime(tb);
struct tm *tb;
if (opt == 1 || sm_input)
{
 wncurmov(NUM_WORDS_ROW, NUM_WORDS_COL);
 wnprintf('%-ld', num_words);
// word statistics (number of words counted)
 wncurmov(NUM_SENTS_ROW, NUM_SENTS_COL);
 wnprintf('%-ld', num_sents);
// statistics of sentences (number of sentences counted)
}
if (opt == 1 )
{
 wncurmov(VEGETATION_ROW, VEGETATION_COL);
```

```
 wnprintf('%-ld', vegetation);
// for Vegetation (number of meanings for this subject field)
}
if (opt == 1 )
{
 wncurmov(SCIENCE_ROW, SCIENCE_COL);
 wnprintf('%-ld', science);
// for Science and Technology  (number of meanings for this subject field)
}
if (opt == 1 )
{
 wncurmov(FISH_ROW, FISH_COL);
 wnprintf('%-ld', animal);
// for living being  (number of meanings for this word group)
}
if (opt == 1 )
{
 wncurmov(SPORT_ROW, SPORT_COL);
 wnprintf('%-ld', sport);
// for sport  (number of meanings for this subject field)
}
if (opt == 1 )
{
 wncurmov(HEALTH_ROW, HEALTH_COL);
 wnprintf('%-ld', health);
// for health  (number of meanings for this subject field)
}
if (opt == 1 )
{
 wncurmov(TRANSPORT_ROW, TRANSPORT_COL);
 wnprintf('%-ld', transport);
// for transport  (number of meanings for this subject field)
}
// etc. Subject fields.
```

Last, but not least, we have to design a window where we can display these statistical results. This, however, is outside our scope, because it is not related directly to the linguistic programming.

The method described in the last chapters can be used in the search engines to search for information based on meaning, rather than simply matching words, parts of words or phrases.

11 Information Retrieval

This book will not be complete without saying a few words about Information Retrieval.

This branch of Language Engineering is one of the earliest developed and most widely used up to this date. There is no large enterprise in the world, be it a car manufacturer or a police department, without a computerised Information Retrieval system. The search engines on the Internet peruse the largest collection of textual information in the world to find what we are looking for. Most often, we are not satisfied with what we get. It is rare that we get exactly what we are looking for within the first few pages of information. Luckily, the search engines on the Internet are not biased, otherwise we would get only what other people deemed suitable for us to know.

Because we do not know how the search engines on the Internet operate, we do not know how to phrase our query in order to obtain the best result. We must guess, paraphrase our input text, shorten it or extend it. In principle, the longer our input text (our description of what we want to find), the more accurate the information we get. Regrettably, this is not always the case. The longest and shortest descriptions find the most unwanted material, unless the shortest description is an unique name of a product or firm. Patience has its rewards; after perusing dozens of pages, we sometimes find what we want. Will that change for the better? Will we find exactly what we want in future?

Perhaps not in the near future, but it is worth trying. We have shown that the computer can be made intelligent enough to answer questions, even to engage in a dialogue. In the previous chapters, especially in the chapter 'Representation of Knowledge', we outlined a method to compress words by coding their meanings. We can make a software program that codes the meanings automatically. This program will assign a code to each meaning of each word in every sentence and text in our database (collection of searchable texts). Then, when we phrase our query, the same program will turn it into a sequence of codes representing meanings. The search will be to identify a matching sequence of meanings, not words.

The same piece of source code, as presented in the previous chapter, only slightly altered, can be used to assign a code or codes to every word-meaning in a text:

```
case 14:          /* assign a code to the meaning */
 if (wrd->syn == 'N' || wrd->esyn == 'N') {
 if (wrd->e.N.musicinst == 1 && wrd->musicinst == 1) {
   wnprintfw('\n \%s\ => 2PJ', wrd->inword);
// print 2PJ, the code for musical instrument
// and other codes for types of musical instruments
 }
 else
 if (wrd->e.N.sport == 1 && wrd->e.N.human != 1 &&
   wrd->sport == 1) {
```

```
        wnprintfw('\n \%s\ => 2PO', wrd->inword);
// print 2PO, the code for sport
      }
      else
      if (wrd->e.N.animal == 1 && wrd->animal == 1) {
        wnprintfw('\n \%s\ => 2LD', wrd->inword);
// print 2LD, the code for animal
// and other codes for kinds of animals
      }
      else
      if (wrd->e.N.vehicle == 1 && wrd->vehicle == 1) {
        wnprintfw('\n \%s\ => 2FY', wrd->inword);
// code for vehicle
// and other codes for types of vehicles
      }
      else
      if (wrd->e.N.body == 1 && wrd->body == 1) {
        wnprintfw('\n \%s\ => 2MV', wrd->inword);
// print 2MV, the code for body organ
// and sub codes for different organs
      }
      else
      if (wrd->e.N.tree == 1 && wrd->tree == 1) {
        wnprintfw('\n \%s\ => 2QF', wrd->inword);
// print 2QF, the code for a tree
// other codes for all kinds of trees
      }
      else
        if (wrd->e.N.human != 1 && wrd->e.N.language == 1 &&
          wrd->language == 1) {
        wnprintfw('\n \%s\ => 2AI', wrd->inword);
// print 2AI, the code for a language
// followed by other codes for language families
        }
      else
        if (wrd->e.N.human == 1 && wrd->human == 1 &&
        (wrd->e.N.fgender != 1 ||
        wrd->e.N.mgender != 1)) {
        wnprintfw('\n \%s\ => 6XY', wrd->inword);
// print 6XY, the code for a human being
// codes for sub-divisions of human beings
        }
      }
      else
      if (wrd->e.N.insect == 1 && wrd->insect) {
        wnprintfw('\n \%s\ => 2LH', wrd->inword);
// print 2LH, the code for insect
// followed by other codes for kinds of insects
      }
      else
      if (wrd->e.N.fish == 1 && wrd->fish == 1) {
        wnprintfw('\n \%s\ => 2LI', wrd->inword);
// print 2LI, the code for fish
// other codes for kind of fish
```

```
      }
      else
      if (wrd->e.N.food == 1 && wrd->food == 1) {
        wnprintfw('\n \%s\ => 2LQ', wrd->inword);
// print 2LQ, the code for food
// followed by codes for types of food
      }
      else
      if (wrd->e.N.no_info == 1 && wrd->no_info == 1) {
        wnprintfw('\n \%s\ => 000', wrd->inword);
// print 000, code for unknown and unrecognized word
      }
       }
       i = mpos; continue;
```

Continuation of the above rule in the respective *.h file:

```
{"N",      NULL, 14}, /* prints coded meanings of the noun */
```

Thus, if one enters the query

cost of milk on the market
price of milk on the market
cost of milk in the shop
price of milk in the shop
etc. alternatives,

case 14 above will code this query as follows

5DOW of LQ on the 2QD
5DOW of LQ in the 2QD

where 5DOW codes *price, cost*, etc. synonyms, LQ codes food and 2QD codes all kinds of shops and markets.

Then the program will start to search in our database for the same sequence of codes, and will print the text related to these codes when the sequences match. With the example above, we will get much unwanted information, because all types of food will be found, not only milk. We can restrict the search to dairy products only (LQ-C), by specifying this sub-category in the search.

5DOW of LQ-C in the 2QD

The best result will be obtained when we limit the search to **milk** only, leaving the codes for price and shop. Then we will get the price of milk (sour, fresh) only:

5DOW of milk in the 2QD
5DOW of sour milk in the 2QD
5DOW of fresh milk in the 2QD
5DOW of yoghourt in the 2QD

The codes used above were taken from *Softhesaurus* (Georgiev, H., 1993b).

12 German and French Sequences of Parts of Speech

In a recent publication on English grammar (Georgiev, 2006) we have called a syntactically correct sequence of parts of speech a 'segment', and defined it as a stretch of words encompassed between punctuation marks or auxiliary words (excluding the auxiliary verbs), or between a punctuation mark and an auxiliary word. Sometimes, the new segment begins without an auxiliary word or a punctuation mark, because the previous segment (usually a prepositional one) has ended. In this case, the new segment can start with any part of speech, including an auxiliary verb.

This method of segmentation of the sentence can be successfully applied to any other language. We have applied it to German and French to obtain a list of a syntactically correct sequences of parts of speech. The sequences of parts of speech are language specific. They can be used for language teaching and for programming linguistic tasks, as, for example, when we need to specify in the program which parts of speech can stand between the words we are analysing. The reader of this book will notice that we have always needed this for the *.h file, where we have specified in which context occur the words we are analysing. These lists can be found in the Appendix of this book. Below, we will give a few examples in German and French to elucidate our method.

The German sentence

Das Buch auf dem Tisch ist meines.

will be split into three 'segments'

Das Buch
T N
auf dem Tisch
P T N
ist meines
X O

which will allow us to operate with them and make new sentences such as

Das Buch ist meines.

We have substituted the words in a segment with the abbreviations for parts of speech (see the Index of Abbreviations at the end of the book).

Similarly, the French sentence

C'est un entrelacs de multiples facteurs, qui détermine leur nature.

will be split in two segments

C'est un entrelacs de multiples facteurs
TX T N T A N
qui détermine leur nature
Q V O N

In the last example, the division into segments coincides with the traditional division into independent and dependent clauses.

Index of Abbreviations

(Note: The standard programming code and abbreviations of programming code not directly related to the subjects discussed in this book are omitted from the Index. They are explained, where needed, in the book.)

#	Unrecognised word
?	Unrecognised word Programming code when in square brackets [ ]
=	Separates the word and the coded information about this word, in the DW
=	'equal to' in the *.c(pp) files
~	Unspecified word
<	Programming code
>	
@	Substitute of any Part of Speech in the *.h files
,	comma in the *.h files
*	Full stop (end of sentence) when used as a sigh in *.h files
*/	Closes a comment in C source code
/*	Opens a comment in C source code
//	Comment, in C source code, follows on the same line
\‘\”	Quotes are marked so in the *.h files
$	marks the presence of alternative(s) in the *.h files
->	code used in the DW and in the *.c(pp) files
A	Adjective
a	Adjective (degree form)
Ä	Type of German Adjective used after a Determiner
ä	Type of Adjective used in the German *.h files
AB	Building
AB-C	Religious site
Adj.	Adjective
ALSD	Artificial Language for Semantic Description
B	Particle used with the Verb
BD	Bilingual Dictionary
BDW	Bilingual Dictionary of Wordforms
C	Conjunction
ç	Type of verb used in the German *.h files
Co	Complement Object
Cs	Complement Subject
D	Adverb
d	Adverb
DS	Dictionary of Segments
DW	Dictionary of Wordforms
E	Past or Participle Form of the Verb
e	Verb (basic form) or Past or Participle Form
ë	Type of Part of Speech used in the German *.h files

ET	Parent(s)
EY	Older generation
EV-BC	Next of kin (relative)
F	Participle Form of the Verb in the DW Noun spelt with a capital letter in the DW Abbreviation (DS only).
f	phrase in BDW
FB	Noun denoting time
FB-BD	Subgroup of a Noun denoting time
FB-BE	Subgroup of a Noun denoting time
G	Present Participle, Gerund Relative Pronoun (DS only).
GR-E	Religious institution
g	Present participle in the Dictionary of Segments
H	Numeral, Number Human being when in square brackets and in the List of Segments Personal Pronoun Nominal Case, Noun denoting a person (DS only)
h	Past Form of the Verb Verb used with 'haben' in the German DW
I	Indicative Pronoun or Numeral (quantifier)
i	Interrogative Pronoun (DS only)
Ic	Infinitival Complement
J	Conjunction
K	Negation
k	Negation
L	Conjunction Interrogative Pronoun (DS only)
M	Reflexive Pronoun Numeral (DS only) Pronoun (DW only)
m	Reflexive Pronoun or PPOC Sub-group of R (DS only)
N	Noun
n	Noun plural
N's	Possessive form of the Noun (Genitive of the Noun)
"N"	a noun used in a quotation (only in the dictionary of segments)
O o	Possessive Pronoun
ö	Type of Adjective used in the German *.h files
Od	Object Direct
Oi	Object Indirect
OU	Clergy
P	Preposition
p	Preposition
PAC	Prepositional Adverbial Clause
PPNC	Personal Pronoun Nominal Case
PPOC	Personal Pronoun Objective Case
Pw	Prepositional adverbial clause (in *.h files only)
Q	Interrogative Pronoun; Reciprocal Pronoun in DS Conjunction (in DW)
R	Personal Pronoun
r	Pronoun
RX	Family member
S	Relative Pronoun, Determiner Reflexive Pronoun (DS only)
s	Determiner Verb used with 'sein' in the German DW
Sj	Subject
SO	Religion
T	Article
U	Modal Verb
Û	Type of Noun used in the German *.h files
u	Verb (basic form) or Participle Form
v	Verb (3rd person singular) in the DW, in the *.h files - constituent verb
V	Verb (usually basic form)
w	constituent word or word within a phrase

W	Start of a phrase
X	Auxiliary Verb "be" and its paradigm (also the equivalent in other languages)
x	Auxiliary Verb "shall" and its paradigm (also the equivalent in other languages)
Y	Auxiliary Verb "have" and its paradigm (also the equivalent in other languages)
Z	Ambiguity: Verb or Noun, Verb or Adjective (basic form)
z	Ambiguity: Verb or Noun, Verb or Adjective (3rd person singular form of the Verb)
	Non-reflexive Verb used in the German DW

References

Ahmanova, O.C. (1969), *Dictionary of Linguistic Terminology* (in Russian). Moscow: Sovetskaja Entziklopedia Publishing House.

Bach, A. (1961), *Geschichte der deutschen Sprache*. Heidelberg: Quelle & Meyer.

Brill E. and Mooney R.J. (1997), 'An overview of empirical natural language processing', *AI Magazine*, 18, (4), 13–24.

Briscoe, E.J. and Boguraev, B.K. (1988), *Computational Lexicography for Natural Language Processing*. New York: Longman / Wiley.

Chevalier, J-C., Blanche-Benveniste, C. and Peytard, J. (1964), *Grammaire du français contemporain*. Paris: Larousse.

Chomsky, N. (1957), *Syntactic Structures*. The Hague: Mouton.

Cunningham, H. (1999), 'A definition and short history of language engineering', *Journal of Natural Language Engineering*, vol. 5, 1–16.

Curme, G.O. (1922), *A Grammar of the English Language*. New York: Macmillan.

—*A Grammar of the German Language* (1922), New York: Macmillan.

—*English Grammar* (1955), New York: Barnes and Noble.

Dal, I. (1962), *Kurze deutsche Syntax auf historischer Grundlage*. Tübingen: Niemeyer.

Davies Paul (1995), *The Indispensable Guide to C*. New York: Addison-Wesley.

Davis, R.E. (1989), *Truth, Deduction and Computation*. New York: Computer Science Press.

Dowty, D.R., Karttunen, Lauri and Zwicky, Arnold, M. (eds) (1985), *Natural Language Parsing*. Cambridge: Cambridge University Press.

Duden (1996), *Die deutsche Rechtschreibung*, hrsg. Vom Wissenschaftlichen Rat der Dudenredaktion, Mannheim, Leipzig, Wien, Zürich: Dudenverlag.

Eisenberg, P. (1986), *Grundriß der deutschen Grammatik*. Stuttgart: Metzler.

Engel, U. (1977), *Syntax der deutschen Gegenwartssprache*. Berlin: Erich Schmidt.

Engel, U. (1988), *Deutsche Grammatik*. Heidelberg: Groos.

Fodor, J.A. and Katz, J.J. (1964), *The Structure of Language*. New Jersey: Prentice Hall.

Fox, A. (1990), *The Structure of English*. Oxford: Clarendon Press.

—*The Structure of German* (1990), Oxford: Clarendon Press.

Garrison, W. Cottrell (1989), *A Connectionist Approach to Word Sense Disambiguation*. London: Pitman.

Garside, R. (1986), 'The CLAWS word – tagging system', in R. Garside, G. Leech, and G. Sampson (eds), *The Computational Analysis of English*. Harlow: Longman.

Gazdar, G. and Mellish, C. (1989), *Natural Language Processing in POP-11*. Reading, UK: Addison-Wesley.

Georgiev, H. (1974), 'Frequency dictionary of Bulgarian foreign policy' (in Russian), in *Statistics of Speech and Automatic Analysis of Texts*. Leningrad, The Soviet Union: Nauka.

—'Brief lexico-semantical description of the subject field oil and gas' (1979), in *t.a. informations, Revue International du traitement automatique du langage*, Vingtieme anee, 1, 47–59.

—*Syntparse, Software Program for Parsing of English Text* (1993), LANGSOFT, Sprachlernmittel, Switzerland, platform: DOS/Windows.

—*Syntcheck, a Computer Software Program for Orthographical and Grammatical Spell-Checking of English Texts* (1993a), LANGSOFT, Sprachlernmittel, Switzerland, platform: DOS/Windows.

—*Softhesaurus, English Electronic Thesaurus* (1993b), LANGSOFT, Sprachlernmittel, Switzerland, platform: DOS/Windows.

—*Linguaterm, Multilingual (English, German, French and Spanish) Electronic Thesaurus of Linguistic Terminology* (1994), LANGSOFT, Sprachlernmittel, Switzerland, platform: DOS/Windows (95, 98).
—*Geoatlas, Multilingual (English, German, French and Italian) Electronic Lexicon of related place names* (1994a), LANGSOFT, Sprachlernmittel, Switzerland, platform: DOS/Windows.
—*Syntcheck, German Orthographical and Grammatical Spellchecker* (1996), LANGSOFT, Sprachlernmittel, Switzerland, platform: DOS/Windows.
—*Syntparse (Satzzerlegung), Software Program for Parsing of German Texts* (1996a), LANGSOFT, Sprachlernmittel, Switzerland, platform: DOS/Windows.
—*Syntparse (Analyse), Software Program for Parsing of French Texts* (1997), LANGSOFT, Sprachlernmittel, Switzerland, platform: DOS/Windows.
—*Syntcheck, French Orthographical and Grammatical Spellchecker* (1997a), LANGSOFT, Sprachlernmittel, Switzerland, platform: DOS/Windows.
—*Syntcheck, Italian Orthographical and Grammatical Spellchecker* (2000), LANGSOFT, Sprachlernmittel, Switzerland, platform: DOS/Windows.
—*Dialogue, Question-Answering Software Program* (2003), LANGSOFT, Sprachlernmittel, Switzerland, platform: DOS/Windows.
—*Word and Text Atribution Software Program* (2003a), LANGSOFT, Sprachlernmittel, Switzerland, platform: DOS/Windows.
—*English Algorithmic Grammar* (2006), London – New York: Continuum.
—*Antwort, German Question Answering Software Program* (2006a), LANGSOFT, Sprachlernmittel, Switzerland, platform: DOS/Windows.
Georgiev, H. and Raynova, D. (1989), 'Words denoting psychic activity in Balkan languages', *Linguistique Balkanique*, XXXII, 3–4, 203–221.
Giorgi, A. and Longobardi, G. (1991), *The Syntax of Noun Phrases: Configuration, Parameters and Empty Categories*. Cambridge: Cambridge University Press.
Glinz, H.(1961), *Der deutsche Satz*. Düsseldorf: Schwann.
Graver, B.D. (1971), *Advanced English Practice*. Oxford: Oxford University Press.
Grey B. Simpson, ed. (1991), *Understanding Word and Sentence*. Amsterdam: North-Holland.
Griesbach, H. and Dora Schlz, (1960), *Grammatik der deutschen Sprache*. München: Hueber.
Griesbach, H. (1986), *Neue deutsche Grammatik*. München, Wien, Zürich: Langenscheidt.
Grisham, R. (1986) *Computational Linguistics*. Cambridge: Cambridge University Press.
Gross, M. and Perrin, D. (eds) (1989), *Electronic Dictionaries and Automata in Computational Linguistics*, Springer.
Hammer's English Grammar and Usage (1995), 2nd edition, revised by Martin Durrell, USA: NTC Publishing Group.
Hammer's German Grammar and Usage (1995), 2nd edition, revised by Martin Durrell, USA: NTC Publishing Group.
Harris, Z. S. (1982), *A Grammar of English on Mathematical Principles*. New York: Wiley.
Hausser, R. (1989), *Computation of Language*. Berlin: Springer.
Heaton, J.B. (1965), *Prepositions and Adverbial Particles*. London: Longman.
Hornby, A.S. (1958), *A Guide to Patterns and Usage in English*. Oxford: Oxford University Press.
Jones, D. (1967), *Everyman's English Pronouncing Dictionary*. 13th edition, Cambridge: Cambridge University Press.
Jung, W. (1966), *Grammatik der deutschen Sprache*. Leipzig: Bibliographisches Institut.
Karen Sparck Jones (1986), *Synonymy and Semantic Classification*. Edinburgh: Edinburgh University Press.
Kathleen Dahlgren (1988), *Naive Semantics for Natural Language Understanding*. Boston: Kluwer.
Katz, B. (1993), *Start, Natural Language Question Answering System*. MIT: http://start.csail.mit.edu/
Kavi, M. and Nirenburg, S. (1997), 'Knowledge-based systems for natural language', in A.B. Tucker Jr. (ed.), *The Computer Science and Engineering Handbook*. Boca Raton, FL: CRC Press, Inc., pp. 637–653.
Dictionnaire Orthographique (1995), Paris: Larousse (de Poche).
Leech, S., Svartvik, J. (1975), *A Communicative Grammar of English*. London: Longman.
Manning, C. and Schütze, H. (1999), *Foundations of Statistical Natural Language Processing*. Cambridge, MA: MIT Press.
Marcus, M.P. (1980), *A Theory of Syntactic Recognition for Natural Language*. Cambridge, MA: MIT Press.
Marx-Moyse, J. (1983), *Untersuchungen zur deutschen Satzsyntax. 'Es' als vorausweisendes Element eines Subjektsatzes*. Wiesbaden: Steiner.
McCarthy, D. (1997), 'Word sense disambiguation for acquisition of selectional preferences', in *Proceedings of the ACL-EACL Workshop on Automatic Information Extraction and Building of Lexical Semantic Resources for NLP Applications*. Madrid, Spain, 52–61.

McEnery, T. (1992), *Computational Linguistics*. Wilmslow, UK: Sigma Press.
Pfeffer, J.A. (1984), *Studies in Descriptive English Grammar*. Heidelberg: Groos.
—*Studies in Descriptive German Grammar* (1984), Heidelberg: Groos.
Primov, U.V., Sorokina, V.A. (1970), 'Algorithm for automatic recognition of the nominal group in English technical texts' (in Russian), in R.G. Piotrovskij (ed.), *Statistika Teksta, II*. Minsk: Politechnical Institute.
Pullum,G.K. (1984), 'On two recent attempts to show that English is not a CFL', *Computational Linguistics*, 10 (3–4), 182–186.
Quirk R., Greenbaum, S., Leech, G. and Svartvic, J. (1972), *Grammar of Contemporary English*. London: Longman.
Quirk, R. and Greenbaum, S. (1983), *A University Grammar of English*. London: Longman.
Reichman, R. (1985), *Getting Computers to Talk like You and Me*. Cambridge, MA: MIT Press.
Roget, Peter Mark (1852), *Roget's Thesaurus of English Words and Phrases*. Harlow, Essex, England: Longman Group Ltd.
Schwarz, A (1978), *Deutsche Sprachlehre*. Lehrmittelverlag des Kantons Zürich.
Sestier, A., Dupuis, L. (1962), 'La place de la syntaxe dans la traduction automatique des langue. Esquisse d'un nouveau systeme de description grammaticale et de son utilisation pour la reconstruction des structures grammaticales', *Ingenieurs et Techniciens*, No. 1555, 43–50.
Schank, R. and Fano, A. (1992), 'Knowledge, memory, learning and teaching. A survey of our research', in *t.a.l., Traitement Automatique des Langues*, Vol. 33, No. 1–2.
Scwartz, A (1978), *Deutsche Sprachlehre*. Lehrmittelverlaq des Kautous Zürich.
Schweizer Weltatlas (1981), Kartentechnische Herstellung, Zuerich: Reproduktion und Druck Orell Fuessli Graphische Betriebe AG.
Shanks, D. (1993), 'Breaking Chomsky's rules', *New Scientist*, February, 26–30.
Shieber, S.M. (1985), 'Evidence against the non-context-freeness of natural language', *Linguistics and Philosophy*, 8, 333–343.
Siebs, Th. (1961), *Deutsche Hochsprache*. Berlin: Mouton de Gruyter.
Stannard, A. (1974), *Living English Structure*. London: Longman.
Urdang, L. (ed.) (1968), *The Random House Dictionary of the English Language* (College Edition), New York: Random House.
The Times Atlas of the World (1992), concise edition, London: Times Books, Harper Collins Publishers.
Trier, J. (1931), *Der deutsche Wortschatz im Sinnbezirk des Verstandes*. Heidelberg.
—'Deutsche Bedeutungsforshung', in Alfred Götze, Wilhelm Horn, Friedrich Maurer (eds), *Germanische Philologie, Ergebnisse und Aufgaben, Festschrift fuer O. Behagel* (1934a), Heidelberg.
—'Das sprachliche Feld. Eine Auseinandersetzung', *Neue Jahrbuecher fuer Wissenschaft und Jugendbildung*, 10 (1934b), Leipzig – Berlin.
Venev, Y. (1990), *Elsevier's Dictionary of Mathematical and Computational Linguistics*. Amsterdam: Elsevier.

Appendices

1 German Dictionary of Segments

Sequences of German parts of speech within the sentence. For the abbreviations used below see the Index of Abbreviations.

AANVlassen
AD
AMNVV
ANDE
ANVNdemN
AN
AVN
A
abRX
aberauch
alsANV
amMFB-BE
anNV
anTNdesN
an
aufND
aufNN'sN
aufTANV
ausANUDN
BV
beiN
beiTN
bis im=PT
bis vorMJahren
DANNN
DAN
DDVIND
DD
DkBV
DkNvielV
DNBV
DNzuV
DRVTNdesN
DTNA
DTNdesNNundN
DTN
DUINDMTN
DVDN
DVHR

AAN
AEx
ANANX
ANdesN
ANV
AundAX
AXDk
abMdesTANE
abTMFB-BEIN
aberdazu=J
als je zuvor=J
amNdesN
anTAANDEp
anTNNdesNN
auchNan
aufNdesNNN
aufNV
auf und ab
ausAN
beiAMN
beiTAANDV
besser als=J
bis jetzt=D
biszu=P
DANN
DA
DDV
DEx
DkE
DMAN
DNNYNNdesNE
DOAN
DRVTN
DTNDD
DTNdesNN
DUHIDV
DundD
DVHAN
DVHTND

AA
AMNVlassen
ANBV
ANE
ANzuV
AundA
AX
abMUhr
abTMFB-BE
alles andere=I
amAFB-B
anMN
anTAN
anTNVzuU
auch wenn=J
aufNdesN
aufON
auf welche vonI
BVV
beiA
beiTANkAN
bis an hin=P
bis vor=P
bis zuMN
DANYN
DDD
DDXH
DHV
DkNDV
DMNV
DNN
DRVTNdesAN
DR
DTND
DTNV
DUHRV
DVDI
DVHD
DVHTN

DVH
DVNR
DVTNan
DVTNP
DV
DXD
DXH
DxNDTN
DxTN
DX
dafür=D
dank des=P
dass auch
der oberhalb des=M
dieNN
die
EHXN
EXD
Ex
EzuV
ein paar=I
erklärtIN
etwa plus
früher oder später=D
fürN
fürTNEx
fürTNV
GAV
GDTNV
GHDD
GHD
GHY
GID
GON's
GSEY
GTANANEY
GTNEX
GTN
GVD
GXNN'sAN
ganz anders=D
ganz gut=D
gegenüberTNN
gibt esDDTN
gibt esD
HA
HDDDVV
HDIV
HDV
HHONAAEY
HH
HkHHBV
HM%V
HNY
HRE
HSVSkID
HS
HTANV
HTNkVU
HTN
HUGk
HURDV
HUTANV
HUTNDV
DVNan
DVN
DVTNdesNNTNb
DVTN
DXDk
DXHN
DXIA
DXNundN
DXviel
DYHIN
damit auch
das eine=JT
dazu=D
dieD
die nur=JD
EBV
ESD
EXx
EY
E
einen oder zwei=M
esgibt=HV
etwa
für denMFB-BE
fürR
fürTNE
GAEX
GAY
GDV
GHDEY
GHEY
GH
GIV
GPNV
GSV
GTANAN
GTNkV
GVAan
GVkD
GX
ganz dem=JT
ganz richtig=D
genügtes
gibt esDD
gibt esD
HBVY
HDDDV
HDTNV
HD
HHONDDEY
HIk
HkNV
HNBVV
HONVU
HR
HSVU
HTANVU
HTANX
HTNSVU
HUD
HUONDV
HURTN
HUTAN
HUTNV
DVNNONan
DVTNAN
DVTNdesNN
DVU
DXDTN
DXHTN
DXID
DXN
Dx
DYHTNE
dank der=P
das einzige=N
dennobschon
die im=JPT
die nurT=JDT
EBY
ES
EX
Ezuhaben
ein bißchen=I
einer der=I
etwa minus
FB-BDYH
für gewöhnlich=D
fürTAN
fürTNNV
GATNV
GBV
GD
GHDV
GHV
GIDEX
GI
GR
GS
GTANV
GTNX
GVDan
GV
G
ganz die=JT
ganz so
gibt es=esgibt
gibt esDTN
gibt esTAN
HBV
HDDDx
HDVU
HEY
HHONDEY
HkBV
HkVU
HNV
HRDV
HSVSID
HSV
HTANVV
HTAN
HTNV
HUGkvielNV
HUONV
HUSk
HUTA
HU

HVAan
HVanBV
HVDDAN
HVDTND
HVHAN
HVONIN
HVRDDTN
HVRD
HVSD
HVTAN
HV
HxAN
HXDE
HxE
HXkN
HXN
HXTAN
HXTN
HYDDE
HYD
HYkN
HYON
HYSI
HYTN
heute abend=D
IAANV
IANYHE
IDkNY
INANXDTNAN
INDEV
INUDDV
INUV
INVNN
INVSDD
INV
ITNVU
IUTNdesN
IVDD
IVND
IV
IXTN
imNN
imNzuX
immer noch=D
inIN
inNV
inTNdesN
insANE
JA
JkNV
JN
JTNV
kBV
kDD
kNVU
kV
L
MAN
MIDBV
MNXTND
MTNXTAN
M
NA
NDDDV
HVABX
HVan
HVDDMN
HVDTN
HVIN
HVON
HVRDD
HVRTN
HVTAAN
HVTNTN
HxAA
HXA
HXDI
HXkAN
HxNV
HxS
HXTDAN
HX
HYDME
HYE
HYkR
HYRDDTN
HYSOE
H
heute morgen=D
IANV
IAN
ID
INANXD
INNundN
INUDV
INVan
INVRD
INVTAN
INx
IURAV
IVan
IVDkTN
IVSA
IXI
I
imNTN
imN
in den vergangenenMJahren
inN"N"
inTAN
inTN
insANV
JBV
Jk
JONN
JVes
kDAN
kE
kNV
k
lautNN
MDAAN
MNM
MN
MundM
mehr als=J
NBVY
NDEx
HVAN
HVDBX
HVDD
HVD
HVkan
HVRAN
HVRDTN
HVR
HVTANdesN
HVTN
HxANdesN
HXDD
HXD
HXkD
HXN
HXsoD
HXTNANE
Hx
HYDTNE
HYkDV
HYMNDS
HYSE
HYSRE
hab's=YI
hin und hau=D
IANV
IA
IHVU
INANX
INOANVON
INUTN
INVNNN
INVR
INVTN
IN
IURDV
IVDan
IVHD
IVSD
IXTAN
im durchschnitt
imNV
immer mehr=D
inINdesTN
inNN
inTNDDVX
in-undAN
JANYU
JD
JNN
JON
J
kDDERD
kNVI
kTN
LDHRV
M%Vk
MDANN
MNTN
ModerM
MVTNANN's
mitTAN
NBV
NDVU

NDV
ND
NdesNdesAN
NdesNdesN
NdesNNVN
NdesNNVR
NdesNXTAN
NdesN
NEx
NEY
NkBV
NkNV
NkVU
NMN
NNdesTNN
NVkan
NNkVU
NNNN
NNN
NNTN
NNU
NNVan
NNVHDan
NNVRDan
NNV
NNXTN
NNYSE
NNYSOE
NNYTNdesN
NN
NONVU
NSVSkID
NTAANX
NTAAN
NTANX
NTNV
NTN
NUD
NUONDV
NUONV
NURauchY
NUR
NUSk
NUTNDV
NUTNV
NundAN
N-undN
NU
NU
NundTN
NVA
NVAan
NVanBV
NVan
NVDD
NVDN
NVD
NVHSD
NVI
NVM
NVN
NVONIN
NVON
NVRAN
NVRDDTN
NVRDD
NVRDTN
NVRD
NVR
NVSA
NVSD
NVS
NVTAAN
NVTNTN
NVTN
NVx
NV
NXAN
NXA
NXDAN
NxDE
NXDIAN
NXIAN
NXkAN
NXkD
NXkN
NXkON
NXNN'sAN
NXN
NXSAD
NXSDD
NXTN
NX
NYDDE
NYDME
NYDTNE
NYD
NYE
NYIE
NYkDV
NYkN
NYkR
NYMNDS
NYSE
NYTN
NY
N
nachANdesNNN
nachANdesNN
nachAN
nichtallein
nicht als=J
nicht mehr=k
noch einmal=D
noch immer=D
O"N"desN
OANEY
OANE
OAN
ONdesN
ONTANEY
ONTAN
ONVD
ONV
ONV
ONXkTN
ONXMND
ONX
ONYE
ON
oberhalb des=P
PAANTDAN
PAAN
PAA
PAINAN
PAINN
PAM
PANAAN
PAND
PANdesNN
PANdesN
PANNV
PANN's
PANN
PANV
PAN
PA
PBV
PDAN
PDD
PDIAN
PDINN
PDM
PD
Pdem einen oder anderenN
PdemHS
PdesN
PGDD
PGD
PGTNEDX
PGTNEX
PGTN
PHBV
PH
PIAAN
PIANundN
PIAN
PIAoderAN
PIA
PIMFB-B
PINdesAN
PINdesN's
PINdesN
PINXTN
PINYTNTN
PIN
PITAN
PITA
PI
PMFB-B
PMNN
PMN
PM
PNAN
PND
PND
PNdesANANVSTNdesANkA
PNdesANANVSTNdesANkD
PNdesANAN
PNdesANNNN
PNdesAN
PNdesNan

PNdesND
PNMdesND
PNND
PNN'sAN
PNoderN
PNVHMN
PNVRMN
PN
POND
PONV
PRN
PRVN
PSANTDAN
PTAAN
PTAFB-BNdesAN
PTAIFB-B
PTANdesAN
PTANdesN
PTANTDAN
PTDAN
PTMNDD
PTMN
PTNAND
PTND
PTNdesNVTANdesN
PTNEx
PTNNundN
PTNON
PTNTN
PTNVNN
PTNV
PTNXHD
PTON
PXTNdesN
P
RNdesN
RVN
RYSE
rundAAN
SV
seitMFB
sondern
TAENV
TANDANX
TANkEYBV
TANTNVU
TANVD
TANVSDan
TANVTNdesN
TANXAE
TANXN
TANYTNdesAN
TDAN
TMAN
TNAX
TNDDX
TNDV
TNdesAN
TNdesNN
TNdesNV
TNdesNXTN
TNEV
TNE
TNNVDTN
PNdesNNN
PNMdesN
PNNN
PNN
PNTN
PNVH
PNV
POANxTNE
PONp
PON
PRp
PRV
PSV
PTAANdesN
PTAFB-BN
PTANDD
PTANdesNN
PTANNN
PTANV
PTIFB-B
PTMND
PTMundMN
PTNAN
PTNdesAN
PTNdesNVTNdesN
PTNNEN
PTNNundTN
PTNREY
PTNundTN
PTNVN
PTNXDA
PTNYHkE
PTSTNV
PX
RDX
RUX
RXDD
RYTNV
SDNV
S
selbst wenn
TAANBV
TANAANX
TANdesAN
TANNN
TANUHEY
TANVI
TANVSDD
TANVTN
TANXDE
TANYDTN
TANY
TMANdesANXTAN
TNAN
TNA
TNDMNV
TNDX
TNdesNAN
TNdesNVSD
TNdesNXA
TNdesN
TNEX
TNHDX
TNNYDTNE
PNdesN
PNM
PNNV
PNONY
PNundN
PNVNDTN
PN'sN
POAN
PONVHTNBV
PRD
PRVI
PR
PS
PTAbisAN
PTAFB-B
PTAND
PTANdesNV
PTANN
PTAN
PTMAN
PTMNN
PTM
PTNan
PTNdesNN
PTNdesN
PTNNN
PTNN
PTNTNV
PTNVH
PTNVx
PTNXDD
PTN
PundP
PzuV
RkDDBV
RVH
RXkON
R
SIN
seit demAJahr
sonder neher=D
TAAN
TANATNX
TANINON
TANON
TANUREY
TANVRan
TANVTANdesN
TANV
TANXD
TANYR
TAN
TMANdesAN
TNAV
TNBV
TNDNV
TND
TNdesNNUTN
TNdesNVTND
TNdesNXD
TNdesN
TNEY
TNNNVD
TNNYDTN

TNN	TNTANx	TNTNN
TNTNx	TNTNX	TNTN
TNTN	TNUDD	TNUDTN
TNUNV	TNU	TNVan
TNVDD	TNVD	TNVIA
TNVIH	TNVINk	TNVkNan
TNVONan	TNVON	TNVRan
TNVR	TNVTAAN	TNVTAN
TNVTDAN	TNVTND	TNVTNdesNNN
TNVTNdesNN	TNVTN	TNVV
TNV	TNXAA	TNxAX
TNXA	TNXDAN	TNXDD
TNXDI	TNXDkD	TNXDTN
TNxDX	TNXD	TNXE
TNXH	TNXkAN	TNXkDD
TNXkD	TNXkNN	TNXkTN
TNXk	TNXNdesN	TNXNN
TNXNundN	TNXN	TNXTAN
TNXTA	TNXTNdesFB-BD	TNXTN
TNx	TNYONE	TNYON
TNYSRE	TNY	TN
teileN'sX	teileN's	UDEx
UD	UeskATNX	UeskDTNX
UHIDV	UHRV	UHSD
UHTNAV	UHTNEV	UHV
UH	UkDNx	UkV
UNV	UON	UTAN
UTNANN'sTNV	UV	U
über die das=PGT	über die der=PGT	überTN
umMUhr	um zuV	undAX
undDX	undIONNN	undNdesNDAN
undNdesNDMN	undNdesNNNN	undNNN
undOIN	undONNN	undS
undTN	und	unterNAN
unterNVHMN	unterNVRMN	unterTANNN
VAan	VAN	VanON
VBV	VDan	VDIN
VDIV	VDRI	VD
VHAAN	VHan	VHDan
VHDAN	VHDD	VHDMN
VHD	VHI	VHkN
VHMN	VHM	VHOANAN
VHOAN	VHON	VHRDan
VHR	VHSan	VHSD
VHS	VHTNBV	VHTND
VHTN	VH	VIAN
VITN	VI	Vkan
VMAN	VNAN	VNan
VNDan	VNDTN	VND
VNdesN	VNMN	VNNan
VNN	VNOANAN	VNOAN
VNR	VNS	VNTND
VNTN	VN	VONBV
VONp	VONTN	VONV
VPTNan	VPTNdesNan	VRAN
VRan	VRD	VRIN
VRMN	VRSDIan	VRSID
VRS	VRTAN	VRTNDTNDD
VRTN	VRX	VR
VSan	VSkDD	VSkD
VSN	VSON	VSV
VS	VTANdesN	VTAN
VTA	VTNan	VTNDMN
VTNdesNN	VTNdesNTANTDDAN	VTNdesN

VTNNNN(usually when the last two Nouns are a name)	VTNN	VTN
VU	VundV	VV
Vx	VY	V
vielAN	vielN	vielTN
vomFB-BH	vomMFB-BE	vomNaus
vomN	vonANAAN	von aussen direkt
vonden=PT	von der=PT	von derAbisAN
vonIN	vonMbisMFB-B	vonMbisMUhr
vonMNanD	vonNaus	vonTINNN
vonTINN	vorallem=D	vor allem=J,when followed by Article)
vorgängig=J(when alone)	wasVTN	wennesdas=JT
wenn es die=JT	wenn noch	wiedasbereits=J
wie möglich=J	XAN	xA
XA	XDAN	xDAN
xDDAN	XDD	xDEX
XDM	XD	xD
XE	XHADA	XHDDD
XHDD	xHDV	XHD
XHE	xHTN	xHV
XH	XINDkDE	xINdesNNN
xI	xkE	XMAN
XMNAN	XMN	xMTNN
xM	xNA	XNDDD
XNDD	XND	xND
XN	xRD	XRkDE
XR	xSNundN	xSN
XTAN	xTNAN	XTNA
XTNDDD	XTNDD	XTND
XTNE	xTNIN	XTNN
XTN	x	X
YAN	YHAN	YHDE
YHkE	YHONDDE	YHONDE
YHTNE	YIN	YMAN
YNNdesN	YRE	YTAN
YTNkNE	YTNNA	YTNND
zuDDN	zuD	zuM%
zuNdesNN	zuNdesN	zuschwer=D
zuTAN	zuTNREY	zuV
zuzweit=D	zumAAN	zumANEx
zumANN's	zum Beispiel=J	zumNdesN
zwischenMundMFB-B	zwischenNundN	

2 French Dictionary of Segments

Sequences of French parts of speech within the sentence. For the abbreviations used below see the Index of Abbreviations.

AN	a priori	AVD
A	après que	après tout
au cas	BKKVYETN	BKKV
BRV	BVA	BVD
BVOAN	BVON	BVTNdeN
BVTN	BV	BXE
bien du mal=D	bien que=J	C
celui de=T	celui du=T	chaqueFB=D
DBRV	DBVTNA	DDD
DD	DI	DRVTN
DRV	DTN	DUNHVON
DYHN	D	de ces=I

deN
de temps en temps=D
de puis long temps=D
EdeN
E
en arrière de=P
en un instant=D
encore très bien=D
GDXH
GIX
GKVK
GKYKEYTNE
GRIV
GRXDA
GRYE
GSV
GUVMAN
GUXTN
GVIAN
GVON
GVTN
GVVIN
GXEN
GYDEN
GYETN
HDYG
HKRV
HKURVKN
HkYkTN
HRhV
HRVINdeN
HRVVTN
HRXE
HU
HVONA
HXDA
HYDEV
HYEV
IANAV
IDKVKTAAN
IDYEETN
IdeIN
IdeNXDDD
IdeN
IKXKTN
IKXK
IMN
INdeA
INdeN
INSV
INV
INXDA
INXE
INYétéE
INYETN
IRVN
iRYE
ITANSV
IVBV
iVVON
IXBSVV
IXE
iXIN
iXNdeN
de nouveau=D(before fullstop)
detrop=D
depuisMFB
ETNdeN
en état de
en avant=D
en un moment=D
fort bien=D
gE
GI
GKVN
GKYKE
GRVTANdeN
GRYEAA
GSVDSV
GTN
GUVTNdeN
GVBVON
GVI
GVRV
gVTN
GV
GXI
GYDE
GYHE
HHVN
HKSVDR
HKURVON
HRHRVTNA
HRRV
HRVN
HRVV
HRYETN
HVD
HVRV
HXEI
HYEBV
HYTNdeN
IANXA
IDKVK
IDYEE
IdeNXDA
IdeNXDD
II
IKXKTNBSVBVD
IMNYETN
INAgTN
INdeNVTNdeNE
INRV
INUYBV
INXAN
INXEIN
INXHA
INYEE
IN
IRVTN
ISVN
iUH
iVHTN
IV
IXBV
IXH
IXIN
IXN
de quoi=G
de puisceFB
ED
ETN
en arrière=D
enFB-BM
envein=D
GDSV
GIV
GKVKD
GKYD
gN
GRV
GRYEDA
GSVD
GURV
GUVTN
GVBV
GVN
GVTAN
GVVBV
GXABV
GXTAAdeN
GYEI
G
HKRVDD
HKUKV
HkVMN
HRHRV
HRVINdeNBRV
HRVTN
HRV
HUV
HVHV
HV
HXE
HYEDG
IANAKVK
IA
IDVVTNBXE
ID
IdeNXDDA
IdeNXD
IKV
IKXKTNBSVBV
IMNYETN
INBV
INdeNV
INSRV
iNV
INXA
INXEN
iNXI
INYETNA
IRKV
iRXDD
ISXE
IUV
IVTN
IXA
iXDTAN
IXINdeN
iXI
IXR

IXTNdeN
IXV
iYA
i
ilyaTNdeN
KHVKA
KNVKA
KRVKXED
KUHKVMFBNTNA
KVHK
KVON
KYHKTNA
K
les autres=I
Mfois
MNdeONV
MN
NBV
NDRYDIN
NDYTNdeN
NdeAA
NdeN
NhV
NKRUV
NKRVK
NKSVDR
NKUKV
NKUVTN
NKVDRRV
NKVI
NKVKD
NKVKSVON
NkVMN
NKV
NKX
NKYDDNBV
NKYIN
NKYKDE
NKYKEBVON
NKYKE
NkYkTN
NKYNBV
NNV
NRHRVTNA
NRIDV
NRUV
NRVD
NRVN
NRVTNDE
NRV
NRXD
NRXE
NRYEDV
NRYEON
NRYETN
NSEV
NSRV
NSVBV
NSVTNdeNIN
NSVTN
NSXEBVI
NTANRYEBV
NUBVTNdeN
NUDV
iXTN
iXV
IYDE
I
ilyaTN
KHVKD
KRRVK
KRVK
KUHKVMFBN
KVK
KV
KYH
la plus large=A
les uns=I
MNBV
MNVON
NA
NCR
NDVD
NDYTN
NdeDABV
NetN
NIRV
NKRVD
NKRV
NKSVD
NKURVAN
NKVAN
NKVD
NKVKBVTNdeN
NKVKSVONTAA
NKVKSV
NKVN
NKXD
NKYANBV
NKYD
NKYKDDV
NKYKDVTN
NKYKEIN
NKYKTANdeN
NKYKVM
NKYN
NNXE
NRHRV
NRIV
NRU
NRVINdeN
NRVON
NRVTON
NRXDA
NRXEBVIN
NRYEBKKVYETN
NRYED
NRYERD
NRYTN
NSRVg
NSVBKVTN
NSVDD
NSVTNdeN
NSVV
NSXEBV
NUA
NUBVTN
NUD
IXTN
IX
IYETNdeN
ilya=HDY
J
KIRVK
KRVKTN
KRYDE
KUHKV
KVN
KYHDKETNBV
KY
leMFB-B
MFB
MNdeNVTNdeNE
MNV
NBVTN
NDRYDIND
NDV
NDY
NdeDA
NetR
NKDYAN
NKRVKV
NKRYE
NKUDYN
NKURVON
NKVDN
NKVIN
NKVKDD
NKVKSVONTDA
NKVK
NKVON
NKXK
NKYDDNBVIN
NKYEIN
NKYKDETN
NKYKDV
NKYKETN
NKYKTAN
NKYNBDV
NKYON
NRHBVTNA
NRhV
NRRV
NRVBV
NRVI
NRVTNA
NRVV
NRXDE
NRXEN
NRYEBKKV
NRYEN
NRYER
NRY
NSRVI
NSVBVTN
NSVTNdeND
NSVTNN
NSV
NSXE
NUBVI
NUBV
NUHVBV

NURVTN
NUTN
NUVON
NUYBV
NVAdeN
NVBRV
NVBVAN
NVBVIN
NVBVTNAdeN
NVBV
NVDIN
NVDVIN
NVE
NVIMN
NVMN
NVONBV
NVRVTN
NVTAN
NVTNdeN
NVTON
NVVR
NV
NXABV
NXDDBVIMD
NXDE
NXEBSV
NXERVTN
NXETNA
NXE
NXTNA
NYBV
NYDEON
NYDEV
NYDVTNBVOAN
NYEAA
NYEDG
NYEDTNV
NYEEON
NYEIND
NYEON
NYETAN
NYETNdeNA
NYEVTON
NYIMN
NYTAN
NYTNBRV
NYUVI
nepas=K
ONCR
ONSXE
ONVBSVD
ONVTN
ONXERV
ONXV
ON
PAN
PDdeN
PdeRD
PGN
Pg
PH
PIGV
PINdeN
PiNSVTN
NURV
NUVBV
NUVTN
NUYTN
NVAN
NVBSV
NVBVD
NVBVN
NVBVTNA
NVDBVTN
NVDONdeN
NVDVTN
NVIMMMN
NVIN
NVNV
NVON
NVTANA
NVTNAA
NVTNdeON
NVVIN
NVVTN
NXABVINdeN
NXA
NXDDBVIM
NXDHX
NXED
NXETAN
NXETN
NXNdeN
NX
NYDDEON
NYDEVI
NYDE
NYDVTN
NYEBVD
NYEDN
NYED
NYEE
NYEIN
NYESVBVN
NYETNA
NYETNdeN
NYEV
NYMN
NYTDAN
NYTNBSV
NYUVN
n'y=K
ONKHVKD
ONUV
ONVBV
ONXBVDTNA
ONXVABV
ONYETNBVD
PAAN
PA
PD
PFB
PgTN
PG
PIAN
PINA
PINE
PIN
NUSV
NUVdeA
NUV
NU
NVA
NVBVANdeNA
NVBVINdeNA
NVBVON
NVBVTN
NVDD
NVDON
NVD
NVIMMN
NVI
NVONA
NVO
NVTANBV
NVTNA
NVTN
NVVMN
NVV
NXABVTNA
NXDA
NXDDBV
NXD
NXEI
NXETNAdeN
NXEVTN
NXN
NYAN
NYDDV
NYDEVN
NYDM
NYDV
NYEBV
NYEDTNSV
NYEEBV
NYEINAgTN
NYEN
NYETANdeN
NYETND
NYETN
NYE
NYTAAN
NYTNA
NYTN
N
ONAXEMfois
ONSVBVTNA
ONVBRVD
ONVN
ONXBVDTNM
ONXVDBV
ONYETNBV
PANdeN
PBRV
PdelaN
PgN
PGV
PHR
PIFB
PIND
PINN
PiN

PION	PITN	PI
PJD	PKVTN	PMFBNA
PMFB	PMN	PNA
PNBVI	PNBVN	PND
PNdeAN	PNdeA	PNdeN
PNON	PNTNA	PNTNdeI
PR	PSAN	PSg
PTAAN	PTANA	PTANdeNAN
PTAN	PTFBD	PTIN
PTNAdeNBVTN	PTNAdeNdeNN	PTNAdeNdeN
PTNAdeN	PTNA	PTND
PTNdeNA	PTNdeNdeN	PTNdeN
PTNE	PTNON	PTNSVVTNdeN
PTN	PVTN	PV
PXN	P	plus tôt=D
plus tard=D	pour que=J	Q
quelqu'un de cesFB	RVD	RVTN
RV	RYE	RYHEVAN
RYHEVIN	R	rien=K(when between 2 Verbs-Auxiliary and Past Participle-only)
SHXTN	SVBV	SVTNAdeN
SVTN	SV	sans doute=D
sans trop=D	TANdeINAVIV	TANdeNA
TANdeNVD	TANdeNVIN	TANRYEBV
TANSV	TANSXE	TANVTN
TANXE	TANYXE	TAN
TFB	TNARV	TNASVTNA
TNAVON	TNAXE	TNAYESVBV
TNAYE	TNA	TNBRVTN
TNBRV	TNCNA	TNCN
TND	TNdeANE	TNdeAN
TNdeI	TNdeNASXETN	TNdeNASXE
TNdeNAVNBVITN	TNdeNAVN	TNdeNAVTNA
TNdeNAVVNBVITN	TNdeNAVVN	TNdeNRV
TNdeNVINA	TNdeNVTNE	TNdeNYEEDTN
TNdeNYETN	TNdeNYE	TNdeNYTNdeMN
TNdeNYTN	TNdeN	TNdeON
TNE	TNKUDV	TNKV
TNKYKE	TNKY	TNSVTN
TNSV	TNS	TNUYBV
TNVBVTN	TNVBX	TNVBXDTNdeI
TNVBXDTNdeN	TNVBXD	TNVDIN
TNVDMN	TNVg	TNVI
TNVMN	TNVN	TNVON
TNVTNA	TNVTNdeN	TNVTN
TNV	TNXDE	TNXED
TNXETNA	TNXETN	TNXE
TNXTNA	TNYDETNA	TNYEE
TNYEON	TNYESVN	TNYETNA
TNYETNBVD	TNYETNBV	TNYETND
TNYETNdeN	TNYETN	TNYEVN
TN	telquel=I	telsdes=I
tenir compte=V	tous ces=I	tout...coup=D
tout ce=I	tout cela=N	tout de suite=D
tout le=I	tout le long=D	tout seul=R
tout seuls=I	toute cette=I	toute une=I
toutes cettes=I	toutes les=I	trop tôt=D
	très bien=D	UHHVON
UHVTN	UHV	UH
UNHVON	UNVTN	UNV
UVTN	UXEBVD	UXEBV
UXVBVD	UXVBV	UYDE
U	un de ces=I	un peu=A

un peud'=A	un peu de=A	VBVN
VBVTN	VBV	VDD
VDVTN	VD	VHOAN
VHON	VHRV	VHTN
VH	VIAN	VIR
VI	VND	VNRV
VN	VON	VRA
VRD	VRH	VRI
VRON	VR	VTAN
VTNdeNA	VTNdeN	VTN
VTON	VVON	V
XABV	XA	XED
XE	XH	XINdeN
XI	XNBV	XN
XTANdeNA	XTAN	XTNdeNA
XTN	X	YHA
YHD	YHE	YHVVIN
YHV	YNVIN	YNV
YRD	YTNE	

3 Sample of source code compilable on a Borland compiler versions 2–4.52

The text below should be copied carefully, exactly as it is, and should be compiled on a Borland compiler (up to version 4.52). The following files are included:

```
// file 'grammar.c'
/* file 'grammar.c' requires the files "chris.h", "gramdic.h", "grammar.h",
"lex.h", "lexicon.h" and
"type.h", see further below for them */
#include <ctype.h>
#include <stdio.h>
#include <conio.h>
#include <alloc.h>
#include <dir.h>

#include <bmenu.h>
#include <bmouse.h>

#include "gramdic.h"
#include "lexicon.h"
#include "chris.h"
#include "lex.h"
#include "type.h"

extern BMENU    *mrus;

#define NB   4

void get_gram(int lang, char *c, WORD *wrd);

int find_words(struct QUE *que[]);

DLIM *enque_dlm(struct QUE *que[], char syn, char ssyn);
WORD *enque_word(struct QUE *que[], char syn, char *word);
struct C_TAB *contr_analys(char *word, int wl, WORD *wrd);
struct M_TAB *morph_analys(char *word, int wl, WORD *wrd, char *ww);
struct PREF_TAB *pref_analys(char *word, WORD *wrd);

/********************* FINDER **********************/

#include "grammar.h"
```

```
struct PREF_TAB *pref_analys(char *word, WORD *wrd)
{
struct PREF_TAB *pref;
int l;

 for ( pref = PREFTAB; pref->prefix; pref++ )
 {
  if ( !strncmp(word, pref->prefix, pref->len) )
  {
   l = pref->len;
   if (wrd->wl == l) {
  strcpy(wrd->outwd, pref->rprefix);
  wrd->syn = 'D';
  wrd->stat = 2;
  return NULL;
   }
   if (word[l] != '-' && strchr(word + l, '-'))
  return NULL;
   strcat(wrd->rprefix, pref->rprefix);
   if (word[l] == '-') {
  l++;
  strcat(wrd->rprefix, "-");
   }
   else
  if ( pref->prefix[0] == 'r' && pref->prefix[1] == 'e') {
    strcat(wrd->rprefix, " ");
   }
   strncat(wrd->eprefix, wrd->inword, l);
   wrd->wl -= l;
   strcpy(wrd->inword, wrd->inword + l);
   strcpy(word, word + l);

   wrd->stat = 1;

   return pref;
  }
 }
 return NULL;
}


struct C_TAB *contr_analys(char *word, int wl, WORD *wrd)
{
struct C_TAB *mor;
int lf, i;
WORD *new;

 for ( mor = CTAB; mor->mflex; mor++ ) {
  if ((lf = isflex(word, wl, mor->mflex)) > 0 ) {
   wl -= lf;
   wrd->stat = 1;

   switch (mor->mgram[0]) {
  case 'M' :
   wl = 3;
   word[wl] = '\0';
   break;

  case 'X' :

     if (!strcmp(word, "there\'s") ||
      !strcmp(word, "here\'s")  ||
      !strcmp(word, "what\'s")  ||
      !strcmp(word, "that\'s")  ||
```

```
    !strcmp(word, "who\'s"))
    {
     word[wl] = '\0';
     break;
    }
    else { /* pronoun or possessive case */
     word[wl] = '\0';
     for (i = 0; PRTAB[i].mflex; i++)
    if (strcmp(PRTAB[i].mflex, word) == 0) break;

     if (PRTAB[i].mflex == NULL && mor->cond == 3) {
    /* possessive case */
    word[wl] = '\'';
    wrd->stat = 0;
    return NULL;
     }
    }
break;

case 'T' :
 word[wl] = '\0';
 if (word[0] != 'i')
 {
  for (i = 1; PRTAB[i].mflex; i++)
   if (strcmp(PRTAB[i].mflex, word) == 0) break;

  if (PRTAB[i].mflex == NULL) i = 1;
 }
break;

default:
 if (!strcmp(word, "can\'t"))
  wl++;
 else if (!strncmp(word, "arn", 3)) {
  strcpy(wrd->inword + 1, "re");
  strcpy(word + 1, "re");
  wl = 3;
 }
 else if (!strncmp(word, "won", 3)) {
  strcpy(wrd->inword + 1, "ill");
  strcpy(word + 1, "ill");
  wl = 4;
 }
 else if (!strncmp(word, "sha", 3)) {
  strcpy(wrd->inword + 3, "ll");
  strcpy(word + 3, "ll");
  wl = 5;
 }
 else if (mor->cond == 2) /* cannot */
  wl = 3;
 wrd->wl = wl;
 word[wl] = '\0';
break;

}

new = enque_word(NULL, mor->mgram[0], mor->ow);
if (new == NULL) {
   wrd->stat = -1;
   break;
}
strcpy(new->inword, mor->iw);
new->stat = 1;
if (new->syn == 'X') new->cflag = '\'';
```

```
    new->wl = strlen(mor->iw);
    new->next = wrd->next;
    wrd->next = new;
    wrd->inword[wl] = '\0';
    wrd->wl = wl;

    return mor;

   }

  }

 return NULL;

}


struct M_TAB *morph_analys(char *word, int wl, WORD *wrd, char *ww)
{
struct M_TAB *mor, *mow;
int lf = 0, l;

 for ( mor = MTAB; mor->mflex; mor++ ) {
  if ((lf = isflex(word, wl, mor->mflex)) > 0 ) {
   wl -= lf;
   if (mor->mflex[0] == 'e') {
     *ww = 'e';
   }
   wrd->syn = mor->mgram[0];

   switch (mor->mgram[0]) {

   case 'G' :
    if( word[wl - 1] == word[wl - 2]) {
     *ww = word[wl - 1];
     wl--;
    }
    else
     *ww = 'e';
    word[wl] = '\0';

   break;

   case 'Z' :
    if(mor->mflex[0] == 'i') {
     word[wl++] = 'y';
    }
    word[wl] = '\0';

    wrd->numb = mor->mgram[1] - '0';
    wrd->person = mor->mgram[2] - '0';
    /*wrd->tcase = C_AKK;*/

    for ( mow = mor + 1; mow->mflex; mow++ ) {
     if (isflex(word, wl, mow->mflex) ) {
      if (mow->mgram[0] == 'V') {
     wrd->syn = 'V';
     wrd->numb = 0;
      }
      else {
     wrd->syn = 'N';
     wrd->tcase = 0;
      }
      break;
```

```
    }
   }

  break;

  case 'E' :
   if(mor->mflex[0] == 'i') {
    word[wl++] = 'y';
   }
   else
    if( word[wl - 1] == word[wl - 2]) {
     *ww = word[wl - 1];
     wl--;
    }
   word[wl] = '\0';
   wrd->tense = T_PAST;
  break;


  case 'A' :
   l = strlen(mor->mflex);
   wrd->cflag = 'a';
   if (mor->mflex[l - 2] == 'e' && mor->mflex[l - 1] == 'r')
    wrd->tense = 1;
   else
   if (mor->mflex[l - 2] == 's' && mor->mflex[l - 1] == 't')
    wrd->tense = 2;

   if (mor->mflex[0] == 'i' && mor->mflex[1] == 'e') {
    word[wl++] = 'y';
    word[wl] = '\0';
   }
   else {
    if (word[wl - 1] == word[wl - 2]) {
     *ww = word[wl - 1];
     wl--;
    }
    word[wl] = '\0';
   }
  break;

  case 'D' :
   word[wl] = '\0';
   wrd->cflag = 'd';
  break;

  case 'N' :
   wrd->numb = mor->mgram[1] - '0';
   wrd->tcase = mor->mgram[2] - '0';
   if (mor->mflex[lf - 1] == '\'' || mor->mflex[0] == '\'')
    word[wl] = '\0';
  break;

  default :
  break;

  }

  wrd->stat = 1;
  strcpy(wrd->inbase, word);

  return mor;

 }
```

```
  }

  return NULL;
}

void get_engram(char *word, char *cw, WORD *wrd)
{
char *wdic;
char *wirr;
  if (!wrd->inbase ||wrd->inbase[0] == '\0')
    strcpy(wrd->inbase, word);
    strcpy(wrd->rprefix, cw);

   switch (wrd->syn)
   {

   case 'X' : case 'x' : case 'Y' :
    if (isdigit(*cw)) wrd->tense = *cw++ - '0';
    if (isdigit(*cw)) wrd->numb =  *cw++ - '0';
    if (isdigit(*cw)) wrd->person = *cw++ - '0';
    if (*cw == '[') {
     while (*cw && *cw != ']') {
      if (isdigit(*cw)) wrd->person = *cw - '0';
      if (*cw == 'P')  wrd->numb = 1;
      if (*cw == '<')  wrd->tense = T_PAST;
      if (*cw == '>')  wrd->tense = T_FUTURE;
      if (*cw == 'd')  wrd->ctran = *cw;
      cw++;
     }
     cw++;
    }
   break;


   case 'R' : case 'M' :
    if (isdigit(*cw)) wrd->numb =  *cw++ - '0';
    if (isdigit(*cw)) wrd->person = *cw++ - '0';
    if (isdigit(*cw)) wrd->gender = *cw++ - '0';
    if (*cw == '[') {
     while (*cw && *cw != ']') {
      if (isdigit(*cw)) wrd->person = *cw - '0';
      if (*cw == 'P')  wrd->numb = 1;
      if (*cw == 'M')  wrd->gender = 1;
      if (*cw == 'F')  wrd->gender = 2;
      cw++;
     }
     cw++;
    }
   break;

   case 'S' : case 'O':
    if (isdigit(*cw)) wrd->numb =  *cw++ - '0';
    if (isdigit(*cw)) wrd->tflag = *cw++ - '0';
    if (isdigit(*cw)) wrd->gender = *cw++ - '0';
    wrd->person = 3;
    if (*cw == '[') {
     while (*cw && *cw != ']') {
      if (*cw == 'P')  wrd->numb = 1;
      if (*cw == 'S') {
       wrd->numb = 0;
       wrd->gflag = 's';
      }
      if (*cw == 'M')  wrd->gender = 1;
      if (*cw == 'F')  wrd->gender = 2;
```

```
      cw++;
     }
    cw++;
   }
  break;


  case 'P':
   if (!stricmp(wrd->inword, "of"))
    wrd->tflag = 1;
   if (*cw == '[') {
    while (*cw && *cw != ']') {
     if (*cw == 'X')  wrd->fflag = 1;
     if (*cw == 'L')  wrd->oflag = 1;
     if (*cw == 'O')  wrd->pflag = 1;
     if (*cw == 'D')  wrd->xflag = 1;
// etc.
     if (*cw == 'u')  wrd->wprep = 1;
     cw++;
    }
    cw++;
   }
  break;

  case 'U' :
   if (isdigit(*cw)) wrd->tense = *cw++ - '0';
   if (isdigit(*cw)) wrd->mood =  *cw++ - '0';
   if (*cw == '[') {
    while (*cw && *cw != ']') {
     if (*cw == '<')  wrd->tense = T_PAST;
     if (*cw == 'M')  wrd->mood = 1;
     cw++;
    }
    cw++;
   }
  break;

  case 'J' : case 'D' :
   if (isdigit(*cw)) wrd->tflag =  *cw++ - '0';
  break;

  case 'N' :
   if (isdigit(*cw)) wrd->tflag =  *cw++ - '0';
   if (isdigit(*cw)) wrd->tense =  *cw++ - '0';
   if (isdigit(*cw)) wrd->gender =  *cw++ - '0';
   if (*cw == '[') {
    while (*cw && *cw != ']') {
     if (*cw == 'C')  wrd->e.N.constant = 1;
     if (*cw == 'S')  wrd->e.N.singular_only = 1;
     if (*cw == 'P')  wrd->e.N.plural_only = 1;
     if (*cw == 'H')  wrd->e.N.human = 1;
     if (*cw == 'J')  wrd->e.N.j_type = 1;
     if (*cw == 'N')  wrd->e.N.name = 1;
     if (*cw == 'T')  wrd->e.N.time = 1;
     if (*cw == 'L')  wrd->e.N.hane_tto = 1;
     if (*cw == 'L')  wrd->oflag = 1;
     if (*cw == 'D')  wrd->e.N.grau_from = 1;
     if (*cw == 'D')  wrd->xflag = 1;
     if (*cw == 'Q')  wrd->e.N.here_oon = 1;
     if (*cw == 'Q')  wrd->nflag = 1;
     if (*cw == 'V')  wrd->e.N.york_prfor = 1;
     if (*cw == 'V')  wrd->kflag = 1;
     if (*cw == 'Z')  wrd->e.N.raz_wth = 1;
     if (*cw == 'Y')  wrd->vflag = 1;
```

```
    if (*cw == 'x')  wrd->uflag = 1;
    if (*cw == 'g')  wrd->e.N.vea_ni = 1;
    if (*cw == 'g')  wrd->iflag = 1;
    if (*cw == 'f')  wrd->e.N.zwei_xot = 1;
    if (*cw == 'f')  wrd->jflag = 1;
    if (*cw == 'l')  wrd->e.N.dorf_orf = 1;
    if (*cw == 'l')  wrd->lflag = 1;
    if (*cw == 'h')  wrd->e.N.natel_hus = 1;
    if (*cw == 'h')  wrd->sflag = 1;
    if (*cw == 'k')  wrd->e.N.grun_rof = 1;
    if (*cw == 'k')  wrd->mflag = 1;
    if (*cw == 'q')  wrd->e.N.xwyn_htiw = 1;
    if (*cw == 'q')  wrd->hflag = 1;
    if (*cw == 'u')  wrd->wprep = 1;
    if (*cw == 'y')  wrd->e.N.vsyg_yb = 1;
    if (*cw == 'y')  wrd->eflag = 1;
    if (*cw == 't')  wrd->e.N.chris_only = 1;
    if (*cw == '^')  wrd->kflag2 = 1;
    if (*cw == 'ª')  wrd->bflag2 = 1;
    if (*cw == '½')  wrd->zflag2 = 1;
    if (*cw == ':')  wrd->spelling = 1;
    if (*cw == 't')  wrd->rflag = 1;
    if (*cw == 'M')  wrd->gender = 1;
    if (*cw == 'F')  wrd->gender = 2;
    cw++;
   }
   cw++;
  }
  if (*cw == '(') {
   wirr = wrd->irrform;
   while (*cw && *cw != ')')
    *wirr++ = *cw++;
   *wirr++ = *cw++;
   *wirr = '\0';
  }
  wrd->person = 3;
break;

case 'n' :
  if (isdigit(*cw)) wrd->tflag = *cw++ - '0';
  if (isdigit(*cw)) wrd->tense = *cw++ - '0';
  if (isdigit(*cw)) wrd->gender = *cw++ - '0';
  if (*cw == '[') {
   while (*cw && *cw != ']') {
    if (*cw == 'P')  wrd->e.N.plural_only = 1;
    if (*cw == 'H')  wrd->e.N.human = 1;
    cw++;
   }
   cw++;
  }
  wrd->numb = 1;
  wrd->person = 3;
break;

case 'A' : case 'd' :
  if (*cw == '[') {
   while (*cw && *cw != ']') {
    if (*cw == 'M')  wrd->e.A.more_most = 1;
    if (*cw == 'E')  wrd->e.A.er_est = 1;
    if (*cw == 'X')  wrd->fflag = 1;
    if (*cw == 'L')  wrd->oflag = 1;
    if (*cw == 'O')  wrd->pflag = 1;
    if (*cw == 'D')  wrd->xflag = 1;
    if (*cw == 'G')  wrd->zflag = 1;
```

```
      if (*cw == 'Q')  wrd->nflag = 1;
      if (*cw == 'V')  wrd->kflag = 1;
      if (*cw == 'Z')  wrd->qflag = 1;
      if (*cw == 'R')  wrd->bflag = 1;
      if (*cw == 'Y')  wrd->vflag = 1;
      if (*cw == 'x')  wrd->uflag = 1;
      if (*cw == 'u')  wrd->wprep = 1;
      if (*cw == '^')  wrd->kflag2 = 1;
      if (*cw == 'ª')  wrd->bflag2 = 1;
      if (*cw == ':')  wrd->spelling = 1;
      if (*cw == 'I' || *cw == 'i') {
       wrd->e.A.irregular = 1;
       wrd->gflag = 'i';
        }
      if (*cw == '-')  wrd->mood = 1;
      if (*cw == 'a')  wrd->e.A.all = 1;
      if (*cw == 'e')  wrd->e.A.e_form = wrd->mood = 1;
      if (*cw == 'p')  wrd->e.A.prefer = 1;
      cw++;
     }
     cw++;
    if (*cw == '(') {
     wirr = wrd->irrform;
     while (*cw && *cw != ')')
      *wirr++ = *cw++;
     *wirr++ = *cw++;
     *wirr = '\0';
    }
    }
    break;

   case 'a' :
    wrd->cflag = 'a';
   break;

   case 'e' :
    if (wrd->stat == 1 && wrd->person == 3)
   wrd->syn = wrd->esyn = 'V';
    goto dig00;
   case 'V': case 'E': case 'F': case 'G': case 'Z':
   case 'h': case 'v': case 'z':
dig00:
    if (isdigit(*cw)) wrd->e.V.anim = wrd->e.V.control = *cw++ - '0';
    if (isdigit(*cw)) wrd->e.V.controli = wrd->tflag = *cw++ - '0';
    if (isdigit(*cw)) wrd->e.V.control2 = *cw++ - '0';
    if (*cw == '[') {
     while (*cw && *cw != ']') {
      if (isdigit(*cw)) wrd->person = *cw - '0';
      if (*cw == 'i')  wrd->gflag = *cw;
      if (*cw == 'm')  wrd->e.V.master = 1;
      if (*cw == 'n')  wrd->e.V.noto = 1;
      if (*cw == 'p')  wrd->e.V.vpost = 1;
      if (*cw == 'b')  wrd->e.V.controli = wrd->tflag = 1;
      if (*cw == 'd')  wrd->e.V.controld = 1;
      if (*cw == 'o')  wrd->e.V.controlo = wrd->mood = 1;
      if (*cw == 'j')  wrd->e.V.control = 1;
      if (*cw == '<')  wrd->tense = T_PAST;
      if (*cw == 'a')  wrd->e.V.transit = 1;
      if (*cw == 'A')  wrd->e.V.of = 1;
      if (*cw == 's')  wrd->e.V.sein = 1;
      if (*cw == 'X')  wrd->e.V.tom_fo = 1;
      if (*cw == 'X')  wrd->fflag = 1;
      if (*cw == 'L')  wrd->e.V.hane_tto = 1;
      if (*cw == 'L')  wrd->oflag = 1;
```

```
   if (*cw == 'O')  wrd->e.V.chur_tat = 1;
   if (*cw == 'O')  wrd->pflag = 1;
   if (*cw == 'D')  wrd->e.V.grau_from = 1;
   if (*cw == 'D')  wrd->xflag = 1;
   if (*cw == 'G')  wrd->e.V.bravo_nin = 1;
   if (*cw == 'G')  wrd->zflag = 1;
   if (*cw == 'Q')  wrd->e.V.here_oon = 1;
   if (*cw == 'Q')  wrd->nflag = 1;
   if (*cw == 'V')  wrd->e.V.york_prfor = 1;
   if (*cw == 'V')  wrd->kflag = 1;
   if (*cw == 'Z')  wrd->e.V.raz_wth = 1;
   if (*cw == 'Z')  wrd->qflag = 1;
   if (*cw == 'R')  wrd->e.V.theo_bby = 1;
   if (*cw == 'R')  wrd->bflag = 1;
   if (*cw == 'Y')  wrd->vflag = 1;
   if (*cw == 'x')  wrd->uflag = 1;
   if (*cw == 'u')  wrd->wprep = 1;
   if (*cw == '^')  wrd->kflag2 = 1;
   if (*cw == 'ª')  wrd->bflag2 = 1;
   if (*cw == '½')  wrd->zflag2 = 1;
   if (*cw == '~')  wrd->qflag2 = 1;
   if (*cw == ':')  wrd->spelling = 1;
   cw++;
  }
  cw++;
 }
 if (*cw == '(') {
  wirr = wrd->irrform;
  while (*cw && *cw != ')')
   *wirr++ = *cw++;
  *wirr++ = *cw++;
  *wirr = '\0';
 }
 if (wrd->syn == 'E' || wrd->esyn == 'E' || wrd->syn == 'e' ||
  wrd->syn == 'h')
   wrd->tense = T_PAST;
 if (wrd->syn == 'h') {
  wrd->syn = 'V';
  wrd->esyn = 'h';
  wrd->gflag = 'i';
 }
 if (wrd->syn == 'F') {
  wrd->tense = T_PAST;
  wrd->syn = 'E';
  wrd->cflag = 'n';
  wrd->gflag = 'i';
 }
 if (wrd->syn == 'v')
   wrd->person = 3;
 if (wrd->syn == 'z'){
   wrd->person = 3;
   wrd->numb = 1;  // closed Nov. 1999

 }
 break;


default :
 break;
}

if (wrd->syn != 'e' && wrd->syn != 'k' && wrd->syn != 'x' &&
 wrd->syn != 'j' && wrd->syn != 't' && wrd->syn != 'u' &&
 wrd->syn != 'd' && wrd->syn != 'b' && wrd->syn != 'i' &&
```

```
   wrd->syn != 'p' && wrd->syn != 'l' && wrd->syn != 'y' &&
   wrd->syn != 'f' && wrd->syn != 'g' && wrd->syn != 'a' &&
   wrd->syn != 'c' && wrd->syn != 'o' && wrd->syn != 'm' &&
   wrd->syn != 'z' && wrd->syn != 'h' && wrd->syn != 'q' &&
   wrd->syn != 'w' && wrd->syn != 'v' && wrd->syn != 's')

    wrd->syn = toupper(wrd->syn);

   wrd->stat = 3;

   strcpy(wrd->outwd, cw);


}

int get_model(WORD *wrd, char *wm)
{
char *wc;
int nm;

 if (wrd->type != 'W') return 0;

 if (*wm == ' ') wm++;

 if ( (wc = strrchr(wm, '*')) && wc[1] == '$')
 {
  nm = wrd->nmodels;
  if (nm < MAXMODELS)
  {
   if (nm == 0)
   if ((wrd->model = (MODELS *) calloc(MAXMODELS, sizeof(MODELS))) == NULL )
   return 0;
   wc[0] = 0;
   wc[1] = 0;

   strcpy(wrd->model[nm].inst, wm);
   strcpy(wrd->model[nm].outwd, wc + 2);

   wrd->nmodels = nm + 1;

  }
 }
 return 1;
}

WORD * find_wc(WORD *wrd, char *wcomb, WORD **wd)
{
char *wcc, *wm;
char wlex[81];
WORD *pre, *pd, *wrd1;
   wm = wcomb;
   *wd = NULL;
   wrd1 = pre = wrd;
   wrd = wrd->next;
   wcc = strlex(wcomb, " *", wlex);

   while ( wrd ) {

      if (*wlex == '~')
      {
       *wd = wrd;
       pd = pre;
       wcc = strlex(NULL, " *", wlex);
       if ( stricmp(wrd->inword, wlex)) {
```

```
      if (stricmp(wrd->next->inword, wlex))
      {
       get_model(wrd1, wm);
       *wd = NULL;
       return NULL;
      }
      else
       wrd = wrd->next;
       }
       else
      *wd = NULL;
     }
     else
     {
      if ( stricmp(wrd->inword, wlex))
       {
      get_model(wrd1, wm);
      *wd = NULL;
      return NULL;
       }
      }

     if ( *lex_last == '*' || wcc == NULL ) {
      break;
      }
     wcc = strlex(NULL, " *", wlex);

    pre = wrd;
    wrd = wrd->next;
   }

  if (*wd) {
   pd->next = (*wd)->next;
   (*wd)->cflag = 'r';
  }
  return wrd;
 }

WORD * handle_wc( char *wdic, WORD *wrd, WORD **pre, WORD *wrdq, WORD *wd)
{
char *cw, *wcc;
WORD *musor, *next, *pd = NULL, *w;
char syn, nextsyn, fsyn;
int clit = 0;

 next = wrdq->next;
 wcc = cw = strchr(wdic, '*'); cw++;

 if (toupper(*cw) != 'W') {
    wrd->esyn = toupper(*cw);
    if ((wrd->esyn == 'V' || wrd->esyn == 'Z') &&
       (wrd->syn == 'E' || wrd->syn == 'e' || wrd->syn == 'G'))
      ;
    else
     wrd->syn = *cw;
    if (wrd->syn == 'V' && wrd->inword[wrd->wl - 1] != '\'')
     wrd->numb = 0;  /* !!! */
    cw++;
    get_engram(wdic, cw, wrd);

    wrd->cflag = 'w';

    if ( wrd->cflag == '=' || wrd->cflag == '%')
     clit = '=';
```

```
    if (*cw) *pre = wrd;
    w = wrd;
    if (*cw) wrd = wrd->next;
    (*pre)->next = next;
    while ( wrd != next ) {
      musor = wrd;
      if (musor == wd) wd = NULL;
      if (w->syn == '#' || clit) {
       strcat(w->inword, " ");
       strcat(w->inword, wrd->inword);
      }
      wrd = wrd->next;
      free(musor);
    }

}
else {
 unsigned char xy_numb = 0xFF, fnumb; //, fpers;
 unsigned char xy_tense;

    if (!cw[1]) {
       (*pre)->next = next;
       while ( wrd != next ) {
      musor = wrd;
      if (musor == wd) wd = NULL;
      wrd = wrd->next;
      free(musor);
       }
       if (wd) free(wd);
       return next;
    }
    fsyn = wrd->syn;
    fnumb = wrd->numb;
    if (*cw == 'w') {
     *pre = wrd;
     wrd = wrd->next;
    }
    else if (wrd->syn == 'X' || wrd->syn == 'Y') {
     xy_numb = wrd->numb;
     xy_tense = wrd->tense;
    }

    pd = NULL;
    cw++;
    if (*cw == '~') {
     if (wd) {
       wd->next = (*pre)->next;
       (*pre)->next = wd;
       pd = *pre;
       *pre = wd;
       wrd = wd->next;
     }
     cw++;
    }
    if (isalpha(*cw) || *cw == '#') syn = *cw;
    else         syn = 'w';
    for (; wrd != wrdq->next;
        *pre = wrd, wrd = wrd->next, syn = nextsyn ) {

     if ( !syn ) {
       (*pre)->next = next;
       while ( wrd != next ) {
      musor = wrd;
      if (musor == wd) wd = NULL;
```

```
 wrd = wrd->next;
 free(musor);
  }
  goto exit_wc;
 }

wcc = ++cw;

if (syn == 'S' || syn == 'O')
{
  if (*cw == '[') {
  while (*cw && *cw != ']') {
    if (*cw == 'M')   wrd->gender = 1;
    if (*cw == 'F')   wrd->gender = 2;
    if (*cw == 'P')   wrd->numb = 1;
    if (*cw == 'S') {
     wrd->numb = 0;
     wrd->gflag = 's';
    }
    cw++;
  }
  cw++;
  }
  wrd->person = 3;
}
else
 while(*cw && !(isalpha(*cw) ||
   *cw == ' ' || *cw == '~' || *cw == '#')) cw++;
nextsyn = *cw;
if (nextsyn == ' ') nextsyn = 'w';
*cw = '\0';

if (syn == 'n')
{
 wrd->numb = 1;
 syn = 'N';
}
else
if (syn == 'V' || syn == 'E' || syn == 'u' || syn == 'e') {
 if (fsyn == 'G' || fsyn == 'E' || fsyn == 'h' || fsyn == 'F') {
 syn = fsyn;
 if (wrd->syn == 'E')
   wrd->tense = T_PAST;
  }
 else if (fsyn == 'v') {
   wrd->person = 3;
   wrd->syn = syn = 'V';
 }
  else if (fsyn == 'z') {
   wrd->person = 3;
   wrd->numb =1;
   wrd->syn = syn = 'Z';
 }
 else if (xy_numb != 0xFF) {
 wrd->numb = xy_numb;
 wrd->tense = xy_tense;
  }
}
else if (syn == 'e') {
 if (fsyn == 'G') {
 syn = fsyn;
  }
}
strcpy(wrd->outwd, wcc);
```

```
wrd->syn = syn;
if (syn == 'h')
  wrd->esyn = syn;
else
  wrd->esyn = toupper(syn);
wrd->stat = 2;
wrd->cflag = 'w';

if (nextsyn == '~')
{
 if (wd) {
 wd->next = wrd->next;
 wrd->next = wd;
 pd = *pre;
 wrd = wrd->next;
  }
 cw++;
 nextsyn = *cw;
 if (nextsyn == ' ') nextsyn = 'w';
}

}

for (next = wrd; syn; syn = nextsyn)
{
 wcc = ++cw;
 if (syn == '#') {
  while(*cw && *cw != '#') cw++;
  if (*cw) *cw++ = '\0';
 }
 else
  while(*cw && !(isalpha(*cw) ||
    *cw == ' ' || *cw == '~' || *cw == '#')) cw++;
 nextsyn = *cw;
 if (nextsyn == ' ') nextsyn = 'w';
 *cw = '\0';

 wrd = enque_word(NULL, syn, wcc);
 if (wrd == NULL) {
  wrd = (*pre)->next;
  *cw = nextsyn;
  wrd->stat = -1;
  break;
 }
 wrd->cflag = 'w';
 wrd->stat = 2;
 if (syn == 'n')
 {
  wrd->numb = 1;
  wrd->syn = 'N';
 }
 else
 if (syn == 'N')
 {
  if (isdigit(*wcc)) wrd->tflag = *wcc++ - '0';
  if (fnumb) wrd->numb = 1;
 }
 else
 if (syn == 'V' || syn == 'E') {
  if (fsyn == 'G' || fsyn == 'E') {
  wrd->syn = syn = fsyn;
  if (wrd->syn == 'E')
   wrd->tense = T_PAST;
  }
```

```
      else if (xy_numb != 0xFF) {
     wrd->numb = xy_numb;
     wrd->tense = xy_tense;
      }
    }
    else if (syn == '#' || syn == 'S' || syn == 'O')
    {
     wrd->person = 3;
     strcpy(wrd->outwd, wcc);
    }

    wrd->esyn = toupper(syn);

    (*pre)->next = wrd;

    if (nextsyn == '~')
    {
     if (wd) {
     wrd->next = wd;
     pd = *pre;
     wrd = wd;
     }
     cw++;
     nextsyn = *cw;
     if (nextsyn == ' ') nextsyn = 'w';
    }

    *pre = wrd;
    wrd->next = next;

   }

 }


 exit_wc:

 if (pd == NULL && wd) {
  free(wd);
  wd = NULL;
 }

 if (wd) {
  *pre = pd;
  return wd;
 }
 else
  return next;

}

WORD * find_word( WORD *wrd, WORD **pre)
{
int len, flen, wcflen;
int sform;
char *cw, *wdic, *grcw = NULL, *wordc;
char ww[2] = "";
char word[81], word1[81];
char inword[81];
int word_found, wc_found, findwc;
int nextword, match;
char vb[NB][256];
WORD *wrdq, *wd, *wrc, *wrdc;
struct M_TAB *mor;
```

```
struct PREF_TAB *pref = NULL;
char *dash = NULL, *dot;
char morsyn, syn, esyn;
DLIM *dlm;
DICTIONARY *dic;

 strcpy(inword, wrd->inword);
 strlwr(inword);

 do {
  syn = '\0';
  findwc = 1;
  dic_current = NULL;
  strcpy(word, inword);

  if (contr_analys(word, wrd->wl, wrd))
   strcpy(inword, word);;

  len = flen = wrd->wl;
  inword[len] = '\0';

  for (;;)
  {

  wdic = dic_find(dic_que, inword, 0);

  if (!wdic)   break;

   dic = dic_current;
   match = MATCH_FULL;
   word_found = 2;
   strcpy(vb[word_found], wdic);
   cw = strchr(vb[word_found], '*');
   if (cw && cw[1] == '=') {
  strcpy(inword, cw + 2);
  strcpy(wrd->inword, inword);
  strcpy(word, inword);
  len = flen = wrd->wl = strlen(word);
  syn = '\0';
  findwc = 1;
  continue;
   }
   if ( !cw )
   {
  *pre = wrd;
  return wrd->next;
   }

   *cw++ = '\0';
   wrd->syn = *cw;
   wrd->esyn = toupper(*cw);
   cw++;
   if (*cw != ':' && wrd->syn != ':')
   {

    wordc = strchr(cw, '\\');
    if (wordc) *wordc++ = '\0';

    if (wrd->syn == 'X' || wrd->syn == 'Y') {
     get_engram(vb[word_found], cw, wrd);
     grcw = NULL;
    }
    else {
     grcw = cw;
```

```
    strcpy(wrd->outwd, cw);
   }
   cw = wordc;

   if (cw && syn != ':')
   {
    strcpy(wrd->inbase, cw);
    strcat(wrd->inbase, " ");
    strcpy(word1, word);
    strcat(word1, " ");
    sform = 1;
   }
   else {
    sform = 0;
   }
   syn = wrd->syn;
  }
  else {
   if (syn == ':')
    findwc = 0;
   else
    syn = ':';
  }
  if (findwc)
  {
   strcat(word, " ");

     wrc = NULL;
     wrdc = wrd;

     wdic = dic_find(dic_que, word, 1);
     do
     {

    if (wdic)
    {

     flen = strlen(word);
     do {
      wrdq = find_wc(wrdc, wdic + flen, &wd);
      if (wrdq != NULL) {
       wrdc = wrc = wrdq;
       wcflen = flen;
       strcpy(vb[0], wdic);
       strcpy(word, wdic);
       cw = strchr(word, '*');
       *cw++ = ' '; *cw = 0;
       flen = strlen(word);
      }
      wdic = dicnext(dic_current);
     } while (wdic && strncmp(word, wdic, flen) == 0);

     if (wrc) {
      wrdq = handle_wc(vb[0] + wcflen, wrd, pre, wrc, wd);
      return wrdq;
     }

    }
    if (sform) {
      sform = 0;
      strcpy(word, wrd->inbase);
      dic_current = dic;
      dic_next = dic_current->next;
    }
```

```
     else {
      if (wrd->inbase[0]) {
       sform = 1;
       strcpy(word, word1);
      }
      dic_current = dic;
      dic_next = dic_current->next;
      wdic = dic_find_next(dic_que, word, 1);
      if (wdic == NULL) break;
      dic = dic_current;
     }

     wdic = dicfind(dic_current, word, 1);
      } while (1);

     word[--flen] = '\0';
      wrd->inbase[0] = '\0';
  }

  if (syn != ':') {
    if (grcw)
    get_engram(vb[word_found], grcw, wrd);
    if (dash && wrd->syn == 'Z') {
     wrd->syn = 'N';
    }

 *pre = wrd;
 return wrd->next;
  }

  dic_current = dic;
  dic_next = dic_current->next;
  wdic = dic_find_next(dic_que, word, 1);
 if (wdic == NULL) break;

  wdic = dicfind(dic_current, word, 1);
 }

 if ((len < 4 && !strpbrk(inword, "-/")) || (dot = strchr(inword, '.')))
 {
  *pre = wrd;
 if (save_unknown) {
  if (wrd->eprefix[0]) {
   strcpy(word1, wrd->eprefix);
   strcat(word1, inword);
  }
 }
 if (dot || syn == ':' || len < 4)
  wrd->syn = '#';
 pref = pref_analys(inword, wrd);
 wrd->person = 3;
 wrd->gender = G_M;

  return wrd->next;
 }
 morsyn = '\0';
 esyn = wrd->syn;

 mor = morph_analys(word, len, wrd, ww);
 if (wrd->syn == 'D')
  wrd->esyn = esyn;
 if (mor != NULL)
 {
  morsyn = wrd->syn;
```

```
 flen = strlen(word);

 findwc = 1;
 syn = '\0';

 dic_current = NULL;

 wdic = dic_find(dic_que, word, 1);

 for (;wdic;) {
match = -1;
wc_found = word_found = -1;
nextword = 0;
dic = dic_current;

do {

  if (wdic[flen] == '*' || wdic[flen] == ' ' ) {

   if ( wdic[flen] == '*' ) {
    match = MATCH_FULL;
    word_found = 0;
    strcpy(vb[word_found], wdic);
   }
   else if ( wdic[flen] == ' ')
    wc_found = 1;
  }
  else if (wdic[flen] == *ww &&
     (wdic[flen + 1] == '*' || wdic[flen + 1] == ' ' ) ) {

   if ( wdic[flen + 1] == '*' ) {
    match = MATCH_FULL;
    strcat(word, ww);
    word_found = 1;
    strcpy(vb[word_found], wdic);
   }
   else if ( wdic[flen + 1] == ' ')
    wc_found = 1;

  }

  if (match == MATCH_FULL)
  {
   cw = strchr(wdic, '*');
   if (cw && cw[1] == '=') {
    strcpy(inword, cw + 2);
    strcpy(wrd->inword, inword);
    strcpy(word, inword);
    len = flen = wrd->wl = strlen(word);
    syn = '\0';
    findwc = 1;
    goto tryref;
   }
   if ( !cw )
   { /* end if selected */
    *pre = wrd;
    return wrd->next;
   }
  }

  if (findwc && (match != -1 || wc_found == 1)) {
   strcat(word, " ");
   flen = strlen(word);
```

```
if ( wdic[flen - 1] != ' ') {
 nextword = 1;
 wdic = dicnext(dic_current);
}

wrc = NULL;
wrdc = wrd;

do
{
 while (wdic && !strncmp(word, wdic, flen) )
 {
wrdq = find_wc(wrdc, wdic + flen, &wd);
if (wrdq != NULL) {
 wrdc = wrc = wrdq;
 wcflen = flen;
 strcpy(vb[0], wdic);
 strcpy(word, wdic);
 cw = strchr(word, '*');
 *cw++ = ' '; *cw = 0;
 flen = strlen(word);
}
wdic = dicnext(dic_current);
 }
 if (wrc) {
wrdq = handle_wc(vb[0] + wcflen, wrd, pre, wrc, wd);

if (wrd->syn == 'e' && wrd->person == 3)
 wrd->syn = wrd->esyn = 'V';
else if (wrd->esyn == '#')
 wrd->syn = wrd->esyn;
else
if (morsyn == 'A' && wrd->tense &&
   (strstr(wrd->outwd, "A.") || strchr(wrd->outwd, 'A')) &&
   (wrd->syn == 'Z' || wrd->syn == 'N')) {
   wrd->syn = morsyn;
}
else
if (morsyn == 'G' || morsyn == 'E' || morsyn == 'D' ||
   wrd->inword[wrd->wl - 1] == '\'' ||
   wrd->inword[wrd->wl - 2] == '\'') {
   wrd->syn = morsyn;
}
else if (wrd->syn == 'V' &&
   (wrd->inword[wrd->wl - 1] != '\'')) {
 wrd->numb = 0;
 wrd->syn = wrd->esyn = 'V';
}
else
if (wrd->syn == 'G' && wrd->numb)
 wrd->syn = wrd->esyn = 'N';

return wrdq;
 }

 wdic = dic_find_next(dic_que, word, 1);
 if (wdic == NULL)                        {
dic_current = dic;
dic_next = dic_current->next;
break;
 }
 wdic = dicfind(dic_current, word, 1);
```

```
    } while (1);

    wc_found = -1;

    word[--flen] = '\0';
    if (word_found == 1) {
     findwc = 0;
     break;
    }

  }

  if ( nextword )
   nextword = 0;
  else
   wdic = dicnext(dic_current);

} while (wdic && strncmp(word, wdic, flen) == 0 );

if (match == MATCH_FULL) {


  if (( cw = strchr(vb[word_found], '*')))
  {
   *cw++ = '\0';
   wrd->esyn = toupper(*cw);

    if (wrd->esyn == 'e' && wrd->person == 3)
     wrd->syn = wrd->esyn = 'V';
    else if (wrd->esyn == '#')
     wrd->syn = wrd->esyn;
    else
    if (morsyn == 'A' && wrd->tense &&
       (strstr(cw, "A.") || strchr(cw, 'A')) &&
       (wrd->esyn == 'Z' || wrd->esyn == 'N'  ||
        wrd->esyn == 'E' || wrd->esyn == 'e')) {
      wrd->syn = morsyn;
    }
    else
    if (morsyn == 'G' || morsyn == 'E' || morsyn == 'D' ||
      wrd->inword[wrd->wl - 1] == '\'' ||
      wrd->inword[wrd->wl - 2] == '\'') {
      wrd->syn = morsyn;
    }
    else if (wrd->esyn == 'V' &&
     (wrd->inword[wrd->wl - 1] != '\'')) {
     wrd->numb = 0;
     wrd->syn = 'V';
    }

    else
     wrd->syn = *cw;

   cw++;
   if (*cw != ':' && wrd->syn != ':') {
    get_engram(vb[word_found], cw, wrd);
    if (dash && wrd->syn == 'Z') {
   wrd->syn = 'N';
    }
    if (wrd->syn == 'G' && wrd->numb)
   wrd->syn = wrd->esyn = 'N';
    strcpy(wrd->inbase, word);
    *pre = wrd;
    return wrd->next;
```

```
    }
    else
      syn = ':';
  }
 }
 wdic = (char *) dic_find_next(dic_que, word, 1);

 if (wdic == NULL) {
  break;
 }

 tryref:
 if (word_found == -1)
  wdic = dic_find_rest(dic_que, word, 1);
 else
 wdic = dicfind(dic_current, word, findwc);
  }

}


if (!strchr(inword, '/'))
 pref = pref_analys(inword, wrd);

if (pref)
 ;
else if ((dash = strpbrk(inword, "-/"))) {
 if (save_unknown) {
  if (wrd->eprefix[0]) {
   strcpy(word1, wrd->eprefix);
   strcat(word1, inword);
   }
  }
  dlm = NULL;
 dlm = enque_dlm(NULL, *dash, '\0');
 if (dlm != NULL) {
  dlm->next = wrd->next;
  wrd->next = dlm;
  dlm->cflag = '/';
 }
 if (*dash == '/') wrd->cflag = '/';

  *dash = '\0';
  len = wrd->wl = strlen(inword);
  wrd->inword[wrd->wl] = '\0';
  if (wrd->inword[len + 1] == '-') {
 len++;
  }
  wrd->syn = '?'; wrd->numb = 0; wrd->person = 0;
  wd = enque_word(NULL, '?', wrd->inword + len + 1);
  if (wd != NULL) {
 if (dlm == NULL) {
  wd->next = wrd->next;
  wrd->next = wd;
 }
 else {
  wd->next = dlm->next;
  dlm->next = wd;
 }
  }
}
else {
 if (save_unknown) {
  if (wrd->eprefix[0]) {
```

```
      strcpy(word1, wrd->eprefix);
      strcat(word1, inword);
     }
    }
    if (wrd->syn == 'Z')
     wrd->syn = '#';

    if (wrd->syn == 'A') {
     wrd->syn = '#';
    }

    wrd->person = 3;
    wrd->gender = G_M;
    }

  } while (dash || pref);

  ex:;

  *pre = wrd;
  return wrd->next;

}

int find_words(struct QUE *que[])
{
WORD *wrd, *pre;

  pre = wrd = (WORD *) que[0];

  while ( wrd ) {
   if (wrd->type == 'W' &&
    (wrd->syn == '?' || wrd->stat == 1) && wrd->wl > 0 && wrd->wl < 40 &&
    isalpha(wrd->inword[0]) &&
    (isalpha(wrd->inword[1])  || wrd->inword[1] == '\0' ||
      wrd->inword[1] == '.' || wrd->inword[1] == '-'  ||
      wrd->inword[1] == '/' ||
      wrd->inword[1] == ' ' || wrd->inword[1] == '\''))
   {
    if  ( wrd->inword[0] == 'i' && wrd->inword[1] == '\0')
    {
   wrd->syn = '#';
   pre = wrd;
   wrd = wrd->next;
    }
    else
    {
   wrd = find_word(wrd, &pre);
    }
   }
   else if (wrd->syn == '#' && isdigit(wrd->inword[wrd->wl - 3]) &&
     (isflex(wrd->inword, wrd->wl, "st") ||
     isflex(wrd->inword, wrd->wl, "nd") ||
     isflex(wrd->inword, wrd->wl, "th") ||
     isflex(wrd->inword, wrd->wl, "rd") ))
   {
    wrd->syn = 'A';
    wrd->cflag = 'h';
    wrd->inword[wrd->wl - 2] = 0;
    wrd->stat = 1;
    pre = wrd;
    wrd = wrd->next;
   }
   else {
```

```
    pre = wrd;
    wrd = wrd->next;
   }
  }
 return 1;
}

// end of file 'grammar.c'
```

```
// -----------------------------------------------------------------------
// file 'chris.h'
#define LWORD 40
#define LMAX  80
#define LRMAX 255
#define MAXMODELS 10
#define MAXWORDS  512
#define CR '\n'


typedef union {
 NOUN N;
 ADJ  A;
 VERB V;
 VERB VP;

 nOUN n;
 aDJ  a;
 vERB v;
 PRON pron;
 PREP prep;

 char z[5];
} GRAMINFO;


typedef struct gr_models {
 char inst[LMAX];
 char outwd[LRMAX];
} MODELS;


typedef struct in_word
{
  struct in_word *next, *back;
  unsigned char id;
  unsigned char did;
  unsigned char prty;
  unsigned char stat;
  unsigned char syn;
  unsigned char ssyn;
  unsigned char type;
  char      cflag;
  int       ll;
  char   inword[LMAX];
  char      esyn;
  GRAMINFO    e;
  char      rsyn;
  GRAMINFO    r;
  unsigned char numb;
  unsigned char tense;
  unsigned char person;
  unsigned char tflag;
  unsigned char gflag;
  unsigned char pflag;
```

```
  unsigned char oflag;
  unsigned char xflag;
  unsigned char zflag;
  unsigned char nflag;
  unsigned char kflag;
  unsigned char qflag;
  unsigned char bflag;
  unsigned char fflag;
  unsigned char jflag;
  unsigned char aflag;
  unsigned char lflag;
  unsigned char iflag;
  unsigned char rflag;
  unsigned char sflag;
  unsigned char mflag;
  unsigned char hflag;
  unsigned char wflag;
  unsigned char eflag;
  unsigned char uflag;
  unsigned char wprep;
  unsigned char vflag;
  unsigned char kflag2;
  unsigned char bflag2;
  unsigned char zflag2;
  unsigned char qflag2;
  unsigned char spelling;
  unsigned char tcase;
  unsigned char gender;
  unsigned char mood;
  unsigned char tcase2;
  unsigned char voice;
  unsigned char shortf;
  char       sem[9];
  int       npar;
  int       wl;
  unsigned char ntrans;
  unsigned char ctran;
  char       *cw;
  char       outwd[LRMAX];
  char       *insyns;
  char       eprefix[LWORD];
  char       rprefix[LWORD];
  char       inbase[LMAX];
  char       irrform[LWORD];
  char       reform[LWORD];
  struct in_word *lex;
  struct in_word *cwrd;
  unsigned char nmodels;
  MODELS             *model;

} WORD;

typedef struct in_delm
{
  struct in_delm *next, *back;
  unsigned char id;
  unsigned char did;
  unsigned char prty;
  unsigned char stat;
  unsigned char syn;
  unsigned char ssyn;
  unsigned char type;
  char       cflag;
  int       ll;
```

```
  char   inword[3];
} DLIM;


enum FIND_MATCH {NO_MATCH = -1, MATCH_PART = 0, MATCH_PART1, MATCH_FULL};


extern struct QUE *tr_que[];

// end of file 'chris.h'
```

```
// file 'gramdic.h'
enum CASE_TYPE  {C_NOM = 1, C_GEN = 2, C_DAT = 4,
      C_AKK = 8, C_INS = 16, C_PRE = 32};


enum R_GENDER_TYPE {G_N, G_U, G_M, G_F, G_B};

enum E_NUMBER_TYPE {N_SG, N_PL};

enum R_PARTS_TYPE {P_NONE, P_NOUN, P_ADJ, P_VERB, P_ADV, P_PRON, P_NUM,
  P_PRE, P_PREP, P_CONJ, P_VMOD, P_PART, P_INTJ, P_ING, P_ART};

enum E_TENSE_TYPE {T_PRESENT, T_PAST, T_FUTURE};

enum E_MOOD_TYPE {M_NULL, M_REFLEX, M_SUBJ, M_3, M_IMPER,
      M_INF = 8, M_SUBQ = 16};


typedef struct {

unsigned        nom             :       1;
unsigned        gen             :       1;
unsigned        dat             :       1;
unsigned        akk             :       1;
unsigned        ins             :       1;
unsigned        pre             :       1;
unsigned        reserve_case    :       1;
unsigned        dummy_case      :       1;

} CASE;


typedef struct {

unsigned        name            :       1;
unsigned        human           :       1;
unsigned        compound        :       1;
unsigned        fem             :       1;
unsigned        neuter          :       1;
unsigned        masculin        :       1;
unsigned        tom_fo          :       1;
unsigned        chur_tat        :       1;
unsigned        spelling        :       1;
unsigned        wzat_toa        :       1;
unsigned        grau_from       :       1;
unsigned        dorf_orf        :       1;
unsigned        here_oon        :       1;
unsigned        natel_hus       :       1;
unsigned        bravo_nin       :       1;
unsigned        vea_ni          :       1;
unsigned        chris_only      :       1;
unsigned        york_prfor      :       1;
unsigned        grun_rof        :       1;
```

```
unsigned         hane_tto           :        1;
unsigned         zwei_xot           :        1;
unsigned         raz_wth            :        1;
unsigned         xwyn_htiw          :        1;
unsigned         theo_bby           :        1;
unsigned         vsyg_yb            :        1;
unsigned         concrete           :        1;
unsigned         material           :        1;
unsigned         j_type             :        1;
unsigned         constant           :        1;
unsigned         time               :        1;
unsigned         dummy1             :        1;

unsigned         mgender            :        1;
unsigned         fgender            :        1;
unsigned         ngender            :        1;
unsigned         singular_only      :        1;
unsigned         plural_only        :        1;
unsigned         reform             :        1;
unsigned         adj                :        1;
unsigned         reserve2           :        2;
unsigned         dummy2             :        1;

unsigned         paradigm           :        7;
unsigned         dummy3             :        1;

} NOUN;


typedef struct {

unsigned         mgender            :        1;
unsigned         fgender            :        1;
unsigned         ngender            :        1;
unsigned         singular           :        1;
unsigned         plural             :        1;
unsigned         person             :        2;
unsigned         oblique            :        1;
unsigned         dummy0             :        1;

unsigned         nom                :        1;
unsigned         gen                :        1;
unsigned         dat                :        1;
unsigned         akk                :        1;
unsigned         ins                :        1;
unsigned         pre                :        1;
unsigned         reserve_case       :        1;
unsigned         dummy_case         :        1;

} nOUN;


typedef struct {

unsigned         no_ly              :        1;
unsigned         prefer             :        1;
unsigned         all                :        1;
unsigned         none               :        1;
unsigned         irregular          :        1;
unsigned         spelling           :        1;
unsigned         reform             :        1;
unsigned         recht              :        1;
unsigned         more_most          :        1;
```

```
unsigned        er_est              :       1;
unsigned        dummy1              :       1;


unsigned        e_form              :       1;
unsigned        analcomparative     :       1;
unsigned        syntsuperlative     :       1;
unsigned        analsuperlative     :       1;
unsigned        noun                :       1;
unsigned        reserve2            :       2;
unsigned        dummy2              :       1;

unsigned        paradigm            :       7;
unsigned        dummy3              :       1;

} ADJ;


typedef struct {

unsigned        mgender             :       1;
unsigned        fgender             :       1;
unsigned        ngender             :       1;
unsigned        singular            :       1;
unsigned        plural              :       1;
unsigned        person              :       2;
unsigned        oblique             :       1;
unsigned        dummy0              :       1;

unsigned        qualitative         :       1;
unsigned        ordinal             :       1;
unsigned        possesive           :       1;
unsigned        prelative           :       1;
unsigned        shortf              :       1;
unsigned        comparative         :       1;
unsigned        superlative         :       1;
unsigned        dummy1              :       1;

unsigned        nom                 :       1;
unsigned        gen                 :       1;
unsigned        dat                 :       1;
unsigned        akk                 :       1;
unsigned        ins                 :       1;
unsigned        pre                 :       1;
unsigned        reserve_case        :       1;
unsigned        dummy_case          :       1;


} aDJ;


typedef struct {
unsigned        transitive          :       1;
unsigned        intransitive        :       1;
unsigned        controlg            :       1;
unsigned        noto                :       1;
unsigned        controli            :       1;
unsigned        control             :       1;
unsigned        irregular           :       1;
unsigned        reform              :       1;
unsigned        haben               :       1;
unsigned        sein                :       1;
unsigned        reflexive           :       1;
```

```
unsigned          transit          :        1;
unsigned          intransit        :        1;
unsigned          dativ            :        1;
unsigned          genitiv          :        1;
unsigned          dummy1           :        1;
unsigned          of               :        1;
unsigned          tom_fo           :        1;
unsigned          chur_tat         :        1;
unsigned          grau_from        :        1;
unsigned          here_oon         :        1;
unsigned          bravo_nin        :        1;
unsigned          york_prfor       :        1;
unsigned          hane_tto         :        1;
unsigned          raz_wth          :        1;
unsigned          theo_bby         :        1;
unsigned          spelling         :        1;
unsigned          anim             :        1;
unsigned          controld         :        1;
unsigned          controlo         :        1;
unsigned          vpost            :        1;
unsigned          master           :        1;
unsigned          reserve          :        2;
unsigned          newspell         :        2;
unsigned          dummy2           :        1;

unsigned          paradigm         :        7;
unsigned          dummy3           :        1;

unsigned          control2         :        7;
unsigned          dummy4           :        1;

} VERB;


typedef struct {

unsigned          mgender          :        1;
unsigned          fgender          :        1;
unsigned          ngender          :        1;
unsigned          singular         :        1;
unsigned          plural           :        1;
unsigned          person           :        2;
unsigned          oblique          :        1;
unsigned          dummy0           :        1;

unsigned          transitive       :        1;
unsigned          perfective       :        1;
unsigned          past             :        1;
unsigned          passive          :        1;
unsigned          imperative       :        1;
unsigned          shortf           :        1;
unsigned          reserve1         :        1;
unsigned          dummy1           :        1;

unsigned          nom              :        1;
unsigned          gen              :        1;
unsigned          dat              :        1;
unsigned          akk              :        1;
unsigned          ins              :        1;
unsigned          pre              :        1;
unsigned          reserve_case     :        1;
unsigned          dummy_case       :        1;

} vERB;
```

```
typedef struct {

unsigned        mgender         :       1;
unsigned        fgender         :       1;
unsigned        ngender         :       1;
unsigned        singular        :       1;
unsigned        plural          :       1;
unsigned        person          :       2;
unsigned        not             :       1;
unsigned        dummy0          :       1;

unsigned        nom             :       1;
unsigned        gen             :       1;
unsigned        dat             :       1;
unsigned        akk             :       1;
unsigned        ins             :       1;
unsigned        pre             :       1;
unsigned        reserve_case    :       1;
unsigned        dummy_case      :       1;

} PRON;


typedef struct {

unsigned        nom             :       1;
unsigned        gen             :       1;
unsigned        dat             :       1;
unsigned        akk             :       1;
unsigned        ins             :       1;
unsigned        pre             :       1;
unsigned        reserve_case    :       1;
unsigned        dummy_case      :       1;
unsigned        tom_fo          :       1;
unsigned        chur_tat        :       1;
unsigned        grau_from       :       1;
unsigned        here_oon        :       1;
unsigned        bravo_nin       :       1;
unsigned        york_prfor      :       1;
unsigned        hane_tto        :       1;
unsigned        raz_wth         :       1;
unsigned        theo_bby        :       1;

} PREP;

struct SYNPARTS {
  char syn;
  char part;
};

int getpart( char synt );

// end of file 'gramdic.h'
```

```
// file 'grammar.h'
struct M_TAB {
char *mflex;
char *mgram;
int cond;
};

struct M_TAB MTAB[] = {
{"ies\'", "N12",},
```

```
{"es\'", "N12",},
{"s\'",  "N12",},
{"\'s",  "N02",},
{"ing",  "G8",},

{"ied",  "E",},
{"ed",   "E",},

{"ness", "N00",},
{"ous",  "A",},
{"less", "A",},

/*      NP */
{"ies",  "Z13",},
{"es",   "Z13",},
{"s",    "Z13",},

{"fy",   "V",},


{"ment", "N00",},
{"ion",  "N00",},
{"ence",  "N00",},
{"ance",  "N00",},
{"ity",  "N00",},
{"age",  "N00",},
{"ure",  "N00",},
{"or",   "N00",},

{"iest", "A",},
{"ier",  "A",},
{"est",  "A",},
{"eur",  "A",},
{"er",   "A",},
{"ical", "A",},
{"ible", "A",},
{"able", "A",},
{"ory",  "A",},
{"ary",  "A",},
{"les",  "A",},

{"ily",   "D",},
{"ly",   "D",},


{NULL,  NULL, }
};


struct C_TAB {
char *mflex;
char *mgram;
char *iw;
char *ow;
int cond;
};

struct C_TAB CTAB[] = {

{"let\'s","M",  "us",  NULL, 4},
{"\'s", "X",  "is",   NULL, 3},

{"n\'t", "K",  "not",  "NOT", 0},
```

```
{"\'ll", "X",  "will", NULL, 0},
{"\'d", "X",  "would", NULL, 1},

{"\'m", "T",  "am",  NULL, 0},
{"\'re", "T",  "are",  NULL, 0},
{"\'ve", "X",  "have",  "have", 0},
{"cannot", "K", "not",  "not", 2},
{NULL,  NULL,  NULL, NULL,}
};


struct PR_TAB {
char *mflex;
char *mgram;
char *ow;
};


struct PR_TAB PRTAB[] = {

{"i",    "R01",   "i"},
{"you",   "R12",   "you"},
{"he",   "R031",  "he"},
{"she",   "R032",  "she"},
{"it",   "R03",   "it"},
{"we",   "R11",   "we"},
{"they",  "R13",   "they"},

{NULL,  NULL,  NULL}
};


struct PREF_TAB {
char *prefix;
int len;
char *rprefix;
};

struct PREF_TAB PREFTAB[] =
{
{"non",   3,  "non"   },
{"sub",   3,  "sub"  },
{"pre",   3,  "pre"  },
{"de",   2,  "de"   },
{"re",   2,  "re" },
{"infra",  5,  "infra" },
{"pseudo", 6,  "pseudo" },
{"stereo", 6,  "stereo" },
{"video",  5,  "video" },
{"radio",  5,  "radio" },
{"photo",  5,  "photo"  },
{"tele",  4,  "tele"  },
{"trans",  5,  "trans" },
{"super",  5,  "super" },
{"hyper",  5,  "hyper" },
{"multi",  5,  "multi" },
{"semi",  4,  "semi"  },
// etc.
{NULL,  0,  NULL }
};

// end of file 'grammar.h'

// file 'lex.h'
```

```
extern char *lex_last;

char *strlex(char *str, const char *pic, char *lex);
int isflex(char *word, int lw, char *flex);

// end of file 'lex.h'
```

```
// file 'lexicon.h'
#define DIC_SIGN_SIZE                    20



typedef struct
{
  char   file_sign[20];
  char   text_terminator;
  char   language;
  char   type;
  char   scr;
  unsigned          version;
  int    xdim;
  int    nabc;
  unsigned long index_offset;
  unsigned long file_size;
  unsigned          csum;
} DIC_FILE_HEADER;


typedef union dic_index_data
{
  unsigned long r2[32][33];
  unsigned long r1[32];
  unsigned long e2[26][27];
  unsigned long e1[26];
} DIC_INDEX_DATA;

typedef struct dictionary
{
  struct dictionary *next, *back;
  unsigned char id;
  unsigned char did;
  unsigned char prty;
  unsigned char stat;
  char    path[MAXPATH];
  char    language;
  char    type;
  int     xdim;
  int     nabc;
  long    len;
  unsigned long  index_offset;
  int              fd;
  long    buflen;
  char    *data;
  char    *word;
  char    *last;
  DIC_INDEX_DATA *x;
} DICTIONARY;



extern int dic_buflen, dic_diff;
extern int dic_gbuflen, dic_errno;
extern char *dic_buf;
extern char *dic_gbuf;
```

```
extern DICTIONARY *dic_current, *dic_next;
extern DICTIONARY *dic_current_eng, *dic_next_eng;
extern DICTIONARY *dic_current_rus, *dic_next_rus;

extern struct QUE *load_que[];
extern struct QUE *dic_que[];
extern struct QUE *rus_que[];
extern struct QUE *eng_que[];


DICTIONARY *cdecl dicopen(const char *, int );
void   cdecl dicclose(DICTIONARY *);
char  *cdecl dicfind(DICTIONARY *, const char *word, int);
int dicseek(DICTIONARY *d, const char *word);
char *dicnext(DICTIONARY *d);
int diccmp(const char *str1, const char *str2);

int dic_init(void);
int load_dic(char *dicarray[]);
DICTIONARY * dic_load(char n, char *path, int mode);
DICTIONARY * dic_unload(char *path);
char *dic_find(struct QUE *que[], const char *word, int mode);
char *dic_find_rest(struct QUE *que[], const char *word, int mode);
char *dic_find_next(struct QUE *que[], const char *word, int mode);
long offset(DICTIONARY *d, char *s);
long artlen(DICTIONARY *d, char *s);
unsigned set_csd(DIC_FILE_HEADER *fh);
int chk_csd(DIC_FILE_HEADER *fh);

char *find_id(const char *word, int mode);
int ids_load(const char *path);


// end of file 'lexicon.h'
// ---------------------------------------------------------------------
// file 'type.h'
extern int save_unknown;

enum FORMAT_TYPE {F_ASCII, F_MAC};

// end of file 'type.h'
```

Index